Adobe

ADOBE COLDFUSION 10
ColdFusion 10 Enhancements and Improvements

web application construction kit

Ben Forta

with Charlie Arehart , Rob Brooks-Bilson, Raymond Camden, Kenneth Fricklas, Hemant Khandelwal, and Chandan Kumar

Adobe® ColdFusion® 10
Web Application Construction Kit:
ColdFusion® 10 Enhancements and Improvements
Copyright © 2013 by Ben Forta

Adobe Press Editor: Victor Gavenda
Project Editor: Nancy Peterson
Production Editor: Tracey Croom
Development Editor: Judy Ziajka
Proofreaders: Liz Welch and Scout Festa
Technical Editor: Hemant Khandelwal
Compositor: Danielle Foster
Indexer: Jack Lewis
Cover Designer: Charlene Charles-Will
Cover Compositor: Mike Tanamachi

Adobe Press books are published by Peachpit, a division of Pearson Education located in San Francisco, California. For the latest information about Adobe Press books, go to www.adobepress.com. To report errors, please send a note to errata@peachpit.com. For information about getting permission for reprints and excerpts, contact permissions@peachpit.com.

Printed and bound in the United States of America

ISBN-13: 978-0-321-89096-2
ISBN-10:   0-321-89096-5

9 8 7 6 5 4 3 2 1

Dedications

Charlie Arehart

I'd like to dedicate this volume with thanks to the hundreds of speakers who've presented on the Online ColdFusion Meetup (coldfusion-metup.com), stepping up to the plate to share their knowledge and experience in all things ColdFusion.

Raymond Camden

To my wife, Jeanne. I love you.

Kenneth Fricklas

I dedicate this book to my wife and son, whom I told I wouldn't do this again, but here we are.

Hemant Khandelwal

To my wife, Meera, and my two kids, Tishya and Tarush, who all have brought tremendous joy into my life.

Chandan Kumar

To mom with love.

AUTHOR BIOGRAPHIES

Ben Forta has more than two decades of experience in the computer industry, in product development, support, training, and marketing. As Adobe's director of developer relations, he is responsible for the company's technical evangelism, community relations, and developer education programs and is a primary liaison between the company and the Adobe developer community. Ben is the author of more than 40 books, including best-selling titles on SQL and ColdFusion and titles on Microsoft Windows development, Regular Expressions, and Java. Over half a million Ben Forta books have been printed in English, and titles have been translated into 15 languages. Ben continues to write and blog at http://forta.com/ and present on web and application development topics worldwide. You can also find him on Twitter at @benforta.

A veteran ColdFusion developer and troubleshooter since 1997, with more than three decades in enterprise IT, **Charlie Arehart** is a longtime contributor to the ColdFusion community and has for several years been a recognized Adobe Community Professional, Adobe Forums MVP, ColdFusion Customer Advisory Board member, and more. An independent consultant, he provides short-term, remote, on-demand troubleshooting and tuning assistance for organizations of all sizes and ColdFusion experience levels (carehart.org/consulting). Besides running the 2800-member Online ColdFusion Meetup (coldfusionmeetup.com, an online ColdFusion user group), he hosts the UGTV repository for recorded presentations from hundreds of speakers (carehart.org/ugtv), the CF411 site offering more than 1800 tools and resources for ColdFusion users (cf411.com), and the CF911 site offering troubleshooting resources (cf911.com). A Certified Advanced ColdFusion developer and instructor for each version since ColdFusion 4, Charlie has spoken at nearly all the ColdFusion conferences worldwide and was a contributor to all three volumes of the ColdFusion 8 and 9 ColdFusion Web Application Construction Kit books.

Rob Brooks-Bilson is a consultant and author and the director of architecture and application development at Amkor Technology. He's a frequent speaker at industry conferences and at local user groups. He is also the author of two O'Reilly books: *Programming ColdFusion* and *Programming ColdFusion MX*. Outside work, Rob is a technophile, blogger, photographer, bed jumper, world traveler, hiker, mountain biker, and Adobe Community Professional for ColdFusion. You can subscribe to Rob's blog at rob.brooks-bilson.com and follow him on Twitter at @styggiti.

Raymond Camden is a senior developer evangelist for Adobe. His work focuses on web standards, mobile development, and ColdFusion. He is a published author and presents at conferences and user groups on a variety of topics. Raymond can be reached at his blog (www.raymondcamden.com), at @cfjedimaster on Twitter, or by email at raymondcamden@gmail.com.

Kenneth Fricklas has been using ColdFusion since Version 1.5 and teaching it since Version 3.0. A well-known speaker and author, he is currently the vice president of software engineering at Placewise Media in Denver, Colorado.

Hemant Khandelwal manages the ColdFusion products at Adobe and has built and shipped ColdFusion Server 8, 9, and 10 and ColdFusion Builder 1 and 2. He has several years of R&D experience in application-server internal design and Internet architecture and wrote the world's first EJB2.0 container. He was part of the expert group committee for the J2EE 1.4, EJB2.0, and EJB3.0 specifications. He is a regular speaker at conferences and is passionate about ColdFusion and the role it plays in making hard things easy. He can be reached on Twitter at @khandelwalh.

Chandan Kumar has been part of the core development team at Adobe for ColdFusion for almost seven years and has been involved in managing its language and runtime application and keeping it current with the latest trends, including closures, REST support, caching upgrades, and PDF features. He has been a speaker at several conferences throughout the world, including Adobe MAX, SOTR, WebDU, CFUnited, and CFUG conferences and many e-seminars. He is a graduate of the Indian Institute of Technology.

ACKNOWLEDGMENTS

Ben Forta: Thanks to my co-authors, Charlie Arehart, Rob Brooks-Bilson, Raymond Camden, Kenneth Fricklas, Hemant Khandelwal, and Chandan Kumar, for their outstanding contributions. Although this book is affectionately known to thousands as "the Ben Forta book," it is, in truth, as much theirs as it is mine. An extra thank you to Hemant Khandelwal for his tech review and for stepping up and taking on extra work when we needed additional contributing authors. Thanks to Nancy Peterson and Judy Ziajka for so ably shepherding this book through the publication process yet again. Thanks to the thousands of you who write to me with comments, suggestions, and criticism (thankfully not too much of the latter)—I do read each and every message (and even attempt to reply to them all, eventually), and all are appreciated. And last, but by no means least, a loving thank you to my wife, Marcy, and our children for putting up with (and allowing) my often hectic work schedule. Their love and support make all that I do possible.

Charlie Arehart: Where would we all be, in terms of our ColdFusion experiences, without Ben?! Most of us learned ColdFusion from him and/or this series, or from the official ColdFusion training that he helped shape, or from his blog, etc. He's been the rock of the ColdFusion world from the beginning. (And he's been a rock star, too. Those of us who saw him roll out on stage in the Hummer at "Powered by Detroit" in 2005 will never forget that scene!) And I've had the sincere pleasure and honor of contributing to the past seven volumes in this series and can attest to his being the glue that holds it all together. Thanks also to my fellow authors, and indeed to all in the community and at Adobe, who've contributed knowledge and experience that has helped all of us learn and improve over the years and even decades. This book is just one more reflection of the ColdFusion community's continued, valuable support for one another. Finally, you see most writers thank their spouses, and it's not just a formality, as they lose us for long periods of time during such projects, especially when we write on top of doing our other work. Kim, as I say daily for some reason or another, "Thank you, my love." I thank God for bringing you into my life, and indeed for all I have and am.

Raymond Camden: I'd like to thank Ben for inviting me back to the book again and to thank the ColdFusion team for their help and support in writing this book.

Hemant Khandelwal: I would like to thank Ben for giving me the opportunity to be part of this book. A special thanks to Judy Ziajka for her help during chapter reviews and to my teammates at the ColdFusion product team who are the real heroes in building these features. I also want to thank my mom for what she has taught me. And finally, I want to thank my wife for her love.

Chandan Kumar: First, I would like to thank Ben Forta and Peachpit for believing in me and giving me this great opportunity to write. Then I would like to thank my manager, Hemant Khandelwal, for his continuous help and guidance throughout my career. I also want to thank my family and friends for their love and support and, finally, my lovely wife, Sudha Singh, for standing by me all along.

CONTENTS AT A GLANCE

CONTENTS

INTRODUCTION

What Is This Book?

ColdFusion needs no introduction: It helped usher in the era of web-based applications over a decade and a half ago, and it remains an innovator in this space to this day. With each update, ColdFusion has further empowered us to build and create the ultimate online experiences, and ColdFusion 10 is no exception.

ColdFusion 10 is indeed a very important release: one that builds on the success of ColdFusion 9 by adding invaluable new features and functions. And that is key: ColdFusion 10 does not change much about the previous release; it adds features and functions. This means that ColdFusion 9 code and applications should run just as is in ColdFusion 10, and any books and tutorials on ColdFusion 9 apply to ColdFusion 10 as well.

And this presented the publishers and authors with a dilemma. *ColdFusion Web Application Construction Kit* (affectionately known as *CFWACK*) started off as a single volume, and then grew to two volumes in ColdFusion 4, and has been three volumes since ColdFusion 8. Recognizing that so much of the existing content for ColdFusion 9 applied as-is to ColdFusion 10, we could not in good conscience justify updating all the books and making readers buy them all over again. Plus, to make room to cover the new features in ColdFusion 10, we would have needed to remove chapters from the existing books, and as ColdFusion's breadth and scope has increased, removing content has proven to be a difficult task.

After lengthy discussions with the publisher, the ColdFusion product team, and the authors, we opted not to update the three *CFWACK* volumes for ColdFusion 10. Instead, we decided to create a fourth volume to focus exclusively on what is new and improved in ColdFusion 10. And this is the book you are now holding in your hands.

This book, and indeed the entire *ColdFusion Web Application Construction Kit* series, is written for anyone who wants to create cutting-edge web-based applications.

If you are just starting creating your web presence, but know you want to serve more than just static information, this book, in conjunction with the ColdFusion 9 books, will help get you there. If you are a webmaster or web page designer and want to create dynamic, data-driven web pages, this book is for you as well. If you are an experienced database administrator who wants to take advantage of the web to publish or collect data, this book is for you, too. If you have used ColdFusion before and want to learn what's new in ColdFusion 10, this book is also for you. Even if you are an experienced ColdFusion user, this book provides you with invaluable tips and tricks and serves as a definitive ColdFusion developer's reference.

This book teaches you how to create real-world applications that solve real-world problems. Along the way, you acquire all the skills you need to design, implement, test, and roll out world-class applications.

How to Use This Book

As already noted, this book is designed to extend and enhance the three existing *ColdFusion 9 Web Application Construction Kit*. The four books are organized as follows:

- **Volume 1—*Adobe ColdFusion 9 Web Application Construction Kit, Volume 1: Getting Started* (ISBN 0-321-66034-X)** contains Chapters 1–21 and is targeted at beginning ColdFusion developers.

- **Volume 2—*Adobe ColdFusion 9 Web Application Construction Kit, Volume 2: Application Development* (ISBN 0-321-67919-9)** contains Chapters 22–45 and covers the ColdFusion features and language elements that are used by most ColdFusion developers most of the time.

- **Volume 3—*Adobe ColdFusion 9 Web Application Construction Kit, Volume 3: Advanced Application Development* (ISBN 0-321-67920-2)** contains Chapters 46–71 and covers the more advanced ColdFusion functions, including extensibility features, as well as security and management features that will be of interest primarily to those responsible for larger and more critical applications.

- *Adobe ColdFusion 10 Web Application Construction Kit, ColdFusion 10 Enhancements and Improvements* (ISBN 0-321-89096-5) contains 19 new chapters focusing on what's new in ColdFusion 10, and is intended to be used in conjunction with the three other titles listed here.

These books are designed to serve two different, but complementary, purposes.

First, as the books used by most ColdFusion developers, they are a complete tutorial covering everything you need to know to harness ColdFusion's power. As such, the books are divided into parts, or sections, and each section introduces new topics building on what has been discussed in prior sections. Ideally, you will work through these sections in order, starting with ColdFusion basics and then moving on to advanced topics. This is especially true for the first two books.

Second, the books are invaluable desktop references. The appendixes and accompanying website contain reference chapters that will be of use to you while developing ColdFusion applications. Those reference chapters are cross-referenced to the appropriate tutorial sections, so that step-by-step information is always readily available to you.

The following sections describe the contents of this new volume

Part I: Web Technology Innovation

ColdFusion is predominantly used to power web applications, and so Part I of this book focuses on ColdFusion web technology enhancements and innovations:

- Chapter 1, "ColdFusion 10 and HTML5," introduces new HTML5 tags and features and explains how these are supported by ColdFusion.

- Chapter 2, "Using WebSocket," introduces an additional HTML5 enhancement, WebSocket, and explores the ways that it changes server-to-browser communication.

- Charting and graphing has long been a ColdFusion staple, and Chapter 3, "Charting Revisited," introduces new HTML5 charting options.

- In Chapter 4, "Web Services," you learn how to implement and use the latest generation of web services technologies.

- The web services discussion continues in Chapter 5, "Using REST Web Services," which introduces REST as an alternative to traditional web services.

- Extensive video support is new to ColdFusion 10, and Chapter 6, "Embedding Video," explains what you can do and provides useful tips and tricks.

Part II: (Even More) Rapid Development

ColdFusion has always been about productivity and rapid development, and ColdFusion 10 continues to innovate to help make developers even more productive:

- The CFML language is the magic that makes ColdFusion coding so productive and simple, but that simplicity need not be at the expense of power and flexibility. Chapter 7, "CFML Enhancements," introduces closures and additional CFML enhancements.

- CFScript is the scripting alternative to CFML, and it too gains new features in Cold-Fusion 10, as discussed in Chapter 8, "CFScript Enhancements."

- Chapter 9, "Object Relational Mapping Enhancements," focuses on what's new in Cold-Fusion's ORM support, including new search options, HQL logging, and more.

- ColdFusion has been built on Java since ColdFusion MX (aka ColdFusion 6), and experienced ColdFusion developers quickly learn how to leverage the underlying Java engine to build more powerful applications. Chapter 10, "Enhanced Java Integration," teaches you how to use custom class paths, dynamic proxies, and more.

- Chapter 11, "XML Enhancements," explains the new and improved XPath support, which provides greater XML processing flexibility.

Part III: Enterprise Ready

Some of the most significant enhancements in ColdFusion 10 focus on administration and security:

- In Chapter 12, "ColdFusion in the Cloud," you learn how to take advantage of innovations in cloud computing, and ColdFusion's new support for simplified cloud deployment and hosting.

- Chapter 13, "Improved Administration," teaches you all you need to know about the updated ColdFusion Administrator, including the critically important hotfix and update installer.

- Chapter 14, "Scheduling," introduces the new and improved scheduler and explains grouping, prioritization, event chaining, and more.

- Chapter 15, "Security Enhancements," introduces the latest security risks and concepts and explains which you should worry about and why.

- Caching has always been an important part of performance optimization, and Chapter 16, "Improving Performance," presents the latest and greatest caching techniques.

- Microsoft Exchange and Microsoft Office are critical to most organizations, and Chapter 17, "Improved Integration," focuses on integration with the latest versions of these applications.

- Apache Solr was introduced in ColdFusion 9 as an alternative to the existing full-text search engine. In ColdFusion 10, Solr is the default engine, and Chapter 18, "Apache Solr," explains how to use this new technology.

- In addition to everything covered thus far, ColdFusion 10 offers a long list of smaller (but no less useful) enhancements, as enumerated in Chapter 19, "Miscellaneous Enhancements."

The Website

This book's accompanying website contains everything you need to start writing ColdFusion applications, including:

- Links to obtain ColdFusion 10

- Links to obtain Adobe ColdFusion Builder

- Source code and databases for all the examples in this book

- An errata sheet, should one be required

- An online discussion forum

The book web page is at http://www.forta.com/books/0321890965/.

And with that, turn the page and start reading. In no time, you'll be creating powerful applications powered by ColdFusion 10.

PART

Web Technology Innovation

ColdFusion 10 and HTML5

In this book, we'll be discussing most of the new features of ColdFusion 10 and how to use them in creating applications. ColdFusion has always embraced the latest technologies available on the web, and a major goal of new versions of ColdFusion has been to make these available to programmers in a standardized, easy-to-use, platform-independent way. Recent versions of ColdFusion have made it possible to create client-side code for form validation, page layout, and navigation without writing JavaScript directly; respond to requests using protocols other than HTTP; and create and call web services without a huge amount of manual coding. Now many of HTML5's features are available to you in the integrated, cutting-edge way you expect from ColdFusion.

This chapter starts by introducing the new features of HTML5 that are beginning to become standard in most web browsers, and it continues with an introduction to the new geolocation features in `<cfmap>`. More HTML5 features of ColdFusion are discussed in Chapters 2, 3, and 6 of this book.

What's New in HTML5?

HTML5 is the new standard in programming for the World Wide Web.

HTML5 standardizes many of the approaches programmers have been using for a long time on the web and makes a lot of other tasks easier. HTML5 addresses many of the shortcomings of earlier versions of HTML and adds a lot of new functions. Improvements include:

- Video and audio tags for embedding rich content in web pages, and timed media playback that allows synchronization of multiple rich elements on a page

- A canvas element that allows the use of bitmaps and 2D graphic rendering and the rendering of scalable vector graphics (SVG) and Mathematical Markup Language (MathML)

- Semantic tags that allow the HTML to indicate what a part of a page *means*, rather than just how it looks (for example, `<article>`, `<nav>`, `<article>`, `<aside>`, `<figure>`, etc.)

- CSS3 support, which allows a much richer set of rules and selectors than earlier style sheets and includes features such as word wrap, rounded corners, variable opacity (semi-transparent layers), and standardization across all browsers

- Offline storage, allowing a web application to store local data on the user's computer (with permission) as well as entire local applications that don't require a user to be connected to the Internet (especially important in mobile web applications)

- Geolocation, which allows a web browser to retrieve location data from a user's computer for use in an application, particularly important in mobile applications

- Drag-and-drop extensions to JavaScript

- WebSocket technology, which allows a web browser to receive data asynchronously from a web server without an additional request

- Support for other technologies including microdata (microformats), document editing, browser history management, and MIME type registration

NOTE

The full HTML5 specification is available at http://www.w3.org/TR/html5/. HTML5, in spite of its broad support, is a work in progress, and a final draft is not expected until 2014.

Can I Use the New HTML5 Features?

Most of these HTML5 features have been implemented in current browsers on all major mobile and desktop computing platforms, including Mozilla Firefox, Microsoft Internet Explorer, Opera, Google Chrome, and Apple Safari and their mobile equivalents. As of fall 2012, about 75 percent of the world's web browsers support the current version of HTML5.

NOTE

For a list of the browsers that support various HTML5 and CSS3 features, see http://html5test.com/.

Most programmers who want to provide applications that use HTML5 but need to support a wide audience currently have to use JavaScript libraries to support earlier browsers. ColdFusion 10 avoids most of the issues for users who aren't using a state-of-the-art browser by providing the option to fall back to non-HTML5 plug-ins that provide the same capabilities.

TIP

Some popular JavaScript-based HTML5 compatibility plug-ins include jPlayer, a jQuery plug-in for audio and video (http://www.jplayer.org/); htmlshiv, which provides some HTML5 syntax support for Internet Explorer versions earlier than IE 9 (http://code.google.com/p/html5shiv/); and selectivizr, which adds CSS3 selectors to IE (http://selectivizr.com/).

ColdFusion 10 HTML 5 Support

The first part of this book discusses the HTML5 features of ColdFusion 10. HTML5 support in ColdFusion 10 includes the features listed in Table 1.1.

Table 1.1 ColdFusion 10 HTML 5 Support

HTML5 FEATURE	COLDFUSION SUPPORT	FOR MORE INFORMATION
Geolocation	`<cfmap>` enhancements	Discussed in this chapter
WebSocket	Provided through listener components	See Chapter 2, "Using WebSocket"
Canvas	HTML5 charting	See Chapter 3, "Charting Revisited"
HTML5 embedded video and audio	`<cfmediaplayer>`	See Chapter 6, "Embedding Video"

Geolocation and the `<cfmap>` Tag

One way in which ColdFusion 10 supports HTML5 is through an extension to the `<cfmap>` tag (which has been around since ColdFusion 9). This tag allows you to embed a Google map with many options, including options to specify the map location by either address or latitude and longitude, show markers, zoom, enable click behavior, and display tooltips.

A new feature in HTML5, the Geolocation API, adds some tags to HTML and JavaScript that allow a script running in the browser to determine the end user's physical location (latitude and longitude, not whether you're on the chair or the couch). HTML5 JavaScript adds a new function, `getCurrentPosition()`, which returns a structure that contains the coordinates of the user. (Since this information is a potential security breach, the browser first asks the user to approve the use of this information.)

ColdFusion 10 adds a new attribute to `<cfmap>`, called `showuser`, that adds this same function to Google Maps. If `showuser` is set to `true`, the user is prompted to allow the application to use the user's location, and if use is allowed, the map is centered at that point. If the user doesn't allow the browser to use the location, or if the browser can't tell where the user is, the map falls back to the location specified in the tag attributes `centeraddress` or `centerlatitude` and `centerlongitude`.

A subset of `<cfmap>` attributes is shown in Table 1.2.

Table 1.2 `<cfmap>` Attributes

ATTRIBUTE	REQUIRED OR OPTIONAL	DEFAULT	DESCRIPTION
centeraddress	Required if centerlatitude and centerlongitude are not specified		This attribute specified the address of the location, which is set as the center of the map.
centerlatitude	Required if centeraddress is not specified		This attribute specifies the latitude value for the location, in degrees. This value is set as the center of the map.
			This attribute must be used with the centerlatitude attribute.
			The valid values for centerlatitude are –90 to 90.
centerlongitude	Required if centeraddress is not specified		This attribute specifies the longitude value for the location, in degrees. This value is set as the center of the map.
			This attribute must be used with the centerlongitude attribute.
			The valid values for centerlongitude are –180 to 180.
name	Required		The name of the map.
			The name attribute is required to invoke JavaScript functions.
showmarkerwindow	Optional	false	If set to true, this attribute displays the marker window. If the attribute markerbind is used, unless you set this attribute to true, the marker window is not displayed.
			This attribute is ignored if markerwindowcontent is set to true.
showUser	Optional	false	If this attribute is set to true, on HTML compliant browsers, the user location is shown on the map.
			For browsers that are not HTML5 compliant, the address falls back to the value you specify for centeraddress. If no value is specified, it falls back to the values specified for centerlatitude and centerlongitude.
			The user has to authenticate the site so that it tracks user location. For example, in Google Chrome you are prompted to allow the browser to track your physical location.
Type	Optional	map	This attribute specifies the type of Google map: map satellite hybrid terrain earth
			If you specify type="earth", you are prompted to download the Google Earth 3D plug-in.
Width	Optional	400 pixels	This attribute specifies the map width, in pixels.

NOTE

Twenty-two other attributes are available for setting markers, callback, and so on. See the documentation for more information, or see Chapter 9, "Object Relational Mapping Enhancements."

Here's a simple example showing the use of the `<cfmap>` tag to map the White House, with the user's location included:

```
<cfmap name="hqmap"
       centeraddress="1600 Pennsylvania Avenue Northwest, Washington, DC"
       showuser="true">
```

Getting a Google Maps API Key

Unfortunately, you need to do more than just use `<cfmap>` to map a location. Google requires a use key for Version 2 of its API, so you need to get a Google API key. Google monitors the number of map loads per day and limits use to 25,000 loads per URL per day (at this time) for noncommercial users; if you exceed that number, you have to purchase a commercial license.

To get a Google API key, visit `https://code.google.com/apis/console/` and log in using a Google user ID (you can register and get one for free if you don't already have one). Click Services in the left menu and then activate Google Maps API Version 2 by clicking the box next to its name. Next, click API Access; your key should now be visible in the Simple API Access area.

You can add your Google API key to your application in either of two ways.

In the application.cfc file, specify:

```
<cfset this.googleMapKey = "<your-google-map-key>">
```

Alternatively, in your template, specify:

```
<cfset mapparams = {googlemapkey="<your-google-map-key>"}
<cfajaximport params="#mapparams#">
```

Using the second solution, here's our current template:

```
<!DOCTYPE html PUBLIC "-//W3C//DTD XHTML 1.0 Transitional//EN"
➥ "http://www.w3.org/TR/xhtml1/DTD/xhtml1-transitional.dtd">
<html xmlns="http://www.w3.org/1999/xhtml">
<head>
<meta http-equiv="Content-Type" content="text/html; charset=utf-8" />
<title>Map Example</title>
</head>

<body>
<!---
  Chapter 1 Example
  FileName: map1.cfm
  Author: Ken Fricklas (KF)
  Purpose: Sample CFMap Tag using the showuser attribute.
--->
<cfset mapparams = {googlemapkey = "AIzaSyCkqZfniiOnZwpBbz8NmR-wBssXUwR1M8k"}>
<cfajaximport params="#mapparams#">
```

```
<h1>Your House, or the White House</h1>
<cfmap name="hqmap" centeraddress="1600 Pennsylvania Avenue Northwest,
➡Washington, DC" zoomlevel="4" showuser="true" tip="White House" type="hybrid">
</body>
</html>
```

Now you can run that map. When it loads, you'll see the prompt for the user to allow access to the location (Figure 1.1).

Figure 1.1

The access location prompt in Firefox.

After you allow the location to be shared, you'll see the map centered on my house in Boulder, Colorado (Figure 1.2).

Figure 1.2

The Google Map created by <cfmap> centered on the author's home.

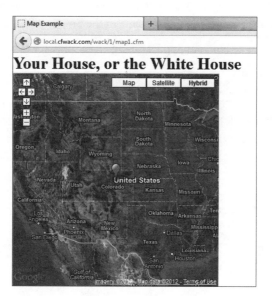

NOTE

You can't run Google Maps against your local host or 127.0.0.1 test server; you need to provide a real URL. The examples here used http://local.cfwack.com/, which is just an entry put in the host's file that points to 127.0.0.1.

One of the most powerful and innovative HTML5-related technologies is WebSocket. WebSocket provides a way to instantly connect your ColdFusion server with any number of web browsers. Users can instantly receive information and share messages with each other using the most up-to-date and speediest protocol available for data.

What Exactly Is WebSocket?

If you consult Wikipedia.org, you may find this definition:

WebSocket is a web technology providing for multiplexing bi-directional, full-duplex communications channels over a single TCP connection.

Clear as mud, right? If you are part of the 98 percent of the population not quite nerdy enough to understand that description, here's another way to think about WebSocket.

When you request a web page, your browser is making a TCP connection to a remote server. You can think of using a TCP connection as almost like sending a message via mail. (And no, not email, but good old reliable postal mail.) This process works well in most cases. In some cases, however, it can be inefficient.

Consider the shiny new Ajax-based web application of an e-commerce site. It wants to use Ajax to ask the server when a new order has been placed. Every time this occurs, the application will update the web page.

Pretty simple, right?

But consider what the browser has to do. Since the browser isn't on the server itself, it has to open a new TCP connection every few seconds to ask the server if a new order has been placed. Using the mail analogy, the process is a bit like your sending a letter every day to your cousin to ask him if he finally popped the question to his significant other.

WebSocket provides a way around this. Instead of sending messages to the server and waiting for a response, WebSocket creates an open line of communication between your browser and the server. If using TCP is like sending letters back and forth, using WebSocket is more akin to simply getting someone on the phone and having a conversation. Your application can stop asking the server when a new order has been placed and simply listen for the server to tell it instead.

The benefits of this approach become even more apparent when you switch to a multiuser application. For instance, consider a chat application. Using plain-old Ajax, each user of the chat application would need to send a TCP request to the server every second or so to see if new messages are waiting. Switching to WebSocket allows the clients to simply wait for new messages. When one user posts to the chat room, every single client can get the new message instantly.

ColdFusion 10 provides a WebSocket implementation that is easy to use and scalable to an incredible number of listening clients. In this chapter, we'll discuss how you can use WebSocket with ColdFusion 10.

Before we dig in, though, be warned. Many of ColdFusion's earlier Ajax-related features allowed developers to build powerful JavaScript-based applications without having to actually write JavaScript. WebSocket is different. You *will* be writing JavaScript. It won't be terribly difficult JavaScript, but if you've never written a line of JavaScript before, you may want to familiarize yourself with some of the basic syntax rules and concepts before continuing.

What About Browser Support?

You're probably wondering: what happens when a browser doesn't support WebSocket technology? Currently, approximately 48 percent of the installed browser market supports WebSocket. The excellent site caniuse.com provides a table showing the current level of support for WebSocket as of late summer 2012, shown in Figure 2.1.

Figure 2.1

Current browser support for WebSocket technology.

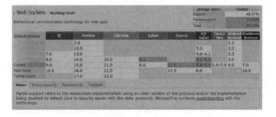

While it is encouraging that support is almost halfway there, you probably are concerned about the entire *other* half of the world out there. Luckily, ColdFusion provides an automatic fallback to Adobe Flash. Adobe Flash has incredible penetration in the browser market. Even better, this fallback is automatic. None of your code has to worry about it or otherwise do anything to create this handle. At a minimum, you can provide a message to those browsers that support neither WebSocket nor Adobe Flash. An example of such a message will be provided later in the chapter.

Getting Started

Before you begin working with WebSocket, you must define what are known as *channels*. A channel is simply one bucket, or one collection, of WebSocket data. When you send messages, they will always be on one particular channel. When you listen for messages, you will always listen for messages from a particular channel. A ColdFusion application can make use of as many channels as you would like, but before you actually use them, you must define them.

Channels are defined in a ColdFusion application with a setting in your Application.cfc file. Listing 2.1 provides an example of a channel definition.

Listing 2.1 /2/demo1/Application.cfc

```
component {

    this.name="cfwack2_1";

    this.wschannels = [{name:"news"}];

}
```

The setting `wschannels` is defined as an array of structures. In the example in Listing 2.1, we've defined one channel with a name value of `news`. You may be wondering why an array of structs is used instead of simply an array of names. Later you will see an example of a more complex WebSocket definition.

Defining the valid WebSocket channels is the first step. To actually make use of a WebSocket instance within a CFM file, you'll make use of the `<cfwebsocket>` tag. This tag handles quite a few things. First, it loads all the necessary JavaScript files into your page. Second, it provides a basic handle, or alias, for a JavaScript object that will integrate with the WebSocket API. Next, it defines the name of a JavaScript function to run when messages are received. And finally, you can specify channels to automatically connect to when the page is loaded. Listing 2.2 provides a simple example of a WebSocket definition.

Listing 2.2 /2/demo1/index.cfm

```
<!DOCTYPE html>
<html>

<head>
<title>Example One</title>
<script language="javascript">
function messageHandler(msg) {
    console.log("messageHandler Run");
    console.dir(msg);
}
</script>
</head>

<body>
```

Listing 2.2 (CONTINUED)

```
<h1>Example One</h1>

</body>
</html>

<cfwebsocket name="myWS" onMessage="messageHandler" subscribeTo="news">
```

Let's tackle this application from the bottom up. The last tag in this template is the `<cfwebsocket>` tag. The name attribute value, `myWS`, is telling ColdFusion to create a JavaScript variable of the same name. If we wanted to do anything with the WebSocket, such as send a message, we would do it via an API provided in that variable. The next attribute, `onMessage`, specifies the name of the JavaScript event handler that will handle messages received by the WebSocket. Note that you must write this handler yourself. If you do not, your code will not work. The final attribute in our template, `subscribeTo`, says that we should automatically connect to the news channel when the page loads. This is not a requirement for WebSocket applications, but for many of them, you will automatically want to connect when the page loads.

Moving up the file, the only other interesting part of the template is the JavaScript function `messageHandler`. To make this template as simple as possible, all it does is use the console API to log a quick message and dump out the value passed to the function.

At the beginning of the chapter, you were warned that some JavaScript experience was going to be required. If this is the first time you've seen the console API in use in JavaScript code, it may be unfamiliar. Essentially, it is a simple logging mechanism for your browser. In Chrome, the browser we'll be using for screen images and testing in this chapter, you can view the console by clicking the wrench icon in the upper-right corner of your browser. Click Tools and then select the JavaScript console. You should see something similar to Figure 2.2.

Figure 2.2

The JavaScript console.

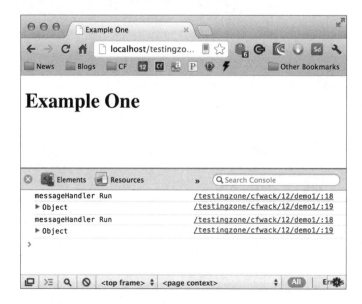

In the figure, you can see something interesting. All our CFM file did was, basically, subscribe to the news channel. We aren't broadcasting messages or actually doing anything interactive either. But notice that we've received two messages already. This is an important detail to note. The message handler is used for *all* messages sent over the WebSocket, which includes a variety of types of messages. When we ran `console.dir(msg)`, we asked the browser to dump (as with `<cfdump>`) the value of the message object. In Chrome, you can click to expand and explore these objects. Figure 2.3 shows the details for the two messages we received upon loading the page.

Figure 2.3

Messages received
upon loading the page.

```
messageHandler Run
▼ Object
    clientid: 91575817
    code: 0
    msg: "ok"
    ns: "coldfusion.websocket.channels"
    reqType: "welcome"
    type: "response"
  ▶ __proto__: Object
messageHandler Run
▼ Object
    channelssubscribedto: "news"
    clientid: 91575817
    code: 0
    msg: "ok"
    ns: "coldfusion.websocket.channels"
    reqType: "subscribeTo"
    type: "response"
  ▶ __proto__: Object
```

Notice that both messages have similar (but not the exact same) keys. Of particular note are the `reqType` and `type` keys. The first message has a welcome `reqType` value. You can probably guess that this is just the WebSocket's way of letting you know that the connection has been opened. The next message has a `reqType` of `"subscribeTo"`. You can see the channel we subscribed to as well as a `msg` value of `"ok"`, indicating the subscription was successful. Later you will learn that you can, on a case-by-case basis, restrict access to channels programmatically. We're spending time looking at these objects because our code later will check these values to determine what actions to take. If you ever forget what's in the message result, simply enter the `console.dir()` command again.

Using the JavaScript API

As described previously, the `<cfwebsocket>` tag is responsible for the setup of WebSocket support on your web page. Along with the channel listing in Application.cfc, this tag will prepare you to begin writing full applications using WebSocket. Now that you've done the setup work, it's time to begin writing JavaScript. The `<cfwebsocket>` tag creates a JavaScript object that you will interact with using custom JavaScript.

The API consists of the features listed in Table 2.1.

Table 2.1 JavaScript API

API	DESCRIPTION
Publish	Used to publish (send) a message to everyone listening. Note that a message need not be a simple string. It can be just about anything.
openConnection and closeConnection	Used to open or close the connection to the WebSocket server.
isConnectionOpen	A simple method that returns a Boolean representing your current connection state.
subscribe and unsubscribe	Used to subscribe (or unsubscribe) from a WebSocket channel. Remember that the `<cfwebsocket>` tag allows you to subscribe automatically. Sometimes you won't want to do so.
getSubscriptions	Returns an array of channels to which the current user is subscribed.
getSubscriberCount	Returns the total number of people subscribed to a channel.
Authenticate	Later in the chapter, we will discuss security options with WebSocket. One of them, authentication, allows you to ensure that only certain people use certain channels.
invoke and invokeAndPublish	Both of these APIs let you use WebSocket to call ColdFusion components (CFCs). These APIs are useful for times when you need to do something on the server side rather than within JavaScript.

Listing 2.3 provides a simple example that uses this API. Be sure you have copied all the files from the zip file you downloaded earlier.

Listing 2.3 /2/demo2/index.cfm

```
<!DOCTYPE html>
<html>

<head>
<title>Example Two</title>
<script language="javascript">
function messageHandler(msg) {
   console.log("messageHandler Run");
   console.dir(msg);

   if(msg.reqType == "getSubscriberCount") {
      document.querySelector("#subscriberCount").innerHTML =
      ➥"There are "+msg.subscriberCount + " subscriber(s).";
   }

   if(msg.type == "data") {
    document.querySelector("#messageResponseArea").innerHTML += msg.data + "<br/>";
   }
}
```

Listing 2.3   (CONTINUED)

```
function init() {

    //Handle the request to get subscriber count
    document.querySelector("#subscriberButton").addEventListener("click", function() {
        myWS.getSubscriberCount("news");
    },false);

    //Handle message send test
    document.querySelector("#messageButton").addEventListener("click", function() {
        var text = document.querySelector("#message").value;
        myWS.publish("news", text);
    },false);

}

</script>
</head>

<body onload="init()">

<h1>Example Two</h1>

<p>
<input type="text" id="message"> <button id="messageButton">Send Message</button>
<div id="messageResponseArea"></div>
</p>

<p>
<button id="subscriberButton">Get Subscriber Count</button>
<div id="subscriberCount"></div>
</p>

</body>
</html>

<cfwebsocket name="myWS" onMessage="messageHandler" subscribeTo="news">
```

Let's tackle this application from the bottom. Notice that the very last line is our `<cfwebsocket>` tag. We've assigned the name `myWS` and a message handler named `messageHander` and are automatically subscribing to a channel called `news`.

Moving up, we have a bit of HTML. Notice the two main paragraphs. The first (top) paragraph defines a text field with a button next to it. Below it is an empty div area. This UI will be used to let you test message sending.

The next paragraph defines a button that lets you get a subscription count. It also has a blank div area underneath. We're going to use JavaScript to enable the functionality for these two paragraphs. Let's start digging into that now.

When the page loads, we'll run a function called `init`. It makes use of `document.querySelector` to find both `subscriberButton` and `messageButton`. The `document.querySelector` function works in most modern browsers. If you have used jQuery in the past, this function is the same as `$("something")`.

When the user clicks the subscriber button, we use the JavaScript API to run `getSubscriberCount`. Notice that we pass in a channel. If the user clicks the button to send a message, we run the publish API. The message we publish is whatever value is in the text field.

Note that for both of these functions, we don't have a result. Why? WebSocket calls are asynchronous. Although they run fast, they aren't instantaneous. Instead, the result of both these calls will be sent to the message handler.

Now look at the message handler function, `messageHandler`. Everything goes through this handler, so we have to add a bit of code so that the handler recognizes the responses. As in the last demonstration, two responses are going to occur right away: one for the initial connection, and another for channel subscription. We don't really care about this. Instead, we want to know when we get a response for a subscriber count and when we get a response for a message.

Figuring out exactly what response was received can be tricky. You can see that we've included the `console.dir()` function for the message object. This function can be helpful during development because no one can be expected to remember the form of every WebSocket message response. You may want to remove this line, though, before putting the code into your production environment.

If you run this code in your browser, you should be able to use both buttons to test the WebSocket connection. However, to make things more interesting, try opening the CFM in *two* tabs. When you type a message in one tab, notice that it shows up in the second tab. This is part of the magic of WebSocket. All connected clients get messages—nearly instantly. Try opening the CFM in three or four tabs or in multiple browsers. Send a message in one, and all will display it. The subscriber count will also increase as you add more and more clients.

Working with CFC Handlers

You've seen now how to set up and connect to a WebSocket instance. You've also seen how to write some basic JavaScript to handle the sending and receiving of messages. ColdFusion's Web-Socket implementation also enables a deeper integration between WebSocket messages and CFML. Recall that before you can use a WebSocket instance in ColdFusion, you must define a list of supported channels in your Application.cfc file. This list was defined as an array of structs. We mentioned that the name value is required for each channel, but that other information can also be provided. That other information is the name of a CFC handler. This feature allows you to associate a CFC handler with a WebSocket channel. It provides a way to use CFML to provide detailed control over the behavior of your WebSocket instances. This handler doesn't replace the JavaScript code you write, but rather provides a complementary server-side association for your WebSocket instances. So what can you do with a CFC handler?

- You can determine programmatically whether someone is allowed to subscribe to a channel.

- You can prevent or modify a message that a client sends.

- You can prevent or modify a message before it is sent to a client.

- You can notice when a client stops listening.

Making use of a CFC handler is a two-step process. First, when you define your channel in the Application.cfc file, you must specify the name of the CFC that will act as a handler. Listing 2.4 shows an example of this.

Listing 2.4 /2/demo3/Application.cfc

```
component {

    this.name = "cfwack2_3";
    this.wschannels = [{name:"news",cfclistener:"newsHandler"}];

}
```

Notice now that along with defining a name for the channel, we've also defined the cfclistener property. We don't provide a filename (no .cfc is included in the value), but rather a "dot" path to the CFC, much like what is used for createObject.

Now let's take a look at newsHandler.cfc (Listing 2.5).

Listing 2.5 /2/demo3/newsHandler.cfc

```
component extends="CFIDE.websocket.ChannelListener" {

    public boolean function allowSubscribe(struct subscriberInfo) {
        if(!structKeyExists(arguments.subscriberInfo,"username")) return false;

        //Poor bob
        if(arguments.subscriberInfo.username == "bob") return false;
        return true;
    }

    public any function beforePublish(any message, struct subscriberInfo) {
        arguments.message = rereplace(arguments.message, "<.*?>","","all");
        return arguments.message;
    }

    public any function canSendMessage(any message, struct subscriberInfo,
    ➥struct publisherInfo) {
        if(findNoCase("darn", arguments.message) && subscriberInfo.username == "mary")
        ➥return false;
        return true;
    }

    public any function beforeSendMessage(any message, struct subscriberInfo,
    ➥struct publisherInfo) {
        message = "For #arguments.subscriberInfo.username#: " & arguments.message;
        return message;
    }

    public any function afterUnsubscribe(struct subscriberInfo) {
        wsPublish("news", "#arguments.subscriberInfo.username# left the
        ➥application.");
        return true;
    }

}
```

So what's going on here? To begin, all CFC handlers for WebSocket instances must extend CFIDE. websocket.ChannelListener. This is a core CFC that defines all the basic methods of a CFC listener (and worth reading yourself; the code isn't encrypted and can be a useful reminder of the available methods). After that, the methods you choose to add to your CFC are entirely dependent on your needs.

The first method defined in this example is allowSubscribe. As mentioned earlier, you can programmatically determine which clients are allowed to connect to a channel. A structure, subscriberInfo, is passed to this method. This structure will contain some metadata, including a unique client ID and connection time, and it will also contain any additional information passed when you subscribe to a channel. Shortly, we'll look at an example of this additional information in the front-end code. For now, though, assume that we've passed a username value. If the value isn't there at all, or if the value is "bob", the code returns false. Otherwise, a true value is returned. The end result is that Bob, for whatever reason we've determined, is not allowed to subscribe to this channel.

The next method, beforePublish, is fired whenever a user sends a message. You can use this method to make modifications to the message before clients start receiving it. In this case, we are using the method to remove any HTML from the message. You could perform this operation on the client side in JavaScript, but that approach would be insecure because a user could use the JavaScript console to bypass it. By using a server-side method, we ensure that the message is safe for others.

Compare beforePublish to the method beforeSendMessage. Imagine that five people are running your application at once. When the first user sends a message, beforePublish is run once. Then beforeSendMessage is run five times: once for each person listening to the channel. In this case, we've modified the message to specify the name of the person getting the message. This change may seem a bit silly because users should remember the usernames they chose, but it demonstrates that the same username that was used when subscribing will persist through the connection. We'll talk more about this when we switch to the front-end code. In theory, we could also remove HTML in this method, but that would be wasteful. By using beforePublish instead, we run this method one time only.

The method canSendMessage is fired before beforeSendMessage and is also sent to the receiver. Whereas beforeSendMessage allows you to dynamically modify the message, canSendMessage allows you to simply block the message completely. In this case, we've done some basic content checking. If the curse word *darn* is in the message and the username is Mary, the message is blocked from being sent to the user.

The final method in our handler is afterUnsubscribe. This method is run automatically when a user disconnects from a WebSocket channel. If you have been testing with multiple tabs in your browser, the easiest way to test this method is to connect with two tabs and then close one. When this event fires, we use the server-side method wsPublish to fire off a message to the remaining listeners. Later in the chapter, we'll discuss the server-side functions for WebSocket instances, but for now, just assume that they will all get a message stating that a particular user has left.

Whew! That's a lot—and we haven't even gotten to the front end yet. Let's take a look at that in Listing 2.6.

Listing 2.6   /2/demo3/index.cfm

```
<!DOCTYPE html>
<html>

<head>
<title>Example Three</title>
<script type="text/javascript" src="https://ajax.googleapis.com/ajax/libs/
➥ jquery/1.7.2/jquery.min.js"></script>
<script language="javascript">
function messageHandler(msg) {
   console.log("messageHandler Run");
   console.dir(msg);

   if(msg.type == "subscribe" && msg.code == -1) {
      alert("I'm sorry, but you were not able to subscribe.");
   }

   if(msg.type == "response" && msg.reqType == "subscribe") {
      $("#stepone").hide();
      $("#chattest").show();
      $("#messageButton").on("click", function () {
         var msg = $("#message").val();
         if(msg == '') return;
         myWS.publish("news",msg);
      })
   }

   if(msg.type == "data") {
      $("#messageResponseArea").append(msg.data + "<br/>");
   }
}

$(document).ready(function() {

   //Handle message send test
   $("#signinButton").on("click", function() {
      var name =$("#name").val();
      if(name.length) {
         myWS.subscribe("news", { username:name })
      }
   });

});

</script>
</head>

<body >

<h1>Example Three</h1>

<div id="stepone">
   Tell us your name please:
```

Listing 2.6 (CONTINUED)

```
    <input type="text" id="name"> <button id="signinButton">Sign In</button>

  </div>

  <div id="chattest" style="display:none">
    <p>
    <input type="text" id="message"> <button id="messageButton">Send Message</button>
    <div id="messageResponseArea"></div>
    </p>
  </div>

  <cfwebsocket name="myWS" onMessage="messageHandler">
```

As before, it makes sense to tackle this listing from the bottom up. The first thing you'll see (at the bottom of course) is that our `<cfwebsocket>` tag is *not* using the `subscribeTo` attribute. Unlike in our earlier demonstrations, we aren't going to automatically connect to a channel. Instead, we will connect through JavaScript later.

Moving up, our application is composed of two main UI items. The first div element, `stepone`, is used to prompt the user for a username. The second div element, `chattest`, is set to not appear. Basically, this application has two forms. On startup, it's going to ask you for a username, and after you enter one, code will be used to switch it to a simple chat application.

Now turn your attention to the JavaScript code. We've made use of jQuery in this demonstration to simplify some of the steps we have to take. You absolutely do not need to be a jQuery user to work with WebSocket.

For those unfamiliar with jQuery, note that the code in `$(document).ready(function() { … }` will fire when the document is loaded. An event listener for the Sign In button is defined. It simply gets the value from the text field and checks to ensure that the field isn't blank. If we have a username, we make use of the JavaScript API for our WebSocket object to run the subscribe method. We haven't used this method before because our `<cfwebsocket>` tag was handling this process for us. There is only one required argument for this API: the channel to subscribe to. But you are allowed to send along any additional information you choose. In this case, we're sending a username value that contains whatever was typed in the field.

Finally, turn your attention to the message handler. As we've stated a few times now, since the message handler is run for *everything*, it needs to be intelligent about handling the messages it receives. Our handler has three main parts to it.

The first part notices a subscribe response with a code of –1. This code represents a subscribe request that was denied. We use a simple alert to tell the user about this. To test this, remember to use the username Bob (Figure 2.4).

The next block will handle a successful subscription. It needs to hide the first div element, display the second, and create a listener to send chat messages. The listener uses the publish API described before. The final portion handles chat messages in general. It does this by appending to a div tag. Figure 2.5 shows an example of a chat session.

Figure 2.4

Testing the subscribe response.

Figure 2.5

Example of successful subscription.

Using Server-Side Functions

In the preceding example, you were introduced to one of the server-side WebSocket functions, wsPublish. You should be aware of two other functions:

- The wsGetSubscribers function will return all the subscribers for a particular channel.

- The wsGetAllChannels function will return the names of all the channels in an application.

Let's look at a simple example of these functions in Listing 2.7.

Listing 2.7   /2/demo4/test.cfm

```
<cfdump var="#wsGetSubscribers('news')#" label="Subscribers">

<cfdump var="#wsGetAllChannels()#" label="All Channels">

<cfif structKeyExists(form, "newmsg") and len(trim(form.newmsg))>
    <cfset wsPublish("news", form.newmsg)>
</cfif>

<form method="post">
    <input type="text" name="newmsg"> <input type="submit" value="Send">
</form>
```

Before going any further, let's be clear that this is one file in a folder with an Application.cfc file and other related files. If you run demo4 in your browser, you can see that the index.cfm file is very similar to the file in the previous example. The file in Listing 2.7 is a related file and wouldn't stand alone. It does, however, demonstrate the various server-side functions that are available. The first two dumps show the results from retrieving all the subscribers for the news channel and simply asking for existing channel names. The rest of the template provides a simple form-based way to broadcast messages. If you enter a message and click the Submit button, the message will be broadcast using `wsPublish`.

After you log into two tabs, Figure 2.6 shows what test.cfm will display if you run it.

Figure 2.6

Example of ColdFusion's server-side WebSocket support.

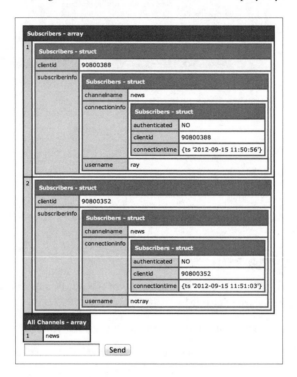

The result from retrieving a list of all the channels isn't that interesting, but the subscriber list provides a more interesting result. We've mentioned before that metadata is included in the subscriber data. You can see that in the figure. But also note that all the custom data (in this case, the username) is also included. Finally, if you enter text in the field and click Send, the clients will all get a copy of it.

Filtering Messages

By default, any time that a client subscribes to a channel, the client will get each and every message sent to that channel. A CFC handler can restrict this behavior, of course, but the default action is for all messages to be received by subscribers. There are options, however, that allow you to create filters that limit the messages received. ColdFusion provides two features that make this filtering easy to implement: subchannels and selectors.

Working with Subchannels

Subchannels are, as you can probably guess, subsets of channels. What's interesting, though, is that while channels must be defined in your Application.cfc file, subchannels are free form. Let's consider some examples.

Imagine an application that defines two channels: News and Stocks. When you subscribe to a channel, it must be one of those two values. But you can also choose to subscribe to a subchannel under News or Stocks. Subchannels are defined by adding a period and a label. So instead of subscribing to News, a client could subscribe to News.Sports. The client could also subscribe to News.Tech and News.Korea. Another user may subscribe to News.Art. Although the higher-level channel News must match one of the channels defined in your Application.cfc file, you can subscribe to any subchannel you desire. You can also go deeper. Instead of subscribing to News.Sports, you could subscribe to News.Sports.Football.

Subscribing to a subchannel filters the messages you get. The more specific the subscription, the fewer messages you will receive. For example, imagine three people: Raymond, Scott, and Todd. Raymond subscribes to News. Scott subscribes to News.Sports. Todd subscribes to News.Sports. Football.

If a message is published to News, then only Raymond gets it. Scott and Todd don't get it because they asked for a more filtered subscription.

If a message is published to News.Sports, then Raymond and Scott get it. Raymond is going to get *everything* under News, and Scott had asked for News.Sports, so obviously he will get it.

Finally, if a message is published to News.Sports.Football, then all three people will get it.

Listing 2.8 provides an example.

Listing 2.8   /2/demo5/index.cfm

```
<!DOCTYPE html>
<html>

<head>
<title>Example Five</title>
<script type="text/javascript" src="https://ajax.googleapis.com/ajax/libs/
➡ jquery/1.7.2/jquery.min.js"></script>
<script language="javascript">
var subscribedChannel;

function messageHandler(msg) {
    console.log("messageHandler Run");
    console.dir(msg);

    if(msg.type == "response" && msg.reqType == "subscribe") {
        $("#stepone").hide();
        $("#chattest").show();
        $("#messageButton").on("click", function () {
            var msg = $("#message").val();
            if(msg == '') return;
```

Listing 2.8 (CONTINUED)

```
            myWS.publish(subscribedChannel,msg);
        })
    }

    if(msg.type == "data") {
        $("#messageResponseArea").append(msg.data + "<br/>");
    }
}

$(document).ready(function() {

    //Handle message send test
    $("#signinButton").on("click", function() {
        var name =$("#name").val();
        subscribedChannel = $("#newstype option:selected").val();
        if(name.length) {
            myWS.subscribe(subscribedChannel,
                    {
                            username:name
                    })
        }
    });

});

</script>
</head>

<body >

<h1>Example Five</h1>

<div id="stepone">
    <input type="text" id="name" placeholder="Your Name:">
    <select id="newstype">
    <option value="news">All News</option>
    <option value="news.tech">Tech News</option>
    <option value="news.sports">Sports News</option>
    <option value="news.sports.football">Sports(Football) News</option>
    </select>
    <button id="signinButton">Sign In</button>

</div>

<div id="chattest" style="display:none">
    <p>
    <input type="text" id="message"> <button id="messageButton">Send Message</button>
    <div id="messageResponseArea"></div>
    </p>
</div>

</body>
</html>

<cfwebsocket name="myWS" onMessage="messageHandler">
```

This example is much like the previous one. It makes use of the username prompt in a div statement. But note the use of the select tag. This time we are prompting our users for the type of news they want to hear. The option tag values match a channel plus a subchannel value, whereas we use readable English in the text.

If you look back up at the JavaScript code, the only difference here is the subscribe call. Instead of subscribing to a particular channel, we take the value from the drop-down menu and use that. To test this, try opening the template in two tabs. In one, subscribe to News, and in the other, subscribe to one of the other options. Then chat in both tabs and note that the tab with the filtered selection receives fewer messages than the other.

Using Selectors

In the previous section, you learned how subchannels allow you to listen to a subset of all messages broadcast to a channel. Now you'll learn about a more precise method, using selectors.

Selectors work by adding a simple conditional statement to your subscription. Previously our messages have all been strings: simple text values. But you are allowed to publish any form of data you want. Imagine that we published a set of data that looks like this:

{ "Stock": "ADBE", "Price": 32, "Change": 5}

That JavaScript Object Notation (JSON)–formatted string represents a stock price. It contains a name, a price, and a change. Imagine then that you care about stock prices only when the change is large, such as 10 points higher or lower. To allow for this, you simply pass in a selector as that condition in the publish API:

```
myWS.subscribe("stockchanges", {selector:"change gt 15"});
```

Notice the use of gt, not <. This condition is passed to ColdFusion, and even though ColdFusion supports < and > operators in CFScript, you need to use gt or lt (or gte or let) in your selector. Let's look at a simple example of how selectors can be used (Listing 2.9).

Listing 2.9 /2/demo6/index.cfm

```
<!DOCTYPE html>
<html>

<head>
<title>Example Six</title>
<script language="javascript">

function doSubscription() {
    myWS.subscribe("stockchanges", {selector:"change gt 15"});
}

function alertHandler(msg) {
    console.log("alertHandler Run");

    if(msg.type == "data") {
        console.dir(msg);
```

Listing 2.9 (CONTINUED)

```
        document.querySelector("#alerts").innerHTML += "Stock "+msg.data.STOCK+"
        ➥changed "+msg.data.CHANGE+" for a price of "+msg.data.PRICE+"<br/>";
    }

}
</script>
</head>

<body>

<h1>Stock Alerts</h1>

<div id="alerts"></div>

</body>
</html>

<cfwebsocket name="myWS" onMessage="alertHandler" onOpen="doSubscription">
```

As before, we'll start at the bottom of the listing with the <cfwebsocket> tag. We've used a new attribute here, onOpen, to specify a function to run when the WebSocket connection is opened. Looking at that function, doSubscription, you can see the subscribe call passing the selector. When a message is received, we know it has passed that selector filter. It is simply appended to a div element as a rolling alert system of stocks. To test this function, we've created a file that simulates market activity (Listing 2.10). It's random, unlike the rational, sensible changes in our markets today.

Listing 2.10 /2/demo6/test.cfm

```
<cfsetting requesttimeout="999">
<cfset x = 1>
<cfloop condition="x lt 100">

    <cfscript>
    stockList = ["APPL","ADBE","MSFT","GOOG","IBM","WOPR","CAT","DOG"];

    arrayEach(stockList, function(itm) {

        if(!structKeyExists(application.stocks, itm)) {
            application.stocks[itm] = { stock:itm, price:randRange(100,120)};
        } else {
            change = randRange(-20,20);
            application.stocks[itm].price += change;
            //broadcast the change
            wsPublish("stockchanges", {stock:itm, change:abs(change),
            ➥price:application.stocks[itm].price});
        }
    });

    </cfscript>

    <cfoutput>
        Pushed an update...<br/>
    </cfoutput>
```

Listing 2.10 (CONTINUED)

```
      <cfflush>
      <cfset sleep(4000)>
      <cfset x++>
</cfloop>

<p>Done generating demo content...</p>
```

This template, test.cfm, simply loops from 1 to a 100 and generates changes to a set of hard-coded stock values. Notice the use of sleep to intentionally slow the output. Messages are published every time, but the client will see the message only if the selector condition passes. You can imagine multiple clients selecting different change values that they care about. The broadcaster will send out information, but clients get only what they care about. To test this code, open the index.cfm file in one tab and test.cfm in another tab. Return to the first tab and be patient.

Providing Security

ColdFusion 10's WebSocket implementation provides multiple ways to secure your applications. You can either log in via a JavaScript API or use an existing login. Your decision basically depends on whether you expect a user to log in when using the WebSocket application, or whether you expect the user to be logged in already. Let's look at the first method.

Using onWSAuthenticate

When logging in via JavaScript, your code will make use of the authenticate API in your JavaScript WebSocket object along with a new method in Application.cfc: onWSAuthenticate. The combination of the two allows you to control who can subscribe or publish to a channel. First, let's look at the index.cfm file (Listing 2.11).

Listing 2.11 /2/demo7/index.cfm

```
<!DOCTYPE html>
<html>

<head>
<title>Example Seven</title>
<script type="text/javascript" src="https://ajax.googleapis.com/ajax/libs/
➥ jquery/1.7.2/jquery.min.js"></script>
<script language="javascript">
var username;

function messageHandler(msg) {
   console.log("messageHandler Run");
   console.dir(msg);

   if(msg.type == "subscribe" && msg.code == -1) {
      alert("I'm sorry, but you were not able to subscribe.");
   }

   if(msg.type == "response" && msg.reqType == "authenticate") {
      if(msg.code == -1) {
         alert("Authentication failed.\nHint:try admin or bob");
```

Listing 2.11 (CONTINUED)

```
        } else if(msg.code == 0) {
            myWS.subscribe('news', {username:name });
        }
    }

    if(msg.type == "response" && msg.reqType == "subscribe") {
        $("#stepone").hide();
        $("#chattest").show();
        $("#messageButton").on("click", function () {
            var msg = $("#message").val();
            if(msg == '') return;
            myWS.publish('news',msg);
        })
    }

    if(msg.type == "data") {
        $("#messageResponseArea").append(msg.data + "<br/>");
    }
}

$(document).ready(function() {

    //Handle message send test
    $("#signinButton").on("click", function() {
        username = $("#name").val();
        var password = $("#password").val();
        if(!username.length || !password.length) return false;
        myWS.authenticate(username, password);
    });

});

</script>
</head>

<body >

<h1>Example Seven</h1>

<div id="stepone">
    <input type="text" id="name" placeholder="Your Name:">
    <input type="password" id="password" placeholder="Your Password:">
    <button id="signinButton">Sign In</button>

</div>

<div id="chattest" style="display:none">
    <p>
    <input type="text" id="message"> <button id="messageButton">Send Message</button>
    <div id="messageResponseArea"></div>
    </p>
</div>

</body>
</html>

<cfwebsocket name="myWS" onMessage="messageHandler">
```

This listing is similar to previous examples, but note the use of a username and password field. Before trying to subscribe to a channel, we first have to authenticate. You can see that code in the JavaScript event handler for the Sign In button.

As with every other call, the result is passed back to the message handler. You can see a new block in here that looks for a reqType value (think request type) of authenticate. If the code is –1, then the authentication failed, and we tell the user. The rest of the code is similar to earlier examples so we don't need to discuss it again.

Now let's look at the authentication code in Application.cfc (Listing 2.12).

Listing 2.12 /2/demo7/Application.cfc

```
component {
    this.name = "cfwack2_7";
    this.wschannels = [{name="news",cfclistener:"newsHandler"}];

    public boolean function onWSAuthenticate(string username, string password,
    ➥struct connectionInfo) {
        if(username == "admin" || username == "bob") {
            connectionInfo.authenticated=true;

            //random additional key
            connectionInfo.starwars = 1;

            if(username == "admin") connectionInfo.role = "admin";

            return true;
        } else {
            return false;
        }

    }
}
```

The new onWSAuthenticate method is fired when the JavaScript code runs the authenticate method. It's passed the username, password, and a struct of connection information. Actual authentication would check a database or some other code, but for now, we simply check the username.

Here's the crucial part. To mark a user as logged in, you set a flag in the connectionInfo structure passed in. The flag must be authenticated, and it must be set to true. You can also add any metadata at this point. Here, for all users, we're setting a key called starwars to 1, but for one user, the admin user, we're specifying a role. What's cool then is that all of this information will be available in the CFC handler. We could use the role, for example, to determine certain permissions.

We aren't done yet, though. To completely secure the application, we must check for an authenticated user in the CFC handler as well (Listing 2.13).

Listing 2.13   /2/demo7/newsHander.cfc

```
component extends="CFIDE.websocket.ChannelListener" {

    public boolean function allowSubscribe(struct subscriberInfo) {

        //I am crucial. You must use me. Or else.
        if(!arguments.subscriberInfo.connectionInfo.authenticated) return false;

        //I'm an optional check just to be extra secure
        if(!structKeyExists(arguments.subscriberInfo,"username")) return false;

        return true;
    }

    //Required because publishing != subscribing
    public boolean function allowPublish(struct publisherInfo) {
        return arguments.publisherInfo.connectionInfo.authenticated;
    }

    public any function beforePublish(any message, struct subscriberInfo) {
        message = rereplace(message, "<.*?>","","all");
        return message;
    }

}
```

To truly lock down the application, both `allowSubscribe` and `allowPublish` have to check the authenticated key. If you don't do this, users can still subscribe or publish to your channel. Note too that we've used a bit of additional logic in `allowSubscribe` to ensure that the user also has passed a username along with the request.

Using Single Sign-On Mode

The second form of authentication is called single sign-on mode. Basically, it assumes that you are logged in already. To use this feature, you must use <cflogin>-based security. Listing 2.14 provides a basic <cflogin>-secured application.

Listing 2.14   /2/demo8/Application.cfc

```
<cfcomponent>

    <cfset this.name = "cfwack2_8">
    <cfset this.wschannels = [{name="news",cfclistener:"newsHandler"}]>
    <cfset this.sessionManagement=true>
    <cfset this.loginStorage="session">

    <cffunction name="onRequestStart" returnType="boolean">
        <cfargument name="req" type="string" required="true">
        <cfset var doLogin = true>

        <cfif not findNoCase("login.cfm", arguments.req)>
            <cflogin>

                <cfif isDefined("cflogin")>
                    <cfif cflogin.name is "admin" or cflogin.name is "bob">
```

Listing 2.14   (CONTINUED)

```
                <cfset var roles = "">
                <cfif cflogin.name is "admin">
                   <cfset roles = "admin">
                </cfif>
                <cfloginuser name="#cflogin.name#" password="#cflogin.password#"
                ➥roles="#roles#">
                <cfset doLogin = false>
             </cfif>
          </cfif>

          <cfif doLogin>
             <cflocation url="login.cfm" addToken="false">
          </cfif>

       </cflogin>
    </cfif>
    <cfreturn true>
  </cffunction>

</cfcomponent>
```

Note how `onRequestStart` uses `<cflogin>` to ensure that every request for a CFM file must be made by an authenticated user. If the user is not logged in, the user is forced to login.cfm. (You can find that file in the downloaded code. It's just a username and password prompt.) We're going to skip the display of the index.cfm file as well because it is so similar to earlier examples. Since authentication is now baked into the ColdFusion side, there is nothing of it left in the JavaScript side: It isn't necessary. However, the CFC handler still checks for it. Instead of showing you the entire file (`allowSubscribe` and `allowPublish` are virtually the same), we'll look at one method, `beforePublish`:

```
public any function beforePublish(any message, struct subscriberInfo) {
    message = rereplace(message, "<.*?>","","all");
    return "From: #arguments.subscriberInfo.connectionInfo.username#: " & message;
}
```

This method shows that the username from `<cflogin>` will be available in the `connectionInfo` structure as well. We use it here to mark the message as being from a particular user.

Generating Messages with CFCs

So far, you've seen examples of messages published from the JavaScript API as well as server-side calls published with `wsPublish`. ColdFusion also provides a few other ways to publish messages that may be of use to you. One method is the `invokeAndPublish` API. This API allows you to access any ad hoc CFC within your application and run a method on it. That CFC message takes an incoming packet of arguments and can do ... whatever! But the result of the CFC will then be broadcast to other clients. So why would you use it? You may have existing functionality that you want to reuse in a WebSocket application. You may want to create a message that is just too complex to build in JavaScript. For whatever reason you may have, if you want to use a CFC to formulate the message, use the `invokeAndPublish` API.

You can see a demonstration of this method in the demo9 folder. Since the code is similar to the earlier examples, let's focus on the changes. Instead of running myWS.publish, we will use this format:

```
myWS.invokeAndPublish('news', "root.chat", "doChat", [msg]);
```

The method's arguments are the channel, the CFC (not the dot path, in this case using a ColdFusion mapping called root), the method, and finally an argument of values. The arguments that you send will depend on your particular logic. The CFC in question is shown in Listing 2.15.

Listing 2.15 /2/demo9/chat.cfc

```
component {

    public function doChat(string input) {
        return len(input) & " * " & input;
    }

}
```

Notice that there is nothing WebSocket related in this code. All we have is a method and a result. In this case, we're taking a message and prefixing it with the length of the message and an asterisk. The result then ends up in the browser. If you send the message "Ray", all the connected clients would see "3 * Ray".

Point-to-Point WebSocket

Another variant of this code is used in point-to-point WebSocket applications. These are single-client applications in which you aren't sharing messages between multiple clients. Instead, the WebSocket communication is between only one client and the server. In these applications, channels aren't used at all, so no settings are required in Application.cfc. Listing 2.16 provides an example of this code.

Listing 2.16 /2/demo10/index.cfm

```
<!DOCTYPE html>
<html>
<head>
<title>Example 10</title>
<script>
var respDiv;

function messageHandler(msg) {
    console.dir(msg);

    if(msg.reqType == "invoke" && msg.type == "response") {
        respDiv.innerHTML += msg.data + "<br/>";
    }

    if(msg.type == "data") {
        respDiv.innerHTML += "The computer said: <b>" + msg.data + "</b><br/>";
    }
}

function init() {
```

Listing 2.16 (CONTINUED)

```
        respDiv = document.querySelector("#response");

        document.querySelector("#testButton").addEventListener("click", function(e) {
            var input = document.querySelector("#input").value;

            myWS.invoke("root.responder", "testResponse", [input]);

            return false;
        });

    }

    </script>
    <style>
    #response {
        font-size: 12px;
        background-color: yellow;
        width: 50%;
        padding: 10px;
    }
    </style>
    </head>

    <body onload="init()">

        <input type="text" id="input" placeholder="Enter Something">
        <button id="testButton">Test</button>

        <p/>

        <div id="response"></div>

    </body>
    </html>

    <cfwebsocket name="myWS" onMessage="messageHandler">
```

First note that the <cfwebsocket> tag is still being used. This tag is necessary to load the proper JavaScript libraries and define the JavaScript handle for API calls. The application consists of a simple input field and a button with a response div area beneath it.

In the JavaScript, note that the button will send the user input using a new API: `invoke`. Like `invokeAndPublish`, this API needs to know the CFC and the method to call. But it does not use a channel name because, again, channels are not involved.

Now let's look at the CFC called (Listing 2.17).

Listing 2.17 /2/demo10/responder.cfc

```
    component {

        public function testResponse(string str) {
            if(str == "beer") {
                wsSendMessage("You like beer!");
            }
```

Listing 2.17 (CONTINUED)

```
        return reverse(str);
    }

}
```

The CFC's `testResponse` method takes in a string, and most of the time, it just returns the reverse of the string. However, it can also use another server-side function, `wsSendMessage`, to pass along an additional message. If you return to Listing 2.16, you can see that the message handler handles both types of responses. Where and when you use this function really depends on the application you are designing.

Error Handling and Unsupported Browsers

As mentioned at the very beginning of this chapter, WebSocket still is not universally supported. Luckily, ColdFusion will switch to Adobe Flash to handle those cases without your needing to modify anything in your code at all. But you may sometimes have a visitor who uses a browser that doesn't support WebSocket *or* Adobe Flash. In those cases, and to handle errors in general, you can use the `onError` attribute of the `<cfwebsocket>` tag. This method can be used as easily as this:

```
<cfwebsocket name="myWS" onMessage="messageHandler" subscribeTo="news"
➥onError="errorHandler">
```

In the preceding example, the expectation is that you will define a JavaScript function called `errorHandler`. You can find an example of this function in the demo11 folder. Here is that particular function from the file:

```
function errorHandler(e) {
    console.log("Error");
    console.dir(e);
    alert(e.msg);
}
```

How you handle the error is up to you. Also keep in mind that this error handler will be fired for *any* error. You will need to work with the Exception object to determine what error was thrown and how best to handle it.

ColdFusion Administrator Options

The ColdFusion Administrator has a WebSocket page that allows you to modify four options:

- You can disable WebSocket completely.

- You can specify the port.

- You can set a maximum size for data packets sent back and forth.

- You can disable the Adobe Flash fallback support.

In most cases, end users will never need to worry about these options.

CHAPTER 3

Charting Revisited

Charting and ColdFusion 10

ColdFusion 10 has increased its support of HTML5 with enhancements to the `<cfchart>` tag. Most important, to support more browsers, including those on mobile devices that don't support the Adobe Flash–based charts in earlier versions, ColdFusion 10 supports chart rendering using the HTML canvas. ColdFusion 10 also offers more than 25 new attributes that allow customization of the HTML and JavaScript code that is generated on your page when the tag is used.

ColdFusion supports bar graphs, pie charts, line graphs, scatter charts, and many other chart types, and it can render them in 3D and in combinations on the same chart.

Getting Started with `<cfchart>`

Let's create a simple chart just to get familiar with the tags involved. For these examples, we'll use the OWS sample movie database and chart the cost of the movies made by the directors in 2001. In Listing 3.1, you can see the tags needed to create a simple 2D pie chart for three of the directors.

Listing 3.1   Basic Chart Example

```
<!DOCTYPE html>
<html>
<!---
   Chapter 3 Basic Chart Example
   FileName: Basic.cfm
   Author: Ken Fricklas (KF)
   Purpose: Sample cfchart example
--->
<head>
<meta http-equiv="Content-Type" content="text/html; charset=utf-8" />
<title>Basic Chart</title>
</head>

<body>
```

Listing 3.1 (CONTINUED)

```
<cfchart>
  <cfchartseries>
  <cfchartdata item="Woody" value="55001">
  <cfchartdata item="Steven" value="17090">
  <cfchartdata item="George" value="15000">
  </cfchartseries>
</cfchart>
</body>
</html>
```

The tags required to create a chart are `<cfchart>`, `<cfchartseries>`, and `<cfchartdata>`. The chart is enclosed in a `<cfchart>` tag. Inside that tag, we include a single chart series, in the `<cfchartseries>` tag, which indicates a set of data points that will be plotted together. Inside this tag are the chart data points—three data points have been manually inserted—each of which has a value that will be plotted on the chart.

Figure 3.1 shows the result.

Figure 3.1

Simple bar chart using `<cfchart>`.

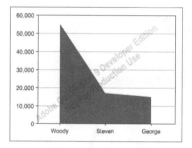

This chart uses all the default values; it renders the chart using Adobe Flash and creates a bar chart. The chart is the default height and width: 240 pixels wide by 320 pixels tall.

We'd actually prefer a pie chart that is 500 x 400 pixels and has a title and a legend. All we need to do all this is add the `showlegend`, `title`, `height`, and `width` attributes to the `<cfchart>` tag and add a `type` of `"pie"` to the `<cfchartseries>`. In addition, we want to support HTML5 browsers that don't handle Adobe Flash by default, so we add `format="html"` to the `<cfchart>` tag as well. Finally, to specify exactly which colors are used for each slice of the pie, we add the `colorlist` attribute, which simply takes a list of colors (names or hexadecimal values) in the same order as the `<cfchartdata>` values to which they correspond.

The resulting code and text are shown in Listing 3.2 and Figure 3.2.

Listing 3.2   Slightly Less Basic **`<cfchart>`** Tag, with Attributes

```
<!DOCTYPE html>
<!---
  Chapter 3 Slightly Less Basic Chart Example
  FileName: Basic2.cfm
  Author: Ken Fricklas (KF)
  Purpose: Sample cfchart example
--->
```

Listing 3.2 (CONTINUED)

```html
<html>
<head>
<meta http-equiv="Content-Type" content="text/html; charset=utf-8" />
<title>Basic HTML Chart</title>
</head>

<body>
<cfchart format="html" showlegend="true"
    height="400" width="500" title="2001 Movie Cost By Director">
    <cfchartseries type="pie" colorlist="red,blue,green">
    <cfchartdata item="Woody" value="55001">
    <cfchartdata item="Steven" value="17090">
    <cfchartdata item="George" value="15000">
    </cfchartseries>
</cfchart>
</body>
</html>
```

Figure 3.2

Slightly less basic
<cfchart> example.

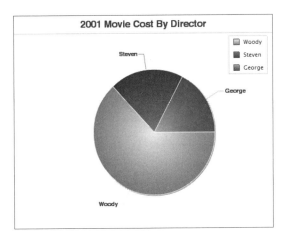

Updating <cfchart>

Unfortunately, the version of <cfchart> that ships with ColdFusion 10 is an old version of ZingChart, which has several bugs when you use it in HTML5 mode. (The most noticeable ones are tips that aren't positioned correctly in Chrome and draggable legends that sometimes don't drag). Hopefully, these bugs will be fixed in a ColdFusion 10 update, but in the meantime you can put better code in place.

It's really easy to upgrade your installation with the current scripts. You can get the latest version of the scripts from www.zingchart.com: download the free trial version of ZingChart and install it.

To upgrade ColdFusion, find the <coldfusion install>/wwwroot/CFIDE/scripts/chart directory. Rename the two files cfchart-lite.js and cfchart-html.js and keep them as backups. Then, from the ZingChart installation folder, copy the file /flash_scripts/zingchart-lite-1.1.js into the directory and rename it as cfchart-lite.js, and copy the file /html5_scripts/zingchart-html5-min.js into the directory and rename it cfchart-html.js. That's it!

Using Query Data in Charts

Our simple example was useful as a starting point, but rarely do we want to just plot a few fixed points with values that we already know. To put live data in your chart, you create a query and pass it to a `<cfchartseries>` tag using a process similar to that for `<cfselect>`, telling the ColdFusion interpreter what query to use, and which columns are the items and the values to be charted. The syntax looks like the following:

```
<cfchartseries query="qData" itemcolumn="myItem" valuecolumn="myValue">
```

Listing 3.3 in the next section provides an example.

Note that you can still include chart data points that are not part of the query in the data, by adding in a `<cfchartdata>` tag, in this case to add a fixed cost for the studio to the amount being spent on actual movies.

> **TIP**
>
> The somewhat complicated-looking `select` clause just provides an easy way to show the data rounded to thousands. By casting the float value as an integer, the tooltip will (for example) show 51 as the value instead of perhaps 51.007.

Previewing and Zooming

A cool feature of `<cfchart>` is the capability to create a block that shows you a small preview of the chart and allows you to zoom in on parts of the chart. Zooming requires you to use the `preview` attribute, and either `xaxis` or `yaxis`, depending on which way you want to allow the user to zoom.

To display the preview area, add the attribute `preview=#{"visible":true}#` to your `<cfchart>` tag. Then add `xaxis=#{'zooming':true}#` or `yaxis=#{'zooming':true}#` to your chart, as required. You can also add style attributes to position and style the preview and axes if needed.

Listing 3.3 shows an example of `<cfchart>`, using a query to create the data and with zooming turned on. Figure 3.3 shows the results of running this code.

Listing 3.3 Advanced Chart with Preview, Zoom, and Query

```
<!DOCTYPE html PUBLIC "-//W3C//DTD XHTML 1.0 Transitional//EN"
➡ "http://www.w3.org/TR/xhtml1/DTD/xhtml1-transitional.dtd">
<html xmlns="http://www.w3.org/1999/xhtml">
<head>
<meta http-equiv="Content-Type" content="text/html; charset=utf-8" />
<title>Advanced Chart with Query Data and Zooming</title>
</head>
<!---
    Chapter 3 Query Data Chart
    FileName: query.cfm
    Author: Ken Fricklas (KF)
    Purpose: Create a chart series from a query result set, and allow the user to
➡ zoom in on part of the data.
--->
```

Listing 3.3 (CONTINUED)

```
<body>
<cfquery name="qFilms" datasource="ows">
    select cast (sum(e.expenseamount / 1000) as int) as filmcost,
        substr(d.firstname, 1, 1) || substr(d.lastname, 1, 1) as initials
      from expenses e, directors d, filmsdirectors fd, films f
    where e.filmid = fd.filmid
        and fd.directorid = d.directorid
        and fd.filmid = f.filmid
        and year(f.dateintheaters) = 2001
      group by substr(d.firstname, 1, 1) || substr(d.lastname, 1, 1), d.directorid
</cfquery>
<cfchart format="html" showlegend="true"
    height="400" width="500" title="Budget By Director, in 1000s"
    preview=#{"visible":true}#
    xaxis=#{'zooming':true}#
    >
    <cfchartseries type="bar" query="qFilms" valuecolumn="filmcost"
    ➥itemcolumn="initials" serieslabel="Film Cost"
    >
    <cfchartdata item="Fixed Cost" value="250">
    </cfchartseries>
</cfchart>
</body>
</html>
```

Figure 3.3

Query result with zooming.

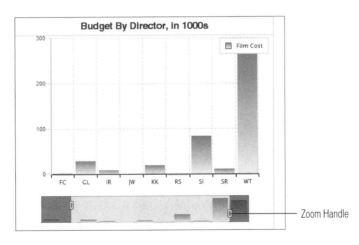

ColdFusion 10 Chart Types

ColdFusion 10's charting engine is based on a product called ZingChart (for more information, go to http//www.zingchart.com). All the chart types supported by ZingChart are available in ColdFusion10. Figure 3.4 shows many of the 33 chart types available.

Figure 3.4

Chart types.

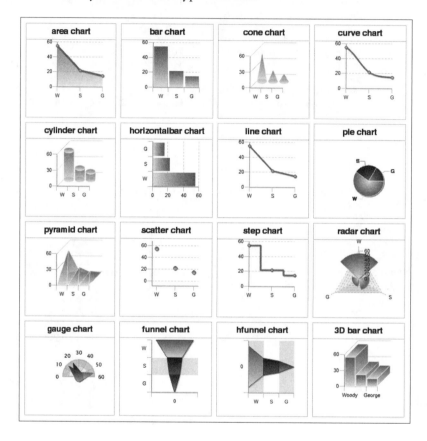

Most chart types can be created easily by using simple `<cfchartdata>` tags as discussed earlier, but some types require more complex data than simple key-value pairs, as listed in Table 3.1. For example, a stock chart requires a target value rather than just a single value on the plot.

NOTE

As of this writing, four additional chart types–rose, Venn, sparkline, and Pareto–are supported by ZingChart but not by ColdFusion.

Table 3.1 The `<cfchart>` Chart Types

TYPE	CHART TYPE ATTRIBUTE VALUE	3D VERSION	NOTES
BAR CHARTS			
Bar	Bar	bar3d	
Stacked Bar	Bar	bar3d	Requires multiple series.
Horizontal Bar	hbar	hbar3d	
Stacked Horizontal Bar	hbar	hbar3d	Requires multiple series.
PIE CHARTS			
Pie	Pie	pie3d	
Nested Pie	pie	pie3d	Requires multiple series.
Ring	pie	pie3d	This is just a pie chart with an additional attribute, "slice", in the JSON style.
X-Y CHARTS			
Line	line	line3d	Can add spline.
Scatter	scatter	scatter3d	
Area	area	area3d	
Stacked Area	area	area3d	Requires multiple series.
ADVANCED CHART TYPES (SEE DOCUMENTATION FOR MORE INFORMATION)			
Vertical Funnel	vfunnel	vfunnel3d	Requires two sets of values. Can add labels to y-axis via a parameter.
Horizontal Funnel	hfunnel	hfunnel3d	Requires two sets of values. Can add labels to x-axis via a parameter.
Bubble	bubble		Uses a complex series, with three axes.
Gauge	gauge		Requires multiple series.
Bullet	hbullet, vbullet		Requires goals and values in series.
Piano	Piano		Requires multiple series and scale values.
Radar	radar		Requires multiple series; many options available.
Stock	stock		Uses four values (open, high, low, and close) for series. Note: The default style file is not included with ColdFusion.

Styling a Chart

If your chart doesn't look exactly the way you would like, you can set the style of the chart or any of the chart ranges. Chart styling in ColdFusion 10 is provided by a JSON document (not the XML of earlier versions), which is documented on the ZingChart website. There's a tool (Figure 3.5) you can use to generate the JSON you need, available at http://www.zingchart.com/builder/. To use the JSON you've generated, simply copy it to a file, and to the <cfchart> tag add an attribute, style, containing the name of the file that contains the JSON. (At this time, Cold-Fusion does not support JSON directly in the contents of the style attribute; instead, it must be in an external file.)

In Figure 3.5, the bar chart we created earlier has been styled, creating the JSON file shown in Listing 3.4. Note that we don't need to bother copying the sample data points from the chart builder to the JSON file; they'll be overridden by the data in the file.

Figure 3.5

ZingChart Builder.

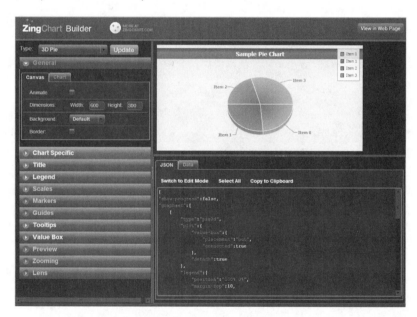

The code here is the same as in Listing 3.3, except that now the <cfchart> tag has a style attribute added. We've modified a few things to make the chart more interesting: the heading has been styled, the tooltips have been modified to show a dollar amount instead of just a number, and the legend is both clickable—which lets you turn series on and off—and draggable—in case the legend covers some of the data in the chart. You can also modify the style of the context menu, show guides when a user moves the mouse over the data, and much, much more.

Listing 3.4 Sample Custom JSON File Created in ZingChart Builder (Slightly Edited)

```
<cfchart format="html" showlegend="true"
  height="400" width="500" title="Budget By Director, in 1000s" show3d="yes"
  style="barcustom.json">
{
```

Listing 3.4 (CONTINUED)

```
"show-progress":false,
"graphset":[
    {
        "plot":{
            "highlight":false,
            "tooltip-text":"$%v,000",
            "color":"#ffffff",
            "value-box":{
                "type":"max,min",
                "text":"%v",
                "color":"#000000"
            }
        },
        "type":"bar",
        "title":{
            "text":"2001 Movie Data",
            "border-color":"#000000",
            "border-width":1,
            "alpha":1,
            "background-color":"#eeeeee",
            "background-color-2":"#eeeeee",
            "position":"0% 0%",
            "font-size":12,
            "color":"#000000",
            "font-family":"Lucida Handwriting"
        },
        "legend":{
            "position":"100% 0%",
            "margin-top":10,
            "margin-right":10,
            "margin-left":10,
            "margin-bottom":10,
            "layout":"x1",
            "alpha":1,
            "background-color":"#000000",
            "background-color-2":"#000000",
            "draggable":true,
            "drag-handler":"header",
            "minimize":false,
            "item":{
                "toggle":true,
                "toggle-action":"hide",
                "margin-top":5,
                "margin-right":5,
                "margin-left":5,
                "margin-bottom":5,
                "font-size":11,
                "color":"#cccccc",
                "text-align":"center"
            },
            "header":{
                "text":"Series"
            }
        }
    }
]
}
```

Figure 3.6 shows the result of this styling.

Figure 3.6

Custom styled chart.

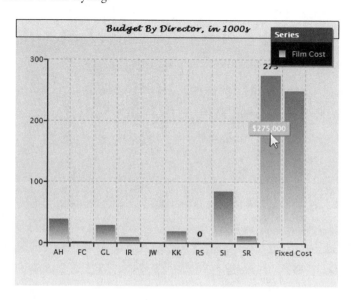

TIP

When you use the chart builder, it's frequently useful to have it use your live data so you can see how your chart looks. An easy trick for getting the live data into your chart is to render your chart without custom styling, view the page source code, and look for the part of the code that looks like this:

```
"series":[{"text":"Alfred ","values":[39],"background-color-2":"#699EBF",
➡ "background-color":"#F0F1F2"},{"text":"Francis ","values":[2],…}]
```

The code will start with `"series"` and end with a squiggly brace and square bracket: `}]`. Click the Data tab below the chart preview in the editor, choose Edit as the data source, and JSON as the source code, and copy all the data between the square brackets to the text field (don't include the square brackets at the end of the data). Clicking back and forth between Canvas and Chart on the left side of the screen will reset the viewport to use your data. You'll probably also want to set a size (height and width) in the editor to display the chart correctly.

TIP

The default style files for each of the chart types is in <ColdFusion Install Directory>/cfusion/charting/styles. You can edit these files to better suit your needs, but make sure to first back them up because otherwise a future update to ColdFusion may over-write your customizations. Style files have the same name as the chart type values and no extension. You can use the ZingChart online chart builder at http://www.zingchart.com/builder/ to easily create these files.

Rendering Options and Fallback

The `<cfchart>` tag has an attribute, `renderer`, with several options: `flash`, `vml`, `svg`, and `canvas`. For Adobe Flash files, the renderer will always use Flash, so you won't need to use the `flash` option. However, in browsers you can use VML (an XML language), SVG (or Scalable Vector Graphics, an older format that Microsoft Internet Explorer browsers support well), or the default, Canvas (to implement the new HTML5 way of doing things). Adobe Flash has a lot of advantages, but many mobile browsers—notably, Apple iOS on the iPad and iPhone—don't support Adobe Flash. If you use `flash`, `<cfchart>` will automatically fall back to an HTML-based approach if the browser doesn't support Adobe Flash.

TIP

The choice among VML, SVG, and Canvas has a lot to do with the kind of users you are trying to support. As browsers provide better support for Canvas, it should be the clear winner, but unfortunately in the iPad before version 3 and the iPhone earlier than the iPhone 4S, Canvas performance is severely lacking. VML is not supported by most browsers, so if you expect to support a lot of iPhone and iPad users, your best bet is to use the SVG rendering engine because it will perform much better than Canvas, especially for users running iOS 5 and later. It's a good idea to test your charts on any device and browser you are supporting, and see how they work. See http://caniuse.com/#feat=svg-html5 for a chart that shows the browsers that support SVG.

Plotting Multiple Series in a Chart

Frequently when creating charts, you need to put multiple series in a single chart. For example, in our previous example, it might be nice to plot the number of movies made per year on the same chart as the cost of movies per director. This is easy to do in ColdFusion: Just add multiple `<cfchartseries>` tags to your chart. Each tag can have its own data and styles associated with it.

Some chart types have interesting variations when you plot multiple series. For example, bar charts can be stacked, and you can add a histogram to the style to show all the values (see the example that follows in Listing 3.5).

Using Clickable URLs and JavaScript

A feature commonly desired when building online charts is the capability to make URLs clickable and to have that action take you to a detail page or show detail data.

This feature isn't the easiest to implement in ColdFusion 10—ColdFusion 10 doesn't officially support URLs via the `<cfchart>` tag—but the process for adding it is pretty straightforward.

ColdFusion exposes all the events from ZingChart, if you know how to get at them. To get at the `Chart` object, you use the JavaScript function `ColdFusion.Chart.getChartHandle()`. The `getChartHandle()` function takes as an argument the name of the chart, which you can set via the `name` attribute of `<cfchart>`, and it returns the `Chart` object.

The `Chart` object is a ZingChart object, and any of the API methods documented at http://www.zingchart.com/learn/api/api.php are available to you.

Here's the code to add a click handler to each node on the chart:

```
cObj = ColdFusion.Chart.getChartHandle("filmchart");
   cObj.complete = function(chartobj){
      // chartobj.id will now contain the handle of the chart,
      ➥so we can set up events.
      cObj.node_click = function(node){
   // log the node so we can look at it
         console.log(node);
   }
```

Among other items returned in the node are the position in the series of the clicked item (nodeindex), the text in the legend for the item (scaletext), and the value where it was clicked. Listings 3.5 and 3.6 show how to create a nice Ajax detail page for a chart. Figure 3.7 later in this chapter shows the result.

Listing 3.5 Multiple Series and Ajax

```
<!DOCTYPE html>
<html>
<head>
<meta http-equiv="Content-Type" content="text/html; charset=utf-8" />
<title>Multiple Series and Click Handler</title>
</head>
<!---
   Chapter 3 Multiple Series and Click Handler
   FileName: 3.5 multiple.cfm
   Author: Ken Fricklas (KF)
   Purpose: Demonstrate a click handler and multiple series in <cfchart>
--->
<body style="font-family:Verdana, Geneva, sans-serif">
<cfajaximport tags="cfdiv">
<cfquery name="qFilms" datasource="ows">
   select cast (sum(e.expenseamount / 1000) as int) as filmcost, cast
   ➥(avg(e.expenseamount / 1000) as int) as avgcost, substr(d.firstname, 1, 1) ||
   ➥substr(d.lastname, 1, 1) as initials, d.directorid
    from expenses e, directors d, filmsdirectors fd, films f
    where e.filmid = fd.filmid
      and fd.directorid = d.directorid
      and fd.filmid = f.filmid
      and year(f.dateintheaters) = 2001
    group by substr(d.firstname, 1, 1) || substr(d.lastname, 1, 1), d.directorid
</cfquery>
<!--
   Create an array which holds a matchup from the position to the directorid we need
   on the detail page. Note we need the offset zero, so we subtract 1 from the
   ➥current row.
   --->
<cfset aFilms = structNew()>
<cfloop query="qFilms">
   <cfset aFilms[qFilms.currentRow - 1] = qFilms.directorid>
</cfloop>
<!--- Convert the array to a javascript variable so we can use it on the
➥client side --->
<cfwddx action="cfml2js" input="#aFilms#" output="jsFilms"
➥toplevelvariable="aFilms">
```

Listing 3.5 (CONTINUED)

```
<script>
  <cfoutput>#jsFilms#</cfoutput>
  cObj = ColdFusion.Chart.getChartHandle("filmchart");
  cObj.complete = function(chartobj){
      // chartobj.id will now contain the handle of the chart,
      ➥so we can set up events.
      cObj.node_click = function(node){
          // grab the director by getting the nodeindex, and looking in the
          ➥array we created
          directorID = aFilms[node.nodeindex];
          // use ColdFusion.navigate to load the detail div with the detail
          ➥page for this director.
          ColdFusion.navigate('detail.cfm?mftest=1&id='+directorID, 'detail');
      }
  }
</script>
<cfchart name="filmchart" format="html" showlegend="true"
    height="400" width="600" title="Budget By Director, in 1000s"
    >
    <cfchartseries type="bar" query="qFilms" valuecolumn="filmcost"
    ➥itemcolumn="initials" serieslabel="Total Cost" animate=#{"effect":"slideup"}#>
    </cfchartseries>
    <cfchartseries type="line" query="qFilms" valuecolumn="avgcost"
    ➥itemcolumn="initials" serieslabel="Avg Cost">
    </cfchartseries>
</cfchart>
<!--- click status div --->
<cfdiv ID="detail"
        style="border: 1px solid grey; text-align: center; width: 598px; height:150"
        ➥bindonload="false">
        Click in chart to see details
</cfdiv>
</body>
</html>
```

Listing 3.6 Multiple Series and Ajax: Detail Page

```
<!DOCTYPE html>
<html>
<head>
<meta http-equiv="Content-Type" content="text/html; charset=utf-8" />
<title>Director Details</title>
<style>
body, td, th {font-family:Verdana, Geneva, sans-serif; font-size:9pt;}
h1 {font-size: 12pt}
table {border-collapse: collapse}
td, th {border: 1px solid black; padding: 2px}
</style>
</head>
<!---
  Chapter 3 Multiple Series and Click Handler - Detail page
  FileName: detail.cfm
  Author: Ken Fricklas (KF)
--->
<!--- ajax request, don't show debug --->
<cfsetting showdebugoutput="no">
```

Listing 3.6 (CONTINUED)

```
<body>
<cfif not isdefined("URL.id")>
    No director id.
    <cfabort>
</cfif>
<!--- grab the director's name and display --->
<cfquery name="qDirector" datasource="ows">
    select firstname, lastname from directors
    where directorid = <cfqueryparam cfsqltype="cf_sql_integer" value="#URL.id#">
</cfquery>
<!--- get budget and expenses for this director's movies --->
<cfquery name="qMovies" datasource="ows">
    select fd.salary, f.dateintheaters, f.movietitle, sum(e.expenseamount) as filmcost
    from filmsdirectors fd, films f, expenses e
    where
        fd.filmid = f.filmid
        and f.filmid = e.filmid
        and fd.directorid = <cfqueryparam cfsqltype="cf_sql_integer" value="#URL.id#">
    group by fd.salary, f.dateintheaters, f.movietitle
    order by f.dateintheaters
</cfquery>
<cfoutput>
<div align="center">
<h1>#qDirector.firstname# #qDirector.lastname#</h1>
<table>
<thead>
    <tr><th>Date</th><th>Title</th><th>Expense Cost</th><th>Director Salary</th></tr>
</thead>
<tbody>
<cfloop query="qMovies">
    <tr>
    <td>#dateformat(qMovies.dateintheaters, "mm/dd/yyyy")#</td>
    <td>#qMovies.movieTitle#</td>
    <td>#DollarFormat(qMovies.filmCost)#</td>
    <td>#DollarFormat(qMovies.salary)#</td>
    </tr>
</cfloop>
</tbody>
</table>
</cfoutput>
</div>
</body>
</html>
```

NOTE

This code uses `<cfdiv>`, `<cfajaximport>`, and the JavaScript function `ColdFusion.navigate`. More information about these functions can be found in the online documentation and in *Adobe ColdFusion 9 Web Application Construction Kit*, Volume 2, Chapter 30.

Highlighting Important Data

Another cool feature of ColdFusion 10 and ZingChart is the capability to have the chart automatically alter the formatting (generally by color) of data that meets certain criteria, such as data that exceeds a specific value or data that is the highest or lowest value in a data set.

To set a criterion, use the `plot` attribute on the `<cfchart>` tag. The argument passed will be a JSON struct with rules in it. You can set rules to highlight values based on their position or value, by adding rules to those values.

Listing 3.7 uses an updated version of the `<cfchart>` tag in Listing 3.6, adding a `plot` attribute with two rules: to set the maximum value for making a background image (a ColdFusion Builder logo) and all other values over 35 an alternate color.

Listing 3.7   Adding a Highlight (Excerpt)

```
<cfchart name="filmchart" format="html" showlegend="true"
   height="400" width="600" title="Budget By Director, in 1000s"
   plot="#{
  "rules": [
    {"rule":"'%node-value' == '%plot-max-value'", "background-image" :
      "CF.png"},
    {"rule":"'%node-value' > '35'", "background-color":"gold"}
  ]
  }#">
```

The rules can include the tokens listed in Table 3.2, as well as many others.

Table 3.2   Tokens for Use in Rules

TOKEN	TYPE	LONG FORMAT	DESCRIPTION
%N	Node	%node-count	Number of nodes
%nv	Node	%node-value	Value of this node
%nmv	Node	%node-min-value	Node minimum value
%npv	Node	%node-percent-value	Node percentage value
%nxv	Node	%node-max-value	Node maximum value
%pavg	Node	%plot-average	Plot average value
%pmi	Node	%plot-min-index	Plot minimum value
%pmv	Node	%plot-min-value	Plot or node minimum value
%v	Scale	%scale-value	Value

You can use these and many other tokens in many of the values that you can set using the new attributes in ColdFusion 10.

Figure 3.7 shows examples of these attributes added to the chart in Figure 3.3.

Figure 3.7

Multiple series, click handler, and highlighting added to the chart in Figure 3.3.

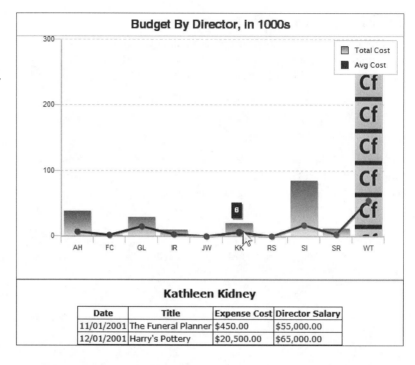

Refreshing Data and Using Live Data

ColdFusion 10 and ZingChart support two methods for updating chart data while the chart is being displayed.

The first approach is to update the entire chart. This approach can be useful when all the data on the chart is changing, or when you want to show multiple views of your data. To use this feature, all you need to do is specify a refresh interval and a URL from which to load the data. Listing 3.8 shows the little bit of code needed for this approach.

Listing 3.8 Updating the Entire Chart

```
<!DOCTYPE html>
<html>
<head>
<!---
   Chapter 3 Refresh Entire Chart
   FileName: 3.8 refresh.cfm
   Author: Ken Fricklas (KF)
   Purpose: Chart with Full Refresh
--->
<meta http-equiv="Content-Type" content="text/html; charset=utf-8" />
<title>Full Refresh Chart</title>
</head>
```

Listing 3.8 (CONTINUED)

```
<body>
<!--- load some random data from 3.9 data.cfm, and refresh every 2 seconds --->
<cfchart format="html" refresh="#{"type"="full","interval":"2",
➡ "url":"3.9%20data.cfm"}#" > </cfchart>
</body>
</html>
```

The data for this feed needs to be in JSON format. The JSON structure that is returned must contain a graph-set array. The graph-set array contains at a minimum a refresh attribute and an array of values structure, in which each series is an array of values. It can also contain all the other attributes we've used to define ColdFusion charts.

Listing 3.9 shows a minimal set of random data used to generate a refreshing chart. Just for fun, in this example it also sets a random chart type, so the chart will change every time it reloads.

Listing 3.9   Refreshing Chart with a Random Chart Type

```
<!---
   Chapter 3.9 JSON data example
   FileName: 3.9 data.cfm
   Author: Ken Fricklas (KF)
   Purpose:  Refresh Data for example 3.8
--->
<!--- this file is JSON data - make sure no debug output on the page --->
<cfsetting showdebugoutput="no">
<cfscript>
// generate some random data
aValues1 = arrayNew(1);
for (i = 1; i LTE 6; i++)
   aValues1[i] = randRange(0,20);
aValues2 = arrayNew(1);
for (i = 1; i LTE 6; i++)
   aValues2[i] = randRange(0,20);
aValues3 = arrayNew(1);
for (i = 1; i LTE 6; i++)
   aValues3[i] = randRange(0,20);
// Each graphset is an element in the graphset array
// While we're at it, we'll pick a random chart time for this page load.
lChartTypes = 'bar,bar3d,area,area3d,line,line3d';
thisChartType = listGetAt(lChartTypes, randrange(1, listLen(lChartTypes)));
jData = structNew();
jData["graphset"] = arrayNew(1);
jData["graphset"][1]["type"] = thisChartType;
// Be sure to include the refresh interval for the next load.  Note that if
//   you want to load a chart from a ColdFusion program, you can simply not set an
//   interval on the next page load.
jData["graphset"][1]["refresh"] = {'type':'full', 'interval':2};
jData["graphset"][1]["title"] = {'text':'Full Refresh Chart'};
// Each series is an array of values; we're putting 3 series in this chart.
jData["graphset"][1]["series"] = [{'values':aValues1}, {'values':aValues2},
➡ {'values':aValues3}];
// write data to output as JSON string
writeOutput(serializeJSON(jData));
</cfscript>
```

Refreshing in Real Time

Another way to update data in a ColdFusion chart in real time is to feed the data continuously into the chart. For this approach to work, you have to define some starting parameters for the chart. Since all the data isn't available when the chart first loads, the system can't figure out where to put default values that will work with your data set, so you should provide the maximum and minimum values to be displayed in the chart, the interval for the chart ticks, and so on.

Listing 3.10 shows an example of a stock ticker chart with a real-time feed, with the feed data in Listing 3.11. The data will load (at the rate specified in the refresh interval) until the chart is full, and then it will roll off the left side of the chart to provide a continuously animated series. The system is very smart as well about adding caption data to the bottom of the chart, as you can see in the example.

Figure 3.8 shows the resulting chart.

Listing 3.10 Continuously Refreshed Chart

```
<!DOCTYPE html>
<html>
<head>
<!---
  Chapter 3
  FileName: 3.10 refresh series.cfm
  Author: Ken Fricklas (KF)
  Purpose: Chart Which Loads Data Continuously
--->
<meta http-equiv="Content-Type" content="text/html; charset=utf-8" />
<title>Feed Refresh Chart - Series</title>
</head>

<body>
<cfscript>
  // start at 50 and 75, we'll alter these in the feed
  application.Plot0Value = 50;
  application.Plot1Value = 75;
</cfscript>
<!--- note the type as feed
  max-ticks is most shown before they roll off (2 min at 1 per second)
  URL is the feed url for the new data
  Reload every second
  Reset timeout - if no data is received in this much time (ms) reset the chart.
--->
<cfchart format="html" type="line"
  refresh=#{"type" : "feed",
          "max-ticks" : 120,
            "url" : "3.11%20feed.cfm",
            "interval" : 1,
            "reset-timeout":20000}#
  height=400
  width=900
  showlegend="yes"
  title="Refresh Chart"
  xaxistitle="Time" yaxistitle="Stock Price"
  >
```

Listing 3.10 (CONTINUED)

```
    <cfchartseries type="line" label="MSFT" >
      <cfchartdata item="#timeformat(now(), "MM:SS")#" value="50">
    </cfchartseries>
    <cfchartseries type="line" label="APPL" >
      <cfchartdata item="#timeformat(now(), "MM:SS")#" value="75">
    </cfchartseries>
  </cfchart>
</body>
</html>
```

Listing 3.11 Continuous Refresh Data Feed

```
<!---
  Chapter 3 Continuous Refresh
  FileName: 3.11 continuous refresh series - datafeed.cfm
  Author: Ken Fricklas (KF)
  Purpose: Chart Which Loads Data Continuously
--->
<!--- this file is JSON data - make sure no debug output on the page --->
<cfsetting showdebugoutput="no">
<cfscript>
time = timeformat(now(),"MM-SS");
application.Plot0Value += randRange(-2,+2);
application.Plot1Value += randRange(-2,+2);
feed = '{"scale-x" :
  "#time#",
  "plot0" : #application.Plot0Value#,
  "plot1" : #application.Plot1Value#}';
writeoutput(feed);
</cfscript>
```

Figure 3.8

Chart with continuous refresh data feed.

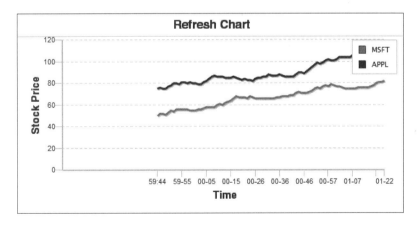

Conclusion

There's much more available in ColdFusion 10 charts than we've covered here. You can add value labeling, create advanced charts, change the markers used in charts, create theme charts, and more. You can discover these features by visiting the ZingChart documentation and using custom styling features.

CHAPTER 4

Web Services

Integration has always been a key strength and an important focus for ColdFusion. ColdFusion supports most of the messaging frameworks and protocols required to effectively communicate with different platforms, and web services are no exception.

On the basis of architectural style, two primary categories of web services are available: traditional Simple Object Access Protocol (SOAP)–based services and Representational State Transfer (REST)–complaint services. ColdFusion has long made it easy to create and consume SOAP-based web services. ColdFusion 10 builds on this foundation by upgrading the underlying engine for SOAP-based web services and supporting creation of REST-based web services. In this chapter we focus primarily on SOAP-based web services. Chapter 5 covers REST-based web services in detail.

NOTE

Web services support in ColdFusion 10 builds on that of prior versions. Basic web services support is covered extensively in *Adobe ColdFusion 9 Web Application Construction Kit, Volume 3: Advanced Application Development*, in Chapter 59, "Creating and Consuming Web Services."

What Are Web Services?

A web service is a web-based application or a network-accessible interface that can communicate and exchange data with other such applications over the Internet without regard for application, platform, syntax, or architecture.

At its core, it's a messaging framework built on open standards through which different applications interact with each other over the Internet, abiding by a definite contract. As simple as it may sound, it truly enabled disparate applications to seamlessly interact and provide integrated solutions. It streamlined the integration of new applications among vendors, partners, and customers without the need for the centralized or proprietary software of enterprise application integration (EAI).

There are many reasons for the success of the web services framework, but these are the most important:

- **Standard communication:** It is based on widely adopted open standards such as Hypertext Transfer Protocol (HTTP) and Extensible Markup Language (XML).

- **Platform independence:** It provides an unambiguous way of defining, invoking, and consuming a service through Web Services Description Language (WSDL) and SOAP.

- **Loose coupling:** Web services components are loosely coupled. A web service requires almost no knowledge of the definitions of other separate components.

- **Effortless integration:** It's widely adopted and has great tooling support. Creating, publishing, and consuming a web service on any platform is basically like creating any other component, with no additional effort.

For now, don't worry about all the acronyms referred to here; we will look at them closely in subsequent sections.

A Typical Web Service Invocation

Let's now look at the steps involved in a complete web service invocation and see how the process works (Figure 4.1).

Figure 4.1

Typical web service invocation.

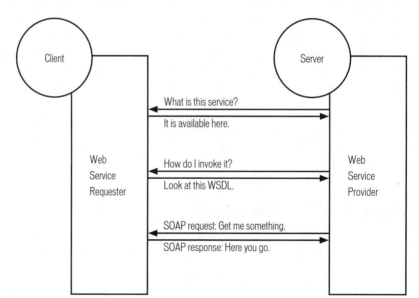

1. (Optional) If a client has no knowledge of a web service it is going to invoke, it may ask a discovery service (usually on a separate server) to provide a service registered with it that meets the client's requirements. However, in most cases, clients will know which service they want to invoke; hence, this step is optional.

2. (Optional) On receiving an inquiry, the discovery service will return the available service details registered with it.

3. The client needs to know how to invoke the service. It asks the web service to describe itself.

4. The web service replies with an XML document describing the methods, arguments, and types in WSDL.

5. Now that the client knows where the service is located and how to invoke it, using the WSDL provided the web service creates the artifacts necessary to invoke and consume the web service. It then sends a request over HTTP with all the details required in its body in SOAP format.

6. The web service returns the result of the operation in a response over HTTP, again in SOAP format.

Web Services Architecture

Now let's look at the web services architecture and the key technologies that make web services possible. For completeness, Figure 4.2 shows the main components of the architecture.

Figure 4.2

Web services architecture.

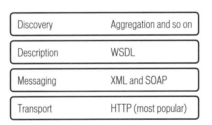

Discovery	Aggregation and so on
Description	WSDL
Messaging	XML and SOAP
Transport	HTTP (most popular)

A web service uses a transport medium such as HTTP to send messages in SOAP format, which is based on XML, abiding by the contract between a client and a server described using WSDL.

Several technologies are absolutely central to the distributed architecture of web services. Among these are HTTP, XML, and SOAP. Additionally, WSDL, a descendent technology, standardizes the syntax for describing a web service and its operations.

HTTP

HTTP is a communications protocol for exchanging information over the Internet. It is the common transport mechanism that allows web service providers and consumers to communicate.

XML

XML is similar to HTML in that it uses tags to describe and encode information for transmission over the Internet. HTML has preset tags that define the way that information is displayed. XML lets you create your own tags to represent not only data but also a multitude of data types, which helps ensure accurate data transmission among web service providers and consumers.

SOAP

SOAP is a lightweight protocol for the exchange of information in a distributed environment. SOAP can be used in messaging systems or for invoking remote procedure calls. It is based on XML and consists of three logical parts:

- A framework for describing what is in a message and how to process it

- A set of encoding rules for interpreting application-defined data types

- A convention for representing remote procedure calls and responses

SOAP handles the onerous job of translating data and converting data types between consumers and web service providers.

Currently, two versions of SOAP are available: Version 1.1, and Version 1.2, which was an upgrade of Version 1.1. Both are World Wide Web Consortium (W3C) standards, and web services can be deployed using either version. However, Version 1.2 offers some significant advantages over its predecessor, as you will see in the coming section.

NOTE

To learn more about the SOAP specification, see the W3C's note about SOAP at http://www.w3.org/TR/soap.

WSDL

WSDL is an XML-based language specification that defines web services and describes how to access them.

WSDL is used to explain the details needed to invoke a web service over the Internet. WSDL defines XML syntax for describing services between a set of endpoints: usually a client and a server that exchange messages. This documentation can then act as a road map for automating the details of a web service. WSDL describes the service interaction rather than the formats or network protocols used to communicate. It simply defines the endpoints and their data, regardless of the implementation detail.

Thankfully, today's ColdFusion developers do not need to concern themselves with such intricacies, or with the need to write documentation by hand, because ColdFusion generates WSDL automatically. To view the generated WSDL for a ColdFusion component deployed as a web service, append the string `?wsdl` to the component's URL. The WSDL document is then displayed in your web browser.

NOTE

To learn more about the WSDL, see the W3C's WSDL specification at http://www.w3.org/TR/wsdl.

The W3C's Web Services Description Working Group has published a new specification, WSDL Version 2.0, which is based on SOAP Version 1.2. It is significantly different and not compatible with WSDL's earlier specification (Version 1.1); hence, it is called Version 2.0, not Version 1.2. We will look at the differences between the two versions and the advantages provided by WSDL 2.0 in the next section.

ColdFusion Web Service Engine

ColdFusion uses Apache Axis, a proven and reliable implementation of SOAP, as its underlying engine to implement SOAP-based web services. ColdFusion Version 9 uses Axis 1, which supports only WSDL 1.1 and SOAP 1.1. Therefore, ColdFusion 9 cannot create web services using these specifications and cannot consume external web services that used newer versions of WSDL and SOAP.

ColdFusion 10 has upgraded its web services support and includes implementation based on Axis 2 as well. ColdFusion now supports both versions of the WSDL and SOAP specifications simultaneously while maintaining backward compatibility.

We have already noted that support for newer specifications is important for ColdFusion to play well with external web services that use these specifications. This support also provides other benefits, discussed in upcoming sections.

In the subsequent sections, we will treat Apache Axis as a web service engine.

SOAP 1.2

SOAP 1.2 can do everything that SOAP 1.1 does and more. Among others the most notable differences between the two versions are the following:

- **SOAP 1.1 is based on XML 1.0, and SOAP 1.2 is based on XML Information Set (XML Infoset).** XML Infoset provides a way to describe the XML document with an XSD schema but is not bound to serialize using XML 1.0 serialization. Thus, SOAP 1.2 places no restriction on the way that the Infoset data is transported.

- **SOAP 1.2 provides a binding framework.** You can use SOAP 1.2's specification of a binding to an underlying protocol to determine which XML serialization is used in the underlying protocol data units, thus making SOAP truly protocol independent.

- **SOAP 1.2 includes HTTP binding.** It provides support for both HTTP GET and POST operations and conforms better to web architectural principles. Thus, it uses established web technologies for improved performance.

- **SOAP 1.2 provides a clear processing model.** SOAP 1.2 is more robust and less ambiguous because it has resolved many of the interoperability issues that were concerns with SOAP 1.1.

To conclude, SOAP 1.2 is truly protocol agnostic, extensible, unambiguous, and more HTTP friendly than SOAP 1.1.

TIP

To visually differentiate between SOAP 1.2 and SOAP 1.1, look for xmlns:soapenv in the soap message. SOAP 1.2 will use http://www.w3.org/2003/05/soap-envelope, and SOAP 1.1 will use http://schemas.xmlsoap.org/soap/envelope/.

WSDL 2.0

WSDL 2.0 is the newer version of WSDL and a W3C standard. It is significantly different from WSDL 1.1 and provides additional benefits since it:

- **Uses SOAP 1.2:** WSDL 2.0 uses SOAP 1.2 to provide all the benefits of SOAP 1.2 such as better extensibility.

- **Supports interface inheritance:** As with Object-Oriented Programming (OOP), a WSDL document can inherit from another WSDL document, providing reusability and component-based architecture.

- **Supports additional schemas:** Along with the XML schema, WSDL 2.0 supports the use of RelaxNG and DTD as type definitions.

- **Supports additional message patterns:** WSDL 2.0 supports eight new patterns, including only single messages.

Although it is an enhanced version, WSDL 2.0 is mainly used to create SOAP-based REST-complaint web services. One reason for its lower rate of adoption is that WSDL 1.1 is sufficient for most common needs of most applications.

To view the generated WSDL 2.0 for a ColdFusion component deployed as a web service, append the string `?wsdl2` to the component's URL. Note that WSDL 2.0 is available only with Web Service Engine Version 2.

Building Your First Web Service

Now it's time to get started building a web service with ColdFusion.

To build a web service in ColdFusion, all we need to do is to write a ColdFusion component (CFC). CFCs take an object-like approach to the grouping of related functions and encapsulation of business logic. They also play a pivotal role in defining and accessing a web service.

We can create or reuse a prebuilt CFC with the operations we want to expose as functions and make the CFC accessible to remote calls by specifying `access="remote"`. The CFC location then becomes the endpoint for the web service, and its remote functions become operations that can be invoked on this web service.

NOTE

For more information about CFCs, read Chapter 24, "Creating Advanced ColdFusion Components," in *Adobe ColdFusion 9 Web Application Construction Kit, Volume 2: Application Development*.

Now let's create our first web service. We'll start with the component in Listing 4.1.

Listing 4.1   /cfwack/4/hello.cfc

```
<cfcomponent>
    <cffunction name="helloWorld" returnType="string" access="remote">
        <cfreturn "Hello World!">
    </cffunction>
</cfcomponent>
```

The `hello` CFC starts with a `<cfcomponent>` tag, which wraps the component's content. Then the `<cffunction>` tag with a name and return type defines a single function, which simply returns a static string. The optional `access` attribute is set to `remote`, which exposes this CFC as a web service. And now we have a simple CFC-based web service, which we can publish and allow to be called by web service clients across the web.

To quickly verify that this web service works, open http://localhost:8500/cfwack/4/hello.cfc?wsdl in a browser. It should output the generated WSDL. Listing 4.2 shows part of the generated WSDL for this `hello` CFC.

Listing 4.2   Part of the WSDL Generated for hello.cfc

```
<!-- Some attributes have been omitted to keep focus only on elements
➥relevant to our discussion later in this section-->
<wsdl:binding name="cfwack.4.hello.cfcSoap12Binding" ...>
    <soap12:binding ... style="document"/>
    <wsdl:operation name="helloWorld">
        <soap12:operation ... style="document"/>
        <wsdl:input>
            <soap12:body use="literal"/>
        </wsdl:input>
        <wsdl:output>
            <soap12:body use="literal"/>
        </wsdl:output>
        <wsdl:fault ...>
            <soap12:fault use="literal" .../>
        </wsdl:fault>
    </wsdl:operation>
</wsdl:binding>
<wsdl:service name="cfwack.4.hello.cfc">
    <wsdl:port name="cfwack.4.hello.cfcHttpSoap11Endpoint" ...>
    <wsdl:port name="cfwack.4.hello.cfcHttpSoap12Endpoint" ...>
</wsdl:service>
```

Here are a few details that you will observe here:

- An operation `"helloWorld"` is listed with the same name as that of the `<cffunction>` function.

- The WSDL has all the information such as types, endpoints, and message style required to execute this operation.

- Both SOAP 1.1 and SOAP 1.2 endpoints are supported through the same WSDL.

- The default WSDL style generated is Document Literal. You can change this style, as you will see later in this chapter.

ColdFusion will additionally log the web service engine used to deploy and access this web service on the console. This log can come in handy when you want to verify that the WSDL was refreshed and identify which web service engine was used for that particular operation.

Consuming a Web Service

Next we will see how to invoke this web service from ColdFusion. There are several ways to invoke any web service in ColdFusion, and we will look at them one by one.

Let's start with the `<cfinvoke>` tag. This tag can be used to invoke a web service by specifying the `webservice` attribute, as shown in Listing 4.3.

Listing 4.3   Calling a Web Service with `<cfinvoke>`

```
<cfset wsURL = "http://localhost:8500/cfwack/4/hello.cfc?wsdl">
<cfinvoke
  webservice = "#wsURL#"
  method = "helloWorld"
  returnVariable = "result">
<cfoutput> <H1> #result# </H1></cfoutput>
```

Here we are trying to invoke the `hello` CFC that we wrote earlier, using the `<cfinvoke>` tag. We specified the CFC's WSDL using the `webservice` attribute, the method to be invoked as "helloWorld" uses the same name as the function, and `returnVariable` is used to store the result of this operation. Then we simply output the result using `<cfoutput>` wrapped with HTML `<H1>` tags. If you run this code in a browser, you should get output similar to that in Figure 4.3.

Figure 4.3

Output generated from `hello` CFC.

Also, since web services are built on top of HTTP, you may need to provide other attributes such as proxy details if you are using an HTTP proxy server to connect to the web service provider and passwords similar to those for the `<cfhttp>` tag for calls using the `<cfinvoke>` tag.

Similarly, you can use the `<cfobject>` tag to create a web service proxy object. Then you can invoke methods on this object, which will be delegated as web service calls to actual endpoints. Listing 4.4 uses `<cfobject>` to call the same `hello` web service described earlier, by specifying the type as `webservice`.

Listing 4.4   Calling a Web Service with `<cfobject>`

```
<cfset wsURL = "http://localhost:8500/cfwack/4/hello.cfc?wsdl">
<cfobject
  name = "ws"
  webservice= "#wsURL#"
  type = "webservice">
<cfset result = ws.helloWorld()>
<H1><cfoutput>#result#</cfoutput></H1>
```

When in script mode—that is, within a `<cfscript>` block or when writing CFCs in script syntax—you can use the `CreateObject()` method to invoke a web service. It is the script equivalent of the `<cfobject>` tag. Listing 4.5 shows how to use `CreateObject` to invoke a web service.

Listing 4.5 Calling a Web Service with `CreateObject`

```
<cfscript>
  wsURL = "http://localhost:8500/cfwack/4/hello.cfc?wsdl";
  ws = CreateObject("webservice", wsURL);
  result = ws.helloWorld();
  writeoutput(result);
</cfscript>
```

Refreshing Stubs

Recall the steps we have discussed for calling a web service. Creation of a web service proxy with `<cfobject>` or `CreateObject()` consists of steps 3 and 4 in Figure 4.1. Any call to a web service using this proxy will be steps 5 and 6. A web service call using `<cfinvoke>` involves steps 3 through 6.

However, steps 3 and 4 are computationally heavy operations and should be performed only once for a WSDL that is not changing. Hence, ColdFusion optimizes this operation significantly. ColdFusion makes a call to get the WSDL and generates the required stubs and artifacts only for the first call to the web service, using `<cfinvoke>` or `<cfobject>`. From the next call onward, it uses the generated stubs themselves, eliminating the need for steps 3 and 4.

This optimization creates a challenge in a development environment in which CFCs are being constantly modified. ColdFusion does not implicitly refresh the stubs for changed WSDL. The clients themselves have to refresh these stubs every time the WSDL changes. This operation can be accomplished by setting the `refreshWSDL` attribute as `true` with `<cfinvoke>` or `<cfobject>`. Although in a production environment `refreshWSDL` should be `false`, this is its default value, too.

Using Complex Data Types

In this section, you will see how to work with different ColdFusion data types. For that purpose, let's look at another CFC, this one with several functions that take some complex data types, such as a struct or query, as arguments (Listing 4.6). Here we will focus on two processes: how to pass an argument to a web service call and how to work on the result.

Listing 4.6 /cfwack/4/complex.cfc

```
<cfcomponent hint="echoes back the input specified">

<!---
The purpose of these functions merely is to demo accepting
and returning a complex object
--->

    <cffunction name="echoStruct" returntype="struct" access="remote">
    <cfargument type="struct" name="argStruct"/>

        <!---
```

Listing 4.6 (CONTINUED)

```
            outputs argument passed to this function to console
            good for debugging while developing the service
            --->
            <cfdump var="#argStruct#" output="console">
            <!--- typically your logic goes here --->
            <cfreturn argStruct>
        </cffunction>

        <cffunction name="echoQuery" returntype="query" access="remote">
        <cfargument type="query" name="argQuery"/>

        <cfreturn argQuery>
        </cffunction>

        <cffunction name="echoDocument" returntype="xml" access="remote">
        <cfargument type="xml" name="argDocument"/>

        <cfreturn argDocument>
        </cffunction>

        <cffunction name="echoAny" returntype="any" access="remote">
        <cfargument type="any" name="argAny"/>

        <cfreturn argAny>
        </cffunction>

    </cfcomponent>
```

Let's analyze what's going on here. We have created a complex CFC that isn't actually very complicated. As you can see, it simply takes native ColdFusion data types as arguments and returns them back: the function echoStruct takes a struct as an argument, the function echoQuery takes a query as an argument, and the function echoAny can take any type as an argument.

Note that no special treatment is required to handle web service calls, and this CFC can work directly by creating its object and can also serve Ajax Remoting and Adobe Flash Remoting calls. You get the same data types to work with. It is ColdFusion's responsibility to internally serialize the given data type to XML format before sending the web service call as a client, and to deserialize this XML back to the desired data type and pass it as an argument to the invoked function when it receives the web service to process it as a server.

Passing Arguments

Next, let's see how to invoke this web service with ColdFusion. We have already talked about different ways to invoke web services, and for this example we will use <cfinvoke>. Let's look at how to pass an argument and work with the returned object (Listing 4.7).

Listing 4.7   /cfwack/4/complex.cfm

```
<cfset wsURL = "http://localhost:8500/cfwack/4/complex.cfc?wsdl">

<cfset varStruct = {key1:"value 1", key2:"value 2"} >
<!-- Passing arguments with cfinvokeparam --->
<cfinvoke webservice = "#wsURL#"
          method = "echoStruct"
          returnVariable = "result">
    <cfinvokeargument name="argStruct" value="#varStruct#" >
</cfinvoke>

<h2> Dumping struct </h2>
<cfdump var="#result#"/>

<cfset varQuery = QueryNew("column1,column2,column3") >
<cfset QueryAddRow(varQuery,["row 1", "row 2", "row 3"])>

<!-- Passing arguments inline as key value pair --->
<cfinvoke webservice = "#wsURL#"
          method = "echoQuery"
          argQuery = "#varQuery#"
          returnVariable = "result">
</cfinvoke>

<h2> Dumping query </h2>
<cfdump var="#result#"/>

<!-- Passing arguments as argument collection --->
<cfinvoke webservice = "#wsURL#"
          method = "echoAny"
          argumentcollection = "#{argAny:'passing a string'}#"
          returnVariable = "result">
</cfinvoke>

<h2> Dumping String </h2>
<cfdump var="#result#"/>
```

As shown here, there are three ways to pass arguments to web service calls. Let's look at them one by one.

First we will see how to pass an argument using the <cfinvokeparam> tag. We begin by creating the WSDL URL to be passed with <cfinvoke>. We then create a struct with implicit notation. And in case the syntax confuses you, ColdFusion also supports JavaScript-style syntax for declaring the struct. Next we use <cfinvoke> to call the web service by using <cfinvokeparam> as its child tag and passing the arguments specified as a key-value pair. This key will be matched with the arguments declared in the function and will be populated likewise.

Alternatively, you can pass arguments as superfluous attributes in the <cfinvoke> tag itself, as shown in next call to echoQuery. Again, the attribute name is the argument name, and its value is the value that we want to pass to the call.

Finally, you can also use `argumentcollection` to pass a struct with the argument name as the key and the value to be passed as its corresponding value as shown for the call `echoAny` call.

Note that you cannot use positional arguments with `<cfinvoke>` because the key is a mandatory attribute in all three scenarios described here. To use positional arguments, you can use `<cfobject>` or `CreateObject()` to generate a web service proxy and call methods on it. This call will behave similarly to any other method invocation for components and supports positional arguments, key-value syntax, and argument collection.

Also note that we passed a simple string to `echoAny`. We did this because the type definition of "any" in generated WSDL supports only simple data types. If you passed any complex object instead, it would fail with the "unknown type cannot serialize" exception.

We have now seen various ways to pass complex objects as arguments and get back complex objects as the result of that particular web service call. What's interesting is that there is almost no difference between calling a web service and calling a component locally. That is the beauty of ColdFusion: the capability to abstract the hard wiring required to perform a complex task such as a web service call and expose it as something simple that we already know such as calling a component. This ease of use lets us focus on the actual business logic and not to be bothered with the underlying technology or mundane boilerplate code.

Working with Multiple Arguments

So far in our examples, we have seen functions with only one argument. But your real-world functions more likely will have more than one argument. And though the mechanism to call these functions as web services remains the same, there are a few details that you need to take care of.

When your function has more than one argument, you may want to make a few arguments required and the rest optional. However, the `<cffunction>` attribute `Required` is ignored when a CFC is called as a web service; for a web service, all arguments are required. ColdFusion doesn't support method overloading, so in in cases in which you want to pass only a few arguments, you need to use either of two approaches:

- You can make the function private and define different public methods for all parameter combinations. These methods will internally invoke this private function within the CFC, which performs the actual processing and also honors the defaults.

- The second possible solution is to use a special value for arguments that you don't want to pass: for example, NULL. Then within the function body, you can check `IsNull()` and place default values instead. If you use `<cfinvoke>`, then you can set the `<cfinvokeargument>` tag's attribute `omit` as `true`. If you are using a proxy object created with `<cfobject>` or the `CreateObject()` method, you can simply pass NULL.

TIP

To create NULL in ColdFusion, you can either use `javaCast( "null", 0 )` or call a function that returns nothing: for example, `function null(){}`.

Securing Your Web Service

Security is a very important aspect to consider when developing your services. As more and more business functions are exposed as web services, the boundary of interaction keeps expanding, and so does your responsibility to address all security requirements such as authentication, access control, data integrity, and privacy. In this section, we explore some ways to secure your web services.

To begin, you can always publish your web service over HTTPS. This approach will guarantee point-to-point security because SSL secures communications at the transport level. However, these scheme has limitations such as scalability issues, and you may not be able to use it.

You can also use your web server to control access to the directories containing your web services, or you can use ColdFusion security in the same way that you use it to control access to any Cold-Fusion page. The <cfinvoke> tag includes the username and password attributes that let you pass login information to a web server using HTTP basic authentication.

Using ColdFusion to Control Access

Let's look at how to secure our web services from within ColdFusion. There are many possible ways to do so, and we will discuss just some of them here. You can pick the approach best suited to your particular needs.

One scheme that you can use uses <cflogin>. Rather than letting web servers handle authorization, you can implement authentication at the application level with Application.cfm (Listing 4.8).

Listing 4.8   /cfwack/4/secure/Application.cfm

```
<cfapplication name="wack4_secure">

<cflogin>
    <cfset authorized = false>
    <!--- verify username and password --->
    <cfif isDefined("cflogin")
          and cflogin.name eq "foo"
          and cflogin.password eq "bar">
       <cfset authorized = true>
    </cfif>
</cflogin>

<cfif not authorized>
    <cfsetting enablecfoutputonly="yes"
               showdebugoutput="no">
    <cfheader statuscode="401">
    <cfheader name="WWW-Authenticate"
              value="Basic realm=""Web Services""">
    <cfabort>
</cfif>
```

This Application.cfm example includes a <cflogin> tag. As you may know, the body of this tag runs only if there is no logged-in user. Therefore, the example includes some logic to validate the user in the body of the <cflogin> tag. In a real-world scenario, you would be validating users against a data source, LDAP, and so on. If the check here fails, the request is simply aborted, with a few authentication headers set. The same logic can be placed in the Application.cfc file's method OnRequestStart. This method is executed for all types of requests and is invoked before the actual call to the web service method is made.

You can also use <cfloginuser> from within the <cflogin> tag to identify an authenticated user to ColdFusion and specify the user ID and roles. This approach lets you set allowed roles in <cffunction>, which can invoke that function.

Next, we explore how to invoke the same old hello web service, using the code snippet shown in Listing 4.9.

Listing 4.9   /cfwack/4/secureclient/basic.cfm

```
<cfset wsURL = "http://localhost:1234/cfwack/4/secure/hello.cfc?wsdl">

<cfinvoke webservice="#wsURL#"
          method="helloWorld"
          returnvariable="result"
          username="foo"
          password="bar">

<h1> <cfoutput>#result#</cfoutput> </h1>
```

As you can see, we are using the same <cfinvoke> tag that we have been using to additionally pass username and password information. This information will be populated in the cflogin struct, accessible within the <cflogin> tag as the name and password that we will use to validate our user.

Another approach is to use Open Standard for Authorization (OAuth) authentication. This authentication protocol allows applications to access a user's data in a secure way. Several good libraries for both publishing and consuming OAuth integrations are available in ColdFusion for you to investigate.

Finally, you can use SOAP headers for authorization purposes: for example, you can set Web Service Security (WSS) headers and validate them either at the application level or the component level, as described in the next section.

Working with SOAP Requests

ColdFusion offers a variety of ways to work with the SOAP requests and responses involved in web services. Let's look at them closely with an example.

We have already talked about CFCs and how the same components can be used to serve different types of requests such as Adobe Flash Remoting and Ajax Remoting calls. When you want to handle SOAP requests differently and to know whether the call originated as a web service call, you can use the function IsSOAPRequest(). This function will return true if the CFC is being called as a web service.

Also we have talked about how SOAP requests for web services use HTTP as the transport medium. You also may know that HTTP uses headers to pass additional workable information about the request and its response. So depending on the use case, you may need to read SOAP request headers—for example, to get the username—or add headers to your SOAP responses—for example, an authorization header. ColdFusion provides functions that let you read and add headers to your SOAP request or SOAP response. Listing 4.10 provides an example.

Listing 4.10   /cfwack/4/soap.cfc

```
<cfcomponent hint="Test for SOAP headers">

    <cffunction name="test" returntype="string" access="remote">

        <cfset isSOAP = isSOAPRequest()>
        <cfif isSOAP>
        <!--- Get the first header as a string. --->
            <cfset username = getSOAPRequestHeader("http://somenamespace/",
            ➥"username")>
            <cfset result = "username: " & username>

            <!--- Get the second header as a string. --->
            <cfset password = getSOAPRequestHeader("http://somenamespace/",
            ➥"password")>
            <cfset result = result & " and password: " & password>

            <!--- Add a header as a string. --->
            <cfset addSOAPResponseHeader("http://somenamespace/",
            "returnheader", "AUTHORIZED", false)>
        <cfelse>
            <cfset result = "Not invoked as a web service">
        </cfif>

        <cfreturn result>
    </cffunction>

</cfcomponent>
```

As you can see, we have a simple soap CFC that has only one function test. Within this function, we check whether the call is a SOAP request with isSOAPRequest(). If the result is true, we get the headers from the request—that is, username and password—using getSOAPRequestHeader() and set a returnheader header in the response using addSOAPResponseHeader(). If the result is false, then we send back the result "Not invoked as a web service." This example is very simple, but you can see how different logic can be applied to perform various operations such as actual authentication.

Now let's see this CFC in action by invoking the CFC once as a web service and for a second time as a local method on a component (Listing 4.11).

Listing 4.11   /cfwack/4/soap.cfm

```
<cfscript>
wsURL = "http://localhost:8500/cfwack/4/soap.cfc?wsdl";
ws = CreateObject("webservice", wsURL);

// Set the username and passwordheader as a string.
addSOAPRequestHeader(ws, "http://somenamespace/", "username", "user");
addSOAPRequestHeader(ws, "http://somenamespace/", "password", "pass");
```

Listing 4.11 (CONTINUED)

```
    // Invoke the web service operation.
    result = ws.test();

    // Get the first header as an object (string) and as XML.
    header = getSOAPResponseHeader(ws, "http://somenamespace/", "returnheader");
</cfscript>

<cfoutput>
    SOAP Return value: #result#<br>
    SOAP Header value: #header#<br>
</cfoutput>


<cfinvoke component="soap" method="test" returnvariable="result">
</cfinvoke>
<cfoutput>The cfinvoke tag returned: #result#</cfoutput>
```

Here we created a proxy for the SOAP web service using CreateObject(). Then we added two headers, username and password, for this proxy. These headers will be added to the SOAP request when the actual call is made, which is when the test method is called. We get back the result of this web service call in result. Additionally, we extract the response header that was set in the CFC from the proxy object. Next, we call a function on the SOAP CFC directly and output its results.

The output of this template when executed in a browser is obvious. For the SOAP request, the output will return the username and password that were sent as headers, and it will also return returnheader as "AUTHORIZED". For a local call, it would simply return "Not invoked as a web service."

Application Settings

Four application-level web service settings can be used to apply certain properties related to web services across a given application. These settings are defined in Application.cfc in the this.wssettings struct, shown in Listing 4.12, which we will discuss one by one. Note that these application settings are introduced in ColdFusion 10 and are not available in previous ColdFusion versions.

Listing 4.12   /cfwack/4/Application.cfc

```
<cfcomponent>

    <cfset this.name="cfwack_4">

    <cfset this.wssettings.version.publish = 2>
    <cfset this.wssettings.version.consume = 2>
    <cfset this.wssettings.style = "wrapped">
    <cfset this.wssettings.includeCFTypesInWSDL = false>

</cfcomponent>
```

Including ColdFusion Types in WSDL

In our discussion of complex data types, we looked at the use of ColdFusion native data types with web services. These data types are similar to a number of data types in C++ and Java, but they do not exactly match any of the data types defined in the XML schema used by WSDL and SOAP for data-type representation and conversion.

This lack of a match is fine if a web service is published and consumed within ColdFusion because ColdFusion expects and understands its own data types and can serialize or deserialize them. However, when clients other than ColdFusion call this web service, they will need additional information to convert arguments to be sent with the web service call to data types that ColdFusion expects and understands.

Here is where `this.wssettings.includeCFTypesInWSDL` comes to our rescue. It tells ColdFusion whether to include ColdFusion's native type information as an XML schema defined in the WSDL itself. Using this schema, other platforms can understand the arguments and result types.

If your web services will be used only with ColdFusion clients, there is no need to include this type information as it will increase the WSDL size. By default, it is set to `false`.

Deciding Which Web Service Engine to Use

Let's step back a bit from our original topic of application settings. We said earlier that there are two web service engines available to us with ColdFusion 10. You can choose the web service engine to use according to your requirements:

- Web Service Engine Version 1: Use this version if you want to publish WSDL in RPC style, or if you do not want all your existing web service clients to refresh their generated stubs. You should also use this version when you have web service clients on Cold-Fusion 9 and you use complex data types.

- Web Service Engine Version 2: Use this version if you want to consume any web service that is based on WSDL 2.0, or if you want to publish WSDL in wrapped style. With ColdFusion 10, this is the default engine for publishing a web service.

- Either engine: For all other scenarios, you can use either of the web service engines.

Specifying the Web Service Engine

ColdFusion uses Web Service Engine Version 2 by default to publish any component as a web service. However, you can override this behavior and tell ColdFusion which engine to use. You can specify the web service engine used to publish your ColdFusion components in any of three places:

- Component level: You can specify `wsversion` with `<cfcomponent>` to declare the web service engine to use to publish that particular component. The possible values are `1` and `2`. This setting takes the precedence over application- and server-level version declarations.

- Application level: You can specify `this.wssettings.version.publish` in your Application. cfm file to declare the web service engine at the application level. All the components in the application will then be published using this setting. This setting takes precedence over the server-level setting.

- Server level: You can specify the web service engine to be used across the server. Select the version on the Web Services page in the Data and Services section of ColdFusion Administrator, shown in Figure 4.4.

Figure 4.4

Changing the web
service version
in ColdFusion
Administrator.

While consuming a web service, ColdFusion will try to understand the WSDL style. If the style is Document Literal or Document Literal Wrapped, ColdFusion automatically uses Web Service Engine Version 2, and if the style is RPC Literal, ColdFusion automatically uses Web Service Engine Version 1. However, the caller can override this behavior by specifying the web service engine to be used while consuming web services. There are two places to provide this option:

- While consuming a service: You can provide `wsversion` with `<cfinvoke>` to tell Cold-Fusion which web service engine to use to consume the web service. The possible values are 1 and 2, and this setting takes precedence over the application-level setting.

- Application level: You can specify `this.wssettings.version.consume` in your Application. cfm file. Any call to consume web services will now use the specified version of the web service engine.

Choosing the WSDL Style

ColdFusion can publish WSDL and consume web services that publish WSDL in the following styles:

- RPC Encoded: Specified with the `<cfcomponent>` attribute `style="rpc"`, this style considers web services as XML-based forms of Remote Procedure Calls (RPCs). Here the SOAP message body contains only one element, which is named after the operation, and all parameters must be represented as subelements of this wrapper element. This style is available only with Web Service Engine Version 1.

- Document Literal: Specified with the `<cfcomponent>` attribute `style="document"`, this style considers web services as a means of moving XML information from one place to another. Here, the SOAP message body must follow the XML schema defined in WSDL as types. This style is available with both web service engine versions.

- Document Literal Wrapped: Specified with the `<cfcomponent>` attribute `style="wrapped"`, this style is similar to the Document Literal style, except that the SOAP message body is wrapped within a root element. This style is available only with Web Service Engine Version 2.

Alternatively, you can specify the WSDL style to use at the application level as `this.wssettings.style`. ColdFusion will use this information to generate WSDL in the specified style for all the CFCs in this application. You can individually override this setting with the `<cfcomponent>` attribute `style`, which takes precedence over application-level settings.

Configuring Web Services in ColdFusion Administrator

The ColdFusion Administrator lets you register a web service with a name. You can do so by adding a web service on the Web Services page in the ColdFusion Administrator in the Data and Services section. When you reference that web service in your code with this name, you won't have to specify the URL or any other details for the web service call. For example, any time you invoke a web service registered as `ZipCodeWS` on a particular server, you can refer to it as `WebService="ZipCodeWS"`. The URL can then be changed to point to another URL without the need to modify the invocation code throughout the application. This approach represents a type of code encapsulation, which you could also implement using application or request scope variables.

With ColdFusion 10, you can also specify proxy settings such as the proxy server, proxy port, proxy username, and proxy password, and a server-level setting to cause any web service request to time out at a particular time. When you call this web service by its name at the time of registration, you need not specify these settings again. However, settings provided at the time of the actual web service call, such as a `<cfinvoke>` call, will override server-level settings.

Note that just accessing any web service from user code will not autoregister or change that web service in ColdFusion Administrator, which used to happen until ColdFusion 9. With ColdFusion 10, to register a web service in ColdFusion Administrator you need to add or modify it from the Administrator only.

NOTE
> To learn more about ColdFusion Administrator changes, visit http://www.adobe.com/devnet/coldfusion/articles/axis2-web-services.html.

Best Practices

Web services have been around for a while and have generated significant hype. Along with the advantages of cross-platform compatibility are some drawbacks. Although the distributed computing environment of web services is widely recognized as the way of the future, it carries the baggage of network latency and additional translation time. The actual overhead of running a web service is not as bad as perceived, but it is a factor to consider when selecting parts of systems to expose to the world. Careful testing and optimization can reduce this potential problem significantly. Here are several general principles to consider when programming and designing web services:

- Use coarse-grained web services. Network latency can be the biggest performance bottleneck. Try to reduce calls to the server. Call a web service once and use a query of queries to return the detailed information for display.

- Secure your services. Never publish your web service without proper security in place. See the discussion about securing your web services earlier in this chapter for details.

- Use a server-level timeout. Aim for a timeout value of 1 to 3 seconds; waiting for a web service from a busy server to return can eat up all threads on your server and potentially can bring it down.

- Preferably, call long running web services from a scheduler or <cfthread> and look for caching possibilities. See Chapter 14 for information about schedulers and Chapter 16 for information about caching.

- Use stateless web services whenever possible.

- Include ColdFusion types in WSDL and limit the use of complex data types in web services that interact with other platforms. Other platforms may not be able to understand deeply nested types.

- Monitor your web service calls to understand their use. You can use ColdFusion server monitoring, which monitors web service calls separately from other types of request. With just the basic monitoring enabled, you can get valuable information about web service requests, running or queued. And on the basis of this information, you can tweak your server settings and also change the application code.

Troubleshooting

No matter how carefully you code, you can always end up with unexpected results. In such cases, you will want to see what is happening and to pinpoint the code that is causing the problem. Debugging can be difficult when there is client-server communication as in the case of web services. Here are a few tips to help you identify and fix common problems that you may face:

- Check the WSDL. As explained earlier, append ?wsdl to the CFC URL and run the URL in a browser to see whether the CFC has any compilation problems and whether the generated WSDL is correct and accessible.

- Use <cfdump> to output to the console to check whether the call is coming to your application and see what arguments are being passed. Remember to remove this function when implementing your application for production.

- Use refreshWSDL. It is possible that the CFC you are accessing through the web service has changed. Use this attribute with <cfinvoke> to regenerate the stubs. Remember to remove it when implementing your application for production.

- If wsversion is not defined while consuming a web service, ColdFusion checks the WSDL to determine which web service engine it should use to consume that particular web service. You can force ColdFusion to use a specific web service engine by specifying wsversion with <cfinvoke>.

- You can use the `GetSOAPRequest` function to get the actual SOAP request sent and the `GetSOAPResponse` function to get the actual response received. This information can help you determine whether correct information is being sent and whether you are receiving the correct response.

- You can use a TCP monitor such as TCPMon to track exactly what is being sent and received over the wire. The monitor acts like a proxy between the client and the server and shows you the communication that occurred in between them.

SOAP or REST?

If you have ever wondered which form of web services you should use, you are not alone. However, there is no easy answer. In this section, we list the key differences between SOAP and REST services to help you decide which style to choose for your particular case.

- SOAP-based web services are object oriented, and REST-based web services are representation oriented. Without going into detail, this distinction means that you can get started easily with a SOAP-based solution, but a REST-based solution will need additional planning to create a logical hierarchy.

- SOAP-based web services are declarative, use the standard WSDL format to describe them, and have great tooling support. REST-based web services do not yet have a standard for describing services.

- SOAP-based web services support only XML, and REST-based web services can support numerous content types, including JavaScript Object Notation (JSON), and can be accessed directly from JavaScript.

- SOAP 1.1–based solutions do not conform to the HTTP model and hence cannot take advantage of HTTP caching, security, and so on. REST is fully HTTP complaint.

- XML use makes the SOAP format verbose and its performance slower than REST using JSON. However, REST clients may take a longer time when using XML.

- REST generates search-engine optimization (SEO)–friendly endpoints.

As a general rule, REST benefits web services directly accessed from web pages as in the case of `XMLHTTPRequests` (XHR) , and SOAP benefits web services accessed by an intermediate server or middleware.

CHAPTER 5

Using REST Web Services

ColdFusion has long made it easy to create consumable services. Whether you are using Simple Object Access Protocol (SOAP), Adobe Flash Remoting, or pure Ajax calls, ColdFusion makes it easy for remote clients to use ColdFusion's server-side features. In ColdFusion 10, developers can now use fully REST-compliant services.

What Is REST?

Representational State Transfer, or REST, was first introduced as a concept by Roy Fielding in 2000. Closely tied to HTTP, REST defines a way to uniquely identify a resource as well as the action that should be performed on that resource. For example, the same HTTP method GET that is used to access a home page can be used in REST to retrieve a particular user resource. The HTTP method DELETE pointed at the same resource implies that the resource should be removed.

You may be wondering then why someone would bother with REST. ColdFusion components (CFCs) supports similar behavior now. You can get a user resource via a CFC call such as this:

```
http://localhost/some.cfc?method=getUser&userid=1
```

Given that we create services like this now, what benefit does REST give us?

First, by reusing the HTTP verb commonly used, we can simplify the call. Second, by defining one uniform resource locator (URL) for a resource, we can perform different actions simply by changing the HTTP verb used. Therefore, you can retrieve the same user record via an HTTP GET call to this URL: http://localhost/userService/user/1.

And then you can delete the user by using the exact same URL but with the HTTP DELETE call. There isn't any guessing at the method (removeUser? deleteUser? eraseUser?); you simply change the HTTP verb used.

Best of all, REST services in ColdFusion are created using the same type of file you've used in the past: a CFC file. By following a few simple rules, you can build your own REST service in Cold-Fusion in just a few steps.

Registering REST Services

Before you work with REST services in ColdFusion, you must perform one critical step. You must register all REST services in ColdFusion before they are used. Also, you must update this regis-tration every time you update the service. Even if you just correct a typo, you will need to refresh the registration.

REST registration can be performed in two ways. The simplest way is via the ColdFusion Admin-istrator. After logging in to the ColdFusion Administrator, click the REST Services link under Data & Services (Figure 5.1).

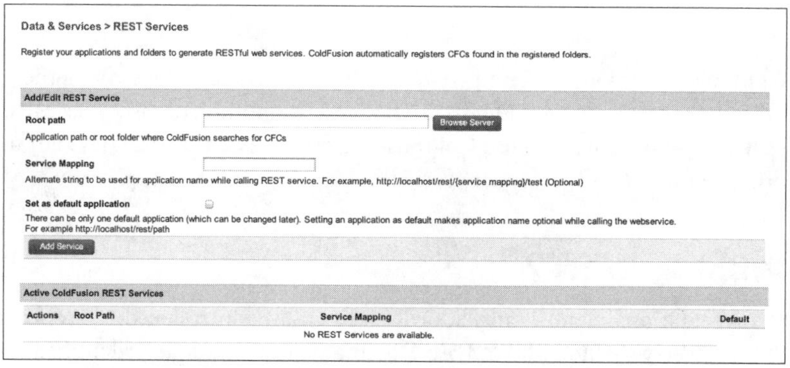

Figure 5.1

The ColdFusion Administrator UI for registering REST services.

You will use this interface to add, edit, and delete REST services. However, do not think of this as a process of defining each individual REST file, but rather as a process of defining a collection of REST files within an application.

We'll discuss the second option for REST registration later in this chapter.

Each REST service is defined by three settings. The first, Root Path, specifies the folder that contains the application with your REST services. This path should point to the directory that contains your Application.cfc file. If your REST-enabled CFCs are beneath this directory in a subdirectory, they will automatically be located.

The second setting, Service Mapping, defines a logical URL group for your REST services. The default name is the name of the application. Assume that your application contains an Applica-tion.cfc file with `this.name` set to `myBlog`. Any REST service within this application will then use `myBlog` in the URL. You will see an example of this soon. You can choose an alternative name if you want; this is purely a cosmetic decision.

The third setting, Set as Default Application, provides a way to override the Service Mapping setting. Only one REST service can be the default on the server. Setting this option to true allows you to skip the Service Mapping setting when you share the URL of a REST service. As with the Service Mapping setting, your choice is mainly a cosmetic decision. If you are certain that this particular REST service will be the only one on the server, or that it will be the most important service, then set this option.

We're going to assume that you've extracted the files from the CFWACK zip file into a folder under your ColdFusion 10 wwwroot folder. For example, your Chapter 5 files may be located in a folder such as this: /Application/ColdFusion10/cfusion/wwwroot/5.

All of our testing will be performed with the files here, so we need to register the service only once. On the ColdFusion Administrator REST Services page, enter that directory for the Root Path setting and leave the other two settings alone. Click Add Service, and you should receive a confirmation. Note that after you do, you have options to edit, refresh, and delete the service. Remember: **Every time you edit a REST-based CFC, you need to refresh the service.** This process can become annoying, but if you keep the ColdFusion Administrator page open in a separate tab, you can make the process less painful.

Building Your First REST CFC

When you registered the REST service earlier, you actually prepared your server to run all the REST services we will discuss in this chapter. Let's begin, though, by looking at the Application. cfc file for our demonstrations (Listing 5.1). Since this chapter focuses just on REST services, the Application.cfc file isn't that interesting. In a real application, there would be much more here.

Listing 5.1   /cfwack/5/Application.cfc
```
component {
    this.name="cfwack5_root";

    this.restsettings.cfclocation = "./restcfcs";
    this.restsettings.skipCFCWithError = false;
}
```

Of note here are two settings, both of which are optional. The `this.restsettings.cfclocation` setting is just what it sounds like: the folder in which REST-enabled CFCs can be found. If this folder is not specified, the ColdFusion Administrator will check all CFCs under the main directory. The `this.restsettings.skipCFCWithError` setting specifies what ColdFusion should do when it finds a bad CFC during the scan for REST CFCs. By default, ColdFusion will ignore the CFC and carry on. There is no logical reason (well, most likely no logical reason) to ever allow this to happen, so we always recommend changing this setting to false.

Now let's move on to our very first REST CFC (Listing 5.2).

Listing 5.2 /cfwack/5/restcfcs/hello.cfc

```
component rest="true" restPath="helloService" {

    remote string function helloWorld() httpmethod="get" {
        return "Hello World!";
    }

}
```

Note that all of our REST-enabled CFCs will be using script-based components. However, you do *not* need to write your components this way.

Let's tackle the important settings in this CFC one by one.

First is the rest="true" setting in the component tag. As you can probably guess, this setting flags the component as a REST service.

Next is restPath. This setting determines the URL by which people will access the service—more about this in a moment.

In the only method in the CFC, helloWorld, we've set the remote attribute so that it can be used by remote clients. Your REST CFCs may create private methods that you do not intend others to use.

Finally, httpmethod defines how the service can be accessed. We discussed earlier that REST services make use of HTTP verbs. By defining httpmethod="get" for this method, we've said that when an HTTP GET request is issued for this service, this is the method that will be executed.

Testing Your First REST CFC

So how now do you test this REST service? If you were doing this the "old way" (that is, building a simple service for Adobe Flash Remoting or Ajax), your URL would look something like this:

http://localhost/cfwack5/restcfcs/helloworld.cfc?method=helloworld

Notice that we specify the method to run within the component. Now let's look at the REST version of this:

http://localhost/rest/cfwack5_root/helloService

A bit simpler, right? Let's break down how we generated the URL:

- /rest is a prefix for all REST services. All REST services begin with this.

- /cfwack5_root is the name of the application. Remember that when we defined the REST service in the ColdFusion Administrator, we had an option to specify a service mapping. Since we didn't, the URL defaulted to our application name. If we'd wanted something else, we could have modified this setting.

- /helloService comes from the restPath setting in our CFC.

Together, these elements form the URL. When you run this URL in your browser, you should see "Hello World." Note that this URL is *not* WDDX-encoded. That is the default for CFCs you write for Ajax-based applications. As you will see soon, you can generate JSON, XML, and plain string results like you do in any other Ajax applications.

How did the REST service know which method to call? Remember the `httpmethod="get"` specification we added to the method in the CFC? This is what responded to the GET request you made in your browser.

Now consider the modified version in Listing 5.3.

Listing 5.3 /cfwack/5/restcfcs/helloworld2.cfc

```
component rest="true" restPath="helloService2" {

    remote string function helloWorldSimple() httpmethod="get" {
        return "Hello World 2!";
    }

    remote string function helloWorldForm() httpmethod="post" {
        return "Hello from a Form Post!";
    }

}
```

This component contains two methods. The first, `helloWorldSimple`, is set up to respond to GET requests. The second method, `helloWorldForm`, is set up to respond to POST requests. If you open http://localhost/rest/cfwack5_root/helloService2 in your browser, you will see that `helloWorldSimple` is executed. But how can you test the POST response? Listing 5.4 is a simple CFM file that executes both of these requests at once.

Listing 5.4 /cfwack/5/test1.cfm

```
<cfhttp url="http://localhost:8500/rest/cfwack5_root/helloService2">
<cfdump var="#cfhttp.filecontent#">

<p>

<cfhttp url="http://localhost:8500/rest/cfwack5_root/helloService2" method="post">
    <cfhttpparam type="formfield" name="something" value="somevalue" />
</cfhttp>
<cfdump var="#cfhttp.filecontent#">
```

Note that the `<cfhttp>` tags in Listings 5.3 and 5.4 both use the *exact same URL*. This is a crucial difference between older Ajax-based CFC requests and CFCs. However, the second `<cfhttp>` tag uses a POST request rather than a GET request. Figure 5.2 demonstrates the different output.

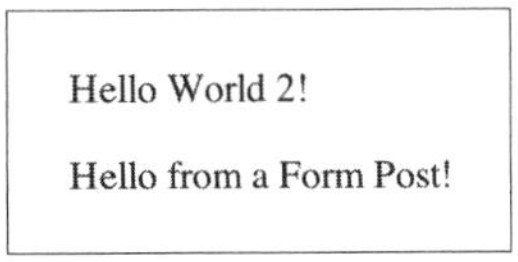

Figure 5.2

Sample output from a call to the REST service.

Hello World 2!

Hello from a Form Post!

ColdFusion will correctly recognize and handle GET, POST, PUT, DELETE, HEAD, and OPTIONS HTTP requests. Note that HEAD will run the GET handler if a specific HEAD-related method is not defined; OPTIONS will return an XML descriptor for the service, again, though, only if an OPTIONS-related method exists.

Specifying Content Types

You've now seen how different HTTP verbs can be automatically handled by specific methods in your components Another aspect of REST is content-type negotiation: that is, when a client makes a request, it can specify the form of the result it wants. So, for example, a client may prefer XML, or it may prefer JSON. ColdFusion lets you take this preference into account and use specific methods to handle each case.

The <cffunction> tag (and its script-based version of course) can use two new attributes to help route and handle particular content-type requests. The first, consumes, defines the types of content-type requests the method handles. These match MIME types and so will look like this: text/plain or text/html. You can also use */* to match any content type. Another example is the use of text/* to match text/plain or text/html.

The second attribute is produces. This attribute specifies the type of result that this method creates. By combining both attributes, you can ensure that your REST methods correctly respond to client requests in the exact format they want.

With these two attributes together, you have a way to handle a client that sends you a specific type of request as well as a way to handle a client that wants a specific type of response.

Listing 5.5 shows a simple REST service that can produce both plain text and JSON responses. (To be fair, JSON *is* plain text, but a specific format of text.)

Listing 5.5   /cfwack/5/restcfcs/contentTypeService.cfc

```
component rest="true" restPath="contentService" {

    remote string function helloWorldSimple()
            httpmethod="get" produces="text/plain" {
        return "Content Simple";
    }

    remote struct function helloWorldJSON()
            httpmethod="get" produces="application/json" {
        return {code:"1", message:"Content Complex"};
    }

}
```

Both methods use produces to specify the type of result they create. Notice the slightly more complex code in helloWorldJSON. It creates a structure for the response. Much the way that older-style Ajax CFCs can produce JSON using returnformat as an argument, REST-based CFCs can automatically serialize results as well. So when would you use one method instead of the other? Let's check Listing 5.6.

Listing 5.6   /cfwack/5/test2.cfm

```
<cfhttp url="http://localhost:8500/rest/cfwack5_root/contentService">
   <cfhttpparam type="header" name="Accept" value="text/plain"/>
</cfhttp>
<cfdump var="#cfhttp.filecontent#">

<p>

<cfhttp url="http://localhost:8500/rest/cfwack5_root/contentService">
   <cfhttpparam type="header" name="Accept" value="application/json" />
</cfhttp>
<cfdump var="#cfhttp.filecontent#">
```

Notice that both HTTP calls in Listing 5.6 use the same URL and the same method. (The default method for <cfhttp> is GET.) The difference here is the addition of the Accept header. This header tells the remote service the form of result that it prefers.

What's interesting is that clients can actually ask for multiple types of responses. In other words, a client can say, "I'll take a response in form X or Y." Clients can even allow for multiple responses with different levels of priorities. So, for example, the client can tell the server, "Hey, buddy, the response I'd most like is application/json, but if I can't have that, send me text/html instead." Listing 5.7 provides an example.

Listing 5.7   /cfwack/5/test3.cfm

```
<cfhttp url="http://localhost:8500/rest/cfwack5_root/contentService">
   <cfhttpparam type="header" name="Accept"
                value="application/uber;q=0.9, application/beer;q=0.8, text/*" />
</cfhttp>
<cfdump var="#cfhttp.filecontent#">
```

This file is using the same REST service as before, but notice that now the Accept header contains three items, separated by commas. The first two content types include a semicolon and q=X string. The q value represents the priority: that is, how strongly one form is preferred over another. This value can range from 0 to 1. Our template has said that its most preferred response type is application/uber, with application/beer being a close second. The third type allowed is text/*. When this script is run, it returns the string "Content Simple" since it supports text/plain.

Using XML Serialization

Developers who have used CFCs for Ajax applications are used to ColdFusion's native JSON serialization. ColdFusion also supports generation of XML in a style called WDDX. REST CFCs in ColdFusion now support a slimmer, simpler XML format. Listing 5.8 defines a newer version of the contentService code listed earlier.

Listing 5.8   /cfwack/5/restcfcs/contentTypeService2.cfc

```
component rest="true" restPath="contentService2" {

    remote string function helloWorldSimple()
           httpmethod="get" produces="text/plain" {
        return "Content Simple";
    }

    remote struct function helloWorldComplex()
           httpmethod="get" produces="application/xml,application/json" {
        return {code:"1", message:"Content Complex"};
    }

}
```

Notice that helloWorldComplex was modified to state that it can produce XML or JSON. The actual logic in the method doesn't have to change. As you will see, ColdFusion will handle the correct serialization. Listing 5.9 shows how to call this service.

Listing 5.9   /cfwack/5/test4.cfm

```
<cfhttp url="http://localhost:8500/rest/cfwack5_root/contentService2">
   <cfhttpparam type="header" name="Accept" value="application/json" />
</cfhttp>
<cfdump var="#cfhttp.filecontent#">

<p>

<cfhttp url="http://localhost:8500/rest/cfwack5_root/contentService2">
   <cfhttpparam type="header" name="Accept" value="application/xml" />
</cfhttp>
<cfdump var="#cfhttp.filecontent#">
```

The result of the first call is a JSON representation of the structure:

```
{"MESSAGE":"Content Complex","CODE":35}
```

But here is how ColdFusion creates the XML format:

```
<STRUCT ID="1"><ENTRY NAME="MESSAGE" TYPE="STRING">Content
➥Complex</ENTRY><ENTRY NAME="CODE" TYPE="NUMBER">35</ENTRY></STRUCT>
```

ColdFusion can serialize complex objects such as CFCs, arrays, and structures (obviously). Note that if you don't like the way that ColdFusion does this, you can create your own XML string.

There's also a URL shortcut for JSON and XML responses. If you open the content service in your browser directly at http://localhost:8500/rest/cfwack5_root/contentService2, you will get the plain string response. But if you append .json or .xml, ColdFusion will act as if you had asked for `application/json` or `application/xml` as the response. So both of these URLs will work:

- http://localhost:8500/rest/cfwack5_root/contentService2.xml

- http://localhost:8500/rest/cfwack5_root/contentService2.json

Working with Subresources

So far you've seen how a REST-based CFC can define a URL for REST calls. You've also seen how methods in the CFC can respond to different HTTP verbs as well as different types of desired responses. Another powerful feature of REST APIs is the use of subresources. As described earlier, a REST-based CFC translates to one particular URL on your server. Subresources allow you to define a URL under the main one. To use subresources, you use the `restPath` argument at the function level. Listing 5.10 provides an example.

Listing 5.10   /cfwack/5/restcfcs/subservice.cfc

```
component rest="true" restPath="subService" {

    remote string function subRoot() httpmethod="get" {
        return "You didn't ask for any particular service";
    }

    remote string function subRoot2() httpmethod="get" restPath="/deep1" {
        return "You asked for deep1";
    }

    remote string function subRoot3() httpmethod="get" restPath="/deep2" {
        return "You asked for deep2";
    }

    remote string function subRoot4() httpmethod="get" restPath="/deep1/evendeeper" {
        return "You asked for deep1 + evendeeper";
    }

}
```

As the basis of what you've seen so far, you know that you can access this service at this URL:

http://localhost:8500/rest/cfwack5_root/subService

But look at the second method. It defines a `restPath` value of `"/deep1"`. This URL is appended to the root URL to provide support for this URL:

http://localhost:8500/rest/cfwack5_root/subService/deep1

As you can see, you can define more subresources. The third method provides support for `/deep2`, and the final method for `/deep1/evendeeper`. You can define any number of these methods that you want.

And in addition to defining static, or hard-coded, subresources as in the previous example, you can define dynamic paths by using regular expressions in the `restPath` argument. Consider Listing 5.11.

Listing 5.11 `/cfwack/5/restcfcs/cats.cfc`

```
component rest="true" restPath="catService" {

    remote string function root() httpmethod="get" {
        return "You didn't ask for a cat.";
    }

    remote string function catbyname(string cat restArgSource="path")
            httpmethod="get" restPath="{cat}" {
        return "You asked for #arguments.cat#";
    }

    remote string function catbynameweight(string cat restArgSource="path",
            numeric weight restArgSource="path")
            httpmethod="get" restPath="{cat}-{weight:[0-9]+}" {
        return "You asked for #arguments.cat# that weighed #weight# pounds";
    }

}
```

This REST service is a simple cat provider. It makes cats. Much like mommy cats. If you request just the service as is, you get a message specifying that you didn't actually ask for a specific cat. The next method allows you to pass in such a request. First, note that we are defining an argument, `cat`, and assigning metadata called `restArgSource` for the path. The `restArgSource` attribute defines the origin of an argument. In this case, we're saying that the path (the URL) will contain the value. This is, usually, the only value you will use, but you can also use `query` (as in a query string), `form`, `cookie`, `header`, and `matrix`. Note that the REST path now is dynamic. ColdFusion associates { } characters to define dynamic values. The name within the brackets (`cat`) is then linked with the argument for the method. (You can also specify the `restArgName` value for an argument to associate an argument in the method with another value in `restPath`, if you so choose.) The end result is that we can now use the following URL:

http://localhost:8500/rest/cfwack5_root/catService/Luna

This URL returns, "You asked for Luna".

The third method, `catbynameweight`, defines a more complex REST path. Notice that it contains both a simple value and a value that includes a regular expression. The `weight` argument will match any set of one or more numbers. Together with the dash between then, we now support a method that will match the following:

```
Set of characters - Set of numbers
```

So the method will match this URL, for example:

http://localhost:8500/rest/cfwack5_root/catService/Luna-10

The URL returns, "You asked for Luna that weighed 10 pounds".

You can mix and match these methods as much as you want. The form of the URL is really up to you.

Putting It All Together

Let's look at a complete, simple application that demonstrates many of the principles we've discussed so far. We're going to build a simple movie viewer. The application will list all the films when it is initially loaded (Figure 5.3).

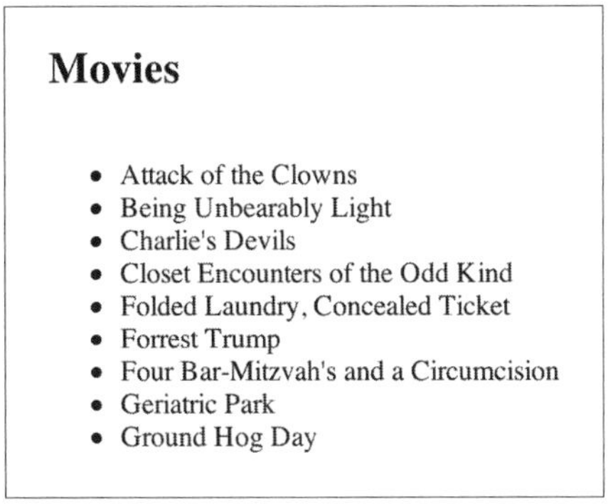

Figure 5.3

The application by default lists all the films.

Movies

- Attack of the Clowns
- Being Unbearably Light
- Charlie's Devils
- Closet Encounters of the Odd Kind
- Folded Laundry, Concealed Ticket
- Forrest Trump
- Four Bar-Mitzvah's and a Circumcision
- Geriatric Park
- Ground Hog Day

Selecting a film displays a detailed view that lets you update the budget or delete the film completely (Figure 5.4).

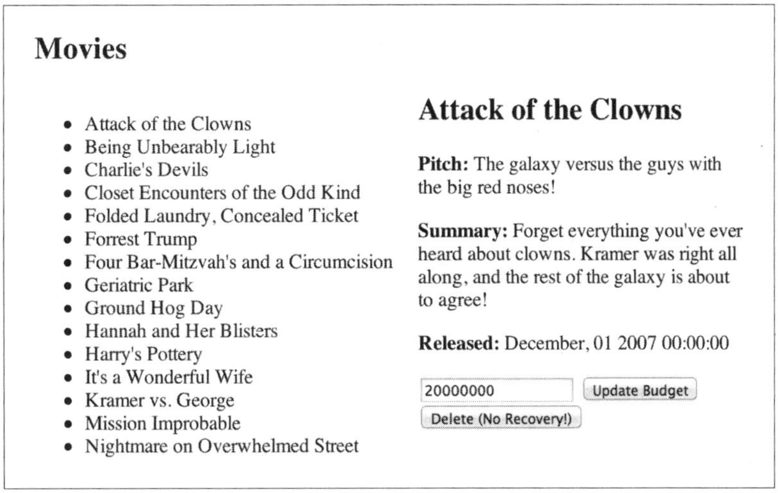

Figure 5.4

You can click for details about the films.

Movies

- Attack of the Clowns
- Being Unbearably Light
- Charlie's Devils
- Closet Encounters of the Odd Kind
- Folded Laundry, Concealed Ticket
- Forrest Trump
- Four Bar-Mitzvah's and a Circumcision
- Geriatric Park
- Ground Hog Day
- Hannah and Her Blisters
- Harry's Pottery
- It's a Wonderful Wife
- Kramer vs. George
- Mission Improbable
- Nightmare on Overwhelmed Street

Attack of the Clowns

Pitch: The galaxy versus the guys with the big red noses!

Summary: Forget everything you've ever heard about clowns. Kramer was right all along, and the rest of the galaxy is about to agree!

Released: December, 01 2007 00:00:00

[20000000] [Update Budget]

[Delete (No Recovery!)]

We will begin by creating a REST-based service. It needs to be able to list all the movies, get details about a film, allow updates, and process deletions. Listing 5.12 creates this service.

Listing 5.12 /cfwack/5/restcfcs/movie.cfc

```
component rest="true" restPath="movieService" {

    remote query function list() httpmethod="get" {
        var q = new com.adobe.coldfusion.query();
        q.setDatasource("ows");
        q.setSQL("select filmid, movietitle from films
            order by movietitle asc");
        var results = q.execute().getResult();

        return results;
    }

    remote struct function detail(numeric id restArgSource="path")
            httpmethod="get" restPath="{id:[0-9]+}" {
        var q = new com.adobe.coldfusion.query();
        q.setDatasource("ows");
        q.setSQL("select filmid, movietitle, pitchtext, amountbudgeted,
            summary, dateintheaters, rating
            from films left join filmsratings
            on films.ratingid = filmsratings.ratingid
            where filmid=:id");
        q.addParam(name="id",value="#arguments.id#",cfsqltype="cf_sql_integer");

        var results = q.execute().getResult();
        var item = {"id":results.filmid, "title":results.movietitle,
                    "pitch":results.pitchtext,
                    "budget":results.amountbudgeted,
                    "summary":results.summary,
                    "released":results.dateintheaters,
                    "rating":results.rating};
        return item;
    }

    remote void function update(numeric id restArgSource="path",
                numeric budget restArgSource="form")
                httpmethod="put" restPath="{id:[0-9]+}" {
        var q = new com.adobe.coldfusion.query();
        q.setDatasource("ows");
        q.setSQL("update films set amountbudgeted=:budget
                where filmid=:id");
        q.addParam(name="id",value="#arguments.id#",
                cfsqltype="cf_sql_integer");
        q.addParam(name="budget",value="#arguments.budget#",
                cfsqltype="cf_sql_numeric");

        q.execute().getResult();

    }

    remote string function delete(numeric id restArgSource="path")
            httpmethod="delete" restPath="{id:[0-9]+}" {
```

Listing 5.12 (CONTINUED)

```
        var q = new com.adobe.coldfusion.query();
        q.setDatasource("ows");
        q.setSQL("delete from expenses where filmid=:id");
        q.addParam(name="id",value="#arguments.id#",
                    cfsqltype="cf_sql_integer");
        q.execute();

        q = new com.adobe.coldfusion.query();
        q.setDatasource("ows");
        q.setSQL("delete from filmsactors where filmid=:id");
        q.addParam(name="id",value="#arguments.id#",
                    cfsqltype="cf_sql_integer");
        q.execute();

        q = new com.adobe.coldfusion.query();
        q.setDatasource("ows");
        q.setSQL("delete from filmsdirectors where filmid=:id");
        q.addParam(name="id",value="#arguments.id#",
                    cfsqltype="cf_sql_integer");
        q.execute();

        q = new com.adobe.coldfusion.query();
        q.setDatasource("ows");
        q.setSQL("delete from merchandise where filmid=:id");
        q.addParam(name="id",value="#arguments.id#",
                    cfsqltype="cf_sql_integer");
        q.execute();

        q = new com.adobe.coldfusion.query();
        q.setDatasource("ows");
        q.setSQL("delete from films where filmid=:id");
        q.addParam(name="id",value="#arguments.id#",
                    cfsqltype="cf_sql_integer");

        q.execute().getResult();
    }

}
```

Most of the code in this service relates to the various queries necessary to perform the actions of our application. Focus your attention on the method declarations, though. The first method, list, simply gets all the content. The detail method handles the use of restPath to notice a request for a specific film.

The third method, update, allows updates. To keep things simple, only the budget is updated. Note that the restAgSource argument for budget is form. Therefore, the new budget value will come from form data. This approach works even though the actual HTTP method will be PUT.

Finally, we have a simple delete handler. It uses the same URL form as detail, but it listens for the HTTP verb delete instead.

Now let's look at the front end (Listing 5.13).

Listing 5.13   /cfwack/5/movieapp/index.html

```html
<!doctype html>
<html lang="en">
<head>
<script type="text/javascript" src="http://ajax.googleapis.com/ajax/libs/jquery/1/
➡jquery.min.js"></script>
<script>
$(document).ready(function() {
    //Modify to match your port, etc
    var service = "http://localhost:8500/rest/cfwack5_root/movieService";

    function getAndDisplayMovies() {
        //I get all the movies
        $.get(service, {}, function(res,code) {
            var s = "";
            for(var i=0;i<res.DATA.length;i++) {
                s+= "<li data-movieid='"+res.DATA[i][0]+"'>"+res.DATA[i][1]+"</li>";
            }
            $("#movies").html(s);
        },"json");
    };

    //on load, run the display
    getAndDisplayMovies();

    //I listen for clicks on the names to get details
    $("body").on("click", "ul#movies li",  function(e) {
        var id = $(this).data("movieid");

        $.get(service + "/" + id, {}, function(movie, code) {
            var s = "<h2>" + movie.title + "</h2>";
            s+= "<p><b>Pitch:</b> "+movie.pitch+"</p>";
            s+= "<p><b>Summary:</b> "+movie.summary+"</p>";
            s+= "<p><b>Released:</b> "+movie.released+"</p>";

            //build a simple form
            s += "<p><input type='text' class='budgetEditField' value='"+
                movie.budget+"'> ";
            s += "<input type='button' class='updateBudgetButton' data-movieid='"+
                movie.id+"' value='Update Budget'><br/>";
            s += "<input type='button' class='movieDelete' data-movieid='"+
                movie.id+"' value='Delete (No Recovery!)'>";
            $("#detail").html(s);
        },"json");

    });

    //I let you update the budget
    $("body").on("click", ".updateBudgetButton", function(e) {
        var id = $(this).data("movieid");
        var newbudget = $(".budgetEditField").val();

        $.ajax(service + "/" + id, {
            type:"put",
```

Listing 5.13 (CONTINUED)

```
            complete:function(xhr,status) {
                console.log("success");
                //We could do something more here...
            },
            data:{budget:newbudget}
        });

    });

    //I let you delete movies
    $("body").on("click", ".movieDelete", function(e) {
        var id = $(this).data("movieid");

        $.ajax(service + "/" + id, {
            type:"delete",
            complete:function(xhr,status) {
                $("#detail").html("");
                getAndDisplayMovies();
            }
        });

    });

});
</script>

<style>
ul#movies {
    float:left;
    padding-right: 20px;
}

li[data-movieid] {
    cursor:pointer;
}
</style>
</head>

<body>

    <h2>Movies</h2>
    <ul id="movies"></ul>

    <div id="detail"></div>

</body>
</html>
```

This application is built entirely in HTML. The REST service is ColdFusion based, but all of the front end is HTML. The code uses jQuery for all data handling and display; therefore, almost all of the code is JavaScript.

When the page initially loads, we run a function called getAndDisplayMovies. It creates a request to the REST URL to get all the movie data.

This data is listed in HTML `<li>` tags within the initially empty `<ul>` tag pair. We have a simple click handler that will detect clicks on these items, fetch the `movieid` value we embedded in the HTML, and then send a request to the REST service for the details. Note that most of the code here handles the result. Most of the code in the CFC was query based; similarly, we can let Cold-Fusion handle most of the REST details for us and focus on our particular business logic. In case it isn't obvious, *that's a good thing.*

The final two functions handle the update (using a `PUT` request) and delete operations. Note that the `delete` function will also automatically request a new listing.

This simple application could be updated to allow full editing of the movie data for the other options as well.

Miscellaneous REST Functions

Although this chapter has discussed most of what you can do with REST in ColdFusion 10, there's still a little bit more that may interest you.

Customizing Responses

If you want to customize the response of a REST call to a fine degree, you can use `restSetResponse`. This function works only when the method is defined to have a `void` return type. It takes in a structure of data that must include the status as well as any other header that you want the caller to receive. This function could be used, for example, to redirect the response of a `PUT` request to a newly created resource.

You can also use `<cfthrow>`. In our demonstration application, we didn't provide support to handle a movie detail request for an ID that doesn't exist. We could easily add this support by using `<cfthrow>` to return a 404 error:

```
<cfthrow type="RestError" errorcode="404">
```

Dynamically Initializing REST Services

At the very beginning of the chapter, we mentioned that the ColdFusion Administrator can be used to register REST services as well as refresh them. You can also do the same via code. The function `restInitApplication` takes two arguments. The first is the directory to scan. The second, which is optional, is the service mappings. There is also a corresponding `restDeleteApplication` function.

CHAPTER 6

Embedding Video

Video is increasingly becoming an important means for a web application to engage and interact with end users. Many Internet and intranet web applications now commonly use videos in some form. To incorporate video into web applications, ColdFusion 9 introduced features to let you create a in-built media player that allows web applications to play several formats supported by Adobe Flash Player. Introduction of HTML5 and its support for video expanded the way that video can be published and consumed on the Internet. To support the rapid expansion of video use and the introduction of new technologies such as HTML5, ColdFusion 10 enhances video support with several new features, including support for HTML5, seamless fallback options, and better viewing support on multiple-screen and mobile devices. This chapter describes the new enhancements for video support in ColdFusion 10.

HTML5 and Video

Before we dig deeper into the new enhancements for video support in ColdFusion 10, let's review the video support with HTML5. Before HTML5, a plug-in such as Adobe Flash was a primary means of showing video on the web. HTML5 tried to standardize the way to show video on a web page by introducing the video element in an HTML page. Listing 6.1 shows an example of video with HTML5.

Listing 6.1   /cfwack10/6/video1.htm

```
<!DOCTYPE html>
<html>
  <body>
    <video height="270" width="360" controls>
      <source src="vid/sample.mp4" type="video/mp4">
      HTML5 video is not supported by your browser.
    </video>
  </body>
</html>
```

The Height and width attributes reserve the space required for video when the page is loaded. The controls attribute adds play, pause, and volume video controls. The type attribute specifies the MIME type of the video. Currently, the following video formats are supported:

- MP4: Uses the H264 video codec and AAC audio codec

- Ogg: Uses the Theora video codec and Vorbis audio codec

- WebM: Uses the VP8 codec and Vorbis audio codec

It is not uncommon for the video element shown in Listing 6.1 to be changed to include multiple source elements, as shown in Listing 6.2.

Listing 6.2 /cfwack10/6/video2.htm

```
<!DOCTYPE html>
<html>
  <body>
    <video height="270" width="360" controls>
      <source src="vid/sample.mp4" type="video/mp4">
      <source src="vid/sample.webm" type="video/webm">
      HTML5 video is not supported by your browser.
    </video>
  </body>
</html>
```

The reason for this change is simple: All browsers—Internet Explorer, Chrome, Firefox, Safari, Opera, and others, and their versions—do not support all the formats. When multiple source inputs are present, the browser tries to play the video in the order that the source elements are specified. On running the code in Listing 6.2, the browser first checks whether it can play the MP4 file. If the browser can, it plays it and renders the video. If it can't, it checks the next source input, the WebM file. If the browser cannot play the WebM file, it prints the message shown in the listing.

Later in this chapter, we discuss how video support in ColdFusion 10 provides an improved and uniform experience with Adobe Flash fallback and a skinning option to deal with such behavior differences in browsers.

HTML5 Video Support

Video support in ColdFusion is provided by the cfmediaplayer tag. The tag was introduced in ColdFusion 9 and supported only Adobe Flash videos. To support HTML5 video and differentiate between Adobe Flash and HTML videos, ColdFusion 10 adds a new attribute, type, to the cfmediaplayer tag. The tag now supports both Adobe Flash and HTML5 videos; the default value of the type attribute is "flash". Listing 6.3 shows how to play an MP4 video using the cfmediaplayer tag in the HTML5 player.

Listing 6.3 /cfwack10/6/mp4Type.cfm

```
<br>Type is set to html
<br>Video should play as html video

<cfmediaplayer name="media02"
               source="vid/sample.mp4"
               type="html"
               controlbar=true/>
```

The example in Listing 6.3 takes an MP4 file as a source and plays it using the HTML5 video capabilities of the browser.

As mentioned for Listing 6.2, multiple sources are required to handle browser support for different formats. You can add multiple sources in the `cfmediaplayer` tag by specifying video elements as shown in Listing 6.4.

Listing 6.4 /cfwack10/6/mp4Type1.cfm

```
<br>Type is set to html
<br>Video should play as html video

<cfmediaplayer name="media02"
               source="vid/sample.mp4"
               type="html"
               controlbar=true>
  <source src="vid/sample.webm" type="video/webm"/>
  <source src="vid/sample.ogg" type="video/ogg"/>
</cfmediaplayer>
```

ColdFusion also provides the JavaScript API `setSource` to set the source on the media player. This API is useful for dynamically setting the source. In ColdFusion 10 the JavaScript-based object name has been changed, from `ColdFusion.Mediaplayer` in ColdFusion 9 to `ColdFusion.MediaPlayer` in ColdFusion 10; note the capital "P." ColdFusion 10 also adds a new function, `getType`, that returns either `"HTML"` or `"Flash"` and is helpful in determining the player type used by `cfmediaplayer`. Other JavaScript functions, including `resize`, `setMute`, `setVolume`, `startPlay`, and `stopPlay`, continue to be supported.

NOTE

ColdFusion resolves video from the web root if the video source begins with "/". Hence, `source="vid/sample.mp4"` is resolved relative to the running page. However, `"/vid/sample.mp4"` is searched from wwwroot in ColdFusion. The two locations are not same. The two locations are the same only when the running ColdFusion page is directly under wwwroot and a vid folder inside wwwroot contains the sample.mp4 file.

Fallback Plan

As discussed earlier, many active browsers lack standardized support for HTML5 video playback, and since Adobe Flash Player is installed as a plug-in, its support may be disabled in some browsers. This lack of standardization increases the complexity of designing a web page with video content because you have to worry about page layout, the uniform look and feel for the page, and browser support for video playback. ColdFusion 10 provides a fallback option in its video player support to deal with this situation. The video fallback capabilities in ColdFusion are transparent to the user, and no additional steps are required in a ColdFusion program.

With the fallback option, ColdFusion checks the playback capability of the browser and creates a playback plan. Both HTML5 and Adobe Flash video fallback are supported.

- If HTML5 video playback is requested using `type="HTML"` and its support is not available in the browser, ColdFusion checks for Adobe Flash Player. If Adobe Flash Player is available, ColdFusion automatically falls back to Adobe Flash and plays the content using it.

- If Adobe Flash video playback is requested using `type="Flash"` and Adobe Flash is not installed or the Adobe Flash plug-in is disabled, ColdFusion falls back to HTML5 video playback.

- If the browser does not support either Adobe Flash and HTML5, an error is displayed in the video pod container.

- If the browser supports both Adobe Flash and HTML5, ColdFusion plays the video using the type specified in the `type` attribute.

Skinning Player Control

If you run the example in Listing 6.3 using `type="HTML"` and then `type="Flash"`, you will notice a similarity in the default layouts of the player control, as shown in Figures 6.1 and 6.2.

This similarity is by design, to provide a uniform look and feel and make it easier to design web pages and layout across various browsers, in which support for video playback is not consistent.

Figure 6.1

MP4 file using the HTML5 video capabilities of the browser.

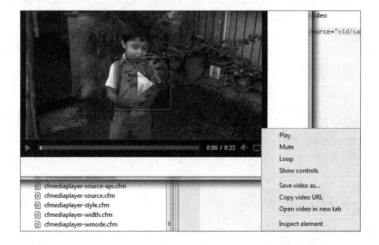

Figure 6.2

MP4 file using the
Adobe Flash plug-in.

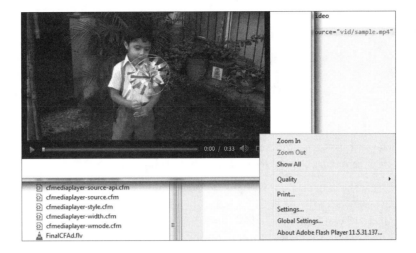

The style attribute introduced with the cfmediaplayer tag in ColdFusion 9 continues to work well with an HTML5-based player. However, for Adobe Flash Player, some elements, such as the control bar and progress bar, cannot be changed with the style attribute. ColdFusion 10 introduces a new attribute, skin, that accepts an XML file to change the Adobe Flash Player skin. A sample skin for the media player is available at http://www.rblank.com/2010/10/06/sample-skin-for-strobeflash-media-playback/.

Callback Events and Error Logging

ColdFusion 10 introduces two new callback functions, onPause and onError, to handle pause and error events, adding to the callback events introduced in ColdFusion 9, including onLoad, onStart, and onComplete.

The example in Listing 6.5 shows how onPause and onError are used with cfmediaplayer.

Listing 6.5   /cfwack10/6/events.cfm

```
<!DOCTYPE html>
<html>
    <head>
    <script type="text/javascript">
    function alertOnPause(){
        alert('Video paused!');
    }
    function logOnError(){
        ColdFusion.MediaPlayer.logError('mp', 'Flash plug-in is missing');
    }
    </script>
    </head>
    <body>
```

Listing 6.5   (CONTINUED)

```
        <cfmediaplayer name="mp"
                       source="vid/sample.flv"
                       type="flash"
                       controlbar=true
                       onpause="alertOnPause"
                       onerror="logOnError"/>
        </body>
    </html>
```

When you run this example and pause the video, ColdFusion invokes the method specified in the onPause attribute and displays a pop-up alert box.

If you run the code in a browser that does not support Adobe Flash, the error message appears in the player since the browser cannot play the FLV file (Figure 6.3). If you have Adobe Flash installed and you want to simulate this behavior, you can disable the Adobe Flash plug-in using the browser settings before running this code.

Figure 6.3

Error message from the media player displayed when the Adobe Flash plug-in is missing or disabled in the browser.

Other Enhancements

ColdFusion 10 also added other enhancements to the cfmediaplayer tag:

- Loop playback support
- Poster image support
- Video title support
- Playlist support

Loop Playback Support

Listing 6.6 provides an example of a repeat attribute that is used to support loop playback. If the repeat attribute is set to true, the media player plays again from the first to the last frame after the media player reaches the end of the video.

Listing 6.6 /cfwack10/6/repeat.cfm

```
<!DOCTYPE html>
<html>
  <body>
    <cfmediaplayer name="mp"
                   source="vid/sample.mp4"
                   controlbar=true
                   autoplay="true"
                   repeat="true"/>
  </body>
</html>
```

When the page runs, the video starts playing automatically since `autoplay` is set to `true`. When the end of the video is reached, the media player starts playing the video from the beginning since the `repeat` attribute also is set to `true`.

Poster Image Support

You can now set a poster image for the video. The poster image is the image that is shown on the video player when it is loaded. The example in Listing 6.7 creates a media player with the supplied image.

Listing 6.7 /cfwack10/6/posterImage.cfm

```
<!DOCTYPE html>
<html>
  <body>
    <cfmediaplayer name="mp"
                   source="vid/sample.mp4"
                   controlbar=true
                   posterimage="vid/pic.jpg"/>
  </body>
</html>
```

Video Title Support

ColdFusion also allows a title to be shown when the media player is loaded, as shown in Figure 6.4. Listing 6.8 shows how a title can be added using the `title` attribute with the `cfmediaplayer` tag.

Listing 6.8 /cfwack10/6/title.cfm

```
<!DOCTYPE html>
<html>
  <body>
    <cfmediaplayer name="mp"
                   source="vid/sample.mp4"
                   controlbar=true
                   posterimage="vid/pic.jpg"
                   title="Windmill song"/>
  </body>
</html>
```

The title also appears when the video is paused. If you want to show the filename instead of a custom title, do not use the `title` attribute and set the `hidetitle` attribute to `false`.

Figure 6.4

Title and poster image displayed on the ColdFusion media player.

Playlist Support

The ColdFusion media player supports playlists. The list of media that is played is embedded in a playlist file that is in the format m3u. The m3u playlist format is a standard supported by many media players, including Microsoft Windows Media Player and Apple iTunes. Listing 6.9 shows a sample m3u file.

Listing 6.9   /cfwack10/6/vid/playlist.m3u

```
# This is a simple playlist.

http://mediapm.edgesuite.net/osmf/content/test/manifest-files/progressive.f4m
http://mediapm.edgesuite.net/osmf/content/test/train_1500.mp3
http://mediapm.edgesuite.net/strobe/content/test/AFaerysTale_sylviaApostol_640_500_
➥short.flv
vid/sample.mp4
vid/pic.jpg
```

To create a playlist, simply specify an m3u file as the source for the `cfmediaplayer` tag, as shown in Listing 6.10.

Listing 6.10   /cfwack10/6/playlist.cfm

```
<!DOCTYPE html>
<html>
  <body>
    <cfmediaplayer source="vid/playlist.m3u" controlbar=true />
  </body>
</html>
```

Playlists are supported for Adobe Flash playback. If you specify `type="html"`, the `cfmediaplayer` tag ignores the `type` attribute and falls back to Adobe Flash Player. If the Adobe Flash plug-in is not available or is disabled in the browser, `cfmediaplayer` does not play the playlist.

Extending the Media Player

If you access the skinning link provided earlier, you can see a reference to Strobe Media Playback. The ColdFusion 10 media player implementation is based on Strobe Media Playback, which in turn is built on the Open Source Media Framework (OSMF).

OSMF allows developers to assemble components to create their own media playback. It provides flexibility, but at the cost of having to create your own playback implementation. You can find more information about OSMF at http://www.osmf.org/.

Strobe Media Playback, which is what ColdFusion 10 uses as the underlying engine for `cfmediaplayer`, is a predefined media player based on OSMF that supports progressive downloading, Real Time Messaging Protocol (RTMP) streaming, live streaming, HTTP dynamic streaming, and so on.

When you use the `cfmediaplayer` tag on your ColdFusion page, it is Strobe Media Playback that is added to your page to support the media playback capabilities. Therefore, if you are looking for media playback support that is not directly available or documented in ColdFusion, you can investigate Strobe Media Playback features and documentation. More information on Strobe Media Playback is available at http://www.osmf.org/strobe_mediaplayback.html.

You can extend the ColdFusion media player in several ways, as the examples in the following sections show.

Playing YouTube Video

You can use the `cfmediaplayer` tag to include the YouTube plug-in. The YouTube plug-in allows playback of YouTube media via the YouTube API. Listing 6.11 presents some sample code.

Listing 6.11   /cfwack10/6/youtube.cfm

```
<!DOCTYPE html >
<html>
  <body>
    <cfmediaplayer name="player_youtube"
                   source="http://www.youtube.com/watch?v=0-kPOJIeOgs"
                   type="flash">
      <param name="flashvars"
             value="plugin_YouTubePlugin=vid/YouTubePlugin.swf"/>
    </cfmediaplayer>
  </body>
</html>
```

To enable the YouTube plug-in, you need to specify two details: the `flashvars` parameter and the YouTube plugin.swf file. The `flashvars` parameter provides a way to pass additional data to Adobe Flash Player. In Listing 6.11, the additional instruction that we want to pass to the media player tells it to play the video using the YouTubePlugin.swf file. You can obtain the YouTubePlugin.swf file from http://osmf.org/dev/1.5-sprint-4/YouTubePlugin.swf or the resource files for this chapter.

Before using this plug-in, make sure that you read and understand the YouTube API terms of service, at http://code.google.com/apis/youtube/terms.html.

As a general rule, you can extend the media player capabilities by using the SWF file for the plug-in that you want to use and specifying it using flashvars.

NOTE

The media player extension works only for Adobe Flash Player and is not applicable for HTML5 playback. HTML5 capabilities are supported through the browser, and any extension of the HTML5 playback capabilities requires browser support.

Streaming

ColdFusion 10 media player support is based on Strobe Media Playback, and Strobe Media Playback supports RTMP streaming, live streaming, and HTTP dynamic streaming. After you have access to the underlying Strobe Media Playback handle, you can use the various streaming options. Listing 6.12 shows how to get hold of the underlying media player and call various operations on the handle.

Listing 6.12 /cfwack10/6/StrobeHandle.cfm

```
<!DOCTYPE html>
<html>
    <head>
        <script type="text/javascript">
        function playerOperation(){
            var player = ColdFusion.MediaPlayer.getPlayer("mp");
            //player.setAutoDynamicStreamSwitch(false);
            //player.switchDynamicStreamIndex(index);
            alert('Player is ' + player);
        }
        function alertOnPause(){
            alert('Video paused! ' + player);
        }
        </script>
    </head>
    <body>

        <cfmediaplayer name="mp"
                       source="vid/sample.flv"
                       type="flash"
                       controlbar=true
                       onpause="alertOnPause"/>
    </body>
</html>
```

The JavaScript function `playerOperation` calls `getPlayer` on `ColdFusion.MediaPlayer` to get a reference to the underlying Strobe Media Playback player. Through this `player` object, all Strobe APIs are available to the ColdFusion page. Commented calls to the API to change the dynamic streaming property are shown in Listing 6.12. Please refer to the API and documentation for Strobe Media Playback at http://www.osmf.org/strobe_mediaplayback.html.

NOTE

The streaming function works with an appropriate media stream hosted on an appropriate media server. For example, the sample code in the Adobe ColdFusion documentation on a dynamic stream would need an F4M file as the source. F4M is an Adobe Flash Media manifest file containing information about codecs, resolution, and the availability of multiple-bit-rate files. A sample F4M file is available at http://mediapm.edgesuite.net/osmf/content/test/manifest-files/dynamic_Streaming.f4m. The sample ColdFusion code is available at http://help.adobe.com/en_US/ColdFusion/10.0/Developing/WSe61e35da8d31851852cc9f7d1353e88b409-7fe0.html.

Digital Rights Management

Support for digital rights management (DRM) in ColdFusion 10 is similar to support for streaming. The ColdFusion media player provides the support required to play a DRM-protected stream. As with streaming, this support comes from the underlying Strobe Media Playback engine and is available for Adobe Flash–based video. When you use the `cfmediaplayer` tag, you need to specify a DRM-protected stream, as shown in Listing 6.13.

Listing 6.13 /cfwack10/6/drm.cfm

```
<!DOCTYPE html>
<html>
  <body>
    <cfmediaplayer source="http://drmtest2.adobe.com:8080/Content/identity.f4v"
                   type="flash"
                   controlbar=true />
  </body>
</html>
```

The example uses a DRM-protected video hosted on an Adobe test server. When this page is run, a login screen appears on which you can specify a username and password, which will be authenticated and authorized by the licensing server (Figure 6.5).

Figure 6.5

Login message for DRM-protected content.

For the example in Listing 16.13, you can use testuser and testpass as the username and password.

Implementation of DRM requires multiple steps: for example, you need to package the stream appropriately and have a licensing server. A detailed description of these steps is beyond the scope of this book. However, note that the `cfmediaplayer` tag can handle a DRM stream and provides the support expected from a media player for Adobe Flash–based media.

PART II

Rapid Development

CFML Enhancements

In every new version of ColdFusion you will find new tags and functions. What you don't always find are dramatic enhancements to the *syntax* of the language itself. Being more low level, these changes are made less often and only after careful consideration and testing. In this chapter, we focus on what ColdFusion 10 adds to the language's syntax. Our primary focus will be on closures (or inner functions). The remainder of the chapter then discusses smaller, but important, changes.

Working with Closures

ColdFusion 10 supports closures—but what exactly are closures and why are they a big deal for the language?

The term *closures* is frequently associated with JavaScript. If you've done any work in JavaScript, especially with jQuery, then you've probably written closures even if you didn't know you were doing so. Lasse Nielsen defines closures as "an expression (typically a function) that can have free variables together with an environment that binds those variables (that 'closes' the expression)."

Practically, this means that a closure, a function itself, can be created by another function. This top-level function closes the inner function and returns it to the rest of the document. You can use this feature to build new functions on the fly, instead of using predefined functions.

ColdFusion 10 allows you to build dynamic functions, and it also allows you to define inline functions to alter application behavior. Some examples of this capability will help clarify the use of closures in ColdFusion 10.

Our first example (http://blog.bittersweetryan.com/) is provided by ColdFusion community member Ryan Anklam. His example is based on work by Ben Alman and provides one of the simplest introductions to the concepts.

Imagine for a moment that you need a user-defined function UDF) that returns the sum of two numbers. Although you can perform the calculation easily enough with a bit of math, say that you want to write a function instead.

Here is our simple add UDF:

```
<cfscript>
public numeric function add(a,b) {
    return a+b;
}
</cfscript>
```

Using this UDF is a simple matter of calling it and passing two values:

```
<cfscript>
sum = add(3,1);
sum1 = add(9,1);
anothersum = add(10,1);
</cfscript>
```

Hopefully, we don't need to share the actual output of that code! Did you notice, though, that every time we used add() we passed some number and 1? A smart developer may see that and build a simpler UDF to allow developers to type a bit less:

```
<cfscript>
public numeric function add1(a){
    return add(1,a);
}
</cfscript>
```

The new function, add1, simply wraps a call to our earlier function, add. But the benefit is that our code can be a bit simpler:

```
<cfscript>
sum = add1(3);
sum1 = add1(9);
anothersum = add1(10);
</cfscript>
```

Everything is great—until you realize that you will soon need, probably, an add2 function or an add3 function. Obviously, this coding can get out of hand; wouldn't it be nice if we could create a generic utility that in itself could generate addX functions?

ColdFusion 10 allows developers to define a new function *within* an existing function. This function can be returned and then used as if it had been defined as a UDF by hand. Listing 7.1 demonstrates a simple version of this feature and a few uses of it.

Listing 7.1 /cfwack10/7/demo1.cfm

```
<cfscript>
public Function function makeAdder(a) {
    return function(b) {
        return a+b;
    };
}
</cfscript>
```

Listing 7.1 (CONTINUED)

```
<cfset add1 = makeAdder(1)>
<cfset add5 = makeAdder(5)>
<cfset sub1 = makeAdder(-1)>

<cfoutput>
<b>Add1 tests:</b><br/>
#add1(10)#<br/>
#add1(11)#<br/>
#add1(12)#<br/>
<p/>

<b>Add5 tests:</b><br/>
#add5(10)#<br/>
#add5(11)#<br/>
#add5(12)#<br/>
<p/>

<b>Sub11 tests:</b><br/>
#sub1(10)#<br/>
#sub1(11)#<br/>
#sub1(12)#<br/>
</cfoutput>
```

The most important part of this example is the UDF makeAdder. Note that the return type of the UDF is Function, which signifies that the function itself returns functions. This specification isn't required, but for completeness it is a good idea to be specific about what your functions return.

The purpose of makeAdder is to create a generic function that adds one static value to a value you pass it. Therefore, makeAdder accepts one argument, a, which represents the number you will always add to the passed values later.

The meat of the function is simply one return statement. We are returning a new function defined inline. This new function takes only one argument. Remember, we are building generic "Add X to a passed in value" functions, so the new function needs only one argument.

Now notice how the returned function has access to the original argument, a. This is where the closure aspect comes in. The parent function is essentially wrapping up the new function as a gift, providing access to its original argument a, and returning it to the caller.

Once we have this generic utility, the test template creates three new functions. These functions are trivial so we won't discuss what each does, but do note that the third example, sub1, shows how we can create a function that performs subtraction as well. Finally, we output some examples that make use of our three new functions.

NOTE

Are you wondering about the capital "F" used for Function as the return type of makeAdder? This is completely unnecessary. But function function may look confusing to people reading your code, so we used the capital letter to make the code easier to read and to remind folks that we are defining a function that returns functions.

In addition to defining functions inside other functions, developers can create functions as arguments. This process will be familiar to people who have used tools like jQuery. Listing 7.2 demonstrates an example of this feature.

Listing 7.2 /cfwack10/7/demo2.cfm

```
<cfscript>
function transformPerson(array input, function transformer) {
    for(var i=1; i<=arrayLen(input); i++) {
        input[i] = transformer(input[i]);
    }
    return input;
}
</cfscript>

<cfset ray = {"name":"Raymond", "age":39, "gender":"male"}>
<cfset scott = {"name":"Scott", "age":44, "gender":"male"}>
<cfset todd = {"name":"Todd", "age":38, "gender":"male"}>
<cfset data = [ray, scott, todd]>

<cfscript>

//Capitalize the name
writeDump(transformPerson(data, function(i) {
    if(structKeyExists(i, "name")) i.name = uCase(i.name);
    return i;
}));

//De-Agify!
writeDump(transformPerson(data, function(i) {
    if(structKeyExists(i, "age")) i.age-=20;
    return i;
}));

</cfscript>
```

This example begins by defining a function called transformPerson. To this function, you will pass an array of people (just simple ColdFusion structs) as well as a function, and this function will be applied to every person passed in. The function then will return the array. Basically, this function provides a quick way to apply some form of logic on every value in an array. (Later you'll see another way of accomplishing the same thing.)

After the function is defined, we have a few lines of simple static data. Then we get to the fun part. In our first use of transformPerson, note how the second argument is actually an inline function. The function assumes one argument, i, which will be a structure of data. If a key called name exists, we capitalize it and return it.

The second example is pretty similar. Instead of modifying the name value, this script looks for, and reduces, the age key. Figure 7.1 shows the output of this script.

Figure 7.1

The output from our inline function.

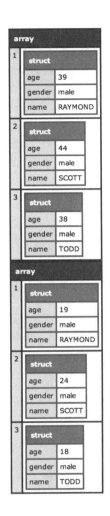

TIP

Careful observers may have noticed another ColdFusion 10 change in the previous example. If you don't see it, don't worry—we'll be discussing it later in the chapter.

In the past, the capability to create UDFs was mainly used to build utilities. (See CFLib.org for a thousand or so examples of this.) These utilities were general-purpose abstractions of some basic function. The main other use of function writing was in ColdFusion components. In that case, your methods (functions) are typically consolidated into one group of related business rules. For example, you may have a CFC with methods related to users.

Utilities and ColdFusion components both are great uses for functions. But closures allow a third use of function writing. There are times when we need to create logic that will *not* be reused throughout the application or that applies only to one set of data. By adding the capability to define inline functions as arguments, we can create ad hoc pieces of logic more quickly and thus will be more likely to create them more often, adding a higher level of functionality to our code.

In fact, this capability is so useful that existing ColdFusion functions were updated to support it. In addition, new functions were added that make use of this feature. Let's take a look at these new and updated functions.

Arrays and Inline Functions

ColdFusion 10 enhances the way that you can work with arrays by adding multiple new functions and features. Let's begin with the simplest new function, arrayEach (Listing 7.3).

Listing 7.3   /cfwack/10/arrayeach.cfm

```
<cfset data = ["Raymond","Scott","Todd","Jeanne","Jacob","Lynn","Noah"]>

<cfscript>

arrayEach(data, function(item) {
   item = left(item, 2);
   writeoutput("Short hand version is #item#<br/>");
});
</cfscript>
```

As you can probably tell by the name, arrayEach provides a simple way to iterate over an array and apply logic, any logic, to it. In the example here, we've defined a simple array of names. The arrayEach function is used to iterate over each name, and an inline function is applied to the value. The argument, item, will be set to each individual value of the array. In the example in Listing 7.3, we simply grab part of the string and output it to the screen, so for example, Raymond becomes Ra, Scott becomes Sc, and so forth.

Now let's look at arrayFind (Listing 7.4).

Listing 7.4   /cfwack/10/arrayfind.cfm

```
<cfset data = ["Raymond","Scott","Todd","Jeanne","Jacob","Lynn","Noah"]>

<cfscript>
shortName = arrayFind(data, function(item) {
   return len(item) lt 5;
});

if(shortName != 0) {
   writeOutput("I found this short name: #data[shortName]#<br/>");
}

weirdName = arrayFind(data, function(item) {
   return left(item,1) == "q" || left(item,1) == "Q";
});

if(weirdName != 0) {
   writeOutput("I found this weird name: #data[weirdName]#<br/>");
} else {
   writeOutput("Sorry, no one has an odd name.<br/>");
}

</cfscript>
```

The `arrayFind` function existed before ColdFusion 10, but it had limited use. ColdFusion 10 enhances it by allowing you to pass an inline function. This function is passed an array element value and should return true or false, depending on the business logic you have in mind.

The example in Listing 7.4 presents a set of names. We call `arrayFind` twice. In the first call, our inline function looks for names that are less than five characters long. In the second call, it looks for names that begin with the letter *q* or *Q*. Note that `arrayFind` returns the index of the value, not the value itself. Also, it returns only the first match. If no match is found, the result is 0.

You may be wondering if there is a corresponding example that will return *all* of the values that match the inline function. Indeed there is: `arrayfindall` (Listing 7.5).

Listing 7.5   /cfwack10/7/arrayfindall.cfm

```
<cfset data = ["Raymond","Scott","Todd","Jeanne","Jacob","Lynn","Noah"]>

<cfscript>
shortNames = arrayFindAll(data, function(item) {
   return len(item) lt 5;
});

if(arrayLen(shortNames)) {
   arrayEach(shortNames, function(x) {
      writeoutput("Short Name: #data[x]#<br>");
   });
}
</cfscript>
```

Listing 7.5 shows a slight variation on our previous example. The data is the same, but `arrayFindAll` is used instead of `arrayFind`. The inline function is the exactly the same, but this time, we get an array of results back instead of one particular index value. The values of the array are still indexes, so to display the values that were returned, we have to use the index with the data array.

Note the use of `arrayLen` on the `shortNames` value. The `arrayFindAll` function will return an empty array if no results were found. Also note that we used `arrayEach` again to iterate over the matches. This step isn't required, of course, but it shows one more example of how inline functions can be useful.

Another new function added to ColdFusion 10 is `arrayFilter`. Unlike the find functions demonstrated earlier, this function allows you to filter an input array to see items that match a particular rule. Listing 7.6 provides an example.

Listing 7.6   /cfwack10/7/arrayfilter.cfm

```
<cfset data = ["Raymond","Scott","Todd","Jeanne","Jacob","Lynn","Noah"]>

<cfscript>
shortNames = arrayFilter(data, function(item) {
   return len(item) lt 5;
});

writeDump(shortNames);
</cfscript>
```

Listing 7.6 (CONTINUED)

```
<p/>

<cfset data2 = [{name:"Ray", age:39}, {name:"Scott", age:42},
                {name:"Jacob", age:12}, {name:"Lynn", age:11 }]>

<cfscript>
logansRun = arrayFilter(data2, function(p) {
   return p.age < 21;
});

writeDump(logansRun);
</cfscript>
```

As with our previous several examples, we begin with a simple array of names. Also, the inline function passed to `arrayFilter` is the same as in the previous examples. The difference is in the result. Instead of the first index value, or an array of indexes, we get an entirely new array. The only values in the array are those that pass the test defined in the inline function.

The second example demonstrates that you can use any of these enhanced array functions with complex data as well. Instead of an array of simple strings, `data2` is an array of structures. Our inline function returns true when the age value is less than 21.

Figure 7.2 shows the output from both of these filters.

Figure 7.2

Sample output from the `arrayFilter` function.

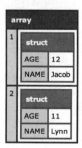

The final array feature we'll look at here is `arraySort`. In earlier versions of ColdFusion, `arraySort` allowed you to sort arrays of simple values. In ColdFusion 10, you can also sort complex values, by using an inline function that defines the way that items should be compared to each other. ColdFusion handles iteration over the array and passes you two values. You must write logic that returns a –1, 1, or 0. A –1 means that the first value is less than the second. A 0 means that the values are equal. A 1 means that the first value is greater than the second value. Consider the example in Listing 7.7.

Listing 7.7   /cfwack10/7/arraysort.cfm

```
<cfset data2 = [{name:"Ray", age:39}, {name:"Scott", age:42},
                {name:"Jacob", age:12}, {name:"Lynn", age:11 },
                {name:"Abby", age:12}]>

<cfscript>

//byAge
arraySort(data2, function(a,b) {
   if(a.age > b.age) return 1;
   if(a.age == b.age) return 0;
   if(a.age < b.age) return -1;
});

writeDump(var=data2,label="By Age");

//byName
arraySort(data2, function(a,b) {
   if(a.name > b.name) return 1;
   if(a.name == b.name) return 0;
   if(a.name < b.name) return -1;
});

writeDump(var=data2,label="By Name");

//by Age, then by Name
arraySort(data2, function(a,b) {
   if(a.age == b.age) {
      if(a.name > b.name) return 1;
      if(a.name == b.name) return 0;
      if(a.name < b.name) return -1;
   }

   if(a.age > b.age) return 1;
   if(a.age < b.age) return -1;
});

writeDump(var=data2,label="By Age, then By Name");
</cfscript>
```

Our template begins with a simple definition of an array of complex data. Each structure in the array consists of a name and an age value. Then we begin sorting. The first sort simply checks the age value. The second sort is pretty much the same, except that it checks the age instead. The third sort is the most interesting. By passing a more complex inline function to arraySort, we've added logic to handle sorting by age and then name. In fact, you could imagine *any* logic here. If you were sorting employees, you could have three levels of comparison: say, hire date, age, and name. The point is that your logic here can be as complex or as simple as you desire.

Lists and Inline Functions

ColdFusion 10 adds one new enhancement for lists: listFilter. Listing 7.8 provides a simple example.

Listing 7.8 /cfwack10/7/listfilter.cfm

```
<cfset list = "Raymond,Jacob,Lynn,Noah,Mary,Nancy,Sam,Barry">

<cfscript>

filteredList = listFilter(list, function(n) {
    return left(n,1) == "R" || left(n,1) == "M" || left(n,1) == "S";
});

</cfscript>

<cfoutput>
The filtered list (people with names beginning with R, M, or S) is #filteredList#.
</cfoutput>
```

The example begins with a simple list of names. We then use listFilter to pare the list to people with names that begin with the *R*, *M*, or *S*. This isn't a terribly exciting example, but obviously this logic can be enhanced to check other things as well. The result of this template is a list containing Raymond, Mary, and Sam.

Structs and Inline Functions

Now let's look at structure-related functions. ColdFusion 10 adds both structEach and structFilter functions. These functions are pretty similar to their array counterparts, so we'll use one simple example that demonstrates both (Listing 7.9).

Listing 7.9 /cfwack10/7/structeachfilter.cfm

```
<cfset data = {
    name:"Ray",
    age:39,
    gender:"Male",
    height:"tall",
    "weight":"over",
    likes:"Beers and Star Wars"
}>

<cfscript>
structEach(data, function(key, value) {
    writeoutput("The value of data.#key# is #value#<br/>");

});
</cfscript>

<p/>

<cfscript>
smaller = structFilter(data, function(key, value) {
    if(key == "name" || key == "age") return true;
    return false;
```

Listing 7.9 (CONTINUED)

```
    });

    writeDump(var=smaller, label="Filtered Struct");
    </cfscript>
```

The template begins with a simple structure that has a few keys. The first example uses `structEach`. The inline function is passed both a key and a value. Here, we simply output the result to the screen:

```
The value of data.NAME is Ray
The value of data.AGE is 39
The value of data.weight is over
The value of data.GENDER is Male
The value of data.HEIGHT is tall
The value of data.LIKES is Beers and Star Wars
```

This result is probably exactly what you expected; however, note the `weight` key. Why is it lowercase? When defining keys for a structure, if you do not quote them (as we did for all the keys except `weight`), ColdFusion will store them in uppercase. If the case is important, wrap the value in quotation marks as we did when defining the structure.

The next example in the template uses `structFilter`. Although both keys and values are passed to the inline function, this simple example checks only for keys called `NAME` or `AGE`. The result is a structure that contains only those two keys and values (Figure 7.3).

Figure 7.3

Using `structFilter`.

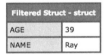

ColdFusion 10 now also provides the `isClosure()` function, which returns true if a value is a closure. Listing 7.10 demonstrates this function.

Listing 7.10 /cfwack10/7/isclosure.cfm

```
    <cfscript>
    public Function function makeAdder(a) {
        return function(b) {
            return a+b;
        };
    }
    </cfscript>

    <cfset add1 = makeAdder(1)>

    <cfoutput>
    is add1 a closure? #isClosure(add1)#<br/>
    is add1 a custom function? #isCustomFunction(add1)#<br/>
    <p/>
    is makeAdder a closure? #isClosure(makeAdder)#<br/>
    is makeAdder a custom function? #isCustomFunction(makeAdder)#<br/>
    </cfoutput>
```

You will probably recognize makeAdder from the beginning of the chapter. We've used makeAdder to create a new function, add1. We then run isClosure and isCustomFunction on both functions. If you run this script yourself, you will see that add1 is reported to be a closure, but not a custom function, whereas makeAdder is the opposite: it is reported to be a custom function, but not a closure. Although isClosure probably won't have much use in most ColdFusion applications, it is another tool at your disposal if you need it.

Miscellaneous Language Enhancements

Now let's look at some of the other language enhancements that developers have access to in ColdFusion 10.

Note that here we will not provide a list of new functions and tags; you can find that in the documentation. Rather, we will look at enhancements that affect syntax and behavior specifically.

<cfinclude> Gets More Intelligent

Let's begin with a simple but useful addition: the runOnce attribute of <cfinclude>.

Many people use <cfinclude> to quickly insert logic into a page. By putting reused code in a template, you enable other templates to use <cfinclude> to include that code multiple times. But what if you want to include a template only once per request? What if including a template more than once will cause problems? ColdFusion 10 introduces a new attribute to <cfinclude> called runOnce. This attribute ensures that no matter how many times you run <cfinclude>, it will actually include the template only once.

Imagine a simple page like the one shown in Listing 7.11.

Listing 7.11   /cfwack10/7/include_test.cfm

```
<cf_layout>

    <cfinclude template="udfs.cfm" runonce="true">

    <h1>Some Page</h1>

</cf_layout>
```

This template uses a custom tag to generate the layout for the page and includes a file called udfs.cfm, shown in Listing 7.12.

Listing 7.12   /cfwack10/7/udfs.cfm

```
<!---
This would normally be a list of UDFs we want to use.
--->
<cfoutput><p><i>Hello, I'm udfs.cfm.</i></p></cfoutput>
```

Where things get interesting is the layout.cfm custom tag (Listing 7.13).

Listing 7.13   /cfwack/10/7/layout.cfm

```
<cfif thisTag.executionMode is "start">

    <cfinclude template="udfs.cfm" runonce="true">

    <html>
        <head></head>

        <body bgcolor="pink">

<cfelse>

        </body>
    </html>

</cfif>
```

While handling basic layout tasks, the template also includes udfs.cfm. But since both files used the runOnce attribute, udfs.cfm is inserted only one time. You can verify this yourself by running include_test.cfm and confirming that the output message from udfs.cfm is shown exactly one time. Note that the script-based version of <cfinclude> also supports this feature.

Application.cfc and Abort Handling

ColdFusion 10 adds a new event to the Application.cfc file: onAbort. This event is fired when the <cfabort> tag (or keyword) is used. The method is passed the name of the currently executing file. The onAbort event will also fire when cfcontent or cflocation is used. Listing 7.14 provides a simple example.

Listing 7.14   /cfwack10/7/appabort/Application.cfc

```
component {

    this.name = "DemoAbortHandling";

    public boolean function onRequestStart(string req) {
        writelog("Yes, onRequestStart fired to get #arguments.req#");
        return true;
    }

    public boolean function onRequestEnd(string req) {
        writelog("Yes, onRequestEnd fired to get #arguments.req#");
        return true;

    }

    public boolean function onAbort(string req) {
        writelog("Yes, onAbort fired in #arguments.req#");
        return true;
    }

}
```

In the folder for this chapter, you will also find three test files. The test.cfm file contains a `<cfabort>` function, test_noabort.cfm does not contain this function, and test_cflocation.cfm simply applies a `<cflocation>` function to test_noabort.cfm.

When you run test.cfm, you will see `onRequestStart` fire and the new `onAbort`. When you run test_noabort.cfm, `onRequestStart` and `onRequestEnd` fire. When you run test_cflocation.cfm, `onRequestStart` and `onAbort` fire for that template. When the user is redirected to test_noabort.cfm, `onRequestStart` fires again, and `onRequestEnd` fires at last.

Handling Form Fields with the Same Name

As long as we're talking about the Application.cfc file, let's discuss another change that applies to it. Normally when working with forms, you assign a unique name to each field. Sometimes, though, you may want multiple form fields to share the same name: for example, when you have checkbox buttons. Listing 7.15 provides a simple example.

Listing 7.15 /cfwack10/7/formarray/test.cfm

```
<form method="post">

<input type="checkbox" name="favorite_movie" value="Star Wars"> Star Wars<br/>
<input type="checkbox" name="favorite_movie" value="Jaws"> Jaws<br/>
<input type="checkbox" name="favorite_movie" value="The Godfather, Part 2">
➡The Godfather, Part 2<br/>
<input type="checkbox" name="favorite_movie" value="Vanilla Sky"> Vanilla Sky<br/>
<input type="submit">

</form>

<cfif structKeyExists(form, "favorite_movie") and len(form.favorite_movie)>
    <cfoutput>
        You selected these favorite movies: #form.favorite_movie#<br/>
        You liked #listLen(form.favorite_movie)# movies.</br>
    </cfoutput>
</cfif>
```

The template consists of a simple form that asks you what your favorite movie is. Checkboxes are used, and each checkbox field has the same name. When the user selects several values, Cold-Fusion will store the selected values in a list. So if the user picks *Star Wars* and *Jaws*, the output would look like this:

```
You selected these favorite movies: Star Wars,Jaws
You liked 2 movies.
```

A simple `listLen` function is used to determine how many movies you selected. But what happens when you add the *Godfather* sequel?

```
You selected these favorite movies: Star Wars,Jaws,The Godfather, Part 2
You liked 4 movies.
```

Four movies? That's not right. The comma in the name of the *Godfather* movie is confusing the listLen function. You could write code specifically to handle that movie, but if you have text fields with the same name, you have no good way to handle this problem. Luckily, ColdFusion 10 offers a simple solution. By adding the setting sameformfieldsasarray to your Application.cfc file, you can change the way that ColdFusion handles values like this. Listing 7.16 provides an example.

Listing 7.16   /cfwack10/7/formarray2/Application.cfc

```
<cfcomponent>
    <cfset this.name = "FormArrayDemo2">
    <cfset this.sameformfieldsasarray = true>
</cfcomponent>
```

Listing 7.17 provides a modified version of the previous form. The only change is that the value is treated as an array, not a list.

Listing 7.17   /cfwack10/7/formarray2/test1.cfm

```
<form method="post">

<input type="checkbox" name="favorite_movie" value="Star Wars"> Star Wars<br/>
<input type="checkbox" name="favorite_movie" value="Jaws"> Jaws<br/>
<input type="checkbox" name="favorite_movie" value="The Godfather, Part 2">
➥The Godfather, Part 2<br/>
<input type="checkbox" name="favorite_movie" value="Vanilla Sky"> Vanilla Sky<br/>
<input type="submit">

</form>

<cfif structKeyExists(form, "favorite_movie") and arrayLen(form.favorite_movie)>
    <cfoutput>
        You selected these favorite movies: #arrayToList(form.favorite_movie)#<br/>
        You liked #arrayLen(form.favorite_movie)# movies.</br.
    </cfoutput>
</cfif>
```

Now if you select a few movies and include *The Godfather, Part 2*, the script will correctly count it as one selection, not two.

ColdFusion Component Updates

ColdFusion components, or CFCs, have probably been the most important enhancement of the ColdFusion language in its entire history. Since their introduction in ColdFusion MX, their basic capabilities have been enhanced with each new update. ColdFusion 10 is no exception: it includes multiple updates to CFCs.

Implicit Constructors

ColdFusion added support for constructors in ColdFusion 9 (although people used them by convention before that). In ColdFusion 10, you can now pretend that your component has a constructor—an implicit constructor—even when it doesn't. This feature allows you to quickly set values without having to actually write a constructor. Consider the CFC in Listing 7.18.

Listing 7.18 /cfwack10/7/cfc1/person.cfc

```
component accessors="true" {

    property name="firstname";
    property name="lastname";
    property name="age";

    public string function toString() {
        return "My name is #variables.firstname# #variables.lastname# and I am
        ➥ #variables.age# years old.";
    }

}
```

This CFC has three properties and a simple toString method to display the values. Note, though, that no init method is defined.

Now let's look at how we can use the implicit constructor (Listing 7.19).

Listing 7.19 /cfwack10/7/cfcs1/test1.cfm

```
<cfset r = new person(firstname="Ray",lastname="Camden",age=39)>
<cfset s = new person({firstname="Scott", lastname="Stroz", age=54})>

<cfoutput>
#r.toString()#<br/>
#s.toString()#<br/>
</cfoutput>
```

Our template creates two instances of the person CFC. In the first instance, we pass three arguments. In the second instance, we pass one argument, but it's a structure with three keys. In both cases, the names of the values match the property tags in the CFC. Because we turned on accessors at the top level, ColdFusion is able to set these values immediately when we created the CFC instance. Again, we didn't need to actually write the init method; we simply had to define properties and ensure that we had accessors turned on. The result is shown here:

```
My name is Ray Camden and I am 39 years old.
My name is Scott Stroz and I am 54 years old.
```

There is no real difference between the list and struct methods. Use whichever feels more natural to you. In case you're curious, if you *had* defined an init method, you would not get the same automatic behavior and would need to update the properties manually.

Method Chaining

Another interesting update is the capability to chain method calls together. This chaining allows you to call one method on a CFC and then call another method immediately after it, in the same line of code. This chaining works for properties with accessors turned on and for methods that set values in a CFC. Using the person CFC defined in the previous example, Listing 7.20 provides an example of method chaining.

Listing 7.20   /cfwack1/7/cfc1/test2.cfm

```
<cfset p = new person()>
<cfset p.setFirstName("Raymond").setLastName("Camden").setAge(39)>

<cfoutput>#p.toString()#</cfoutput>
```

This example actually involves more typing then the earlier example, but it provides an alternative syntax that you may prefer. Note that this feature was available before ColdFusion 10 if your methods returned this as a result. The improvement here is the integration with property values and accessors. (You can mix and match these approaches as well. For additional examples, check out complexperson.cfc and test3.cfm in the same folder as the other examples.)

Implicit Notation

The final new CFC feature we will look at here is implicit notation. Implicit notation is a subtle change and requires an Application.cfc change before it can be used, so let's start by recalling the use of the This and Variables scopes in CFCs. All CFCs have a This scope, which represents the CFC as a whole; it includes things like the methods and any This scoped variable. CFCs also have a corresponding Variables scope.

The This scope can be accessed by code outside a CFC. Imagine that a CFC has this line in its constructor:

```
<cfset this.name = "Ray">
```

If you were to create an instance of this CFC—let's call it thePerson—you could actually output thePerson.name. Conversely, if you specify thePerson.name = "Jacob", any code inside the CFC that references this.name would see the new value.

In general, developers tend to avoid doing this sort of coding. It breaks the idea of encapsulation, in which the CFC with its data inside is considered a black box. Most people only run CFC methods and let the CFC decide if and when values should be stored. There is no rule saying that you must do this, but again, most developers tend to follow this pattern.

ColdFusion 10 allows you to modify this behavior a bit. By adding a new setting in your Application.cfc file, you can allow implicit notation but have it address the Variables scope instead of the This scope. First, let's create an Application.cfc file that shows this new setting (Listing 7.21).

Listing 7.21   /cfwack10/7/cfc2/Application.cfc

```
component {
    this.name = "cfcimpnotation";
    this.invokeImplicitAccessor = true;
}
```

The new setting, invokeImplicitAccessor, defaults to false if nothing is specified. The cfc2 folder contains a copy of the person component from the previous example. We won't repeat the code listing here as it hasn't changed. But consider the modified example in Listing 7.22.

Listing 7.22 /cfwack10/7/cfc2/test1.cfm

```
<cfset p = new person()>

<cfset p.firstName = "Ray">
<cfset p.lastName = "Camden">
<cfset p.age = 99>

<cfoutput>
    #p.toString()#<br/>
    My age again: #p.age#
</cfoutput>
```

By enabling the `invokeImplicitAccessor` setting in the application, we can now directly access properties in the component and have them stored in the `Variables` scope, not the `This` scope.

Now you may be wondering which option you should use. The answer is simple: whichever one you want. The best syntax is the one that makes you most effective as a developer. Play around a bit and see which form makes the most sense for you and your team.

Improvements to `queryNew` and `queryAddRow`

For our final investigation of new language enhancements, we'll look at improvements to `queryNew` and `queryAddRow`. These enhancements are probably not something you will use in day-to-day coding, but they are extremely useful when you do find yourself needing to work with virtual, or self-made, queries.

When would you do that? Typically you use `queryNew` and `queryAddRow` when you need to create fake data. Fake data can be useful in a number of scenarios. For example, imagine that you're building an application that lists users, but the database administrator who has the data is out, and you can't get access to your SQL server. You can instead create a CFC with a `listUsers` method that uses fake queries to return your data. You can then spend time working on the look and feel of the report instead of being stuck because you can't get the actual data.

You can also use fake data to create test cases. Imagine that you've asked someone to help you with a difficult formatting issue. If this person doesn't work at your organization and your template is database driven, the person can't run your code. However, if you replace a real query with `queryNew` and `queryAddRow`, the person can run the template and help you with your problem.

Although these functions can be useful, they are, unfortunately, a bit verbose. Imagine a simple three-column user query with four rows of data. To create the fake query shown here, you need almost 20 lines of code.

```
<cfset users = queryNew("id,username,password", "varchar,varchar,varchar")>
<cfset queryAddRow(users, 4)>

<cfset querySetCell(users, "id", 1, 1)>
<cfset querySetCell(users, "username", "bob", 1)>
<cfset querySetCell(users, "password", "unicoron", 1)>
<cfset querySetCell(users, "id", 2, 2)>
<cfset querySetCell(users, "username", "scott", 2)>
<cfset querySetCell(users, "password", "ilikesoccer", 2)>
```

```
<cfset querySetCell(users, "id", 3, 3)>
<cfset querySetCell(users, "username", "todd", 3)>
<cfset querySetCell(users, "password", "icheatoncod", 3)>
<cfset querySetCell(users, "id", 4, 4)>
<cfset querySetCell(users, "username", "ray", 4)>
<cfset querySetCell(users, "password", "icodesmelly", 4)>
```

That's a heck of a lot of writing! ColdFusion 10, though, makes the process much easier. Both queryNew and queryAddRow have been updated to allow you to specify data immediately and completely skip the querySetCell calls. Listing 7.23 demonstrates this new support.

Listing 7.23   /cfwack10/7/querynew.cfm

```
<cfset users = queryNew("id,username,password","varchar,varchar,varchar",
    [{id:1, username:"bob", password:"unicoron"},
     {id:2, username:"scott", password:"ilikesoccer"},
     {id:3, username:"todd", password:"icheatoncod"},
     {id:4, username:"ray", password:"icodesmelly"}])>
```

This templates accomplishes the *exact* same result as the previous code but takes about one-fourth the space. The queryNew function now takes a third argument: an array of structures. Each array item represents one row, and each struct maps keys to the columns of a query.

Similarly, queryAddRow can take a structure. Given that you have a query object called users already created, you can append a row, like so:

```
<cfset queryAddRow(users, {id:5, username:"vader", password:"whiny"})>
```

CHAPTER **8**

CFScript Enhancements

ColdFusion 10 offers several enhancements related to script-based CFML development, including the following items that are detailed in this chapter:

- Support for colon separators in structures (key:value pairs)

- Enhanced script looping (for-in) over queries and Java arrays

- Two new tag equivalents as script statements (setting and cookie)

- One new tag equivalents as a function (invoke)

- Three new tag equivalents as CFCs (collection, index, and search)

Of course, there are many things discussed elsewhere in this book, which, while not specific to CFScript, would be of interest to script-based developers. Among these are method chaining for ColdFusion components (CFCs), as well as implicit constructors and notation for CFCs; enhancements to the queryNew and queryAddRow functions; new functions such as structeach, arrayeach, and arrayslice (related to closures, but useful separately); the new imageCreateCaptcha function; and much more.

NOTE

This chapter frequently refers to pages in the ColdFusion documentation and other online resources. For your convenience, these links are provided on the book's web page.

Evolving Script-Based Development in CFML

Though ColdFusion has always been a tag-based language, it has also supported script-based CFML (via CFScript) since ColdFusion 4. And since then, features have been added in each release to enhance this scripting functionality.

Recent releases have focused especially on the addition of features that make CFML script-based coding look or work more similarly to other scripting languages, with new operators (such as ++), more flexibility in conditionals (> compared to GT, for instance), and the new keyword (for creating CFC instances).

Other enhancements have been about creating more script equivalents to traditional tags. Some are implemented as statements (to be used only within scripting), and others have been implemented as functions or CFCs (which, although they would be necessary to perform the tag equivalent in script, can also be used outside of scripting).

NOTE

If you wonder why Adobe has implemented such tag equivalents in these different ways (some as statements, some as functions, and some as CFCs), this approach really is not as illogical and random as it may seem on the surface. We'll address this point at the end of this chapter, after introducing the new features that demonstrate the three approaches, in the section, "About the Three Approaches to Tag Equivalents."

ColdFusion 10 continues this evolution, offering the new and enhanced features discussed here. The chapter concludes by offering resources for more information about these script-related enhancements as well as script-based development in general.

Support for Colon Separators in Structures (Key:Value Pairs)

In ColdFusion 10, you can now define the key:value pairs within a structure using colon (:) separators when defining them with implicit structure notation (more about this in a moment). Listing 8.1 provides a simple example, creating a structure named student, with three keys, one being an array.

Listing 8.1 01-colon-notation.cfm

```
<cfscript>
student = {firstName:"Jane", lastName:"Doe", grades:[77, 84, 91]};
writeDump(student);
</cfscript>
```

This style of coding is part of the ongoing evolution of CFScript coding, which started with implicit structure and array definition in ColdFusion 8 (which again, technically, can also be used outside scripts).

The curly braces ({}) surround the structure keys, and the square braces ([]) following the grades key name indicate that the grade numbers form an array of grades. And now in ColdFusion 10 you can use colon where you previously would have used the equal sign (=), for assignment of values to keys, in such an implicit structure creation. (You can, of course, continue to use equal signs. Either key:value separator is acceptable.)

All these elements are typical of similar notation in other scripting languages such as JavaScript (CSS also uses the colon operator for property:value assignment). This approach is a great example of how Adobe ColdFusion engineers listened to CFML developers, who were challenged when moving back and forth between CFML and such other languages.

NOTE

You cannot use this colon notation within simple variable assignments (such as `<cfset name:"Jane">`, or even a single-line script statement, such as `name:"Jane";`.) This notation is supported only when you create a structure with implicit notation (the curly braces). That said, using colon notation within implicit notation is not technically limited to CFScript. You could just as well create a structure in this way in a `<cfset>` tag, like this : `<cfset student = {firstName:"Jane", lastName:"Doe", grades:[77, 84, 91]}>`.

Enhanced Script Looping (`for-in` over Queries and Java Arrays)

Another ColdFusion 10 enhancement for CFScript is the new capability to use the `for-in` looping construct to loop over queries and Java arrays. (ColdFusion has long been able to use the `for-in` statement to loop over structures, and ColdFusion 9.0.1 added the capability to loop over CFML arrays.)

Using `for-in` Looping over Queries

Let's assume we had a query that we had created with CFQUERY as follows:

```
<cfquery name="arts" datasource="cfartgallery">
  select artName, price from art
  </cfquery>
```

Of course, any developer reading this book should know how to loop over that query using CFOUTPUT, and many will also be familiar with the use of CFLOOP. But those familiar with (and preferring) CFScript have chaffed because they could not use the script-based looping construct, for-in, to loop over such a query result. Now in ColdFusion 10, we can:

```
<cfscript>
for(row in arts) {
  writeoutput(row.artName & ' ' & row.price & "<br>");
}
</cfscript>
```

Within the `for()` statement, `row` declares a variable, which will hold a reference to each row as the statements within the braces (`{}`) loop over each record in the arts query.

NOTE

> If this `for-in` statement was being implemented within a function, you could (and should) use the `var` keyword, as in `for (var row in arts)`, if the variable being named has not yet been declared as a function-local scoped variable.

We refer to the column names with a familiar-looking `prefix.columnname` format as might be used in tag-based query loops, though note that we are referring not to the query name but rather to the variable named first in the `for` statement. (But yes, you can still use structure notation to refer to the columns if you prefer, as in `row[columnname]`.)

You can also access the built-in `currentrow` variable, provided in any ColdFusion query loop, which is an incrementing number from 1 through the number of records in the result set. But note that in this case you must refer to the query name and not the row variable as the prefix, as in `arts.currentrow`.

Each of these variations is demonstrated in `02a-for-in-query-loop.cfm`, included in the book's listings for this chapter.

What About a Script-Based Query?

Again, developers who favor CFScript may be cringing at the thought of having to implement the query in a tag and then the loop in script, wondering, "When will we ever be able to perform a query in script?" The good news is that this capability has in fact been available since ColdFusion 9. It's a feature that some might easily have missed, one of many tags that have been implemented as CFCs, as mentioned earlier. Here's a quick demonstration of a script-based query:

```
<cfscript>
arts = new query(datasource="cfartgallery",sql="SELECT artName,
➡price FROM Art" ).execute().getResult();
</cfscript>
```

It's beyond the scope of this chapter to elaborate on script-based queries and `query.cfc`, but this idea of using CFC-based tag equivalents is nevertheless discussed later in this chapter, when the new Solr-based CFCs are discussed. At that point, we'll also discuss the general concept of (and some common challenges with) using CFC-based tag equivalents.

Using `for-in` for Java Arrays

For information about using the `for-in` construct to loop over Java arrays, another new feature in ColdFusion 10, see its discussion in Chapter 10, "Enhanced Java Integration."

Two New Tag Equivalents as Script Statements (`setting` **and** `cookie`)

The remaining three sections of this chapter discuss the general topic of enhancements in ColdFusion 10 that are related to the evolution of CFScript, through which more and more CFML tags are (since ColdFusion 4) being implemented for use within CFScript.

In this first section, we look at the tags implemented as *statements* within script. (Subsequent sections discuss tags implemented as *functions* and as *CFCs*.)

Most tag equivalents in CFScript were originally created as statements, such as `if`, `else`, `for`, and other statements in ColdFusion 4, and more recent ones include `include` for `CFINCLUDE` and `param` for `CFPARAM`, added in ColdFusion 9.

ColdFusion 10 adds the following tag-equivalent CFScript statements:

- `setting` statement (for `CFSETTING`)

- `cookie` statement (for `CFCOOKIE`)

We will discuss these statements in the order that most people are likely use them.

Note that CFML is not case sensitive, so you can enter these statements using any case, although the ColdFusion documentation and many people who write about CFML present CFML tags as all uppercase and CFScript statements as all lowercase or camel-case.

Using the `setting` Statement (for `CFSETTING`)

In ColdFusion 10, you can now use the `setting` statement within CFScript in place of the corresponding `CFSETTING` tag.

The `CFSETTING` tag can be used to set various template-specific attributes, such as the request timeout value in seconds (`RequestTimeout`), whether to display ColdFusion page debugging output (`ShowDebugOutput`), and whether to display page-generated content (or whitespace) other than that generated within a `CFOUTPUT` tag (`EnableCFOutputOnly`). (See the *ColdFusion 10 CFML Reference* for more information about `CFSETTING` and the available settings and their defaults, which remain the same between tag and script syntax.)

Listing 8.2 shows how to set two of these attributes in CFScript.

Listing 8.2   `03a-setting-in-script.cfm`

```
<cfscript>
  setting requesttimeout=20 enablecfoutputonly=true;
</cfscript>
```

This script may be especially well received by those who might have wanted to implement Application.cfc as a purely script-based component (another scripting enhancement introduced in Cold-Fusion 9). Such people have been unable to do that if they needed to use this `CFSETTING` tag, which is commonly used in that file to apply settings to all pages in an application.

But as shown in the example, this scripting approach can be useful in any CFScript template. (And though this is not a point specifically related to scripting, note that you can control Boolean settings in CFML using either a quoted "yes" or "no" value or an unquoted true or false value. Similarly, the time value for requesttimeout can be quoted or not, as is true for all numbers in CFML.)

TIP

> In ColdFusion 10 you can now set the RequestTimeout value to 0, which tells ColdFusion to disable any request timeout for this page (which may have been set in the ColdFusion Administrator or in an Application.cfc/cfm or another template previously executed within the current page request). Note that this capability is not limited to the script-based setting tag.

Using the cookie Statement (for CFCOOKIE)

In ColdFusion 10, you can now use the cookie statement within CFScript in place of the corresponding CFCOOKIE tag to set a cookie.

Of course, it's long been possible to set a cookie in CFML by just creating a variable in the cookie scope (<cfset cookie.firstname="Charlie">). That specification would cause ColdFusion to not only create that variable in memory on the server, but it would also cause ColdFusion to send the cookie to the browser (setting it in the page response).

But that simple approach would allow you to control only the name of the cookie and its value. If you wanted to control attributes such as how long the cookie should last in the browser (the expires property), whether it works for all subdomains for a domain or only the current one (the domains property), and so on, you had to use CFCOOKIE. And of course, you could not use CFCOOKIE in script. Thus, ColdFusion 10 introduces the new cookie statement.

The new cookie statement's arguments are the same as the tag's attributes (including types and defaults). So, for instance, to set a cookie named firstname with a value of "Charlie" and that expires in 10 days, you could use the script shown in Listing 8.3.

Listing 8.3   03b-cookie-in-script.cfm

```
<cfscript>
cookie.firstname = {value="Charlie",expires="10"};
writedump(cookie.firstname);
</cfscript>
```

Note that we are naming the cookie and using a structure to set the other properties (including value) shown here using the implicit structure notation discussed earlier in the chapter. And yes, technically we could also instead use the new colon notation, like this:

```
cookie.firstname = {value:"Charlie",expires:"10"};
```

There are many properties we could set for a cookie, and indeed they are exactly the same ones that can be set with CFCOOKIE: value, expires, domain, path, secure, and httponly. ColdFusion 10 also provides two new properties (attributes for CFCOOKIE): preservecase and encodevalue.

You can find more information about each of these, including their purpose, the kinds of values they take, and their defaults, on the *ColdFusion 10 CFML Reference* page for `CFCOOKIE`.

NOTE

You may notice we are using `writeDump` here rather than `writeOutput`. We are doing so to demonstrate a point: Although we can now set various properties for a cookie, they are not something we can observe as being "set" for the cookie in the cookie scope itself. They are used only to create the cookie (in the response headers for the page) to be sent to the browser. A dump of the cookie has only its name.

One New Tag Equivalent as a Function (`invoke`)

The second way in which Adobe has enabled developers to call tag equivalents in CFScript (since scripting was introduced in Coldfusion 4) is by implementing them as functions, with such examples as `createObject` for `CFOBJECT` and `writeOutput` for `CFOUTPUT` from ColdFusion 4, to `component` for `CFCOMPONENT` and `writeDump` for `CFDUMP`, added in ColdFusion 9. And there is one new function implemented in ColdFusion 10.

Using the `invoke` Function (for `CFINVOKE`)

In ColdFusion 10, you can now invoke CFC and web service methods using the invoke function in place of the corresponding `CFINVOKE` tag.

Here's an example of how to invoke a method in a CFC. Let's begin with a simple CFC with a `helloWorld` method (Listing 8.4).

Listing 8.4   `04a-demo-cfc.cfc`

```
component {
    function helloWorld() {
        return "Hello World";
    }
}
```

We can then call this method using the `invoke` function (Listing 8.5).

Listing 8.5   `04b-invoke-CFC-in-script.cfm`

```
<cfscript>
  retval=invoke("04b-demo-cfc","helloWorld");
  writeOutput(retval);
</cfscript>
```

This call returns "`Hello World`" for display. (Of course, you've also long been able to call methods on components or web services within CFScript using the `createObject` function, which has some advantages. We'll discuss how to choose between these two approaches in a moment, in the section, "Reusing a Saved CFC Instance".)

Passing Arguments

That was simple enough, since there were no arguments to be passed to the method. But what if we need to do that? We can pass in arguments after the first two arguments, but there's a catch: You must provide this third argument (the arguments to the method call) as a structure. An example will make this clear.

Let's consider a new method for our CFC (available in 04a-demo-cfc.cfc):

```
function helloFriend(string name) {
    return "Hello " & arguments.name;
}
```

This example takes a single argument, a name, as a string. To pass the `name` argument to the `helloFriend` method, we need to package it as a structure, which we can do with implicit notation:

```
<cfscript>
    retval=invoke("04a-demo-cfc","helloFriend",{name="Charlie"});
    writeOutput(retval);
</cfscript>
```

(For this example and the two code listings in the next section, see the file 04c-invoke-CFC-in-script-with-args.cfm.)

What happens if you miss or forget this point about needing to pass the third argument as a structure?

```
<cfscript>
    retval=invoke("04a-demo-cfc","helloFriend","Charlie");
    writeOutput(retval &'<br>');
</cfscript>
```

Things will not work as expected. Actually, it's not the `invoke` function that will fail. Indeed, it will seem to work, but really it will have returned nothing (literally, null). So it's on the next line, when it tries to output that result, that ColdFusion will complain: "`Variable RETVAL is undefined.`"

Let's now look at a more complex example.

Passing Complex Arguments

Consider two more methods in the CFC, each expecting an incoming array and structure argument, respectively (as they do in the code in the book's listings file for 04a-demo-cfc.cfc). In this case, you can call them each with the variations of the code shown here. First, here is a call passing an array:

```
<cfscript>
    retval=invoke("04a-demo-cfc","getAvgGrades",{grades=[1,2,3]});
    writeOutput('Avg Grade: ' & retval);
</cfscript>
```

And here is code passing a structure:

```
<cfscript>
  retval=invoke("04a-demo-cfc","getNameCount",{names={name1="bill",name2="bob",
  ➥name3="al"}});
  writeOutput('Count of Names: ' & retval);
</cfscript>
```

There's really nothing more to say about this. These examples are offered simply to demonstrate the capability.

Reusing a Saved CFC Instance

Astute readers might object to the new `invoke` function on two grounds: First, as already mentioned, we can already invoke methods on CFCs and web services in CFScript using `createObject`:

```
helloInstance=createobject("component","04a-demo-cfc");
retval=helloInstance.helloWorld();
```

That approach offers the advantage that we end up with an instance of the CFC (or web service) that we can then use over and over in the request, to call other methods.

Using `invoke` as we did earlier, especially in those last couple examples, we're instead always creating a new instance (by naming the CFC in the first argument as a string) and invoking its methods in one step. When we use `invoke` in this way again, we are really asking ColdFusion to create yet another instance of the CFC and then invoking the named method.

This issue is not new, nor is it unique to scripting. The same issue exists in the choice between the `CFOBJECT` and `CFINVOKE` tags.

With `CFOBJECT` or `createObject`, you save an instance of the indicated CFC in a variable, and then you can reuse that instance over and over in the request to call methods. (You may even be able save the instance to a shared scope, such as `session`, `application`, or `server`, to reuse it over many requests, although that approach has potential risks if you fail to apply the `var` scope to all your variables in the CFC. However, elaboration on this topic is beyond the scope of this discussion.)

You can find a middle ground by using both approaches at once, though. You can pass the variable that names such a saved instance to `CFINVOKE` or the `invoke` function, in place of naming a string that names the CFC. Here's an example using both `createobject` and `invoke`:

```
helloInstance=createobject("component","04a-demo-cfc");
retval=invoke(helloInstance,"helloWorld");
writeOutput(retval);
```

Of course, some would point out that at that point, after you have the instance saved (in `helloInstance`, shown earlier), you can just as well skip the `invoke` method and instead use the traditional format for invoking methods on an object, mentioned earlier:

```
helloInstance=createobject("component","04a-demo-cfc");
retval=helloInstance.helloWorld();
writeOutput(retval);
```

And of course, the last two lines could even be combined:

```
writeOutput(helloInstance.helloWorld());
```

So there are many ways to code CFC method calls. The `invoke` function was added so that those who are already using CFINVOKE (for whatever reason) can easily change it to work nearly the same way in script.

Use whichever style you prefer. If you're invoking many methods in a given CFC in a request, it will generally make sense to save the instance and reuse it by pointing to it (whether with `invoke` or the more traditional *object.method*() notation).

Invoking a Web Service Method

There's one more reason this chapter has demonstrated the aforementioned ability to save an instance of a called object for later reuse: This is, in fact, the only way to use the new `invoke` method when calling a web service.

Currently, you cannot name a web service URL as the first argument of the `invoke` function, the way that you can provide a string naming a CFC. Instead, you must first create an instance of the web service (such as with `createObject`) and then invoke any method you are using after that.

Listing 8.6 presents an example, using a publicly accessible web service (available as of this writing). It's a free temperature service available at http://wsf.cdyne.com/WeatherWS/Weather.asmx?WSDL, and it uses the `GetCityWeatherByZIP` method, which takes an argument of a zip code (named `zip`, which again we will pass as a structure).

That method's result will then have an available property, which we can access as `GetTemperature` (accessed here during the call to `writeOutput`).

Listing 8.6 04d-invoke-websvc-in-script.cfm

```
<cfscript>
tempSvc=createobject("webservice","http://wsf.cdyne.com/WeatherWS/Weather.
asmx?WSDL");
retval=invoke(tempSvc,"GetCityWeatherByZIP",{zip="30005"});
writeOutput('Temp=' & retval.GetTemperature());
</cfscript>
```

Or again, we could eschew the `invoke` function and just call the method the more traditional way:

```
tempSvc=createobject("webservice","http://wsf.cdyne.com/WeatherWS/Weather.
asmx?WSDL");
retval=tempSvc.GetCityWeatherByZIP(zip="30005");
writeOutput('Temp=' & retval.GetTemperature());
```

Note, though, that in this latter case, the argument provided to the web service method is *not* specified as a structure (as it is with the `invoke` method). That's a requirement of the `invoke` method alone.

Three New Tag Equivalents as CFCs (`collection`, `index,` **and** `search`)

The third and final way in which Adobe has (since ColdFusion 9) enabled developers to call tag equivalents in CFScript is by implementing them as CFCs, and there are three new ones implemented in ColdFusion 10. They're all related to processing Solr text indexes, as equivalents for `CFCOLLECTION`, `CFINDEX`, and `CFSEARCH`.

These can be used to add or maintain Solr collections, add or maintain data within a collection, and search a collection, respectively. This chapter discusses each of them, in that order.

(Again, if you wonder why there are three different approaches for tag equivalents—some as statements, some as functions, and some as CFCs—we discuss the reason in a later section, "About the Three Approaches to Tag Equivalents.")

Recall that we've already seen an example of one of these CFCs, in our earlier demonstration of the new CFScript capability to perform a `for-in` loop over a query. Here again is the relevant part of that example, implementing the query itself in script:

```
<cfscript>
arts = new query(datasource="cfartgallery",sql="SELECT artName,
➡price FROM Art" ).execute().getResult();
</cfscript>
```

This type of CFC-based implementation of CFML tags has been provided since ColdFusion 9. Tag equivalents added in ColdFusion 9.0 were `ftp`, `http`, `mail`, `pdf`, `query`, and `storedproc`, and those added in ColdFusion 9.0.1 were `dbinfo`, `feed`, `imap`, `ldap`, and `pop`.

We will not elaborate on the general use of CFC-based implementation of CFML tags here. For more information about the use and features of such CFCs (for both the new and old CFCs), see the section "About These Adobe-Provided CFCs" later in this chapter.

Now let's look at the new CFCs.

Using the `collection` CFC (for `CFCOLLECTION`)

In ColdFusion 10, you can now manage Solr collections using the `collection` CFC and its available functions in place of the corresponding `CFCOLLECTION` tag.

This chapter isn't the place to discuss the use of Solr in general or the `CFCOLLECTION` tag in particular, but a few examples will show how to connect the dots between any `CFCOLLECTION` tag you may have and a corresponding `collection` CFC and its methods. The tag offers several values for `ACTION`, and there is a corresponding method in the CFC for each action value.

A Simple Example: Listing Collections

Let's start with a simple example: If you want to list the collections you have defined in your ColdFusion server, you can (using tags first) use the LIST action for CFCOLLECTION:

```
<cfcollection action="list" name="myCollections">
<cfdump var="#myCollections#">
```

This action returns a query, which we display using the dump.

To implement the corresponding action in CFScript using the new CFC, you need to create an instance of the collection CFC and then call its list method. (To find out more about the available methods, consider the resources discussed in the later section "About These Adobe-Provided CFCs.")

You can create an instance of a CFC either using createObject or the new keyword, which was introduced in ColdFusion 9. Here's an example using the latter approach, which is the style of CFC instantiation that we will use throughout the remainder of this chapter:

```
<cfscript>
myCollections=new collection().list();
writeDump(myCollections.getresult().name)
</cfscript>
```

(This code and the rest of the code in this section about the collection CFC is provided in the book's listings for this chapter in 05a-collection-in-script.cfm.)

Note that we are combining in the first statement both the instantiation of the collection CFC (new collection()) to create an instance of the collection CFC, and then chaining a call to its list method. The list method itself requires no arguments, nor does it require that you provide any arguments for the initialization of the CFC (which we need to perform when working with a particular collection, as we'll see in a moment).

One important difference to note when using this CFC-based approach to get the list is that the result of calling this method is not itself a query we can dump as we saw with the result of the list action in the tag. Instead, for some reason, the query we want to dump is buried inside the result in such a way that we need to call the getresult() method on the object that's returned and within that access the name property. The resulting query then is the same as for CFCOLLECTION ACTION="list".

NOTE

If you don't see any result listed using the list method call shown here, you may have no collections defined. But if you're running ColdFusion on Microsoft Windows, the problem may be that you don't have the needed Microsoft Windows service running. In ColdFusion 10, this service is called ColdFusion10JettyService.

When you try to run these CFCs, if you get errors indicating that ColdFusion can't find the CFC, make sure that you have not deleted the mapping, defined on the ColdFusion Administrator Custom Tag Paths page, pointing to [ColdFusion10]\cfusion\CustomTags.

Creating and Manipulating a Collection

There are also several methods for working with a given Solr collection (`create`, `optimize`, etc.). For those, we need to pass that collection as an argument to the method, as well as perhaps other arguments. Let's look at a few examples, starting first by creating a collection.

To do that, we need to provide a name for the collection (which will be the name by which the ColdFusion Administrator and any code you later run will refer to it) and a place to put the collection, which can be a directory anywhere on the server (and in which ColdFusion will place some subdirectories and files to hold the collection). Note that there's no special place within ColdFusion in which collections must be placed (nor need they even be placed within the ColdFusion directory; it would be wise, though, not to place them in a web-accessible directory).

The following example creates a collection named `merchandise` to be put in a directory to be created called c:\coldfusion10\Collections\. This directory does not exist by default, nor do you need to create it. ColdFusion will create it for you, placing a "merchandise" directory there:

```
<cfscript>
newCollection=new collection();
newCollection.create(collection="merchandise",path="c:\coldfusion10\Collections\");
<cfscript>
```

A Solr collection is really just a directory of files at this point (whose name and location are now registered with ColdFusion). You will see how to populate a collection in the next section, with the `index` CFC.

Technically, we could also specify this on a single line of script:

```
<cfscript>
new collection().create(collection="merchandise",path="c:\coldfusion10\
Collections\");
</cfscript>
```

Note that with the latter approach, no intermediate variable is needed to hold the collection. That may actually lead some readers to wonder, "Well, if I were running several methods against the collection, wouldn't I want to save the collection instance as a variable to reuse?" The answer is yes.

In fact, notice that in the preceding examples we are actually passing the collection name and arguments to the method (`create`), rather than during the creation of the collection instance. Although this approach is not well documented, you could instead pass those arguments on the creation of the CFC instance, accomplishing the same thing as in the preceding examples but using the following:

```
<cfscript>
newCollection=new collection(collection="merchandise",
➥path="c:\coldfusion10\cfusion\Verity\Collections\");
newCollection.create();
<cfscript>
```

Notice that in this case the `create` method has no arguments, because it knows to perform its action against the instance for which it's now a method. Either way, the result is the same: a collection is created. This example just shows a different style that may suit some tastes or situations. Of course, if you try to run these variations consecutively, trying to create a collection that already exists, you will get an error ("Unable to create collection merchandise, collection already exists.").

NOTE

On the other hand, an attempt to create a collection may fail with this message:

```
"Unable to create collection [collectionname]. An error occurred while creating
➥the collection: coldfusion.tagext.search.SolrUtils$UnableToConnectToSolrException:
➥Unable to connect to Solr Server."
```

In this case, the problem may simply be that the Solr (ColdFusion10JettyService) service has not been started.

You could delete a collection using the ColdFusion Administrator, but you can also delete it in code.

Deleting a Collection

If you want to delete this (or any collection), you can do so with the `delete` method, which takes only an argument for the collection name (or no argument, if you created an instance of the collection CFC by passing it the collection name). Here's an example of such a script-based deletion:

```
new Collection.delete(collection="merchandise");
```

Other Methods in the `Collection` CFC

There are several more methods for the `collection` CFC, including `create`, `delete`, `map`, `optimize`, and `categoryList` (the last is new for Solr and did not exist for the older Verity search engine). Syntactically, they are used similarly to the examples presented earlier.

See the documentation for `CFCOLLECTION` to understand the purpose and use of the various methods (which will correspond to `Action` values) and arguments (which for each method will correspond to attributes for a given equivalent action).

Again, you can learn more about the CFC specifically and its methods (including how to view its source code), in the later section "About These Adobe-Provided CFCs."

Errors Returned from Script-Based Tag-Equivalent CFCs

One challenge you may face when using these script-based tag equivalent CFCs is that sometimes the errors are not as clear as when you use the tags. This reflects that fact that the CFC-based tag equivalents are actually simply wrappers for the tags they represent, ultimately calling on the tags themselves for you.

For instance, when you are try to delete a collection, you may be tempted to use this code:

```
<cfscript>
new Collection.delete("merchandise");
</cfscript>
```

Do you see the mistake? It's easy to miss. And in fact, the error message won't really help:

```
Attribute validation error for tag CFCOLLECTION.
It does not allow the attribute(s) 1. The valid attribute(s) are
➡ ACTION,COLLECTION,LANGUAGE,PATH.
```

The problem is that the "collection=" name for the argument was left off.

Similarly, if you use the feature discussed earlier in which you choose to pass the collection name on the creation of the CFC instance, you may make the same mistake:

```
<cfscript>
myCollection=new collection("bookclub");
</cfscript>
```

Fortunately, in this case, the error message is at least closer to being helpful:

```
Attribute validation error for tag CFCOLLECTION.
When the value of the ACTION attribute is OPTIMIZE,
➡ it requires the attribute(s): COLLECTION.
```

It's telling us that we need the collection. Note, however, that the message refers to the CFCOLLECTION tag, even though we are using a CFC. It does reiterate that these CFCs are really just wrappers for the tags, implemented in a way that can be accessed from within CFScript. It doesn't really tell us that we need the "collection=" keyword before the collection name, but it tells more about the solution than did the previous error message discussed.

Using the `index` CFC (for `CFINDEX`)

Now that we have a collection, we can put data into it. In ColdFusion 10, the new `index` CFC corresponds to the `CFINDEX` tag, which is used for adding or maintaining data in a Solr collection. That data can be documents (text files, PDF files, Microsoft Office documents, static web pages, and much more), or it can be query results, all of which can be searched using the `CFSEARCH` tag or the CFScript equivalent `search` CFC, discussed later in this chapter.

Again, this chapter is not really the place to discuss the ins and outs of Solr collections, but a quick example will let us populate our collection, and in the section about the `search` CFC we'll see how to search it. In this example, we'll populate the index with query results.

See the ColdFusion documentation for more information about the broader subject of Solr indexing and searching, including an explanation of when and why it can make sense to store and search query data in a Solr index, as well as information and examples about storing documents instead of query data in Solr. See the later section "Some Final Comments on the Use of Solr in ColdFusion" for detailed references.

Querying a Data Source in Script

Before we can populate the index with query results, we need to run a query. With tags, we would of course do that with CFQUERY. ColdFusion 9 added a query CFC so that we can run a query in CFScript. See the ColdFusion documentation for more information about the query CFC, but here's a quick and simple example, querying the OWS data source provided with this book (there are additional ways to use the query CFC, but this will suffice):

```
<cfscript>
q = new query(datasource="ows");
merch=q.execute(sql="select merchid, merchname,
➥merchdescription from merchandise").getResult();
//WriteDump(merch);
</cfscript>
```

Note that we have a writeDump statement as a comment here, to allow us to see the data returned from the query.

With that query in hand (well, in the merch variable), we can now use it to populate the index.

If we wanted to use a CFINDEX tag to populate this collection from the query, we could use this code (performing an update action, though a refresh action can make sense in some cases, so see the ColdFusion documentation for more about the difference):

```
<cfindex action="update"
         collection="merchandise"
         query="merch"
         key="merchid"
         type="custom"
         title="merchname"
         body="merchdescription">
```

Now we just need to translate this code into a corresponding script equivalent, using the new index CFC. Given our experience working with the collection CFC earlier in this chapter, the index CFC should feel familiar.

We obviously want to create an instance of the CFC and then call the update method (to correspond with the ACTION of the tag), and then we need to pass the rest of the attributes as arguments to the method. There is one gotcha. See if you can spot a difference between one of the tag attribute values and the corresponding argument to the update method.

```
<cfscript>
m=new index();
m.update(collection="merchandise",query=merch,key="merchid",type="custom",
➥title="merchname",body="merchdescription");
</cfscript>
```

Did you spot the difference? Notice that you do not want the value of the query argument to be a quoted string (naming the variable holding the query) as it is with the tag attribute, but instead you want to just provide the variable name, without quotation marks. If you forget and leave the name quoted, you will get the following (not so obvious) error message, because ColdFusion is trying to treat the string as a query:

```
The variable specified in the query attribute, local.query, is not a query.
```

Similarly, when you convert the tag to the method call, you don't want to name the action as an argument (as we did for the tag, using `action="update"`), because that action value is implied by the method being called.

Other Methods in the `index` CFC

Besides the `update` and `refresh` methods, other methods available in the `index` CFC are `delete` (to remove one or more items from the index) and `purge` (to remove all items from the index.)

NOTE
> Although ColdFusion 10 also added new `action` values for `CFINDEX`, there are currently no corresponding methods for the following in the `index` CFC: `abort`, `deltaimport`, `fullimport`, and `status`.

Using the `search` CFC (for CFSEARCH)

The final new ColdFusion 10 tag-equivalent CFC is the `search` CFC, used to search for results in a Solr collection. Again, there is much to discuss about searching Solr collections, including how to define search criteria, choose search keywords, and decide what parts of an index record to search. See the ColdFusion documentation for more information.

To explore the script equivalent of `CFSEARCH`, we will focus on one simple example, but with a couple of observations that may help you with script-based (and even tag-based) dumping of output.

A Basic Search Using Tags

If we want to perform a simple search of the titles of the records stored in our collection (with the title having been set to one of the columns from our query results earlier), we can do that using `CFSEARCH` as follows:

```
<cfsearch collection="Merchandise"
          name="merch"
          criteria="title:ColdFusion"
          maxrows="10">
```

Again, there's a lot more that could be done in such a search. We're keeping things simple, searching the records for any titles that have the phrase "ColdFusion," and limiting the result to the first 10 records. (We don't have that many, but it's helpful to know that you can indeed limit the results in this way if you ever need to do so.) The result of `CFSEARCH`, a query result set, will be stored in a variable named "merch".

We can see this query result of `CFSEARCH` using `CFDUMP`:

```
<cfdump var="#merch#" show="score,title,summary">
```

Figure 8.1 shows the results.

Figure 8.1

04d-invoke-websvc-in-script.cfm

query [Filtered - 3 of 15 columns shown]		
SCORE	SUMMARY	TITLE
1	1.2331685	Free Guns and Roses album with purchase.	ColdFusion Construction Kit
2	1.2331685	Yes, it really shipped on 3.5 inch floppies, and you can have the proof.	ColdFusion 1.x diskettes

You may have noticed we've added an attribute to CFDUMP that you may not often see: show. This is one of many attributes added (especially in ColdFusion 8) to give you greater control over what should be dumped. In the case of show, the attribute limits the display to only the named columns (if this is a query). (There's also a top attribute that can be used to limit the number of records shown.)

The show attribute is especially helpful here, because the results of the CFSEARCH call (or the script equivalent) has many more columns, most of which are not at all interesting for this example; by using show, we are limiting the display to just three columns from the query result: score, title, and summary.

The Basic Search Using Script

Now let's convert those two tags to CFScript. Again, by now the process should feel familiar:

```
<cfscript>
merch=new search().search(collection="merchandise",criteria="title:ColdFusion",
➥ maxRows=10);
writeDump(var=merch.getresult().name,show="score,title,summary");
</cfscript>
```

This script will produce the exact same results as the tags (though note again that, as with the index().list(), we have dumped not just the merch variable, but rather merch.getresult().name, to get the exact same results as we did for the tag-based search result).

The only other detail about this example that may require some explanation is the first line's use of new search().search(), which may look a little awkward. Of course, by now you realize that the first search value is the CFC name, and the second search value is then the method. But there's no ACTION="search" on the CFSEARCH tag to go with this search method, which has been the pattern we saw for the script-based equivalent CFCs for CFCOLLECTION and CFINDEX.

Indeed, there is no ACTION at all for CFSEARCH, so the ColdFusion engineers had to simply pick some name for the method to be used to tell the CFC to go to work. They picked search. The same challenge existed for CFCs created in ColdFusion 9, such as the equivalent of CFQUERY, for which they chose query().execute(), as well as for CFMAIL, for which they chose uses mail().send(), CFHTTP, for which they chose http().send()), and so on.

One other potential gotcha is the variation in the writeDump dump shown. Note that when we have used it previously , we've not added any arguments. We just passed the variable to be dumped, and that works. But if we need to pass other name=value argument pairs, as is the case for the show argument being demonstrated, then ColdFusion requires that we give a name to each argument being passed. If, instead, we had tried to write that dump as:

```
writeDump(merch.getresult().name,show="score,title,summary");
```

we would have received the (rather unhelpful) error message:

```
Invalid CFML construct found on line 12 at column 38.
ColdFusion was looking at the following text:
=
```

Some Final Comments on the Use of Solr in ColdFusion

Again, this chapter provides only a cursory discussion of the use of Solr in ColdFusion. To find out more, see the section "Solr Search Support" in Chapter 7, "Accessing and Using Data," in *Developing ColdFusion 10 Applications*, available in the ColdFusion documentation.

Also, if you have problems that you can't readily solve using the available error messages, documentation, and ColdFusion logs, be aware that you can find Solr logs (for errors and more) at [ColdFusion10]\cfusion\jetty\logs.

Finally, many developers have found that when they've run into challenges or limitations in ColdFusion's implementation of tag- or script-based searching and manipulation of Solr collections, calling the Solr service (built into ColdFusion) directly via HTTP can be helpful. Doing so is beyond the scope of this chapter, nor is this approach documented in the ColdFusion documentation. You can find a nice, quick tutorial by David Faber here: http://www.thefaberfamily.org/search-smith/coldfusion-solr-tutorial/.

What About Crawling a Site?

So we can index files and query data, but can ColdFusion be used to index all or part of a website, including the results of execution of dynamic pages as in ColdFusion? Sadly, the answer is no. At least, this sort of web crawler or spider capability is not built into ColdFusion.

There is, however, an open source project called Nutch (http://nutch.apache.org/), which is a web crawler written in Java, that is built to save its results in a Solr collection. It cannot be directly integrated into ColdFusion (to crawl or search its results), but you could certainly define a collection in ColdFusion that points to a Solr collection created and populated with Nutch, and then use the Solr searching capability within ColdFusion to query it.

About These Adobe-Provided CFCs

After learning about these new ColdFusion 10 tag-equivalent CFCs, perhaps you're intrigued about their use, and about the use of older ones as well. There are three places you can look to find out more: the ColdFusion documentation, the CFML source code (yes, it's open source), and the component metadata and methods.

ColdFusion Documentation for the CFCs

First, you can find more about the CFCs in general in the *ColdFusion 10 CFML Reference*, in the section "Script Functions Implemented as CFCs." You can also refer to the section "Service Tags with Bodies," in *Developing ColdFusion 10 Applications*.

NOTE
> Yes, the fact that the section names in these documents differ indicates that the documents refer to these CFCs as "service tags with bodies" and as "script functions implemented as CFCs" for what we're here calling "tag equivalents as CFCs" or "CFC-based implementation of tags." There's no one right way to refer to them.

CFML Source Code for the CFCs

Second, these CFCs provided by Adobe are also available as CFML source code. They are *not* precompiled, so you can view them with any editor. The source code is especially helpful because the documentation for these CFCs (including those from ColdFusion 9) is often sparse, and there is currently no documentation at all for these new CFCs in ColdFusion 10: collection, index, and search.

You can find all these CFCs installed in ColdFusion by default in the built-in CustomTags directory. In ColdFusion 10, that's located at [ColdFusion10]\cfusion\CustomTags\com\adobe\ coldfusion (where [Coldfusion10] would be C:\ColdFusion10 in Microsoft Windows, where ColdFusion is installed by default).

NOTE

If, when you are trying to execute these CFCs, you get an error because ColdFusion can't find the CFC, make sure that you have not deleted the mapping to these CFCs: [ColdFusion10]\cfusion\CustomTags.

Related to these files is a file used by ColdFusion tags to track and validate tag attributes. Called taglib.cftld, it's at [ColdFusion10]\cfusion\wwwroot\WEB-INF\cftags\META-INF. These CFCs validate their arguments (through code in a base.cfc file that they all extend) against this file.

Component Metadata, Methods, and More

Third, you can also view information about the CFCs and their methods using the available CFC browser, built into ColdFusion (since ColdFusion 6). To view the information about the collection CFC, for instance, set the browser to the following URL: http://[servername]/CFIDE/ componentutils/cfcexplorer.cfc?method=getcfcinhtml&name=com.adobe.coldfusion.collection

You may be prompted to provide your ColdFusion Administrator or RDS password.

Community-Contributed CFC-Based Tag Equivalents

In addition to the three new CFCs in ColdFusion 10 and those existing since ColdFusion 9 and 9.0.1, more tags are available through a community-organized project that creates and shares CFC-based implementations of tags. To learn more, see https://github.com/CFCommunity/ CFScript-Community-Components.

In fact, as you explore those, you will notice that the three added in ColdFusion 10 were created and shared there by one of our fellow authors, Raymond Camden, who works for Adobe. The project website says that anyone can use the CFCs, and that the group would welcome the CFC's being built into the core of ColdFusion, so we may see more of these CFCs in future ColdFusion releases thanks to this project.

Some of the CFCs listed there (as of this writing) that are not yet implemented in ColdFusion are content, execute, flush, header, htmlhead, loginuser, logout, registry, schedule, spreadsheet, wddx, and zip. If you wished that ColdFusion included one of these, you can get it from the project.

Finally, if there's still some other tag that no one has yet converted to a CFC, give the job a try yourself. If you look at the source code for the CFCs included with ColdFusion, you'll see that it's fairly straightforward to convert a tag to a CFC using the approach that's been adopted for the ones already created.

About the Three Approaches to Tag Equivalents

Before we leave the subject of script equivalents to tags, let's revisit a point raised at the beginning of the chapter: how some developers grimace when they notice that Adobe uses three different ways to extend the CFML language to make it easier to execute tag equivalents in CFScript. Why is `setting` implemented as a statement, and `invoke` as a function, and `collection` as a CFC?

This approach is not as illogical as some assert it to be.

Consider that when a tag is implemented as a statement, it performs one very specific task (such as enabling settings or creating a cookie). It may take attributes (though some statements don't: for instance, `break`). But statements don't ever return anything.

Next consider tags implemented as functions, such as `invoke`. The tag may or may not take arguments, but it definitely can return a result, so `invoke` couldn't possibly be implemented as a statement (except perhaps for the very limited purpose of calling a CFC or web service method that returns nothing, but it's not worth implementing that as a statement just for that single use case).

Finally, consider tags implemented as CFCs, such as `collection`. This tag offers an ACTION attribute that allows a variety of values (`create`, `delete`, `list`, and do on), and each of those values may take different additional attributes. The `create` value takes `collectionname`, `path`, and other attributes. The `delete` value takes just a collection name. The `list` value needs no additional attributes and returns a list of collections.

So in implementing tags to be called from script, Adobe could have created different statements (for those that don't return a result), and different standalone functions for those that do. But doesn't it make sense to package them together in a CFC, just as you would if you were defining multiple related methods for your own CFC?

(Consider, for instance, the many `image*` functions that exist in CFML, or the many `spreadsheet*` functions. Some people have lamented that these are not organized better . Although name spaces for functions would be nice, perhaps these too should have been implemented as methods in a CFC.)

Note as well that some of the CFCs discussed in this chapter are defined so that you can pass them arguments to set properties, so that they are essentially stateful, meaning they are really more than just a collection of static methods (to use a Java term for methods or objects without state).

Where to Learn More About CFScript-Based Development

Some of the changes in ColdFusion 10 may motivate you to want to do more script-based development, but many developers assume that there is little documentation for CFScript and script-based development in general.

Part of the challenge stems from the fact that many developers know only about the CFML reference manual (*ColdFusion 10 CFML Reference*). It has some coverage of CFScript, but just as for any tag or function, that manual, because it's a reference, doesn't really teach how to use the various features.

For more tutorial content, instead look to the developer's guide (referred to frequently in this chapter), which has had various names in the different releases of ColdFusion, and which in the latest release is named *Developing 10 ColdFusion Applications*.

With respect to scripting in particular, there is substantial coverage of these in the ColdFusion documentation. For your convenience, links are provided on this book's web page.

CHAPTER 9

Object Relational Mapping Enhancements

ColdFusion 9 introduced object relational mapping (ORM), a persistence framework in which a ColdFusion component (CFC) can be mapped to a relational database without the need to write SQL. This framework is based on Hibernate, a popular persistence framework. ColdFusion 10 improves ORM support by providing ORM search, Hibernate Query Language (HQL) logging, and inheritance mapping enhancements. This chapter discusses these ORM enhancements.

ORM Enhancements Summary

ColdFusion 10 adds the following ORM enhancements:

- ORM search enhancements

- HQL logging enhancements

- Improved handling of persistent parent-child CFCs

The chapter assumes familiarity with the basic concepts of ORM and ORM integration, introduced in ColdFusion 9. For an introduction to ORM concepts, refer to Chapter 38, "Working with ORM," in *Adobe ColdFusion 9 Web Application Construction Kit, Volume 2: Application Development*.

ORM Search Enhancements

A traditional way to search a database is to use SQL. In SQL, you select a table or group of tables to join them and then specify a WHERE clause to match your search condition. Listing 9.1 shows a simple example.

Listing 9.1 /cfwack10/9/querySearch.cfm

```
<cfquery name="result">
SELECT firstname, lastname FROM ARTISTS WHERE state='CA'
</cfquery>

<cfdump var="#result#" metainfo="no">
```

This example searches for all artists living in California and produces the output shown in Figure 9.1.

Figure 9.1

Result of a `cfquery` operation.

query		
	FIRSTNAME	LASTNAME
1	Austin	Weber
2	Elicia	Kim

This scenario in this example is very common, and most ColdFusion programmers are familiar with it.

NOTE

All the examples in this chapter use `cfartgallery` as the data source. It is available in the default ColdFusion installation. The listings for this chapter contain an Application.cfc file in which the `cfartgallery` data source is set for the applications used in this chapter.

Extending this model to ORM requires either HQL or ColdFusion's built-in functions such as `EntityLoad`, `EntityLoadByExample`, and `EntityLoadByPK`. Writing equivalent code for Listing 9.1 in HQL is easy, but here we will use `EntityLoadByExample`, as shown in Listing 9.2.

Listing 9.2 /cfwack10/9/entityLoad.cfm

```
<cfset artist1 = EntityNew("Artist").setState("CA")>
<cfset result = entityLoadbyExample(artist1)>
<cfdump var="#result#" >
```

On running this example, ColdFusion will search for all `Artist` entity objects listed as living in California. The resulting object is a struct listing the two artists that we obtained in the example in Listing 9.1.

Note that a traditional search operation returns entities of the same type. For instance, all entities of either type `Artist` or type `Order` are returned. This behavior can be limiting if you want to search across all entities: for example, if you want to find all artists and customers in the state of California.

ColdFusion already supports general-purpose text searching using `cfindex` and `cfsearch` tags. Now ColdFusion 10 introduces the capability to perform full-text searches across multiple ORM entities using the ORM search function. Using ORM searching, you can provide search criteria and load all the persistent entities that match the search criteria.

But before we perform an ORM search, we need to index data. Full-text searching is a two-step process and is similar to a search operation performed using `<cfsearch>`. The next section briefly describes how to index ORM.

Enabling ORM Entities for Indexing

Three steps are required to enable ORM entities for indexing:

- Enable ORM search for the application.

- Declare the ORM entity to be eligible for indexing.

- Identify ORM entity properties that will be indexed.

ColdFusion uses these hints when it is loading the application.

The first step is to enable ORM search using the `searchenabled` property in Application.cfc as shown in Listing 9.3.

Listing 9.3   /cfwack10/9/Application.cfc

```
<cfset this.name = "Chapter9OrmSearch">
<cfset this.datasource = "cfartgallery">
<cfset this.ormenabled = "true">
<cfset this.ormsettings.searchenabled = "true">
```

The `searchenabled` property is part of `ormsettings` and is applicable to ORM CFCs only. This step is similar to the step required to enable ORM using the `ormenabled` property. You can also set a few other properties related to ORM search in Application.cfc; we will discuss them after we explore our first application using ORM search.

The next step is to make the ORM entity eligible for indexing. You do this by specifying the `indexable` property in the `cfcomponent` tag, as shown in Listing 9.4.

Listing 9.4   /cfwack10/9/Artist.cfc

```
<cfcomponent persistent="true" table="ARTISTS" indexable="true">
    ...
</cfcomponent>
```

The final step is to identify the ORM entity properties that will be indexed. The indexed properties are then available when a text search operation is called using ORM search. Listing 9.5 shows an example in which `state` is marked as the `indexable` property.

Listing 9.5   /cfwack10/9/Artist.cfc

```
<cfcomponent persistent="true" table="ARTISTS" indexable="true">
    <cfproperty name="artistId" fieldtype="id" indexable="true">
    <cfproperty name="firstName">
    <cfproperty name="lastName">
    <cfproperty name="address">
    <cfproperty name="city">
    <cfproperty name="state" indexable="true">
    <cfproperty name="phone">
    <cfproperty name="email">
    <cfproperty name="postalCode">
</cfcomponent>
```

When the ColdFusion application starts, ColdFusion searches for ORM CFCs, if ORM is enabled. In the preceding example, it will locate Artist.cfc. Since search is enabled in Application.cfc, Cold-Fusion additionally checks for ORM entities that are marked as indexable. ColdFusion identifies Artist.cfc and then searches for indexable properties in it. If ColdFusion creates instances of Artist, it will index the state value of Artist instances, which can later be searched.

Indexing an ORM Entity

An ORM entity object is indexed when it is either loaded from persistent store or created inside the ColdFusion environment. If you are using methods such as EntityNew and EntitySave, then the entity object is created in the ColdFusion environment, and hence ColdFusion automatically indexes it using the indexable hints discussed in the previous section.

To index entities that exist in the persistent store, ColdFusion provides the method ormIndex. There are many variations on this method, and we will discuss them in detail after we examine a simple example to put all the pieces together.

Searching an ORM Entity

Let's look at how to search Artist using the index that we created in Listings 9.3, 9.4, and 9.5. Examine Listing 9.6.

Listing 9.6   /cfwack10/9/basicORMSearch.cfm

```
<cfscript>
  /* ormReload() should not be used in production settings */
  ormReload();
  /* Index all instances of Artist existing in the persistent store */
  ormIndex("Artist");
  result = ormSearch("CA", "Artist", ["state"]);
  writedump(result)
</cfscript>
```

The first call is to ormReload. This call makes sure that any ORM code changes are reloaded properly.

The next call is to ormIndex. This call loads all Artist entities from the database and indexes them.

The next call, to ormSearch, adds all the records with a state value of "CA" from the Artist entities.

NOTE

When you are building an ORM application, ormReload makes sure that all your application's new settings are loaded properly. However, ormReload should not be used in a production environment because you are not changing your code and you do not want the additional overhead of loading the same settings repeatedly.

The ormSearch method in Listing 9.6 uses two parameters: a query string and the name of the entity to be searched. Since ColdFusion uses the Apache Lucene engine for the search, the query string uses the same syntax that is required to search an object with the Lucene engine. For more information about Lucene queries, see http://lucene.apache.org/core/old_versioned_docs/versions/3_0_0/queryparsersyntax.html.

Figure 9.2 shows the results of running the page in Listing 9.6.

Figure 9.2

Result struct from an ORM search operation on a single entity type.

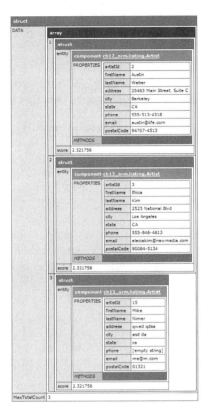

The result is a struct of two keys: `Data` and `MaxTotalCount`. In addition, `Data` is an array of matched entities and scores. The `MaxTotalCount` value is the maximum number of entities matched by ColdFusion while performing the search.

The entry `ORMSearch("query string", "entity name", fields, optionMap)` accepts up to four parameters in the following order:

- The `query string` parameter specifies the search term based on Apache Lucene query syntax.

- The `entity name` parameter specifies name of the ORM entity that you want to search. You can specify multiple entities using a comma-delimited list.

- The `fields` parameter specifies an array of property names for entities in which the search is to be performed. The field should exist in all entities specified in entity name and must be indexable.

- The `optionMap` parameter specifies a map to provide additional hints to ColdFusion while executing the search:

  - The `sort` parameter is used to sort the data based on the field name.

  - The `offset` parameter is used in pagination to specify the position from which to retrieve entity instances.

  - The `maxResults` parameter returns up to a specified number of results.

The first two parameters (`query string` and `entity name`) are mandatory.

NOTE

ColdFusion is case insensitive, whereas Apache Lucene is case sensitive. Therefore, use care when passing any data to Apache Lucene as part of a search operation: for example, a field name.

Searching Multiple Entity Types

The example in Listing 9.6 searches the state of the `Artist` entity type. How do you perform a full-text search across multiple entities? Listing 9.7 performs an ORM search on the `state` field for the `Artist` and `Order` entity types.

Listing 9.7   /cfwack10/9/multiEntitySearch.cfm

```
<cfscript>
  /* ormReload() should not be used in production settings */
  ormReload();

  /* Index all instances of Artist and Order existing in the persistent store */
  ormIndex("Artist,Order");

  /* Search Order and Artist together */
  result = ormSearch("CA", "Order,Artist", ["state"]);

  writedump(result)
</cfscript>
```

The code first indexes both `Artist` and `Order` entities using the `ormIndex()` function. The search is performed in the usual way, except that both the `Order` and `Artist` entities are passed to the `ormSearch` function. ColdFusion automatically converts a comma-separated list of entities to multiple entity objects and applies the index or search operation to the passed entities.

NOTE

There should not be a space after the comma between multiple entities passed to `ormIndex` and `ormSearch`. If you include a space, ColdFusion reports an error, saying that the entity must be indexable. This behavior is a bug and has been reported to the Adobe product team.

When you run Listing 9.7, it returns a result object with six entities. Three orders have been given by customers staying in the state of California, and three artists are staying in California.

Part of returned results is shown in Figure 9.3.

Figure 9.3

Result struct from an
ORM search operation
on multiple entity
types.

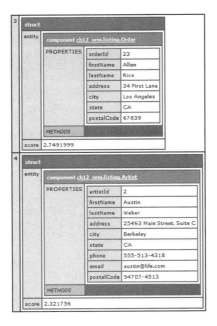

The entities are available in an array of structs, with the array available as the value of the Data key.

Performing Offline Searches

ColdFusion allows you to perform offline searches on ORM entities. A typical ORM search using ormSearch returns a complete object graph. This result can be overkill for applications when large numbers of entities need to be loaded from the database to create the result set. In many cases, only a small subset of properties is required in the result set. ColdFusion enables the offline search option by storing entity properties while indexing and using the stored properties from the index to match and create the result set. This process avoids the need for a database roundtrip while preparing the search result.

This search is achieved using the ormOfflineSearch function and is a two-step process. The first step marks the ORM entity fields for storage in the index store, and the second step uses the marked fields in the search result. These steps are shown in Listing 9.8 and Listing 9.9, respectively.

Listing 9.8 /cfwack10/9/Order.cfc

```
<cfcomponent persistent="true" table="ORDERS" indexable="true">
    <cfproperty name="orderId" fieldtype="id">
    <cfproperty name="firstName" column="CUSTOMERFIRSTNAME" >
    <cfproperty name="lastName" column="CUSTOMERLASTNAME"
                indexable="true" indexstore="true">
    <cfproperty name="address" column="ADDRESS" >
    <cfproperty name="city" column="CITY" >
    <cfproperty name="state" indexable="true">
    <cfproperty name="postalCode">
</cfcomponent>
```

When `indexStore` is specified as a property, ColdFusion stores the value in its original form without tokenizing. This approach is useful in returning search results. You can also specify `indexStore="compressed"`, where the property is stored in a compressed form based on the Lucene implementation.

Listing 9.9 /cfwack10/9/offlineSearch.cfm

```
<cfscript>
  /* ormReload() should not be used in production settings */
  ormReload();

  /* Index all instances of Artist existing in the persistent store */
  ormIndex("Order");

  /* Search query criteria in state and return last name fields */
  result = ormSearchOffline("CA*", "Order", ["lastName"], ["state"]);

  writedump(result)
</cfscript>
```

This code is similar to the code when `ormSearch` is called, except the call to offline searching. When this code is run, ColdFusion finds all `Order` entities from customers in California and returns a struct with the customers' last names. Figure 9.4 shows the result.

Figure 9.4

Result struct from an offline search operation.

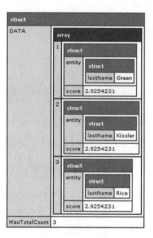

The result contains other keys, such as `Data`, `MaxTotalCount`, and `score`, that have the same behavior as the result struct from `ormSearch()` discussed with Listing 9.6.

The specification `ORMSearchOffline("query string", "entity name", fields_to_select, fields, optionMap)` accepts the following parameters:

- The `query string` parameter specifies the search term based on the Apache Lucene query syntax.

- The `entity name` parameter specifies the name of the ORM entity that you want to search. You can specify multiple entities using a comma-delimited list.

- The `fields_to_select` parameter specifies an array of fields added to the resulting struct.

- The `fields` parameter specifies an array of property names of entities in which the search is to be performed. The field should exists in all entities specified in the entity name parameter and must be indexable.

- The `optionMap` parameter specifies a map to provide additional hints to ColdFusion while executing the search:

- The `sort` parameter sorts the data based on the field name.

- The `offset` parameter is used in pagination to specify the position from which to retrieve entity instances.

- The `maxResults` parameter returns up to a specified number of results.

Searching Relationships

ColdFusion ORM search also support the searching of related entities. You need to set the `indexable` attribute on the relationship property. The second step involves searching using the `ormSearch()` method and navigating to the indexable field in the related entity. For example, `ormSearch("CA", "Art", ["artist.state"])` navigates to the `artist` entity from `Art`; `state` is an indexable property, so the method will search for all `Art` entries in which artists are from California.

Managing Indexes

This section describes how ColdFusion manages indexes and discusses the options available to you to create and purge your own indexes.

Explicit Indexing

ColdFusion allows indexes to be created implicitly as well as explicitly. ColdFusion creates indexes explicitly on a call to the `ormIndex()` method. The example in Listing 9.6. used the `ormIndex()` method. This method has four options:

- `ORMIndex("entity name")` method indexes all records of the given entity name and, if required, loads entity records from the persistent store. This operation can consume a lot of overhead and should be performed separately as part of application initialization.

- The `ORMIndex("entity name list")` method is same as the `"entity name"` method except that this method accepts multiple, comma-delimited entity names. The behavior is the same as when multiple `ormIndex("entity name")` calls are made, each with a single entity name.

- The `ORMIndex(entityObject)` method indexes the specific entity instance that is passed as an argument.

- The `ORMIndex()` method indexes all ORM entities in the current application. This method consumes a lot of overhead and should be performed separately as part of application initialization.

Explicit indexing should be performed offline and not in a typical web request. It is also referred to as offline indexing.

Implicit Indexing

ColdFusion creates indexes implicitly whenever an indexable entity is created, updated, or deleted. ColdFusion checks whether the ORM entity is marked as indexable and creates the indexes along with the page request in which the entity is created, updated, or deleted. This mechanism is also referred to as inline or autoindexing and can be turned on or off using `ormSettings.search.autoindex` setting in Application.cfc. Implicit indexing is performed at the end of a request to optimize and batch multiple index requests.

Purging

ColdFusion provides the `ORMIndexPurge()` method, which clears all indexed data for all or specified entities. This method is useful when you have to rebuild your indexes. The `ORMIndexPurge()` method has three options:

- The `ORMIndexPurge("entity name")` method clears the indexed data for the given entity name.

- The `ORMIndexPurge("entity name list")` method clears indexed data for all entities in a comma-separated list.

- The `ORMIndexPurge()` method clears indexed data for all persistent entities in the current application scope.

Specifying Search Settings

You can specify search settings at the server, application, component, and property levels.

Server Level

You can specify the directory at the server level, where all of the application's indexable data is saved. This index directory is specified by choosing ColdFusion Administrator > Server Settings > Settings, as shown in Figure 9.5.

Figure 9.5

Administrator setting to specify the ORM index directory.

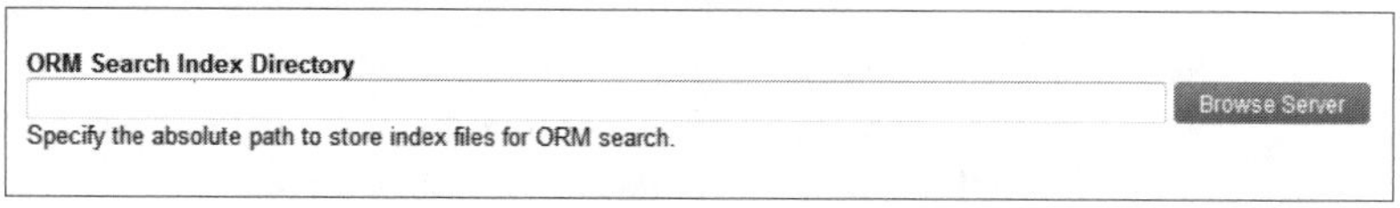

ORM Search Index Directory

[   ] [Browse Server]

Specify the absolute path to store index files for ORM search.

For each application, a directory with the application name is created in the index directory to store the application's indexed data. By default, ColdFusion uses the `ormindex` folder under the `cfusion` folder in the ColdFusion installation directory as the index directory.

Application Level

ColdFusion 10 introduces four new search settings in Application.cfc. These settings are specified using the properties shown in Listing 9.10.

Listing 9.10 /cfwack10/9/extra/Application.cfc

```
component
{
    this.name = "SearchSettings";
    this.ormEnabled = "true";
    this.ormSettings.datasource = "cfartgallery";
    this.ormsettings.searchenabled = "true";
    this.ormSettings.search.autoindex = "true";
    //this.ormSettings.search.indexDir = "C:/CF10/ormindex";
    this.ormSettings.search.language = "English";
}
```

- The `searchenabled` property enables the ORM search. ORM must be enabled using `ormEnabled` for this setting to work.

- The `search.autoindex` property enables automatic or inline or implicit indexing. If automatic indexing is disabled, the application will use `ormIndex` to perform explicit indexing.

- The `search.indexDir` property specifies the directory in which ColdFusion creates a folder with the application name and saves indexed data for this application. This setting overrides server-level settings for the index directory for this application.

- The `search.language` property specifies the language that is used to index and search the ORM entities of this application.

Component Level

ColdFusion 10 introduces three search settings that can be specified in the `cfcomponent` tag, shown in Listing 9.11.

Listing 9.11 /cfwack10/9/extra/Media.cfc

```
<cfcomponent persistent="true"
             table="MEDIA"
             indexable="true"
             indexlanguage="English"
             autoindex="true">
</cfcomponent>
```

- The `indexable` property enables indexing for the ORM component.

- The `indexLanguage` property specifies the language that is used to index and search the ORM component. The value set here overrides the value specified in Application.cfc for this component.

- The `autoindex` property enables automatic or inline or implicit indexing. The value set here overrides the value specified in Application.cfc for this component.

Property Level

The property-level search setting is specified in the `cfproperty` tag for an ORM component, as shown in Listing 9.12.

Listing 9.12 /cfwack10/9/GalleryAdmin.cfc

```
<cfcomponent persistent="true"
              table="GALLERYADMIN"
              indexable="true"
              indexlanguage="English"
              autoindex="true">
    <cfproperty name="galleryAdminId"
                fieldtype="id"/>
    <cfproperty name="firstName"
                indexable="true"
                indexboost="4.0"/>
    <cfproperty name="lastName"
                indexable="true"
                indextokenized="true"
                indexfieldname="surname"/>
    <cfproperty name="email"
                indexstore="true"
                indexlanguage="English"/>
</cfcomponent>
```

- The `indexable` property enables the column for indexing. The primary key or ID properties automatically become indexable if any of the nonprimary keys are marked as indexable. In Listing 9.12, the `galleryAdminId` indexable value is automatically set to `true`.

- The `indexBoost` property prioritizes the search results. In Listing 9.12, the `firstName` field has an index boost value. This means that if a search is performed on the `firstName` and `lastName` fields, the results will show matching results for `firstName` before the results for `lastName`.

- The `indexTokenized` property divides the field text into subkeys for indexing.

- The `indexFieldName` property specifies an alternative name that is used in the search query while indexing and performing the search.

- When `indexStore` is specified for a property, ColdFusion stores the value in original form without tokenizing. This is used in offline searches. We discussed this in Listing 9.8.

- The `indexLanguage` property specifies the language that is used to index and search the field. The value set here overrides the value specified in `cfcomponent` or Application.cfc for this property.

All property-level search settings apply only when the `indexable` attribute of the field property is set to `true`.

Listing 9.13 provides an example of the property-level settings.

Listing 9.13 /cfwack10/9/ propSetting.cfm

```
<cfscript>
  /* ormReload() should not be used in production settings */
  ormReload();

  /* Index all instances of GalleryAdmin */
  ormIndex("GalleryAdmin");

  /* Search firstName and lastName field */
  result = ormSearch('firstName:"Mike" OR surname:"Demo"', "GalleryAdmin",
  ➥["firstName","surname"]);

  writedump(result)
</cfscript>
```

The ORM search in this operation is performed on the firstName and lastName fields. Instead of using lastName, the example uses the indexFieldName value of surname. If you try to use lastName, ColdFusion throws an error because the search engine identifies surname as the indexed field, not lastName.

The search uses a complex query string with OR criteria as allowed by a Lucene query string. Figure 9.6 shows the result struct.

Figure 9.6

Result struct from an ORM search operation with index boost and the index field name.

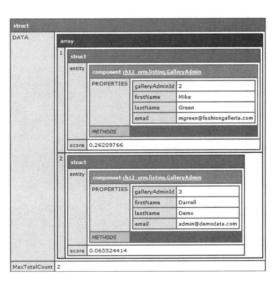

Two records are matched: one with first name Mike, and the second with the last name Demo.

If you remove the indexBoost attribute from firstName and add it to lastName, the results in the struct will be swapped. When indexBoost is specified with lastName, the result that matches Demo as lastName gets priority and will be listed as the first result.

HQL Logging Enhancements

ColdFusion can log the SQL generated by ORM, a capability introduced in ColdFusion 9. To enable SQL logging, set `ormsettings.logsql` to true in Application.cfc. You can also log SQL by directly modifying the log4j.properties file. This second option does not require any settings to be specified in ColdFusion.

Rupesh Kumar from the ColdFusion engineering team has written an excellent article about SQL logging with ORM that you can find at http://www.rupeshk.org/blog/index.php/2009/07/coldfusion-orm-how-to-log-sql/.

ColdFusion 10 added the capability to show HQL logging along with the debug output of the page. To use this feature, enable request debugging output in the ColdFusion Administrator by choosing Debugging & Logging > Debug Output Settings and selecting Enable Request Debugging Output, as shown in Figure 9.7.

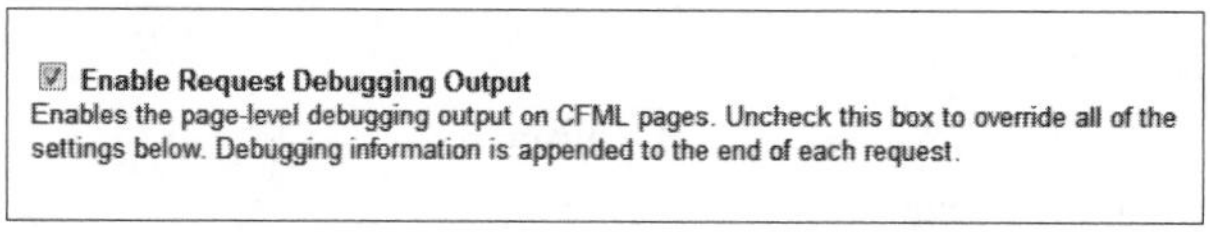

Figure 9.7

Administrator setting to enable request debugging output.

☑ **Enable Request Debugging Output**
Enables the page-level debugging output on CFML pages. Uncheck this box to override all of the settings below. Debugging information is appended to the end of each request.

Listing 9.14 runs a simple page that loads a `Media` entity and dumps the output.

Listing 9.14 /cfwack10/9/logging/logtest.cfm

```
<cfset result = entityLoadbyPK("MediaLog", 1)>
<cfdump var="#result#">
```

When the page runs, it adds debugging output since debugging output is enabled. Because HQL logging is enabled in Application.cfc, ColdFusion adds SQL logging with the output debug information, as shown in Figure 9.8.

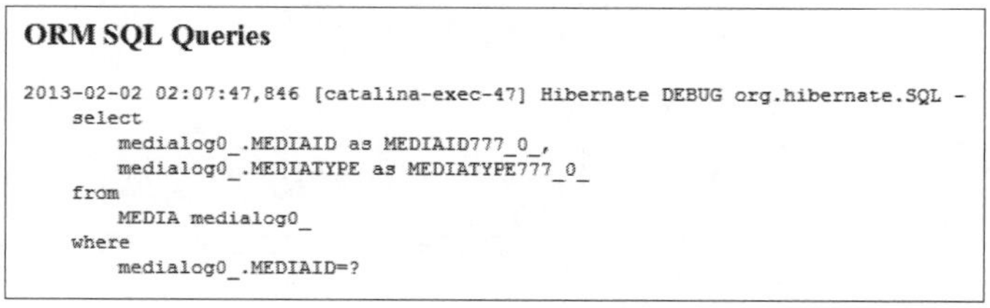

Figure 9.8

Logs from ORM SQL log added to the request output debug information.

ORM SQL Queries

```
2013-02-02 02:07:47,846 [catalina-exec-47] Hibernate DEBUG org.hibernate.SQL -
    select
        medialog0_.MEDIAID as MEDIAID777_0_,
        medialog0_.MEDIATYPE as MEDIATYPE777_0_
    from
        MEDIA medialog0_
    where
        medialog0_.MEDIAID=?
```

Improved Handling of the ORM Hierarchy

ColdFusion 9 contains a bug: the parent-child relationship between persistent entities is not managed properly if there is any nonpersistent entity in the chain. This bug has been fixed in ColdFusion 10.

Consider a hierarchy in which the component AllLivingThing is the parent of the component Mammal, and Mammal is the parent of the component HumanBeing. AllLivingThing and HumanBeing are defined as ORM entities, and Mammal is a non-ORM component. In ColdFusion 9, HumanBeing will not inherit properties of AllLivingThing because of this bug. In ColdFusion 10, HumanBeing inherits all properties of AllLivingThing in ORM operations.

Enhanced Java Integration

ColdFusion 10 enhances CFML support for Java integration, solving various problems that have challenged such integration:

- Dynamic application-specific class loading with `this.javaSettings`

- Enhanced capability to call CFCs from Java with `CFCProxy`

- Capability to proxy CFCs as Java objects with `createDynamicProxy`

- Capability to loop over Java arrays in CFML

Each of these features is available in ColdFusion Standard and Enterprise.

About CFML and Java Integration

CFML has long been able to integrate with Java. Before exploring the new features, we will review this capability, to provide a context for the features that are new or different in ColdFusion 10.

Perhaps the simplest form of integration is the capability of a CFML page to load a Java class, using either `CFOBJECT` or the `createObject()` function, and then invoke methods or access properties within it using CFML.

NOTE

Here's a question for a ColdFusion "bar bet": When was Java integration added to ColdFusion? In other words, when could Cold-Fusion developers first call a Java class with `CFOBJECT` or `createObject()`? Most would say it was with the introduction of ColdFusion MX (CF6), the first release in which ColdFusion itself was built on Java and deployed by default upon Macromedia JRun (preceding its acquisition by Adobe). But technically, we've been able to call Java from within CFML since ColdFusion 4.5.1, released in March 2000. That release added the capability to define a JVM class path in the ColdFusion Administrator, allowing us to add any classes or .jar files in that location, which could then be invoked using `CFOBJECT` or `createObject()`. CF6 certainly added much more in the way of Java integration, of course.

Simple Java Example: DNS Lookup

Here's a simple example of CFML and Java integration. Because ColdFusion is built on Java (since ColdFusion 6, also known as CFMX), and Java has a library for performing a domain name server (DNS) lookup, we can use that library to obtain the IP address for a given domain name.

We can easily access that Java library in just two lines of CFML code. Listing 10.1 obtains the current IP address for the Adobe.com domain.

Listing 10.1 01a-cfobject-demo.cfm

```
<cfobject type="java" class="java.net.InetAddress" name="iaddr">
<cfoutput>#iaddr.getByName("adobe.com").getHostAddress()#</cfoutput>
```

This script calls the InetAddress class, found in the java.net package of the core Java library, and invokes its method, getByName, which returns an object, which then has a getHostAddress method. Notice that we are chaining these methods into one statement here.

The result displayed is the IP address for the Adobe site (at the time of this writing):

```
192.150.16.117.
```

Listing 10.2 shows the same solution implemented instead using createObject with CFScript.

Listing 10.2 01b-createobject-demo.cfm

```
<cfscript>
iaddr = createObject("java","java.net.InetAddress");
writeoutput(iaddr.getByName("adobe.com").gethostaddress());
</cfscript>
```

There's no functional difference between the tag or the function with regard to the results of the loading and calling methods in a Java object. The function-based syntax will be more familiar to those coming from other script-oriented languages. Even so, note that createObject can be used either within CFScript or within tags, as shown here:

```
<cfset iaddr=createObject("java","java.net.InetAddress")>
<cfoutput>#iaddr.getByName("adobe.com").getHostAddress()#</cfoutput>
```

Performing a Reverse-DNS Lookup

After seeing how easily you can perform a DNS lookup, you may want to try a reverse-DNS lookup, to instead get the domain name for a given IP address. The Java InetAddress library offers a method for this as well, and it can be called just as easily with a line of code as shown in Listing 10.3 (which shows just script-based syntax).

Listing 10.3 01c-reversedns-bad-demo.cfm

```
<cfscript>
iaddr = createObject("java","java.net.InetAddress");
writeoutput(iaddr.getByName("192.150.16.11").getHostName());
</cfscript>
```

But there are two problems with this library's functions: In some situations, it may not return anything but the IP address. Worse, it may take several seconds to complete, which is a known issue with this method.

The good news is that there is a helpful third-party library that can easily perform the reverse-DNS lookup job for us, as you'll see later, when we discuss how to easily access such a newly added Java library by using one of the new features in ColdFusion 10: dynamic application-specific class loading.

Using Java Libraries and Classes

Besides using Java and ColdFusion integration to call on Java core libraries (ColdFusion has been deployed on top of a Java server since ColdFusion 6), you can use it to call on any Java library that may be accessible within ColdFusion, including Tomcat libraries (since ColdFusion 10 is deployed by default on Tomcat) as well as any of several industry-standard third-party libraries that are bundled with ColdFusion. These libraries provide capabilities for various tags, functions, and features of ColdFusion, including Ehcache, Jasper reports, and Hibernate. If a CFML tag or function doesn't exist but you can access something of interest using a Java library, you can call it yourself, using `CFOBJECT` or `createObject`.

You can also use any Java class or library that exists, whether within your organization or available from third parties, or that you create. The addition of such classes and libraries to ColdFusion is the subject of the next section, as part of the discussion of improvements in the methods for dynamically specifying and using such newly added libraries.

More About CFML and Java Integration

Since this chapter (and indeed this book) is meant to focus on what's new in ColdFusion 10, we'll not discuss any more fundamentals of CFML and Java integration.

For more information about how to integrate ColdFusion with Java, see the ColdFusion documentation, specifically the (often-missed) manual, *Developing ColdFusion 10 Applications*; in particular, see the section *Integrating J2EE and Java Elements in CFML Applications* in Chapter 15, *Using Web Elements and External Objects*.

That substantial documentation discusses such important topics as how to:

- Use Java objects, including core Java libraries, JEE APIs, and custom-written classes, whether plain-old Java objects (POJOs), JavaBeans, or Enterprise JavaBeans

- Initialize a Java class constructor when loading it, implicitly or using `init()`

- Perform Java and ColdFusion data-type conversions

- Resolve ambiguous data types with the CFML `javaCast` function

- Handle Java exceptions

- Access the Java servlet `pagecontext` (available on any CFML page) using the CFML `getPageContext()` function

- Run JSPs and servlets within ColdFusion

- Integrate CFML with ColdFusion with JSPs and servlets, including the capability to perform include and forward processing between such pages and share variables between them (in the application, session, and request scopes)

- Import and use JSP custom tag libraries

As you can see, the support in ColdFusion for Java integration is indeed substantial. You can also find a discussion of CFML and Java integration in the ColdFusion 9 Web Application Construction Kit, Volume 3, *Adobe ColdFusion 9 Advanced Application Development*, in Chapter 68, *Extending ColdFusion with Java*.

With that introduction as preface, let's now see what's different in ColdFusion 10 with regard to CFML and Java integration.

New: Dynamic Application-Specific Class Loading with `this.javaSettings`

As the previous section demonstrated, ColdFusion has long provided the capability to call Java objects from within CFML. In previous releases, if you wanted to provide a Java library (.jar) or class (.class) files to be loaded, you either had to place these in specific predefined locations or use the ColdFusion Administrator to define a new location, both of which required a server restart to make them take effect.

In ColdFusion 10, you can now provide the location of a Java library or class (or a directory containing them) as a setting within Application.cfc. This approach is more flexible—and more secure, because the classes can be loaded only by CFML within that specific application. You can also optionally configure this feature to watch for changes to the classes. Best of all, both these capabilities work without requiring a ColdFusion server restart (although there are some caveats, discussed later).

About Java Class Loading in ColdFusion

When `CFOBJECT` or `createobject` names a Java class to be loaded, ColdFusion has traditionally searched for the class in the following order:

1. Java archive (.jar) files in `[cf_web_root]/WEB-INF/lib`

2. Class (.class) files in `[cf_web_root]/WEB-INF/classes`

3. The class path specified on the JVM and Java Settings page in the ColdFusion Administrator

4. The default JVM class path

NOTE

In the locations listed here, `[cf_web_root]` refers to the built-in webroot directory within the given instance of ColdFusion in which your code is running. It doesn't matter whether your CFML code is located in some other directory or webroot, such as that of an external web server such as Apache or IIS. The `[cf_web_root]` directory referred to here is always located in the ColdFusion installation directory. For the default `cfusion` instance (the only instance you'll have if you're running ColdFusion 10 Standard), this location (in Microsoft Windows) would be C:\ColdFusion10\cfusion\wwwroot, and the `WEB-INF` instance referred to in options 1 and 2 in the list is within that directory. If you've defined other instances in ColdFusion 10 Enterprise, the location would be C:\ColdFusion10\[instancename]\wwwroot.

If you wanted to use a given Java .class or .jar file, if it did not already exist in ColdFusion or Java, you would need to add it to the appropriate locations listed here. And if you added a new directory location using options 3 or 4 in the list, you would also have to restart ColdFusion for that change to take effect.

Defining an Application-Specific Class Library

ColdFusion 10 adds a new way to name a location from which to load classes, and it takes precedence in the class-loading search order listed in the previous discussion. The feature is a new property in Application.cfc, called `javaSettings`. This property is a structure that can contain the following keys:

- `loadPaths`: An array of paths to the directories that contain Java classes or .jar files. You can also provide the path to a .jar file or a class. If the paths are not resolved, an error occurs when a page runs, accessing this Application.cfc file.

- `loadColdFusionClassPath`: A Boolean that indicates whether to load the classes from the ColdFusion lib directory. In other words, enable this setting if you need to access classes in the ColdFusion lib directory from within any classes that have been loaded from the `loadPaths` array. The default value is `false`.

- `reloadOnChange`: Indicates whether ColdFusion should watch the classes and JAR files in the named `loadPaths` property to reload any updates dynamically, without restarting ColdFusion. The default value is `false`.

- `watchInterval`: Specifies the time interval in seconds in which ColdFusion should watch for such changes if `reloadOnChange` is enabled. The default value is 60 seconds.

- `watchExtensions`: Specifies the extensions of the files to monitor for such changes. By default, only .class and .jar files are monitored.

We'll discuss each of these options, but let's first focus on the simplest example of this feature.

NOTE

There has long been an open-source project offering similar functionality for earlier releases of ColdFusion: JavaLoader, organized by Mark Mandel. For more information, see http://javaloader.riaforge.org/.

Example: Naming a Load Path

The javaSettings structure requires at least the LoadPaths key, which is itself an array of one or more paths, pointing to a .jar file or .class file, or a directory containing either of those files.

Following is an example of an Application.cfc file that sets this property, naming a single directory from which .jar files or classes can be loaded. (Yes, Application.cfc files can be written entirely in CFScript. If you prefer that approach, we'll assume that you know how to convert the example here to script-equivalent syntax.)

```
<cfcomponent>
<cfset this.name = "JavaDemo">
<cfset this.javaSettings = {LoadPaths = ["C:\ColdFusion10\cfusion\wwwroot\cfwack10\
➥ cf10"]}/>
</cfcomponent>
```

While many other settings can be, and are, typically set in the this scope in Application.cfc, here we are setting just this.name, which provides a name for the application.

NOTE
A new feature of ColdFusion 10 enables the ColdFusion Administrator to be configured to require an application name, although the default setting still is not to require one.

In this example, the javaSettings setting of the this scope is set using the implicit structure notation introduced in ColdFusion 8. The curly braces ({}) create a single key (loadPaths) within the javaSettings structure. And the loadPaths key itself should be an array, as is denoted by the square brackets ([]) surrounding its values.

To name multiple paths, you would list them separated by commas; an example is shown in the next subsection. And again, you can either name a directory as shown here, or you can name the path to a specific .jar or .class file. For reasons that will be discussed later, even though naming a directory is indeed most flexible, there may be benefits to naming a .jar or .class file specifically.

WARNING
If you specify a directory or file that does not exist, you will get an error upon the execution of any request that uses this Application.cfc file: "The directory or file [incorrect path] specified in LOADPATHS does not exist".

When you add javaSettings to an application, the settings take effect immediately at the next request that uses this Application.cfc file: no restart of ColdFusion is required to use the classes found in this library path.

WARNING
Note that we said specifically that when "you add javaSettings to an application, the settings take effect immediately." If instead you modify the settings, those changes may not take effect immediately. See the section "Challenges Using Dynamic Class Loading" later in this chapter for more information.

The next section demonstrates the actual use of this feature. Subsequent sections discuss that the benefits this feature provides as well as additional capabilities of this.javaSettings that can help you make changes to classes after they are loaded, dynamically reloading the classes, if you want. The last section discusses some challenges you might experience using the dynamic class-loading feature.

Example: Using a Better Reverse-DNS Java Library

Previously we observed that the built-in Java `InetAddress` library was sometimes slow or inaccurate in performing a reverse-DNS lookup. Fortunately, there is a free third-party library, dnsJava, from Brian Wellington (http://www.dnsjava.org/), which addresses some of these shortcomings.

We will see here how you can use this new dynamic class-loading function. To use the library, simply download the latest .jar file provided, using the download link at the dnsjava.org site. As of this writing, the latest release of the dnsJava library is Version 2.1.3, which is also included in this book's sample code directory.

Prior to ColdFusion 10, you had to decide where (among those four locations listed at the beginning of this section) to place such downloaded Java classes and libraries.

With ColdFusion 10, you can still do that (which again requires a restart), or you can use the new `this.loadPaths` setting to just name a location where you have placed the .jar file. That location can be anywhere on the server, either within the web application directory or not. (An argument could be made that, for security reasons, the class should not be stored in a web-accessible directory.)

Adding Multiple Load Paths

For demonstration purposes, we'll assume that the .jar file is saved in the C:\ColdFusion10\ cfusion\wwwroot\cfwack10\cf10\dnsjava directory. We then add that directory to the previously set `LoadPaths` key. (Note the commas that separate the quoted strings declaring this array of two elements for `LoadPaths`):

```
<cfset this.javaSettings = {LoadPaths = ["C:\ColdFusion10\cfusion\wwwroot\cfwack10\
➥cf10","C:\ColdFusion10\cfusion\wwwroot\cfwack10\cf10\dnsjava"]}>
```

(We could also have named the .jar file specifically, rather than the directory in which it was placed. While on the surface it would seem better to name the directory, to be able to load any and all .jar files and classes within that directory, we'll discuss later situations in which you may want to name a file instead, in the section that discusses potential challenges.)

Calling the New Library

With this configuration code in place, we can load the .jar file's classes from any CFML page within the application under this Application.cfc file, as will be shown in a moment.

To call the library, we need to be aware that the dnsJava library's package name is `org.xbill.DNS`, and it contains a class named `Address`, which has methods to obtain the hostname for a given address, as shown in Listing 10.4.

Listing 10.4   `04-reversedns-bad-demo.cfm`
```
<cfobject type="java" class="org.xbill.DNS.Address" name="addr">
<cfoutput>#addr.getHostName(addr.getByAddress("192.150.16.117"))#</cfoutput>
```

The result is the reverse-DNS lookup of that address, which as of this writing returns www.wip4. adobe.com, and unlike the built-in Java library shown previously, this method runs quickly.

Benefits of Dynamic Class Loading

Besides not needing to restart ColdFusion when you add the javaSettings feature to an application, we gain several additional benefits from the new dynamic application-specific class-loading feature.

First, because the library path location is defined within Application.cfc, this specification is defined on a per-application basis. Per-application definition can be regarded as a security benefit. Prior to CF10, any CFML page could access any Java class that may have been added to ColdFusion (using the other approaches in the list at the beginning of this section), because all pages shared the same class-loading search order. With the new dynamic class-loading feature, a given library will be available only to CFML pages within a given ColdFusion application.

> **TIP**
>
> Of course, the converse is also true. If you really do want to share a Java class or library among all applications in the ColdFusion instance, the wiser approach is to place it in one of those shared locations rather than to define the location with the javaSettings property in each application.

Second, those running their ColdFusion code in a shared hosting environment will not likely be able to make modifications to those other class-path locations discussed earlier, and a hosting provider may not agree to place a Java class or library in the shared locations. With ColdFusion 10, even those with shared hosting providers can now use class libraries of their own choice.

> **WARNING**
>
> While there's not currently any way for a hosting provider to prevent you from using the this.loadPaths feature, a hosting provider, or anyone responsible for administering your ColdFusion server can entirely disable the capability to call Java objects. This is a security feature that can be controlled in the ColdFusion Administrator, under Security> Sandbox Security (or Resource Security in ColdFusion Standard).

Reloading Changed Classes: reloadOnChange, watchInterval, and watchExtensions Arguments

The new dynamic class-loading feature in ColdFusion 10 also supports the capability to indicate whether changes made to classes or .jar files in the named location should be detected, so that they are reloaded when requested. The reloadOnChange key of this.javaSettings is a Boolean that, if set to true, tells ColdFusion to watch the classes (.class or .jar files) in the named locations. (The default is false.)

The following example shows the javaSettings property changed to watch for updated classes:

```
<cfset this.javaSettings = {LoadPaths = ["C:\ColdFusion10\cfusion\wwwroot\cfwack10\
➡cf10"],reloadOnChange=true}/>
```

Note that this key is added as a second key, separated from the LoadPaths key by a comma.

WARNING

> Beware: ColdFusion does note validate these key names in **this.javaSettings**, so if you misname this setting **reloadOnChanges** (plural), for instance, ColdFusion will not generate an error. The expected behavior will not be implemented. Worse, any keys after it (such as **watchInterval**) will be ignored.

The default watchInterval (in seconds) at which ColdFusion watches for changes is 60 seconds. If you want to change this interval, add that value as another key. The following sets the watch interval to 5 minutes:

```
<cfset this.javaSettings = {LoadPaths = ["C:\ColdFusion10\cfusion\wwwroot\cfwack10\
➥cf10"],reloadOnChange=true,watchInterval=300}/>
```

The default behavior is for ColdFusion to watch for changes to files with .class or .jar extensions. If you want to add another extension, specify that as yet another key, with the extensions offered as a list (not an array), as shown here:

```
<cfset this.javaSettings = {LoadPaths = ["C:\ColdFusion10\cfusion\wwwroot\cfwack10\
cf10"],reloadOnChange=true,watchInterval=300, watchExtensions = "jar,class,xml"}/>
```

Challenges Using Dynamic Class Loading

You may experience challenges when using the new dynamic class-loading feature to make changes to the loadPaths setting. These challenges may lead you to question the dynamic nature of the function, but after you understand the problem, you may find the behavior acceptable.

The main challenge is that after the application (the one defined by the Application.cfc file in question) is loaded, some changes that you make to this LoadPaths setting will *not* take effect immediately, such as these:

- Adding a new directory or changing an existing one already listed

- Adding a new .jar file to a directory, regardless of whether its directory is already listed or is newly added (note that a new .class file added to such a directory will indeed be immediately picked up when a request that tries to load it)

- Adding a new path to a .jar file

NOTE

> Don't misunderstand this challenge. As we saw in the previous section, there is indeed provision for the new dynamic class-loading mechanism to pick up changes to classes or .jar files after they are loaded. This section instead refers to changes made to the **loadPaths** value itself, or the addition of a new .jar file to a directory named there, after an application is loaded.

For instance, consider a case in which you have initially configured the loadPaths setting and have run a page that has therefore loaded the application (so that the application is initialized).

If you then change the loadPaths setting to name a new directory or change an existing one, using a directory name that does not exist, you will *not* get an error, at least not on execution of the line that makes the setting (as you normally would if you named an erroneous location, as discussed earlier). Instead, you will get an error when trying to load the class that cannot be found (via CFOBJECT or createObject).

On the other hand, if you add a new directory to `loadPaths` that does in fact exist (after the application is initialized), you *will* get an error in trying to load the class itself, even though you would think that ColdFusion should pick up the change.

Similarly, if you add a new .jar file to a directory named in `loadPaths`, or if you add a new path to a .jar file, after the application is initialized, classes within such .jar files cannot be loaded immediately.

Again, in these cases, you are making changes that you would reasonably think should get picked up by an application-specific dynamic class-loading feature. But in these cases, where you have already initialized the application, such changes will not be detected.

Reason for Challenges

Here's why: Adobe has with this feature implemented an application-specific class loader, which is created on instantiation of the Application.cfc file. Adobe did not want to create a new class loader on every request.

To solve this "problem," you need to reinitialize the application (cause a new application to be loaded, as discussed in the next section), or if you are adding a new .jar file, you can name the path to the .jar file itself, as discussed in a subsequent section.

Solutions to Challenges

If you do need to make changes to the `loadPaths` value or add a new .jar file after the application has been initialized, you have at least three ways to effectively reinitialize the application:

- Use the `applicationstop` function. You can call this CFML function, introduced in ColdFusion 9, which effectively resets the application. The next request to that application will reinitialize it.

- Change the application name. You can change the value in `this.name` (in the Application.cfc file) to a new value, which will create a new application (assuming that there is not an application of that name already defined in the ColdFusion instance). Just be aware that you will lose access to previously set variables in the application scope (for the previously named application) and session variables (because they are connected to the application name).

- You can restart ColdFusion, which of course will reinitialize all applications running in the instance.

After any of these actions, the next request made to the application will pick up any change you made to `loadPaths`, and the application will be able to load classes from any newly added .jar files.

Challenges Adding a New .jar or .class File to `loadPaths`

As mentioned earlier, the challenge described in this section occurs when you try to add a new or changed directory location in the `loadPaths` setting or add a new .jar file to such a directory after the application is initialized.

There is a way to avoid the problem entirely: Instead of naming a directory in loadPaths where the .jar file can be found, provide in loadPaths the complete specific path and name of a .jar file. This change would be detected on the next request to the application, without requiring reinitialization. (Again, .class files can be added to a named directory even after application initialization, and they will be loaded immediately without a restart.)

Also see "Reloading Changed Classes" earlier in this chapter for a discussion of the separate but related feature allowing ColdFusion to detect changes to classes or .jar files after they have been loaded or their locations have been indicated during initialization of the application.

Unexpected Class (or Unexpected Version) Loaded

Here's one more potential challenge, and it's somewhat related to those discussed already. Sometimes you may load a class and get a version that you did not expect (perhaps an older version), or calls to methods that you know exist may fail. How can this happen?

The explanation may lie in the fact that, as discussed in the introduction to this section, there are several other locations from which ColdFusion may load a class. If there is a similar class (in a similar package) in another .class or .jar file elsewhere, ColdFusion may be loading that class.

You may ask, how can that be if this new loadPaths location is supposed to take precedence over the others? However, as discussed earlier, even though you may have named a new class-loading location, if ColdFusion does not process the change to the loadPaths location, then it can't take precedence. Try one of the techniques offered earlier to reinitialize the application and see if now the correct class is loaded.

Similarly, you may be experimenting with different values for loadPaths and remove the path to find some given class. If you then reinitialize the application and find that the class is still loaded, again it may be being loaded from one of these other locations.

Enhancement: Calling CFCs from Java with CFCProxy

Java developers or organizations with an investment in Java program may want to integrate with ColdFusion objects, which are defined as ColdFusion components (CFCs).

The capability to invoke CFCs from Java was added in ColdFusion 7.0.1. In ColdFusion 10, this CFCProxy class has been enhanced with a new optional constructor argument called directinvoke.

Rather than exploring only the new argument, we'll briefly discuss CFCProxy, since it hasn't been (and still is not) well documented in the ColdFusion manuals.

In the example that will be presented, we will define a Java program that will invoke a CFC. We will then define a CFML page that will invoke that Java program.

NOTE

This capability to call CFCs from within Java is limited to Java classes that are loaded by the ColdFusion class loader, such as ones loaded using CFOBJECT or createObject (as discussed previously in this chapter).

Sharp readers may wonder why we would have a CFML page call a Java program only to have that Java program call a CFC. Of course, the CFML program could just call the CFC directly. But consider that a more elaborate Java program (such as one already existing in your environment) might benefit from being able to call a CFC, such as to access an elaborate CFC you may have, bringing important new functionality through this sort of integration.

About the Long-Existent and Little-Known `CFCProxy`

The `CFCProxy` Java class has been provided since ColdFusion 7.0.1, allowing us to call a CFC and invoke a method. The only documentation that ever existed was this: http://www.forta.com/misc/cfcproxy.htm. The information provided there still applies in ColdFusion 10, though it does not mention the new optional constructor argument, which is introduced here.

NOTE

The information at that site is presented in a Javadoc style, simply listing the Java constructors and methods. It assumes that the reader will know how to use that information in creating a Java program. Similarly, the following information must necessarily be brief and assumes that the reader understands the basics of Java application development.

The `CFCProxy` Constructor

The `CFCProxy` class now offers four constructors, listed in Table 10.1.

As depicted in Table 10.1, the first and only required constructor argument is a string naming the path to the CFC to be called. This must be a fully qualified path, including the filename and extension.

NOTE

If this path is being provided directly in the Java program, it must be in Java pathing format, so if the CFC to be called were in a Microsoft Windows directory of C:\ColdFusion10\cfusion\wwwroot\cfwack10\cf10\03b-called.cfc, the format of the path should be specified as either C:/ColdFusion10/cfusion/wwwroot/cfwack10cf10/03b-called.cfc or C:\\ColdFusion10\\cfusion\\ wwwroot\\cfwack10\\cf10\\03b-called.cfc. If instead the path is passed into the Java program, Java will correctly handle a normal Microsoft Windows path.

Table 10.1 CFCProxy Constructors

CONSTRUCTOR	ARGUMENT DESCRIPTION
`CFCProxy(str)`	String `str`: Fully qualified path of the CFC file
`CFCProxy(str directInvoke)`	String `str`: Fully qualified path of the CFC file Boolean `directInvoke`: If true, request does not go through the ColdFusion Filter chain
`CFCProxy(str initThis)`	String `str`: Fully qualified path of the CFC file Map `initThis`: Name-value pairs to initialize the `This` scope of the CFC
`CFCProxy(str initThis directinvoke)`	String `str`: Fully qualified path of the CFC file Map `initThis`: Name-value pairs to initialize the `This` scope of the CFC Boolean directInvoke: If true, request does not go through the ColdFusion Filter chain

So, for instance, here is one variant of CFCProxy instantiation with the simplest constructor:

```
CFCProxy myCFC = new CFCProxy("C:\\ColdFusion10\\cfusion\\wwwroot\\cfwack10\\cf10\\
➥03b-called.cfc");
```

(This code would typically be specified all on one line in a Java program, but it also works if it's split across multiple lines, as here, given the page width limitation.)

Now you would be able to invoke the methods in the named CFC. We'll discuss how to do that next and then look at a complete example of a Java program that instantiates a CFC and invokes a method within it.

The CFCProxy invoke Method

After you have an instance of a proxy to the CFC, you can invoke a method within that CFC by using a method provided in the CFCProxy class named, appropriately, invoke.

This invoke method in the CFCProxy class takes two arguments at minimum:

- String; specifies the name of the method to be invoked in the CFC.

- Object; specifies any arguments to be passed to the CFC method (this argument is required, even if there are no arguments to be passed in).

So, for instance, one variant of the invocation of CFCProxy with the simplest constructor (continuing on from the previous line instantiating the proxy to the CFC as myCFC) is:

```
myCFC.invoke("myFunction1", new Object[] { });
```

This line invokes a method in the CFC named myFunction1 and passes in no arguments. (Again, even if you have no arguments, you need to specify an empty object.)

NOTE

There are a few other forms of the invoke method available in the CFCProxy class (it's loaded with different arguments for various specialized uses). See the documentation at http://www.forta.com/misc/cfcproxy.htm for more information about these other forms of the invoke method as well some other potentially interesting methods available in the CFCProxy class.

Importing the CFCProxy Class

We're almost ready to write the complete Java program, but before we can create an instance of CFCProxy, we need to tell Java where to find the CFCProxy class. The class is available in a package, bundled with ColdFusion, called coldfusion.cfc.

So before we can use the class, we need to import it, with this line:

```
import coldfusion.cfc.CFCProxy;
```

With these fundamentals understood, we can now examine a complete Java program that will tie everything all together. We will create a Java program called MyCFCInvoker_03a.java, shown in Listing 10.5.

Listing 10.5 `MyCFCInvoker_03a.java`

```
import coldfusion.cfc.CFCProxy;
public class MyCFCInvoker_03a {
  public String myInvoke() throws Throwable {
    CFCProxy myCFC = new CFCProxy("C:\\ColdFusion10\\cfusion\\wwwroot\\cfwack10\\
    ➥cf10\\03b-called.cfc");
    return (String)myCFC.invoke("myFunction1", new Object[] { });
  }
}
```

This chapter cannot elaborate on all the details of writing a Java program, but note that the file-name should be the same as the name given for `public class`. Also, we have defined a method within it called `myInvoke`, which we will use shortly, to call this Java program from within ColdFusion.

We will take whatever response we get from the `myFunction1` CFC method (expected here to be a string result), and that result will be returned to the caller (which again will be a CFML program calling this Java program).

NOTE

This simplified example may seem (and indeed is) contrived. It's not a practical example but a greatly simplified version that provides an easy demonstration. There would normally be no reason to have a CFML program invoke a Java program that just then invokes a CFC method, when the CFML program could just invoke the CFC directly.

Note also that Adobe has defined the `CFCProxy` class's `invoke` method to throw exceptions if there are any errors, so you must declare the Java method that performs that call to throw such an exception (a "throwable exception"). Then the ColdFusion program that calls the Java program can handle the error using try-and-catch handling (`CFTRY` and `CFCATCH`, or `try` and `catch` in CFScript).

Compiling the Java Program

Now that we have a Java program that can call a CFC (we will see the CFC soon), we need to compile the program. To compile Java programs, you must have downloaded and installed the Java Developer Kit (JDK), which includes the javac.exe file. (We will refer to Microsoft Windows file-names and paths, leaving those using Linux, Unix, and Mac OS X to translate things accordingly.)

Again, the discussion of how to choose, obtain, install, configure, and run the JDK (including how to compile Java programs, whether at the command line or in a Java IDE) is beyond the scope of this chapter.

NOTE

It's also impractical here to provide compiled Java classes with the examples. The Java compiler creates different results for different operating systems, different JVMs, different versions, and so on. You will need to be able to compile these examples on your own if you want to run them. Fortunately, it's not too difficult.

Let's assume that we have the JDK installed at C:\Program Files\Java\jdk1.6.0_25\bin\, and that we have saved the Java program shown in Listing 10.5 in C:\ColdFusion10\cfusion\wwwroot\ cfwack10\cf10. You can issue the following commands at the Microsoft Windows command line to compile the Java program:

```
cd C:\ColdFusion10\cfusion\wwwroot\cfwack10\cf10
"C:\Program Files\Java\jdk1.6.0_25\bin\javac" javac MyCFCInvoker_03a.java
➡ -cp c:\ColdFusion10\cfusion\lib\cfusion.jar
```

That's just two lines: a cd command and a javac command.

Notice the javac command's -cp argument. That's required so that during the compilation, the CFCProxy class can be located. Although we discussed earlier that it's in a package called coldfusion.cfc, the actual class is in the cfusion.jar file, which is located in c:\ColdFusion10\ cfusion\lib\.

Assuming that there are no errors in compiling the Java program, you will end up with a MyCFCInvoker_03a.class file.

Recall from earlier in the chapter that a Java program that wants to call a CFC in this way needs to import that class, and the compilation will need to include that .jar file in its class path.

Defining the CFC to Be Called

Continuing our greatly simplified example, Listing 10.6 shows the 03b-called.cfc file that our Java program is calling. Recall that the Java program invoked a method in the CFC called myFunction1, which returns a string.

Listing 10.6 03b-called.cfc

```
<cfcomponent>
<cffunction name="myFunction1" returntype="string">
  <cfreturn "Hello stranger" />
</cffunction>
</cfcomponent>
```

So when the Java program invokes this CFC method, it will receive in reply the string "Hello Stranger".

Many readers might want to point out that since ColdFusion 9, it's been possible to define a CFC that is all CFScript. It can be interesting to see how closely CFML can resemble Java (and other scripting languages) when written as CFScript. In fact, in creating script-based components, you don't even need the CFScript tag or the CFCOMPONENT tag. Instead, the 03b-called.cfc file can be written simply like this:

```
component {
  function myFunction1 () {
  return "Hello stranger";
  }
}
```

Variations in Accepting Arguments

Of course, it would be more interesting to have a function that accepted arguments and returned its result based on that incoming data, and in fact if you look at the code in 03b-called.cfc, you will see that such a variation is offered as myFunction2.

Further, if you look at the code in MyCFCInvoker_03a.java (provided in the listings for the book), you will see that such a variation of a Java method also exists. There's an important difference between Java and CFML worth noting: in the Java code, the alternative method has the same name as the original one, myInvoke. Java lets you have different methods with the same name but that have arguments that are different (in type or number), an approach called method overloading. CFML does not allow two methods of the same name, even with different arguments (it does not allow method overloading).

A third variation also exists, which accepts both a name and a string holding the path to the CFC to be executed, which then has the CFCProxy access that named CFC.

You can see variations showing how to call these three methods from CFML in 03c-call_mycfcinvoker_via_java.cfm.

CFML Page That Calls the Java Program

The last program in our trio is the CFML page that will call the Java code we have created (which calls the CFC). Listing 10.7 presents is a CFScript-based variation of such a program.

Listing 10.7 `03c-call_mycfcinvoker_via_java.cfm`

```
<cfscript>
writeOutput(createObject("java","MyCFCInvoker_03a").myInvoke());
</cfscript>
```

Notice that this rather tersely implemented version does three things on one line of code. In the middle, it uses createObject (as we saw earlier in the chapter) to create an instance of the Java program (class) we created, MyCFCInvoker_03a. Chained to that is the invocation of the myInvoke method, which was defined in the Java class.

That method had the code that created CFCproxy and then called the method in our CFC, myFunction1. That returns the "Hello Stranger" string as a result of the invoke code used in the Java method, and that Java method was set to simply return whatever string it was given.

So finally, at the opening of the single CFScript-based line of code here, it uses the writeoutput CFML function to display that string, so that this program displays the "Hello stranger" result. And the circle is complete.

There are some other variants for calling the CFCInvoker code in CFML, commented in the listings for the book for 03c-call_mycfcinvoker_via_java.cfm.

Caveats

You must be sure to follow a few guidelines—ensuring proper filenames, file locations, CFML, and Java code and javaSettings specifications in the Application.cfc file—to avoid tripping up when calling createObject in the CFML program.

In fact, speaking of javaSettings, in some situations this.javaSettings in the Application.cfc file must have the loadColdFusionClassPath=true option enabled, which was discussed earlier in this chapter.

If you change the provided MyInvoker.java program or create your own programs, consider the reloadOnChange and watchInterval keys of this.javaSettings, which control whether ColdFusion watches to pick up changes as you recompile the Java program (of course, that's assuming that you save the compiled file in a directory named in the LoadPaths key).

Also, sometimes when things aren't working as you expect, you may want to run a page that just calls the CFC via CFML (as you may traditionally call a CFC), just as a sanity check to confirm whether any problems are really related to the Java code. See 03d-run_called_cfc_via_cfml.cfm.

Also consider traditional CFML code troubleshooting tools such as CFDUMP and CFLOG, as well as Java logging (System.out.println("somestring");), which displays a log line from Java in ColdFusion 10's coldfusion-out.log.

About the New directInvoke Argument

Now, with all that discussion of CFCProxy as preface, the actual new feature for ColdFusion 10 is the new optional constructor argument for CFCProxy that describes an aspect of the way it should create an instance of the CFC that will be invoked from Java.

We saw earlier that this new optional constructor argument is directinvoke, a Boolean which, if true, indicates that the instantiation of the CFC should *not* go through the normal ColdFusion request filter chain, resulting in somewhat improved performance in certain circumstances.

The following example shows how we can change the line shown earlier creating CFCProxy to use this second argument:

```
CFCProxy myCFC = new CFCProxy("C:\\ColdFusion10\\cfusion\\wwwroot\\cfwack10\\cf10\\
➥ 03b-called.cfc",true);
```

However, if the page being called is fast, and if you're not calling many CFCs in one request, you may not see any real difference in performance.

New: Proxying CFCs as Java Objects with createDynamicProxy

The previous section discussed how to access a ColdFusion Component from within a Java class. This next enhancement in ColdFusion 10 allows a CFC to be passed to a Java program or class.

ColdFusion 10 provides a new CFML function, createDynamicProxy, which creates a dynamic proxy of the CFC that is passed to the Java class. The Java class can then work with the ColdFusion component as if it were itself a native Java object, invoking functions within the CFC directly, without having to use CFCProxy.

Another way to look at this is that with CFCProxy, you're configuring a Java class to explicitly call and work with a CFC, whereas with createDynamicProxy you're allowing a Java class to more implicitly work with a CFC that is passed to it. This function also uses the idea of a Java interface. The approach to use for a given need simply depends on your preference.

With CFCProxy, three programs are involved (a CFC, a Java class that calls the CFC, and a CFML page that calls the Java class).

With createDynamicProxy, four programs are involved: a Java interface, a CFC template that offers implementation of the methods in that interface, a Java class that receives that CFC and works with it as if it's a Java object, and a CFML page to create an instance of that Java class and pass the CFC to it. It's in this final CFML page that we will see the use of createDynamicProxy.

The steps shown here present a very simple "hello world"-type example of how to proxy a CFC to a Java class.

Step 1: Define an Interface

First, we must define a Java interface: a Java program with one or more abstract methods (methods without any implementation code). Our example will ultimately have a single method in our CFC, called sayHello, which will return a string, so we will first define a Java interface doing just that, named MyInterface_04a.java (Listing 10.8).

Listing 10.8 MyInterface_04a.java

```
public interface MyInterface_04a
  {
      public String sayHello();
  }
```

We don't even need to compile this code, because when we refer to it within the later Java class and compile that, the interface will also be compiled if it has not been compiled already.

NOTE

You may wonder why the filename proposed is not 04a-MyInterface.java., as we've been naming files with an incrementing number as a prefix. The problem is that a Java class name must start with a character, and the file in which a Java class is defined must have the same name. Similarly, dashes in class names are not allowed: thus, we use the name MyInterface_04a.java.

Step 2: Create a CFC That Offers an Implementation

Second, we must create a CFC template that implements one or more methods in the defined interface (Listing 10.9).

Listing 10.9   `04b_HelloWorld.cfc`

```
<cfcomponent>
  <cffunction name="sayHello" returntype="string">
    <cfreturn "Hello World! (from inside sayHello method of 04b_HelloWorld.cfc)">
  </cffunction>
</cfcomponent>
```

Again, this is a simple example, offering just one method that implements the one defined in the interface we created earlier, and returning a string to its caller (which will be the Java class defined next). Note that a string has been inserted here to clarify where the result is coming from, just to help you see what's happening when you finally run the code. (Readers who prefer script-based CFCs can convert this code as desired; the tag-based approach is shown here for those who prefer that.)

Note that the method name provided here must be the same as that defined in the interface.

Step 3: Create a Java Class to Work with the CFC

Next, we need to create a Java program and class that will reference the interface as well as be passed the CFC, to work with it as if it's a Java object. Note again the numeric suffix at the end. Also notice that we are referencing our interface by its name in defining a field called `myInterface`, known only to this program (Listing 10.10).

Listing 10.10   `InvokeHelloProxy_04c.java`

```
public class InvokeHelloProxy_04c
{
  private MyInterface_04a myInterface;
  public InvokeHelloProxy_04c (MyInterface_04a myProxy)
  {
    this.myInterface = myProxy;
  }
  public String invokeHello()
  {
    return myInterface.sayHello();
  }
}
```

We are also defining an inner class, having again the same name as the file and class defined in the first line. This inner class will define a constructor argument to receive a proxy (which will be our CFC) that will implement the interface. We'll see our next and last program, the CFML page, creating an instance of this `InvokeHelloProxy_04c` class and passing in a proxied CFC.

It may help to explain now that our CFML program will then call on this Java object's `invokehello` method, which will itself call on the interface's `sayHello` method, which will in turn actually execute the method of that same name (`sayHello`) in the CFC. The point is that this `invokeHello` method could do anything, but it's calling on a CFC method to do what it does. The Java program doesn't refer to the CFC directly (unlike when we use `CFCProxy`), and the CFML page that calls this page won't know how the page has implemented this `invokeHello` method.

To use this class, we need to compile this program. Here's how we might do so from the command line in Microsoft Windows:

```
cd C:\ColdFusion10\cfusion\wwwroot\cfwack10\cf10
"C:\Program Files\Java\jdk1.6.0_25\bin\javac" InvokeHelloProxy_04c.java
```

(While we show here compilation using the Java 1.6 JDK, there's nothing about this program or this feature that requires any specific version of Java.)

Keep in mind when compiling this program that whether ColdFusion picks up the change depends on `this.Javasettings`, especially the `watchInterval` argument that controls the length of time that ColdFusion watches to detect a changed class. These examples use the same `loadPaths` setting created earlier in the chapter, which is defined to point to the directory in which all this code is being created.

Step 4: Create a CFML Page to Pass the CFC to the Java Class

The fourth and final step is to create a CFML page that creates an instance of the Java class and passes the CFC to it for processing. Again, as mentioned earlier, it will create an instance of the Java class we just created, but in doing so it will pass in the proxied CFC, created using the new `createDynamicProxy`. Listing 10.11 shows a tag-based variant of the program.

Listing 10.11 `04d-call_createdynamicproxy.cfm`

```
<cfset dynInstnace = createDynamicProxy("04b_HelloWorld", ["MyInterface_04a"])>
<cfset x = createObject("java","InvokeHelloProxy_04c").init(dynInstnace)>
<cfset y = x.invokeHello()>
<cfoutput>#y#</cfoutput>
```

First, this program creates a variable to hold the dynamic proxy, which maps the CFC (the second file we created) to the interface (the first file we created). (Technically, the second argument could be an array of multiple interfaces, if needed for the application.)

Then the template instantiates the Java class (the third file we created) using `createeObject` with the `init` keyword, which (you may recall from earlier in the chapter) causes ColdFusion to invoke the class's constructor (in this case, the one we saw in the third program). The variable holding the dynamic proxy is what's passed to that `init` keyword.

This CFML program then can invoke methods within that Java class (in the third program), and in this case it outputs the result, which is the message we saw defined in the CFC. (If you are now wondering why you might want to bother with all this CFML and Java integration, we'll discuss that in the next section.)

Before leaving this example, note that we can not only convert the CFML shown here to CFScript, but we can even compress it all into one line of script code. It may not always make sense to do this (for example, you may want to call multiple methods on the object or save some other aspect of the processing for reuse).

But just to show that this conversion is possible, here's the same functionality as 04d-call_ createdynamicproxy.cfm in just one line, chaining `createbject:` (with the nested `init`) with the method invocation:

```
<cfscript>
writeOutput(createObject("java","InvokeHelloProxy_04c").init(createDynamicProxy
➡ ("04b_HelloWorld", ["MyInterface_04a"])).invokeHello());
</cfscript>
```

Still other examples are offered as comments in the version of 04d-call_createdynamicproxy.cfm offered in the book's code listings.

Why Use These New Proxy Features?

As discussed in the earlier section on `CFCProxy`, it may seem extreme overkill to use these new features simply as new ways to invoke CFC methods from CFML. But that's not really the point at all.

The point is that, in the case of `CFCProxy`, the Java program (for whatever reason) wants to call a CFC and use its capabilities. We just happened to use a CFML program to then invoke that Java program.

And here with `createDynamicProxy`, the Java program being executed can do many things (which is why we want to invoke it), but one of the things it does may be something that can be implemented in CFML (in the CFC) for reasons that help improve the Java program. Although here we are simply passing the result of that back to our CFML program, in a real-world implementation, the benefits of calling a CFC from Java would inspire the use of this approach.

Consider, for instance, that ColdFusion 9 exposed many new features of ColdFusion as services, so a Java program might call upon ColdFusion to perform image manipulation, PDF generation, or mail processing. And if the things that the Java program does are valuable to your CFML, you can call upon Java, and so on. Total CFML-Java integration is at your disposal.

New: Looping over Java Arrays in CFML

The fourth and final enhancement to CFML and Java integration in ColdFusion 10 is the new capability to loop over Java arrays in CFML in tags and in CFScript.

Various Java methods return Java arrays. One example is the capability to get the cookies for the currently executing request, which can be obtained by using the CFML `getPageContext` function. This function returns the underlying Java Servlet context for the CFML page (recall that ColdFusion technically runs your CFML atop Tomcat, which is a Java Servlet engine, just as ColdFusion ran atop JRun in prior ColdFusion releases).

The servlet context is itself a Java object that has a getRequest method, and that returns an object that has a getCookies method. The result of a call to getCookies is an array of cookies for the current request. The cookies in each array element are in fact also objects that have various methods for obtaining information such as the cookie's name and value.

The data in this cookie array can be displayed by the CFML shown in Listing 10.12, which loops over that returned cookie array and for each cookie calls its getName and getValue methods.

Listing 10.12   05-java-arrray-loop.cfm

```
<cfscript>
cookiearray = getpagecontext().getrequest().getcookies();
for (acookie in cookiearray) {
    WriteOutput(acookie.getname() & '=' & acookie.getvalue() & '<br>');
}
Writedump(cookiearray);
</cfscript>
```

The writeDump specification at the bottom of the code will dump all the cookies in the array, showing their name and value as well the other available methods and fields for each cookie (writeDump is the script equivalent of CFDUMP and generates the same result as a CFDUMP).

Conclusion

This chapter has discussed a few new capabilities for ColdFusion and Java integration in ColdFusion 10, along with explanations about why to consider them and challenges you might encounter and their solutions.

For more information about ColdFusion and Java integration in general, see the documentation and other references mentioned earlier in the section "More About CFML and Java Integration."

XML Enhancements

Venerable old XML is not quite the popular data format nowadays. Most of the services you use on the Internet use JSON instead. In general, JSON is lighter and therefore more efficient for Ajax applications. But there are still many services out there using XML, and there are still some features that XML offers that are significantly more powerful than those provided by JSON. Two of these features are XPath and XSLT Transforms, and both features are greatly enhanced in ColdFusion 10.

ColdFusion XML and XPath

One of the most compelling tasks for which XML outshines JSON is filtering, or searching, against data. For many years, a technology known as XPath (http://www.w3.org/TR/xpath/) has provided a basic selector-style interface for searching XML data. ColdFusion has supported XPath 1.0 for some time, but ColdFusion 10 now supports Version 2.0 (http://www.w3.org/TR/xpath20/). A discussion of all the changes from XPath Version 1 to Version 2 is beyond the scope of this book; instead, we will focus on some of the interesting things you can do with the enhanced XPath 2.0 support. First, let's quickly review a simple example of XPath.

Here is some sample XML data:

```
<?xml version="1.0" encoding="ISO-8859-1"?>
<bookstore>
<book>
<title lang="eng">Harry Potter</title>
<price>29.99</price>
<pages>200</pages>
<released>2001-01-01</released>
</book>
<book>
<title lang="eng">Learning XML</title>
<price>39.95</price>
<pages>100</pages>
```

```
<released>2003-01-01</released>
</book>
<book>
<title lang="eng">Learning JSON</title>
<price>49.95</price>
<pages>22</pages>
<released>2003-01-01</released>
</book>
<cd>
<title lang="eng">The Downward Spiral</title>
<price>39.95</price>
<released>2009-01-01</released>
</cd>
</bookstore>
```

In this XML packet, three books and one CD are defined. Each product contains a title, price, and released value. The books contain a number of pages. Listing 11.1 shows a simple XPath example that can search for books or CDs separately.

Listing 11.1 /cfwack10/11/test1.cfm

```
<cfxml variable="xmldoc">
(See XML already displayed.)
 </cfxml>

<cfset books = xmlSearch(xmlDoc,"/bookstore/book")>
<cfdump var="#books#" label="Books">

<cfset cds = xmlSearch(xmlDoc,"/bookstore/cd")>
<cfdump var="#cds#" label="CDs">
```

To save space, we haven't repeated the XML code in the listing, but you can see that it is wrapped in a <cfxml> tag pair. This tag pair turns the XML string into a native ColdFusion XML object. Once we have done that, we can use xmlSearch to perform XPath searches against it. The first example requests all XML nodes that match /bookstore/book. The second example is similar except that it looks for cd nodes instead. The end result is two arrays. The Books array will contain all the book-related data, and the CDs array will contain those products. Figure 11.1 shows what these XML nodes look like.

To be clear, the same capability could be accomplished manually by looping over the data and checking each node for a match. XPath makes the process simpler, though, and more powerful. The one XPath statement does all the searching and looping that we need and provides a simple array of results.

Along with basic node matching, you can apply a bit of conditional logic. For example, to get all the products that have a price value of 35 and higher, you could use the following:

```
<cfset specificCost = xmlSearch(xmlDoc,"/bookstore/*[price>35.00]/")>
<cfdump var="#specificCost#" label="Products with pricers higher than 35.">
```

Figure 11.1

XML nodes returned from a sample XML search.

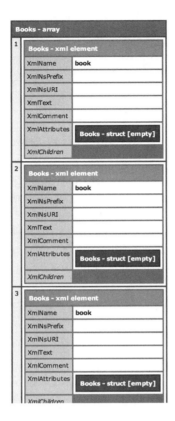

The power of XPath 2.0 can mainly be found in its much richer function syntax. XPath 1.0 had some functions, but XPath 2.0 greatly expands this feature list to provide for many more. Listing 11.2 provides a simple example.

Listing 11.2   /cfwack10/11/test2.cfm

```
<cfset avg = xmlSearch(xmlDoc,"avg(/bookstore/*/price)")>
<cfoutput>The average price is #dollarFormat(avg)#.</cfoutput>
```

NOTE

Many of our examples will be reusing the same XML packet, so to save space, we won't be reshowing this packet in the code samples.

This example uses a new XPath 2.0 function: avg. If passed an XPath selector that returns numerical data, this function will return the average of the values.

Unlike our first example, this example returns one precise value. We can then pass that value to the ColdFusion dollarFormat function for formatting. Of course, if you can average, you can get the min and max values as well (Listing 11.3).

Listing 11.3 /cfwack10/11/test3.cfm

```
<cfset maxprice = xmlSearch(xmlDoc,"max(/bookstore/*/price)")>
<cfdump var="#maxprice#" label="Max Price">

<p/>

<cfset minprice = xmlSearch(xmlDoc,"min(/bookstore/*/price)")>
<cfdump var="#minprice#" label="Min Price">
```

Given the data we've shown before, this listing returns 29.99 and 49.95 as the minimum and maximum values, respectively.

As mentioned earlier, XPath can be especially useful in cases in which you are not permitted to search or filter remote content. Earlier in the book, you learned about REST services in Cold-Fusion 10. You saw a simple list service that returned all the movies in the OWS films database table. Imagine that you need to provide a simple search interface to filter that data. Although you could search by looping over all the results and manually comparing your search results to the data, XPath can make the process simpler, as shown in Listing 11.4.

Listing 11.4 /cfwack10/11/test4.cfm

```
<!--- First, request the data from the REST service. --->
<cfhttp url="http://localhost:8500/rest/cfwack5_root/movieService.xml">

<!--- get the result and check to ensure it is xml --->
<cfset content = cfhttp.filecontent>

<cfif isXML(content)>

    <cfset data = xmlParse(content)>

    <cfparam name="form.search" default="">

    <cfoutput>
    <form method="post">
    Title search: <input type="text" name="search" value="#form.search#">
    ➥<input type="submit" value="Movie Title Search">
    </form>
    </cfoutput>

    <cfif len(trim(form.search))>

        <cfset results = xmlSearch(data,"/QUERY/ROWS/ROW[matches(COLUMN[1],"
        ➥"#form.search#"","i"")]")>

        <cfif arrayLen(results)>

            <cfloop index="r" array="#results#">
                <cfoutput>
                  <p>
                  Title match on #r.column[1].xmltext#<br/>
                  Budget: #dollarFormat(r.column[2].xmltext)#<br/>
                  Release date: #dateFormat(r.column[4].xmltext,"full")#<br/>
                </cfoutput>
```

Listing 11.4 (CONTINUED)

```
            </cfloop>

        <cfelse>

            <p>
                Sorry - there were no matches.
            </p>

        </cfif>

    </cfif>

<cfelse>

    <p>
        Sorry, but the remote service isn't working right today!
    </p>

</cfif>
```

We begin by requesting the XML feed from the REST service. This data really might be cached, but for now, don't worry about that.

The rest of the template is driven by a simple check to see whether the XML is valid. If valid XML was returned, then a form is displayed. This form lets the user enter a simple search term. If the user does enter something, an XPath regular expression (or regex) is run against the XML in this line:

```
<cfset results = xmlSearch(data,"/QUERY/ROWS/ROW[matches(COLUMN[1],"
➥ "#form.search#","""i""")]")>
```

This code may seem a bit confusing, but what it boils down to is a matches function call against the first column in each row of the results. Why the first column? That's simply how the REST service returned the data. The i attribute at the end flags the regular expression search as case-insensitive.

This example could be expanded to perform numeric range checking as well. For example, you may want to limit your results based on a range of movie budgets. Figure 11.2 shows the output from a sample search.

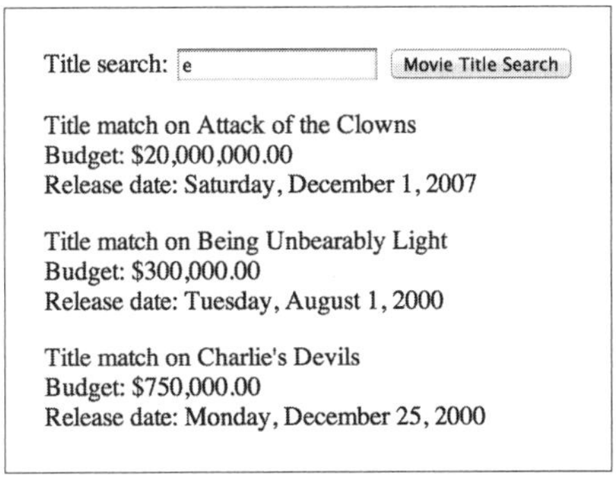

Figure 11.2

Using XMLSearch to filter the results of a REST service call.

Title search: e   [Movie Title Search]

Title match on Attack of the Clowns
Budget: $20,000,000.00
Release date: Saturday, December 1, 2007

Title match on Being Unbearably Light
Budget: $300,000.00
Release date: Tuesday, August 1, 2000

Title match on Charlie's Devils
Budget: $750,000.00
Release date: Monday, December 25, 2000

XPath and Variables

Listing 11.5 provides a final example of what can be accomplished with XPath2 and ColdFusion: You can now pass in a structure of values that map to XPath variables.

Listing 11.5   /cfwack10/11/test5.cfm (Partial)

```
<cfscript>
   params = {"test":"cd"};
</cfscript>

<cfset result = xmlsearch(xmldoc,"/bookstore/*[local-name() eq $test]", params)>
<cfdump var="#result#" label="Example of variable">
```

As in the earlier examples, we're skipping the display of the XML data presented earlier.

You can see that a structure called params is created with a key and a value. Then params is passed to xmlSearch. Note that the test key maps to the $test string in the XPath statement.

You may be wondering what the point is: Couldn't you have simply used #params.text# directly in the XPath string? Sure—but consider this code snippet:

```
<cfscript>
   params = {"test":"cd or 1=1"};
</cfscript>

<cfset result = xmlsearch(xmldoc,"/bookstore/*[local-name() eq $test]", params)>
<cfdump var="#result#" label="Example of variable">

<cfset result = xmlsearch(xmldoc,"/bookstore/*[local-name() eq #params.test#]")>
<cfdump var="#result#" label="Example of variable">
```

Note the modified value for test. Instead of just "cd", the value is "cd or 1=1". When passed as a variable, the or 1=1 portion is escaped, much like a <cfqueryparam> tag. In the second example, in which test is passed as is, it ends up breaking the intended logic of the XPath search and returning everything. If your XPath statement were based on user input, then this form of sanitization would certainly be recommended.

ColdFusion XML and XSLT

ColdFusion's support for Extensible Stylesheet Language Transformations, or XSLT, has also now been upgraded to Version 2. XSLT provides a way to use XML to build a generic text transformer. You create an XSLT document and feed it input in one form, and the output comes out transformed. Listing 11.6 shows a sample XSLT document. Full discussion of the XSLT syntax is beyond the scope of this book, but you should be able to get a feel for what this listing does.

Listing 11.6   `/cfwack10/11/demo.xslt`

```
<?xml version="1.0"?>
<xsl:stylesheet version="2.0" xmlns:xsl="http://www.w3.org/1999/XSL/Transform">
<xsl:output method="html" doctype-public="-//W3C//DTD HTML 4.0 Transitional//EN" />
<xsl:template match="/">
<html>
   <body>

      <table border="1" style="width: 400px;">
      <thead>
      <tr>
      <th>Name</th>
      <th>Released</th>
      <th>Price</th>
      </tr>
      </thead>
      <tbody>
      <xsl:for-each select="bookstore/book">
      <tr>
      <td>
      <xsl:value-of select="title"/>
      </td>
      <td>
      <xsl:value-of select="released"/>
      </td>
      <td>
      <xsl:value-of select="price"/>
      </td>
      </tr>
      </xsl:for-each>
      </tbody>
      </table>

   </body>
</html>
</xsl:template>
</xsl:stylesheet>
```

Pay particular attention to the `for-each` block. As you can guess, this block uses the `select` argument to run an XPath search against the XML input. Inside the `for-each` block, more select arguments act on the data. To use the XSLT stylesheet, you simply use the ColdFusion `XMLTransform()` function (Listing 11.7).

Listing 11.7   `/cfwack10/11/test6.cfm`

```
<cfxml variable="xmldoc">
(Deleted for space…)
</cfxml>

<cfset xsl = fileRead(expandPath("./demo.xsl"))>

<cfoutput>#XmlTransform(xmldoc, xsl)#</cfoutput>
```

The XMLTransform function takes in your input XML (and note that we are using the same list of data as before) and your XSLT file and returns the result. Figure 11.3 shows how the XML data was transformed into HTML.

Figure 11.3

Simple example of an XSLT transform on source XML.

Name	Released	Price
Harry Potter	2001-01-01	29.99
Learning XML	2003-01-01	39.95
Learning JSON	2003-01-01	49.95

What's new in XSLT 2.0? It offers many new features (you can view the full specification at http://www.w3.org/TR/xslt20/), but one of the more interesting is the capability to create a user-defined function with the XSLT document itself. Listing 11.8 provides an updated form of our previous example.

Listing 11.8   /cfwack10/11/demo2.xsl

```
<xsl:transform
  xmlns:xsl="http://www.w3.org/1999/XSL/Transform"
  xmlns:xs="http://www.w3.org/2001/XMLSchema"
  xmlns:str="http://example.com/namespace"
  version="2.0"
  exclude-result-prefixes="str">

<xsl:function name="str:highprice" >
  <xsl:param name="price" as="xs:float"/>
  <xsl:sequence select="if($price > 40.00) then concat('*',$price,'*') else $price"
/>
</xsl:function>

<xsl:output method="html" doctype-public="-//W3C//DTD HTML 4.0 Transitional//EN" />
<xsl:template match="/">
<html>
    <body>

    <table border="1" style="width: 400px;">
    <thead>
    <tr>
    <th>Name</th>
    <th>Released</th>
    <th>Price</th>
    </tr>
    </thead>
    <tbody>
    <xsl:for-each select="bookstore/book">
    <tr>
    <td>
    <xsl:value-of select="title"/>
    </td>
    <td>
    <xsl:value-of select="released"/>
    </td>
    <td>
```

Listing 11.8 (CONTINUED)

```
    <xsl:value-of select="str:highprice(price)"/>
    </td>
    </tr>
    </xsl:for-each>
    </tbody>
    </table>

    </body>
</html>
</xsl:template>
</xsl:transform>
```

Note the addition of a function called highprice. This function will notice a numeric value higher than 40 and wrap the result with asterisks. Further down in the XSL you can see that the price select statement now includes a call to this function.

In the code you can downloaded from the website, you can view test7.cfm. This example is the same as the previous example except that it uses the new XSL stylesheet. The output, however, is a bit more dynamic because of the addition of the user-defined function (Figure 11.4).

Figure 11.4

The effect of a user-defined function in an XSLT transform.

Name	Released	Price
Harry Potter	2001-01-01	29.99
Learning XML	2003-01-01	39.95
Learning JSON	2003-01-01	*49.95*

PART III

Enterprise Ready

CHAPTER 12

ColdFusion in the Cloud

Cloud computing is the latest term for the old dream of computing as a utility, which is now emerging as a commercial reality. The notion of infinite computing resources (hardware and software) available on demand without any upfront commitment and with the ability to pay as you go for only the actual use of these computing resources is indeed fascinating. It has the potential to transform a large part of the IT industry, making software even more attractive as a service and altering organizations' approaches to building IT infrastructure.

This chapter covers the basics of cloud infrastructure and how you can use it to deploy web applications built on top of ColdFusion.

What Is "The Cloud"?

The term *cloud* is used in many contexts: in reference to utility computing, computation, storage, widely distributed or network-based computing, and more. The most broadly applicable and widely accepted definition comes from the United States National Institute of Standards and Technology (NIST), which defines cloud computing as a model for enabling ubiquitous, convenient, on-demand network access to a shared pool of configurable computing resources (networks, servers, storage, applications, and services) that can be rapidly provisioned and released with minimal management effort or service provider interaction.

More casually, you can consider the cloud to be a place you go to use the technology of your choice—software, platform, hardware, and so on—whenever you need it and for as long you need it. You access the technology as services via a web browser or web services API and pay only for what you use.

Certain features of a cloud are essential to enable services that truly represent the cloud computing model and satisfy the expectations of consumers. These include the following:

- **On-demand self-service:** A consumer can unilaterally provision computing capabilities, such as server time and network storage, as needed automatically without the need for human interaction with each service provider.

- **Broad network access:** Capabilities are available over the network and accessed through standard mechanisms via a wide variety of client platforms (for example, mobile phones, tablets, laptops, and workstations).

- **Resource pooling:** The provider's computing resources are pooled to serve multiple consumers using a multitenant model, with different physical and virtual resources dynamically assigned and reassigned according to consumer demand. There is a sense of location independence in that the customer generally has no control over or knowledge of the exact location of the provided resources, but may be able to specify a location at a higher level of abstraction (for example, country, state, or data center). Examples of resources include storage, processing, memory, and network bandwidth.

- **Rapid elasticity:** Capabilities can be elastically provisioned and released, in some cases automatically, to scale rapidly outward and inward commensurate with demand. To the consumer, the capabilities available for provisioning often appear to be unlimited and can be appropriated in any quantity at any time.

- **Measured service:** Cloud systems automatically control and optimize resource use through a metering capability at some level of abstraction appropriate to the type of service (for example, storage, processing, bandwidth, and active user accounts). Resource use can be monitored, controlled, and reported, providing transparency for both the provider and consumer of the service.

Cloud Technology

Cloud computing is the evolution of a variety of technologies that have come together. There is nothing fundamentally new in any of the technologies that make up cloud computing, and most have existed for decades. However, two of these technologies are absolutely central to the cloud computing architecture: virtualization and web services.

- **Virtualization:** Virtualization is the underpinning of the entire cloud: the capability to deliver multitenancy applications and partition use to increase operation performance. Virtualization hides the physical characteristics of a computing platform from users, instead showing another abstract computing platform with the help of a control program commonly known as a hypervisor or virtual machine manager or monitor (VMM). The hypervisor allows several operating systems to share a single hardware host by controlling the host processor and resources, distributing what is needed to each operating system in turn and ensuring that the guest operating systems and virtual machines are unable to disrupt each other.

- Web services: All the technologies are essentially exposed as web services. We discussed web services in detail when discussing Simple Object Access Protocol (SOAP)–based web services in Chapter 4 and Representational State Transfer ((REST)–compliant services in Chapter 5. The maturity of web services has enabled the creation of powerful services that can be accessed on demand, in a uniform way. Clients consume these services either by directly invoking the services or through a web services API provided by the cloud service provider. Most of these services also have easy-to-use web interfaces built on top of the web services API.

Advantages of the Cloud

Cloud infrastructure offers several advantages over the operation of your own servers:

- Flexibility: You can assume that you have infinite computing resources at your disposal and can almost instantly respond to any change in web traffic to your application. You don't have to worry about servers running out of capacity or the need to deprecate a server.

- Availability: Availability describes how often a service can be used over a defined period of time. It can be calculated as a percentage of the mean time between failures of network components compared to the total time that the component should have worked. How much downtime can you afford? Ninety-nine percent availability of your server may sound reasonable, but it could mean 14 minutes of service disruption per day. Cloud infrastructure gives you sufficient ways to increase your application availability.

- Data reliability: Data reliability refers to how well you can trust a system to protect data integrity and execute its transactions. Cloud infrastructure provides number of ways to reliably store your data and handle disaster recovery.

- Time to market: You don't need to worry about IT infrastructure because the provisioning of servers, data stores, and any other network component takes just seconds. This speed saves you time in setting up your IT infrastructure and helps you to deploy your applications quickly.

- Cost: There is no upfront investment, and you pay for only the computing resources you use. You need not worry about the expense of deprecating a server or the cost of space or electricity. The total cost of ownership (TCO) is reduced.

- New application opportunities: Several important classes of existing applications, including mobile interactive applications, parallel batch processing applications, data-heavy applications such as analytics, and computation-intensive applications, can greatly benefit from cloud computing.

Cloud Service Models

We have discussed technologies that make up cloud computing and the general value proposition behind the cloud. Let's take a moment to understand the cloud infrastructure models. Clients interact with the cloud using a service layer. There are three service models for cloud computing:

- Software as a service (SaaS): SaaS enables the consumer to use the provider's applications running on a cloud infrastructure; the service layer exposes the provider's application for the consumer to use. Applications are accessible from various client devices through either a thin client interface such as a web browser (for example, web-based email) or a program interface. The consumer does not control or need to know about the underlying cloud infrastructure, including the network, servers, operating systems, storage, or individual application capabilities, with the possible exception of limited user-specific application configuration settings. Examples of SaaS include Dropbox, Flickr, Google Apps, and Salesforce.com applications.

- Platform as a service (PaaS): PaaS enables the consumer is to deploy on the cloud infrastructure applications created or acquired by the consumer using programming languages, libraries, services, and tools supported by the provider. In this case, the service layer exposes a platform managed by the cloud provider, which is akin to giving the consumer an entire application environment in which to write software. The consumer does not manage or control the underlying cloud infrastructure, including the network, servers, operating systems, and storage, but has control over the deployed applications and possibly configuration settings for the application-hosting environment. Some of the key players are Google App Engine and Force.com

- Infrastructure as a service (IaaS): IaaS enables the consumer to provision processing, storage, networking, and other fundamental computing resources on which the consumer can deploy and run arbitrary software, which can include operating systems and applications. In this case, the service layer exposes infrastructure managed by the cloud provider, and the consumer gets to pick and manage the platform and the software installed on it. The consumer does not manage or control the underlying cloud infrastructure but has control over the operating systems, storage, and deployed applications and possibly has limited control of selected networking components (for example, host firewalls). Some of the key players are Amazon Web Services and RackSpace. IaaS is the focus of this chapter.

Figure 12.1 shows a complete service stack, clearly differentiating each service level and its elements.

Figure 12.1

Complete set of service stack elements.

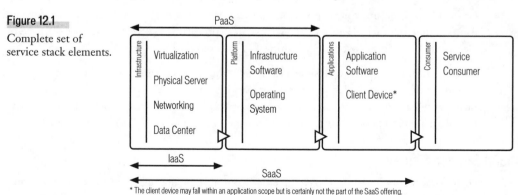

* The client device may fall within an application scope but is certainly not the part of the SaaS offering.

Cloud Deployment Models

There are some general cloud deployment models that are accepted by most cloud stakeholders today:

- Private cloud: The cloud infrastructure is provisioned for exclusive use by a single organization comprising multiple consumers (for example, business units). It be owned, managed, and operated by the organization, a third party, or some combination of these, and it may exist on or off premises. For example, VMware's suite of tools and OpenStack can be used to transform IT infrastructure into a private cloud.

- Community cloud: The cloud infrastructure is provisioned for exclusive use by a specific community of consumers from organizations that have shared concerns (for example, shared mission, security requirements, policy, and compliance considerations). It may be owned, managed, and operated by one or more of the organizations in the community, a third party, or some combination of these, and it may exist on or off premises. One example of an open cloud is OpenCirrus, formed by HP, Intel, Yahoo, and others.

- Public cloud: The cloud infrastructure is provisioned for open use by the general public. It may be owned, managed, and operated by a business, academic, or government organization, or some combination of these. It exists on the premises of the cloud provider. Popular examples of public clouds are Amazon Web Services (AWS), Amazon Elastic Compute Cloud (EC2), and Amazon Simple Storage Service (S3); the Rackspace cloud suite; and the Microsoft Azure service platform.

- Hybrid cloud: The cloud infrastructure is composed of two or more distinct cloud infrastructures (private, community, or public) that remain unique entities, but are bound together by standardized or proprietary technology that enables data and application portability (for example, cloud bursting for load balancing between clouds). Public cloud vendors that offer hybrid cloud capability include Amazon (Amazon Virtual Private Cloud) and Skytap (Skytap Virtual Lab).

For a transactional web application the model that makes most sense is IaaS deployed in a public or hybrid cloud. The model fulfills all the promises of cloud computing and provides all the flexibility required for application development without vendor lock-in as in the case of PaaS, in which the platform is managed by the cloud provider, and the application needs to use the programming interface provided by the vendor.

Amazon Web Services

So far, we have discussed general principles that apply in any cloud environment. In this section, we focus on IaaS for web application development, and we'll use the major player in this environment, Amazon Web Services (AWS), to demonstrate the logical components and key principles.

AWS is Amazon's umbrella for all its web-based technology services. It encompasses a wide variety of services, all of which fall into the category of cloud computing. Also, it offers a complete set of infrastructure and application services that enable you to run almost everything in the cloud: from enterprise applications and big data projects to social games and mobile apps.

At the time of this writing, AWS offers 33 services, excluding Mechanical Turk. For the purposes of this chapter, we will use only the technologies that fit into the AWS infrastructure services.

Registering with AWS

To begin using any of the AWS services, you need to register with AWS. You can sign up at http://aws.amazon.com. You will be asked for your name and address, phone number, and payment details (credit card and so on). AWS will verify your phone number and payment details by charging a nominal one dollar. You will not be billed any more until you use the service.

AWS offers a free-use tier of service, which provides 750 hours per month for one year to run an Amazon EC2 micro instance, Amazon Relational Database Service (RDS), Amazon S3, and more for new clients only. If you've already had an AWS account for more than a year, you do not qualify.

Note that AWS will autocreate certain access credentials for you available under the security credentials in the AWS console. These credentials are used to authenticate your requests to AWS. There are primarily three ways to securely connect to these services:

- REST: You can use an access key ID and a secret access key to send secure REST or Query protocol requests to any AWS API.

- SOAP: You can use an X.509 certificate and private key registered with AWS to send secure SOAP requests to AWS APIs.

- Web UI: You can use the AWS console UI provided by Amazon to use all AWS services. Use the username and password you provided at the time of registration to log in.

Additionally, AWS provides developer toolkits for several languages including Java and command-line utilities built on top of the AWS API. You can use these to consume all AWS services and automate many operations such as build processes.

There are several infrastructure services that are important for understanding AWS cloud infrastructure and for developing web applications. We will discuss these core services next, in order of their importance.

Amazon Elastic Compute Cloud

Amazon EC2 is the heart of the AWS cloud computing platform and the building block of your computational environment. It provides a web services API for acquiring, configuring, and managing virtual servers in the Amazon cloud. In other words, you can launch a virtual server in the Amazon cloud at any time and from any place in the world and will have complete control of your server.

The EC2 infrastructure includes a set of components that you can use to create and manage a computing node, described here.

Region and Availability Zone

To acquire a virtual server, you first need to select a region. At the time of writing, Amazon data centers are located in eight regions. Each region has several availability zones, which are data centers interconnected with a high-speed network and constructed so that service malfunctions from one availability zone don't interfere with the work of services in another availability zone. The resources of one region cannot be used in another region, except for communication between instances using external addresses, which will add to the data transfer charges. The prices for each region vary, so check the rates before you select a region.

Purchasing Model

The next step is to buy an instance or node. Amazon EC2 provides three purchasing models to optimize your costs. On Demand instances allow you to pay a fixed rate by the hour with no commitment; with Reserved instances, you pay a low, one-time fee and in turn receive a significant discount on the hourly charge for that instance. Spot instances enable you to bid whatever price you want for instance capacity. As a general rule, you should buy Reserved instances to serve your estimated base web traffic. Then, when the traffic increases, you can add capacity using the other two models. Figure 12.2 depicts a scenario that uses a Reserved instance for base traffic and an On Demand instance for peak load.

Figure 12.2

Reserved instance compared to On Demand instance use.

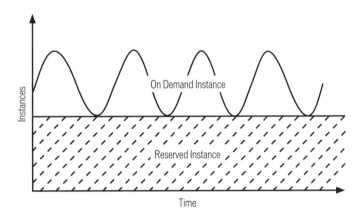

Amazon Machine Image

Next you need to select a predefined Amazon Machine Image (AMI). An AMI is a prepackaged environment that includes all the necessary elements to set up and boot your instance, including preconfigured operating system and application software. It serves as the basic unit of deployment for services delivered using EC2. Most people start with a standard AMI based on their favorite operating system, customize it, create a new image, and then launch their servers based on their custom images.

Note that EC2 has two kinds of storage:

- Ephemeral storage, which is tied to the node and expires with the node
- Elastic block storage (EBS), which acts like a hard drive and persists across time

Along with these two storage options, you can use Amazon S3 to store your data; data stored with Amazon S3 is not bound to any node and will persist across a node restart. The recommended approach is to use a local instance store for temporary data and, for data requiring greater durability, to use EBS volumes or to back up the data to Amazon S3.

An AMI is ultimately an image of a virtual machine and, depending on the type of store used by its boot partition, you can have two kinds of AMI:

- EBS-backed AMI: This AMI uses an EBS volume as a root partition.
- Instance-based AMI: In this AMI, the boot partition is in the ephemeral store of the instance.

If you use an instance-based AMI, your changes will not persist across restarts. If you use an EBS-backed AMI, everything will persist—logs, command history, and so on—which may not be what you want. In general, AMI providers are tending toward EBS-based offerings. Still, you need to be mindful of the type of AMI you are using and plan accordingly.

Instance Types

To start a virtual server in the Amazon environment, you also need to select an instance type. Amazon has many instance types, based on number of CPUs, amount of memory, local storage resources, and CPU use profile. You should select the type that best meets your applications requirements and CPU use profile.

Figure 12.3 shows the ideal CPU use profile for an Amazon micro instance (T1.micro); the allowed CPU use is constantly kept at a lower level, depicted as T1.micro background, and periodically bursts to allow the instance to use approximately two CPUs, depicted as T1.micro max. For a small instance, allowed CPU consumption is kept constant, higher than that of a micro instance's (m1.small) background CPU use. So if your application requires consistently higher CPU use, you should choose a larger instance such as m1.small instead of T1.micro.

Figure 12.3

Typical CPU use profile of a micro instance.

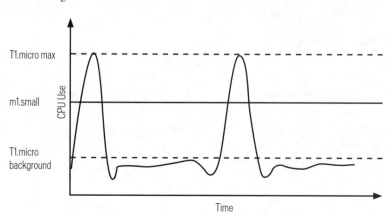

Security Group

To secure your network within the cloud, you can control virtual firewall rules that define the way that traffic is filtered to your virtual nodes by specifying the traffic's security group. The security group acts as a firewall, allowing you to choose which protocols and ports are open to computers over the Internet. You can use the default security group and then customize it, or you can create your own security group. A few ports, such as 8575 for WebSocket and 995 for POP3S, need to be opened for ColdFusion to work properly (in case you are using these in your application).

You can use the web interface and utilities provided by Amazon or a reliable third-party provider to manage your nodes. The preferred way to connect to a Linux-based node is through Secure Shell (SSH). You can use any SSH client: for example, PuTTY. To transfer files, you can use the `wget` command or any Secure File Transfer Protocol (SFTP) client, such as FileZilla. To connect to a Microsoft Windows–based node, you can use Remote Desktop Protocol (RDP) and can map drives to transfer files to the remote node.

Amazon Simple Storage Service

The Amazon S3 AWS component is cloud-based data storage accessible in real time via a web services API from anywhere on the Internet. You can store and retrieve any amount of data by creating special folders called buckets. A bucket acts like a root folder and is a container for objects stored in Amazon S3. When creating a bucket, you can choose a region to optimize for latency, reduce costs, or address regulatory requirements. As with traditional directories, you can hierarchically organize your files and folders inside these buckets.

It is important not to think of Amazon S3 as a file system. First, the bucket namespace is shared by all users of the system, so you need to give it a unique name. There are additional rules governing what is allowed as a bucket name. Since buckets are treated similarly to Internet domain names, as a general convention you can use a name that matches your own domain name.

Second, although Amazon S3 is very fast for an Internet-deployed service, it is nowhere nearly as responsive as a local disk, and there is a wait time with every S3 call. Also, developers need to bear in mind that Amazon S3 is accessed via web services and is not exactly a file system or a Web Distributed Authoring and Versioning (WebDAV) client. Hence, applications must be written specifically to store data in Amazon S3 using APIs provided by technologies like ColdFusion.

Amazon S3 enables you to reliably place persistent data in the Amazon cloud and retrieve it later. Its main benefit is that you can continue to push data to Amazon S3 and never worry about running out of storage space.

Using ColdFusion to Access Amazon S3

Support for Amazon S3 was added in ColdFusion 9, Update 1. ColdFusion lets you treat the Amazon S3 buckets just like any another file system, such as the in-memory file system (ram://). You can use the same file system APIs, such as `FileExists()`, with the only difference being that you will use the s3:// prefix. Note that to access Amazon S3, ColdFusion itself can be deployed anywhere, not necessarily in the cloud, but it should be able to connect to Amazon S3.

Let's look at how to use Amazon S3 with ColdFusion. To connect to your bucket, you need to provide your Amazon security credentials—that is, your access key ID and secret access key— to ColdFusion. You can get these by logging into the AWS console and going to the security credentials section.

You can specify your credentials in two ways:

- At the application level
- At the individual level

If you specify access credentials at the application level, any Amazon S3 calls in this application will use these values. You can pass these credentials as `this.s3.accessKeyId` and `this.s3.awsSecretKey` within your Application.cfm or Application.cfc file. Listing 12.1 shows an example using Application.cfc.

Listing 12.1 /cfwack/12/Application.cfc

```
<cfcomponent>

    <cfset this.name="cfwack_12">

    <cfset this.s3.accessKeyId = "your_access_key_id">
    <cfset this.s3.awsSecretKey = "your_aws_secret_key">
    <!--- Default locaion --->
    <cfset this.s3.defaultLocation = "US">
    <!--- File Size in MB --->
    <cfset this.s3.minsizeformultipart = 4>

</cfcomponent>
```

As you can see, we have specified the secret key and access ID with an `s3` struct as application settings. You can also specify the default location or region of Amazon S3 bucket creation, as discussed earlier. A bucket on Amazon S3 can be set to one of the following regions: US, EU, or US-WEST. The default value is US.

ColdFusion 10 added multipart uploading, in which files are split into multiple parts and the parts are uploaded in parallel. To use this feature, you can set `this.s3.minsizeformultipart` using a file size in megabytes. The size you specify is treated as a minimum above which file uploading is performed as a multipart upload. This option is helpful when you have to upload very large files.

You can also specify individual-level credentials. You specify which credentials to use at the time of individual Amazon S3 calls in the URL itself. The format of the URL should be s3://*accessKeyId:awsSecretKey*@bucket/x/y/sample.txt, where *accessKeyId* is the access key ID, and *awsSecretKey* is the secret key generated for your AWS account by Amazon. Individual-level credentials take precedence over application-level credentials.

Now let's look at file operations in Amazon S3. Because ColdFusion lets you treat Amazon S3 just like any file system, you can use the same file functions, such as `DirectoryExists` and `FileWrite`, to perform the same operations in Amazon S3. Listing 12.2 provides an example.

Listing 12.2 /cfwack/12/fileop.cfm

```
<cfif not directoryExists("s3://examples1.cfwack.com")>
   <cfset directoryCreate("s3://examples1.cfwack.com")>
</cfif>
<cfset fileWrite("s3://examples1.cfwack.com/#createUUID()#.txt", "some stuff!")>
<cfset files = directoryList("s3://examples1.cfwack.com")>
<cfdump var="#files#">
```

Here we are checking whether the bucket examples1.cfwack.com exists; if not, we want to create it using `directoryCreate()`. Then we want to write a file in this bucket using the `fileWrite()` function. Then we want to list all the files in this directory. Figure 12.4 shows the the file has been uploaded in the Amazon S3 bucket.

Figure 12.4

Amazon S3 file listing.

As you can see, we have used normal file functions in our code and have used the s3:// URL prefix for directories and files. You can use a similar process to read or delete files and directories on Amazon S3.

You can also share files by granting permissions to other users to read or modify your files. Cold-Fusion lets you specify an array of structs as `storeACL`, where you can specify permissions for selected users. Listing 12.3 shows how to set and retrieve these permissions.

Listing 12.3 /cfwack/12/permission.cfm

```
<cfif not directoryExists("s3://examples11.cfwack.com")>
   <cfset permissions =
   [
     {group="all", permission="read"},
     {id="your_canonical_used_id", permission="full_control"}
   ]
   >
   <cfdirectory action="create" directory="s3://examples11.cfwack.com"
   ➡ storeacl="#permissions#">
</cfif>
<cfset acls = storeGetACL("s3://examples11.cfwack.com")>
<cfdump var="#acls#">
```

Here we are creating the bucket examples11.cfwack.com if it doesn't exist. We are giving everyone read access, and we are giving only one user with a given canonical user ID (which can be retrieved from the bottom of the security credentials page) all permissions, including read, delete, upload, and view permissions. Then we get all the permissions for this folder using the `storeGetACL()` function and simply dump the list. You can alternatively use `storeSetACL(url, array)` to set these permissions.

Other Notable AWS Components

Other notable AWS components include the following:

- Amazon Virtual Private Cloud (VPC): This is the hybrid cloud model provided by Amazon. It lets you provision a private, isolated section of the AWS cloud, where you can launch AWS resources in a virtual network that you define. It further enables enterprises to connect their existing infrastructure to a set of isolated AWS computing resources via a virtual private network (VPN) connection, and to extend their existing management capabilities such as security services, firewalls, and intrusion-detection systems to include their AWS resources.

- Amazon Elastic Beanstalk: This is Amazon's PaaS offering. It provides an easier way for you to quickly deploy and manage applications in the AWS cloud. You select a platform provided by Amazon, upload your application, and tweak configuration settings such as load balancing and autoscaling. Everything else is handled by Amazon Elastic Beanstalk. Amazon Elastic Beanstalk automatically handles the deployment details of capacity provisioning, load balancing, autoscaling, and application health monitoring.

- Amazon CloudFront: This cloud-based content distribution network (CDN) enables you to place your online content at the edges of the network, so that content is delivered from a location close to the user who is requesting it.

AWS also offers several other application services, such as database, queue, search, and networking services, that you can use while developing your application for the cloud. These services lets you use Amazon's infrastructure to better deploy and manage your applications.

Designing for the Cloud

In this section, we look at some of the key factors to consider when building an application for the AWS cloud and some of the tools you can use.

Main Differences Between Cloud and Traditional Designs

Building applications for the cloud is no different than building a highly scalable web application. The design principles remain the same. Nevertheless, there are some differences between designing for the cloud and for a traditional deployment, particularly in the areas of software licenses, cloud services cost models, and service levels for cloud applications.

Licensing

You need to understand the licensing model of the software that you are using, including Cold-Fusion. In many cloud environments in operation today, you pay for resources by the CPU hour, and the same holds true for the software that you choose, including the publicly available AMI.

Not all software vendors, including ColdFusion as of now, offer licensing terms that match the payment model for the cloud. Traditional software licenses are often based on the number of CPUs, and the CPU count is calculated as the number of computing cores available on the physical server.

With the end-user license agreement (EULA) changes in ColdFusion 10, one enterprise license enables you to use ColdFusion on two CPUs, with each CPU consisting of four cores. Therefore, if you are running ColdFusion on a two-quad-core CPU (eight cores total, which would be deemed two CPUs), you can still continue to run ColdFusion 10 on it; ColdFusion 10 is free for use on development, staging, and testing servers. But when you deploy on a cloud, you need to take into account the number of cores that you actually end up using, calculate the number of licenses that you need, and provision that many ColdFusion licenses.

TIP

Visit http://blogs.coldfusion.com/post.cfm/coldfusion-10-eula to learn more about the changes in the ColdFusion 10 EULA.

All of this is about to change with the new ColdFusion AMIs available at Amazon Marketplace. These prebuilt AMIs provide pay-for-what-you-use licensing, and you can continue to enjoy the flexibility of the cloud without worrying about licensing compliance or the need to buy licenses beforehand. We discuss this ColdFusion offering later in this chapter.

Cloud Cost Model

Pay-for-use is a big shift from the traditional pricing model used to procure hardware and software. With the traditional model, you knew how much you had to pay and usually paid up front. Now with cloud infrastructure, you pay for resources as you use them, by the CPU hour, and you don't know up front how much you will need to pay. The best way to compare costs for cloud computing with costs for other models is to determine the TCO over the course of your hardware depreciation period, which typically is between two and three years. You need to estimate your total server use and the cost of infrastructure, licensing fees, labor, and any other resources. Then, using these estimates, you can select your instances and your infrastructure components such as load balancers and calculate the charge you will incur on cloud infrastructure. You may also want to calculate your return on investment (ROI) by taking into account your business goals, such as customer experience and increased web traffic.

Service Levels

When a company offers a service, it generally provides its customers with a service level agreement (SLA) that identifies key metrics (service levels) that the customer can reasonably expect from the service. The three most important metrics for a cloud-based service are availability, durability, and performance.

Typically, AWS infrastructure services are considered to have high availability. The documented expectation of Amazon EC2 availability is at least 99.95 percent during the service year. That means a downtime of 1 minute and 12 seconds per day. Expectations for Amazon S3 are 99.999999999 percent durability and 99.99 percent availability.

Although the same high-availability concepts apply in the cloud as in a traditional data center, what you might consider a reliable component differs dramatically. Failures such as disk failures and server crashes are common in the cloud environment. You need to design your application for these failures so that there is no loss of service to your end customers. There are several techniques for reducing the downtime of your applications, which we will cover in the next section.

Design Considerations

When building an application for cloud deployment, you should treat a cloud deployment like a multiserver deployment and apply all the best practices that are typical in any multiserver deployment. You want to use the flexibility of cloud and be able to add servers on the fly. Hence, your applications should be programmed in such a way that they are prepared for a multiserver deployment.

Managing the Application State and Transactions

There are times when you require an application's state to be shared across all the nodes that are currently available and serving requests. There are several strategies to handle this scenario. You can use session replication or sticky sessions, but they have overhead and limitations.

Also, web applications require secure transactions to maintain a consistent state. Typically, you handle these transactions by enforcing mutual exclusion, by using <cflock> to take locks on different ColdFusion in-memory scopes: for example, the application scope. This approach will ensure that no two threads on the same server enter the code between these locks; however, it will fail in a multiserver deployment.

To handle both requirements, the best practice is to use a separate database to manage the application state. You push the data in a separate database server and retrieve information whenever required. To maintain transactions, you can use any of several mechanisms.

You can use stored procedures, which enables you to use the database to manage the integrity of your transactions. However, stored procedures are not portable across databases.

If you are not using stored procedures, you can handle transactional integrity either by creating protection against dirty write operations or creating a lock in the database. Two approaches can help you:

- Change your database schema and add the last update timestamp and last update user fields. Then use these properties while querying or updating your database. If these fields have changed, your call will fail, and you can get fresh values and try again to update the table.

- If you do not want to change your table schema, add another table to manage your locks. This table can have locked user and locked timestamp fields. Set these fields whenever you start a transaction and clear them when you are done. Other calls should wait for this transaction to complete.

Additionally, you can use Amazon S3, a different network share server, or an EBS volume (other than the root) to store your persistent files because the ephemeral store does not persist.

Managing the Database

Use a database or an out-of-process distributed cache such as Amazon EC2 to ensure the persistence of any data that needs to survive the destruction of your cloud environment. Then create a line of defense to secure your database's availability and consistency.

For this, you can consider database clustering and replication. In a clustered database scenario, multiple databases act together as a single logical database and can survive failure of any node to maintain data consistency. All the transactions are replicated across nodes, so every node is current with all the changes. A clustered database is less likely to lose any changes unless a particular node goes down without informing the others. However, in a clustered database scenario, you need to manage the primary keys yourself. Several strategies can be applied to generate globally unique primary keys: for example, the user of universally unique IDs (UUIDs).

Alternatively, you can use a master-slave replication strategy. In this strategy, you configure one server as a master server that handles your write operations, and you replicate transactions on a slave server, which can be used as a backup database.

Figure 12.5 shows one possible application deployment model. You have a cluster of Amazon EC2 servers handling your requests behind an Amazon Elastic Load Balancer (ELB). You can have different distributed storage mechanism for various types of data and content: for example, static files over Amazon S3, and user-generated data or content in a cache server such as Amazon EC2. Then you can have a clustered database with a master-slave replication strategy. At each level, you can have redundant nodes on standby, which can help you replace faulty or failed nodes instantly.

Figure 12.5

Sample application
deployment model.

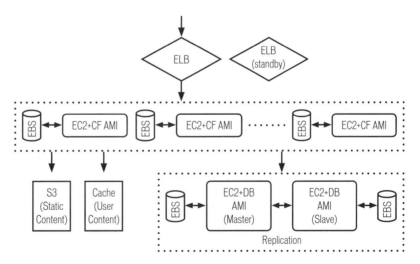

Depending on your need for data consistency and the price that you are willing to pay, you can also take snapshots of your slave server at regular intervals. You can store these in different availability zones, in Amazon S3, or even outside the Amazon cloud.

As a general rule, you should focus on three key elements in your recovery planning:

- Backups: Keep backup copies of your data to recover from failure of your server. Failures can happen at any time, and you should be prepared for the worst.

- Geographic redundancy: Store your backup copies in different geographic locations to recover from failure of an entire data center.

- Organizational redundancy: Cloud providers periodically suffer outages, disruptions, and maintenance events that cause services to be unavailable. To keep your services undisrupted, you can keep backup copies with multiple providers or even with you to handle network outages at the cloud provider. It may be rare for a cloud provider to go down, but the data is yours and you need to safeguard it.

Ensuring Security

A cloud has no defined perimeter, and that opens your application to all possible attacks and security threats. Hence, you need to be extra careful about securing your data and servers in the cloud.

To start, you need to define the traffic that can reach your servers by using security groups as discussed earlier. Allow only traffic that you need, such as HTTP and HTTPS traffic. Try to communicate over secure channels such as HTTPS and SFTP and don't leave any ports opened on your server that your application doesn't require. You should use encryption for any data that is stored or transmitted through a service from a cloud environment.

Also, do not open direct access to your most sensitive data. Use web servers such as Apache and Microsoft Internet Information Services (IIS) and a proxy server that can validate the user before handing over the information. Any attack then will require the attacker to exploit additional attack vectors before reaching actual data.

Most important, your server should be hardened so it is running only the one service that you intend to run on it. Do not enable user accounts on the server except those necessary to support the services running on the server or to provide access for users who need it. All configuration files for common server software should be configured to the most secure settings, and all necessary services should run under a under a user account with a nonprivileged role: for example, nobody.

If you are using ColdFusion, use a secure profile, and use the security lock-down guide for ColdFusion 10, available at https://www.adobe.com/content/dam/Adobe/en/products/coldfusion/pdfs/cf10/cf10-lockdown-guide.pdf, which details all the measures you need to take to secure your server. Use sandboxes to clearly define the boundaries of interactions between your application and the server. Also, be sure to keep logs of important activity and access on your server. Logging can help you identify security attacks and the paths taken and the attack vectors used by an intruder.

To respond to a safety threat, you should always keep a redundant virtual node ready. Whenever you determine that an attack has occurred, you can cut off its access to outside world to analyze the issue and in the meantime have your redundant node service incoming requests.

Safely Publishing a Public AMI

When you create an AMI and make it publicly available, you need to consider your setup carefully. To understand the importance of using care, assume that you could be making available for everyone the exact same machine that you use. It might contain the SSH keys that you used to connect with the instance, log history, web server connection details, command history, unwanted users that you created on the system, temporary files, and other sensitive information that you would not like to share. Extra precaution is required to safely remove this information from your instance before you create an image from it. Use utilities such as `shred` and `sdelete` to permanently delete your files. On Microsoft Windows, run the Amazon EC2Config Settings application to prepare your system before AMI creation.

Monitoring

It is extremely important to monitor your cloud infrastructure. You will be able to execute your recovery plans or replace a failing service only if you know what has failed. You can use AWS CloudWatch service and also implement your own monitoring tools to properly manage your Amazon EC2 infrastructure or enable automated data recovery. For this, you can use the Amazon EC2 monitoring APIs provided by AWS or your own application monitoring tools, such as server monitoring in the case of ColdFusion.

ColdFusion AMI

Wouldn't it be great if ColdFusion were available to you with a pay-for-use model without any upfront fees and prebuilt on the operating system of your choice? You could then enjoy the complete flexibility of cloud infrastructure without having to worry about licensing compliance, and you could start a server with ColdFusion whenever you needed it for as long as you needed it and pay for only that period of use. At the time of this writing, Adobe is about to launch ColdFusion 10–based AMIs for the AWS market. It will be available in two configurations:

- Linux based: The operating system used is Ubuntu 12.0.4 LTS, with ColdFusion Version 10, Update 7, 64-bit Enterprise edition installed, running under nobody, and set to restart on OS reboot. The web server used is Apache 2.2.x, set to restart on OS reboot. MySQL Version 5.5.x is also installed.

- Microsoft Windows based: The operating system used is Microsoft Windows 2008 Server R2, with ColdFusion Version 10, Update 7, 64-bit Enterprise edition installed, and set to restart on OS reboot. The web server used is Microsoft IIS 7.5.x, set to restart on OS reboot. MySQL Version 5.5.x is also installed.

These AMIs are supported only on large (L) and extra-large (XL) Amazon EC2 instances and have a flat price for hourly use. You can build your Amazon EC2 instances by selecting one of the two ColdFusion AMIs, launching it, and customizing it according to your needs: setting up your application, tweaking the configuration, including patches, and so on. Once you have the setup you want and have verified that your application to be working properly, you can create another private AMI from this instance. You can use this new AMI to launch your servers and need not replicate all the effort required to set up your first instance.

ColdFusion will be installed in the AMI in the default configuration, and you will likely want to change these settings. The ColdFusion AMI comes with a jump-start tool, which autostarts the first time you log into your machine and lets you change all the passwords and settings that you could change with an ordinary installer. Also, the ColdFusion AMI does not implement the security lock-down guide. System hardening is left to users to implement based on their requirements.

As mentioned earlier, you need to open a few ports in your security group to allow ColdFusion to work properly, assuming that you use those features. Table 12.1 lists some of these ports and associated features.

Table 12.1 Features and Associated Default Ports

RULE	PORT
SSH	22
HTTP	80
HTTPS	443
POP3S	995
Microsoft SQL	1433
MySQL	3306
LDAP	389
RDP	3389
Custom TCP rule (for SOLR)	8985
Custom TCP rule (for FTP)	20,21
Custom TCP rule (for POP)	110
Custom TCP rule (for IMAP)	143
Custom TCP rule (for Adobe Flash)	843
Custom TCP rule (for Microsoft Outlook)	1237
Custom TCP rule (for a remote ColdFusion instance)	8012
Custom TCP rule (for WebSocket)	8575
Custom TCP rule (for WebSocket Flash fallback)	1234
Custom TCP rule (for PostgreSQL)	5432
Custom TCP rule (for SMTP)	25
Custom TCP rule (for server monitor)	5500

Keep in mind that if you make your AMI public, it will be available to all AWS users. But AWS as of now does not support a multiple-licensing model for an AMI, so to redistribute any software, you need authorization from the software vendor.

Improved Administration

The ColdFusion Administrator has long been the ColdFusion developer's best friend when setting up a new application. In this chapter, we'll discuss some of the updates for the Administrator in ColdFusion 10.

What's Not Covered

Many of the new features in ColdFusion 10, such as REST and WebSocket, also have relevant pages in the Administrator. These features are covered in other chapters in this book and will not be discussed here.

Similarly, updates to the ColdFusion Administrator API are, for the most part, to be expected and should match the changes in the web application. You can expect that a new setting in the Administrator will also be available in the API.

The New Look: Shiny!

One of the first things you may notice about the ColdFusion Administrator is the new theme. The Administrator is still frame based, with a simple menu on the left side, but the colors and chrome have been updated with a slightly more modern look and feel. The default page has also been updated to include more useful information (Figure 13.1). As an example, you can find links to report bugs or enhancements for ColdFusion itself.

Figure 13.1

The updated design of the ColdFusion Administrator.

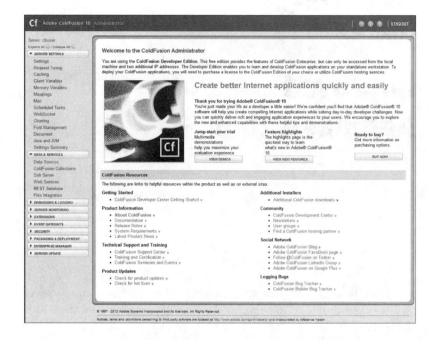

Another welcome change, and one that may go unnoticed, is the removal of the old Java applets used by the file picker. If you've grown accustomed to *not* using the Administrator's file picker controls because of these, good news: you can start using it again. The applets have all been replaced by fancy Ajax-based controls that should work much more smoothly in modern browsers (Figure 13.2).

Figure 13.2

The new Ajax and HTML–based file and directory chooser.

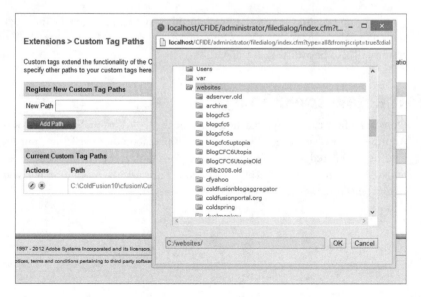

Caching Updates

Two minor, but useful, caching updates may be found in the new Administrator. First is the ability to remove a folder from the trusted cache. The trusted cache is a setting that tells ColdFusion to not check CFM files for updates. This is a cheap, simple performance enhancement but requires you to clear the entire cache when you make any updates. This new option allows you to specify a folder so that only it is removed from the cache.

Along with this enhancement, you may now clear the query cache from the Administrator as well. Figure 13.3 from the Administrator's Caching page shows both of these new options.

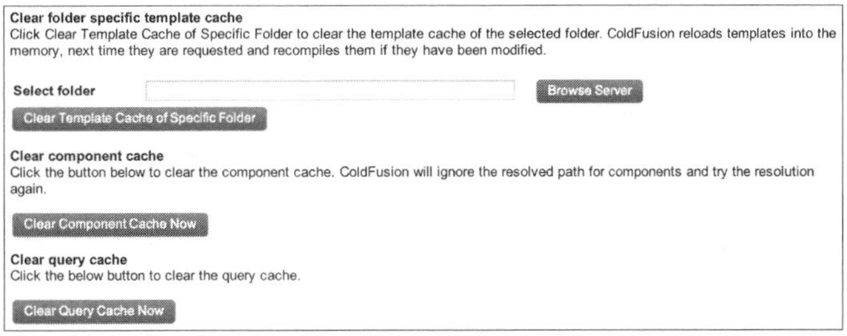

Figure 13.3

New caching options.

Security Updates

ColdFusion 10 includes many security-related updates (see Chapter 15, "Security Enhancements"), and the Administrator includes security improvements as well.

Automatic Logging of Administration Changes

One security improvement is the addition of a new audit log. You can find this new file, named audit.log, with the other ColdFusion log files. You can also view the log directly in the Administrator using the built-in log viewer. The audit file contains records for most changes made in the Administrator. Here's an example of what you may find in the log:

```
"Information","ajp-bio-8012-exec-6","12/04/12","15:22:00","CFADMIN",
➡"User admin logged in."
"Information","ajp-bio-8012-exec-2","12/04/12","16:05:39","CFADMIN",
➡"User admin changed Server-Settings settings.Enable Per Application Settings:
➡From 'YES' to 'NO'."
"Information","ajp-bio-8012-exec-7","12/04/12","16:05:44","CFADMIN",
➡"User admin changed Server-Settings settings.Enable Per Application Settings:
➡From 'NO' to 'YES'.Use UUID for cftoken: From 'YES' to 'NO'."
"Information","ajp-bio-8012-exec-3","12/04/12","16:05:45","CFADMIN",
➡"User admin changed Server-Settings settings.Use UUID for cftoken:
➡From 'NO' to 'YES'."
"Information","ajp-bio-8012-exec-8","12/04/12","16:05:58",,
➡"User admin added datasource galleon2."
"Information","ajp-bio-8012-exec-6","12/04/12","16:14:22","CFADMIN",
➡"User admin logged out"
"Information","ajp-bio-8012-exec-2","12/04/12","16:14:22","CFADMIN",
➡"User admin logged in."
```

The log details both log ins and log outs. It also reports changes to settings. In the example here, you can see that the admin user toggled the "Use UUID for cftoken" setting from yes to no and back again. In an environment with multiple users, this type of logging can be crucial to see who did what. Even if you are working in a single-user environment, it can be helpful to see what changes you've made in the past, especially if you've noted performance degradations.

Password Reset Script

Sooner or later, everybody asks this question: How do I reset my password? You set up a good password for a site—in this case, your ColdFusion Administrator—and then promptly forget what it was. There have been unofficial workarounds in the past, but ColdFusion 10 now ships with an official way to reset the password.

The password reset script can be run only from the command line. In Microsoft Windows, you would use the cmd.exe program, and in OS X and Unix systems, you would use the terminal. You will find the script in the cfusion\bin folder, in the location in which you installed ColdFusion 10. For Windows, you use passwordreset.bat, and for Unix-based systems, you use passwordreset.sh. Figure 13.4 demonstrates the password-reset process.

Figure 13.4

The password reset script running from a Microsoft Windows command prompt.

```
→ bin ./passwordreset.sh
Enter 1 for changing Admin Password and 2 for changing Admin Component(jetty) password :
1
Enter new Admin Password :

Confirm new Password :

Enter new RDS Password :

Confirm new Password :

Your Admin and RDS password has been reset. Re-start the server to reflect the changes.
→ bin ▌
```

Note that you are prompted to specify whether you want to change the main administrator password or the admin component related to the underlying Jetty application server. Typically, you will select the first option. The password reset script will prompt you for both a new administrator password and a new Remote Development Services (RDS) password.

Enable RDS (After Installation)

Another small, but welcome, change is the capability to configure RDS. Previously, RDS (used by tools such as ColdFusion Builder to enable inspection of data sources) could be configured only during installation (unless you wanted to edit the XML files by hand). Now you can enable and disable RDS directly in the ColdFusion Administrator. Figure 13.5 demonstrates this new toggle in the Administrator.

Figure 13.5

You can now enable or disable RDS directly in the Administrator.

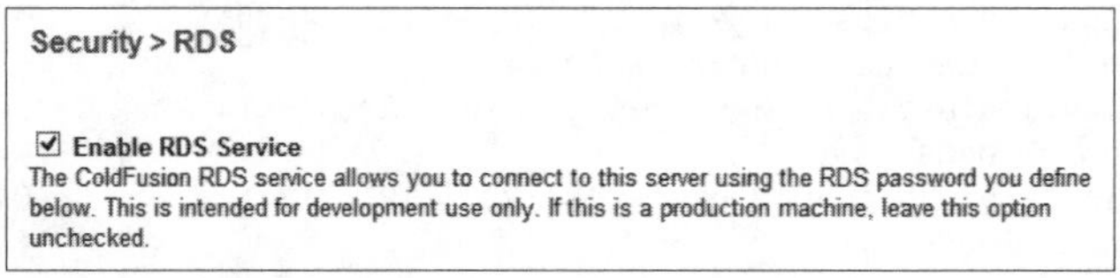

Security > RDS

☑ **Enable RDS Service**
The ColdFusion RDS service allows you to connect to this server using the RDS password you define below. This is intended for development use only. If this is a production machine, leave this option unchecked.

Restrict Admin Access by IP Address

You can also now lock down access by IP address. Figure 13.6 shows the new field added to the Administrator's Security > Allowed IP Addresses for ColdFusion Administrator Access page.

Figure 13.6

Use this form to specify IP addresses that can access the Administrator.

Specify the client IP addresses that can access Administrator. This can be individual IP addresses, IP address ranges of the form 10-30, or * wild cards. Both IPv4 and IPv6 addresses are supported. To include an IP address in the list, enter the address and click Add. To delete an IP address from the list, select the address and click Remove Selected. When no IP addresses are selected, all users are allowed access.

Allowed IP Addresses for ColdFusion Administrator access

IP Address [   ]

[Add]

[Remove Selected]

You can enter both static IP addresses and ranges. So for example, 192.168.1.* would allow for any machine with a matching IP address to access the Admin. Note that if you leave this field blank, the Administrator will allow logins from any IP address.

Server Updates

We've saved the best update for last. Over the years, many updates have been released for ColdFusion. These updates typically include security and bug fixes, and sometimes they include completely new features. Unfortunately, installing these updates has been, historically, something of a pain. First you grab a file from the Adobe.com website. Then you extract the file on the server's desktop. Then you need to copy some files into one folder, other files in another folder, and some more files into yet another folder. Then you need to manually restart the ColdFusion services to make the update take effect, and cross your fingers in the hope that you didn't mess up anything. While everyone appreciates fixes (especially security patches), no one enjoyed the process of applying them.

In ColdFusion 10, this process has been radically improved. You can now download, install, and even uninstall hotfixes directly from within the ColdFusion Administrator.

Upon logging in, you will see a new alert in the upper-right corner if an update is ready. Figure 13.7 shows an example.

Figure 13.7

Updates are available!

In Figure 13.6, two updates are available. Clicking the icon brings you to the new Server Update > Updates page. Figure 13.8 shows how this page may look on your server.

Figure 13.8

The new Server Update > Updates page.

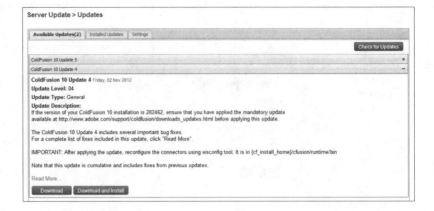

Note that Figure 13.8 uses an accordion display to present information about two updates. If only one update is available, then (obviously) only one update will be displayed. Also note the description of the update, with a link for additional details.

You have the option either to download the update and leave it on your system for installation later or to download and install it at the same time. Figure 13.9 shows what happens when you choose the latter option.

Figure 13.9

You will be warned about the server restarting.

Notice that the Administrator warns you that the server will be restarted.

A progress bar may briefly appear while the file is downloaded. After the download is complete, you are warned again about the restart (Figure 13.10).

Figure 13.10

The Administrator wants to be sure you really know that the server will be restarted.

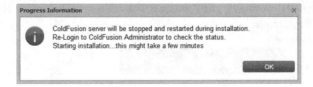

Eventually this pop-up window will go away by itself (even if you don't click OK), and the page will reload after the restart. You can then peruse the list of installed updates (Figure 13.11).

Figure 13.11

You can check the list of installed updates at any time.

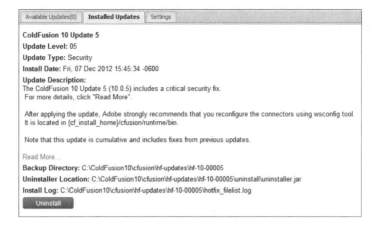

Note the Uninstall button. In the unlikely event that an update breaks something instead of fixing a problem (mistakes do happen), you can use this feature to quickly remove an update.

One other part of this new feature is the Settings tab (Figure 13.12).

Figure 13.12

The Settings tab allows you to tweak the way that updates are handled.

On the Settings tab, you can choose whether to allow or disable automatic updates. If you disable automatic updates, you still can check for updates manually.

You also can choose to have your server send you an email when an update is ready. Figure 13.13 demonstrates what this email may look like.

Figure 13.13

A sample email detailing an available update.

The Settings tab offers one additional feature: if you have set up a proxy server or some other form of update mechanism, you can configure your ColdFusion server to go to another URL instead of the default.

NOTE

Be sure to make a copy of the default URL in case you need to restore it later.

For information about how to set up your own update site, see this blog post: http://www.krishnap.com/2012/09/coldfusion-10-hotfix-update-installer.html.

Scheduling

Task scheduling was added to ColdFusion in version 3.1 and has remained largely unchanged over the years—until now. Those who use scheduled tasks regularly will be pleasantly surprised to see that the scheduler in ColdFusion 10 has received a lot of attention from Adobe. This chapter covers the updates to the scheduling engine, `<cfschedule>` tag, and ColdFusion Administrator, all designed to make scheduling tasks in ColdFusion 10 more flexible and powerful than ever.

A Word About ColdFusion Standard versus Enterprise

Before we get going, it's important to note that there are differences in scheduler features and functions between the Standard and Enterprise versions of ColdFusion. Features that pertain to the Enterprise version only will be noted as we cover them throughout the chapter. For a summary, refer to Table 14.1.

Table 14.1   Enterprise versus Standard Product Comparison

FEATURE	STANDARD	ENTERPRISE
Quartz scheduling engine	✓	✓
Grouping	✓	✓
Task priority	✓	✓
Repeating tasks	✓	✓
Cron expressions	✓	✓
Task listing	✓	✓
Application-level tasks		✓
Chaining		✓
Event listeners		✓
Misfire and exception handling		✓
Clustering		✓

Introducing the Quartz Scheduling Engine

At the heart of the scheduler changes in ColdFusion 10 is a brand-new scheduling engine. This new scheduler is built on the open source Quartz enterprise job scheduler and gives ColdFusion powerful new scheduling capabilities that just weren't possible with the old job scheduler.

The current version of the Quartz scheduler included with ColdFusion 10 is 2.0.2. You can learn more about the Quartz scheduler here: http://quartz-scheduler.org/.

If you are upgrading to ColdFusion 10 from a previous version, all of your existing scheduled tasks are automatically upgraded to run on the new engine during the upgrade process.

Changes to CFSCHEDULE

The <cfschedule> tag provides the main interface for the ColdFusion scheduler, and it's been completely updated in ColdFusion 10. There are a dozen or so new attributes and values you can use with the tag to bend, shape, twist, and cajole scheduled tasks to your will. Before we dive into all the changes, though, we need to set the stage.

Setting the Stage

Almost every example in this chapter creates a task that executes code on a scheduled basis. Rather than call an arbitrary URL at example.com, it's much more useful if you can review the results of your scheduled tasks after they have been executed. With that in mind, let's create a simple .cfm file that we can use with most of our examples. This .cfm file will simply log the successful execution of a scheduled task to a text file in the same directory as our example files. This log will make it easy for you to follow along and to ensure that your scheduled tasks are firing correctly. Listing 14.1 shows the code.

Listing 14.1 /cf10wack/14/myTask.cfm

```
<cffile
  action="append"
  file="#expandPath('./tasklog.txt')#"
  output="#dateFormat(now(), 'mm/dd/yyyy')#, #timeFormat(now(),
          'HH:MM:SS')#, #CGI.SCRIPT_NAME#, Success">
```

Application-Level Tasks

The first piece of functionality we'll discuss is a ColdFusion Enterprise–only feature called application-level tasks. In previous versions of ColdFusion, your only option was to schedule tasks at the server level. This limitation meant that your tasks were accessible to anyone with ColdFusion Administrator access, and programmatically to any application on the server. In addition to making security difficult, especially in shared hosting environments, it also meant that you couldn't have multiple tasks with the same name, even if they were used by different applications. ColdFusion 10 addresses these issues with the addition of application-level tasks.

A few characteristics set application-level tasks apart from server tasks. First, they can be created and edited only programmatically. That means that no one can create or edit an application-level task within the ColdFusion Administrator, although users can run, pause, and delete it. Second, application-level tasks are isolated at the individual application level. This means that tasks scheduled for one application cannot interact with tasks scheduled under another application on the server. This application-level isolation is important in shared hosting environments, as well as in cases in which you want better organization and control over your scheduled tasks.

To create an application-level task, you need two things. First, your application needs to have an Application.cfc file with this.name specified. In this case, we're calling our application CF10WACK (Listing 14.2).

Listing 14.2   /cfwack10/14/Application.cfc

```
<cfcomponent>
  <cfset this.name="CF10WACK">
</cfcomponent>
```

To actually create an application-level scheduled task, use the new Mode attribute of the <cfschedule> tag as in Listing 14.3.

Listing 14.3   /cfwack10/14/createWithMode.cfm

```
<cfschedule
  action="update"
  mode="application"
  task="App_Level_Task"
  url="http://localhost/cf10wack/14/myTask.cfm"
  startdate="#now()#"
  starttime="#dateAdd('n', 1, now())#"
  interval="daily"
  / >

<cfschedule
  action="update"
  mode="server"
  task="Server_Level_Task"
  url="http://localhost/cf10wack/14/myTask.cfm"
  startdate="#now()#"
  starttime="#dateAdd('n', 1, now())#"
  interval="daily"
  / >
```

In our example, the first <cfschedule> tag creates an application-level task by setting mode="application". Everything else in the tag is just as it would be in previous versions of ColdFusion. The second <cfschedule> tag shows how to set a server-level scheduled task. Note that the Mode attribute is optional, with the default being a server-level task.

If you want to verify that the tasks are scheduled correctly, log into your server's ColdFusion Administrator and click the Scheduled Tasks link under Server Settings. You should see output similar to that in Figure 14.1.

Figure 14.1

Server- and
application-level tasks
in the ColdFusion
Administrator.

Grouping

A new feature that's available in both ColdFusion Standard and Enterprise is task grouping. Task grouping lets you organize individual tasks into groups. If you don't specify a group for your scheduled task, it automatically belongs to a group called DEFAULT. Creating a task and adding it to a group is as simple as using the appropriately named Group attribute of the <cfschedule> tag, as shown in Listing 14.4.

Listing 14.4   /cf10wack/14/createGroups.cfm

```
<cfschedule
   action="update"
   task="Task1"
   url="http://localhost/cf10wack/14/myTask.cfm"
   startdate="#now()#"
   starttime="#dateAdd('n', 1, now())#"
   interval="daily"
   / >

<cfschedule
   action="update"
   task="Task1"
   group="Group1"
   url="http://localhost/cf10wack/14/myTask.cfm"
   startdate="#now()#"
   starttime="#dateAdd('n', 2, now())#"
   interval="daily"
   / >

<cfschedule
   action="update"
   task="Task2"
   group="Group1"
   url="http://localhost/cf10wack/14/myTask.cfm"
   startdate="#now()#"
   starttime="#dateAdd('n', 3, now())#"
   interval="daily"
   / >
```

Listing 14.4 (CONTINUED)

```
<cfschedule
  action="update"
  task="Task1"
  group="Group2"
  url="http://localhost/cf10wack/14/myTask.cfm"
  startdate="#now()#"
  starttime="#dateAdd('n', 4, now())#"
  interval="daily"
  / >

<cfschedule
  action="update"
  task="Task2"
  group="Group2"
  url="http://localhost/cf10wack/14/myTask.cfm"
  startdate="#now()#"
  starttime="#dateAdd('n', 5, now())#"
  interval="daily"
  / >

<cfschedule
  action="update"
  task="Task1"
  mode="application"
  group="Group1"
  url="http://localhost/cf10wack/14/myTask.cfm"
  startdate="#now()#"
  starttime="#dateAdd('n', 5, now())#"
  interval="daily"
  / >

<cfschedule
  action="update"
  task="Task2"
  mode="application"
  group="Group1"
  url="http://localhost/cf10wack/14/myTask.cfm"
  startdate="#now()#"
  starttime="#dateAdd('n', 5, now())#"
  interval="daily"
  / >
```

This code creates seven scheduled tasks (you can view them from the Scheduled Tasks section of the ColdFusion Administrator). Because we don't specify a Group or Mode value for the first task, it's automatically assigned to the DEFAULT group of the server-level tasks. The second and third tasks are assigned to a server-level group called Group1, and the fourth and fifth tasks are assigned to a server-level group called Group2. The sixth and seventh tasks are assigned to an application-level group called Group1. Note that more than one task can share the same name, as long as the tasks belong to different groups or one task is a server-level task and the other is an application-level task. The same goes for group names. You can use the same name for two unrelated groups: one for application-level tasks and one for server-level tasks.

Deleting Tasks

You delete tasks in ColdFusion 10 in essentially the same way as in previous versions of ColdFusion, with one caveat. With the addition of application-specific tasks and task groups, it's possible to have more than one task with the same name, so when you delete a task, you can now provide group and mode attributes to specify exactly which task to delete. If no group is provided, ColdFusion will make the deletion from the Default group. If no mode is specified, ColdFusion will delete from the server-specific tasks. Listing 14.5 shows how to delete one of the application-specific tasks from Group1, which we created in Listing 14.4.

Listing 14.5 /cf10wack/14/deleteTask.cfm

```
<cfschedule
  action="delete"
  task="Task1"
  mode="application"
  group="Group1"
  / >
```

Running Tasks

As with task deletion, the addition of groups and application-specific tasks affects the way that you manually run a task using <cfschedule>. To manually launch a task, you optionally specify the mode and group attributes as shown in Listing 14.6. If you don't specify a mode, ColdFusion defaults to a server-specific task. If no group is provided, ColdFusion assumes the Default group.

Listing 14.6 /cf10wack/14/runTask.cfm

```
<cfschedule
  action="run"
  task="Task2"
  mode="application"
  group="Group1"
  / >
```

Running this example launches the application-specific task from Group1 named Task2 that we created in Listing 14.4.

Task Prioritization

Task prioritization is available in both ColdFusion Standard and Enterprise and lets you give tasks higher or lower execution priority relative to other tasks that are scheduled to run at the same time. Task prioritization is useful in situations in which you have fewer threads available to run tasks than you have tasks scheduled at a given time. So if you have 5 threads available to run tasks, and you have 20 tasks set to run at the same time, you can specify the relative priority of each task so that ColdFusion will run the tasks with higher priority first. To set the task priority, use the new Priority argument. The Priority argument accepts any integer, positive or negative (Listing 14.7).

The number of threads available to run tasks is configurable via a properties file called quartz.properties. This process is covered in detail later in this chapter.

Listing 14.7 /cf10wack/14/createPriority.cfm

```
<cfschedule
  action="update"
  task="Priority_Task"
  url="http://localhost/cf10wack/14/myTask.cfm"
  startdate="#now()#"
  starttime="#dateAdd('n', 1, now())#"
  interval="daily"
  priority="10"
  / >
```

This code creates a new task set to run at 8 a.m. with a priority of 10. If several other tasks were also set to run at 8 a.m., this task would run before any tasks that have a priority lower than 10. If you don't specify a priority, a value of 5 is used as the default.

NOTE

If multiple scheduled tasks are scheduled to run at the same time and have the same priority, and if the number of tasks is greater than the number of available threads, the Quartz scheduler will randomly choose which one to run first.

Chaining

Task chaining is a new Enterprise-only feature that you can use to set up dependencies between one or more scheduled tasks so that the completion of a parent task triggers the execution of one or more child tasks. Listing 14.8 shows an example that creates two server tasks and chains them together as parent and child.

Listing 14.8 /cf10wack/14/chainParentChild.cfm

```
<cfschedule
  action="update"
  task="Child_Task"
  group="chainParentChild"
  url=" http://localhost/cf10wack/14/myTask.cfm "
  / >

<cfschedule
  action="update"
  task="Parent_Task"
  group="chainParentChild"
  url="http://localhost/cf10wack/14/myTask.cfm"
  startdate="#now()#"
  starttime="#dateAdd('n', 1, now())#"
  interval="Daily"
  onComplete="Child_Task:chainParentChild:server"
  / >
```

Two details you should notice here right away. The first task we create has no `startDate`, `startTime`, or `interval` value set for it. This is because the task is a child task and generally shouldn't run outside its relationship with its parent task (it is possible to have chained tasks run independently, but this behavior is usually not a good idea). The second task in this example is the parent task, so it gets `startDate`, `startTime`, and `interval` values. It also gets another attribute called `onComplete`, which tells ColdFusion that this is a parent task, and that upon successful completion, it should fire a child task called `Child_Task` from the group `chainParentChild` at the `server` level.

NOTE

> An application-level parent task can call a server-level scheduled task, but a server-level parent task cannot call an application-level child task. Your ColdFusion code won't throw an error if you chain tasks in this way, so be careful: the only indication of a problem will be in the scheduler.log file.

You also can run multiple child tasks in parallel when the parent task completes, as shown in Listing 14.9.

Listing 14.9   /cf10wack/14/chainParentMultipleChildren.cfm

```
<cfschedule
  action="update"
  task="Child_Task1"
  group="chainParentMultipleChildren"
  mode="application"
  url="http://localhost/cf10wack/14/myTask.cfm"
  / >

<cfschedule
  action="update"
  task="Child_Task2"
  group="chainParentMultipleChildren"
  mode="application"
  url="http://localhost/cf10wack/14/myTask.cfm"
  / >

<cfschedule
  action="update"
  task="Parent_Task"
  group="chainParentMultipleChildren"
  mode="application"
  url="http://localhost/cf10wack/14/myTask.cfm"
  startdate="#now()#"
  starttime="#dateAdd('n', 1, now())#"
  interval="Daily"
  onComplete="Child_Task1:chainParentMultipleChildren:application,
             Child_Task2:chainParentMultipleChildren:application"
  />
```

In this case, we specify two different child tasks in the `onComplete` parameter. Upon successful completion of the parent task, both child tasks are fired at the same time.

You also can nest chains so that child tasks can themselves have additional children. In such cases, the child task is a parent to its children, with the relationship defined by an onComplete parameter in the child's <cfschedule> tag. Listing 14.10 illustrates this scenario.

Listing 14.10   /cf10wack/14/chainParentNestedChildren.cfm

```
<cfschedule
  action="update"
  task="Grandchild_Task"
  group="chainParentNestedChildren"
  url="http://localhost/cf10wack/14/myTask.cfm"
  / >

<cfschedule
  action="update"
  task="Child_Task"
  group="chainParentNestedChildren"
  url="http://localhost/cf10wack/14/myTask.cfm"
  onComplete="Grandchild_Task:DEFAULT:server"
  / >

<cfschedule
  action="update"
  task="Parent_Task"
  group="chainParentNestedChildren"
  url="http://localhost/cf10wack/14/myTask.cfm"
  startdate="#now()#"
  starttime="#dateAdd('n', 1, now())#"
  interval="Daily"
  onComplete="Child_Task:DEFAULT:server"
  />
```

Excluding Dates

Another new scheduling feature in ColdFusion 10 is the capability to exclude certain dates from a scheduled task's execution schedule. Say you have a report that's set to run daily, but you don't want it to run on certain company holidays. Using the new Exclude attribute of the <cfschedule> tag, you can tell the scheduler not to run on those days. Listing 14.11 shows how the code might look.

Listing 14.11   /cf10wack/14/excludeDateList.cfm

```
<cfschedule
  action="update"
  task="Exclude_Date_List"
  url="http://localhost/cf10wack/14/myTask.cfm"
  startdate="#now()#"
  starttime="#dateAdd('n', 1, now())#"
  interval="daily"
  exclude="01/01/2013,04/04/2013,5/27/2013"
  / >
```

If you look at the Exclude attribute, you'll see that we've passed in a comma-delimited list of dates to exclude from the schedule.

NOTE

Did you notice that there are no spaces between the dates and commas in the `Exclude` attribute? This is currently (as of Updater 4) a bug in ColdFusion as whitespace between list items shouldn't matter. If you leave any whitespace between the dates and their delimiters, ColdFusion throws an error.

You can also pass in a range of dates by using the format `exclude="03/01/2013 TO 03/31/2013"`, which in this case would exclude the entire month of March. Additionally, you can pass in an array of date strings or objects, as shown in Listing 14.12.

Listing 14.12 /cf10wack/14/excludeDateArray.cfm

```
<cfset excludeDates =
  [
    "01/01/2013",
    "04/04/2013",
    "05/27/2013"
  ]
/>

<cfschedule
  action="update"
  task="Exclude_Date_Array"
  url="http://localhost/cf10wack/14/myTask.cfm"
  startdate="#now()#"
  starttime="#dateAdd('n', 1, now())#"
  interval="daily"
  exclude="#excludeDates#"
  / >
```

Although it's possible to pass a list or an array of dates using the `Exclude` attribute, you can't currently pass both a single date or list of dates *and* a range of dates in the same operation. In other words, you can't specify the following:

```
Exclude="02/14/2013, 12/31/2013 TO 01/01/2014"
```

If you try to do this, ColdFusion throws an exception.

Repeating Tasks

In older versions of ColdFusion, if you wanted a task to repeat a certain number of times, you had to take your start time, figure in your interval, and then calculate an end time based on the interval and the number of times you want the task to repeat. ColdFusion 10 lets you more easily schedule tasks that must repeat several times outside the standard daily, weekly, or monthly interval with the introduction of a new attribute for the `<cfschedule>` tag called `Repeat`. The `Repeat` attribute lets you specify the number of times that a task should repeat for a given interval—so if you want to schedule a task to execute every day at 8 a.m. and repeat five times every five minutes, you could code it as shown in Listing 14.13.

Listing 14.13 `/cf10wack/14/repeatTask.cfm`

```
<cfschedule
  action="update"
  task="My_Repeating_Task"
  url="http://localhost/cf10wack/14/myTask.cfm"
  startdate="#now()#"
  starttime="#dateAdd('n', 1, now())#"
  repeat="5"
  interval="300"
  / >
```

Cron Expressions

Cron expressions for the Quartz scheduler allow you to represent complex scheduling operations using a relatively simple syntax. Cron expressions are made up of six required and one optional field, which gives you fine-grained control over the time that a scheduled task fires. Each field in a Cron expression consists of a string of values or special characters. For example, the Cron expression `0 0 13 ? * MON-FRI` means execute the task at 1 p.m. every weekday. Alternatively, the expression can be written `0 0 13 ? * 2-6`. Table 14.2 lists each field, the range of values for that field, and the special characters you can use.

Table 14.2   Cron Expressions

FIELD	VALUES	SPECIAL CHARACTERS
Seconds	0 to 59	* - , /
Minutes	0 to 59	* - , /
Hours	0 to 23	* - , /
Day of Month	1 to 31	* - , / ? L W
Month	1 to 12 or JAN to DEC	* - , /
Day of Week	1 to 7 or SUN to SAT	* - , / ? L #
Year (optional)	1970 to 2099	* - , /

The special characters in Cron expressions are used to indicate and modify values. Table 14.3 explains the use of each special character.

Table 14.3 Special Characters in Cron Expressions

CHARACTER	DESCRIPTION
*	All values within a field: For example, if you use * in the Day of Week field, the task will run every day.
-	Range of values: For example, if you use MON-FRI in the Day of Week field, the task will run only on weekdays.
,	Delimiter for lists of values: For example, is you use MON, WED, FRI in the Day of Week field, the task will run only on Monday, Wednesday, and Friday.
/	Used to indicate an increment to a given value or range: For example, if you specify 0/15 in the Minutes field, the task will run every 15 minutes starting on the hour. Likewise, if you specify 10/15, the task will run every 15 minutes, starting at 10 minutes past the hour. If you don't specify a value before the / delimiter, Quartz defaults to 0.
?	Used only with the Day of Month and Day of Week fields to indicate a blank value: For example, if you specify ? in the Day of Month field, the day of the month isn't factored into the schedule for the task.
L	Used only in the Day of Month and Day of Week fields: For Day of Month, L indicates the last day of the month (January 31, February 28 or 29, April 30, and so on). For Day of Week, L can be used alone to indicate Saturday (not very useful), or with a day value to indicate things like the last Saturday of the month, which would be written as 7L.
W	Used only with the Day of Month field to indicate the closest weekday (MON-FRI) to a given day: For example, 15W runs the task on the weekday closest to the fifteenth of the month. If the specified day of the month is Saturday, the task will run on the Friday before. Likewise, if the specified day is on Sunday, the task will run on the following Monday. Note that the scheduler will not cross into the previous or next month's days. If you specify 1W and the first day of the month is Saturday, the task will not run until Monday the third. Likewise, if you specify 30W for a month with 30 days, and the thirtieth is on Sunday, the task will run on Friday the twenty-eighth. If you specify LW in the Day of Month field, the task will run the last weekday of the month.
#	Used only in the Day of Week field to specify nth day of the week of the month. For example, to run a task on the third Thursday of the month, you would use THR#3 or 5#3 in the Day of Week field.

To specify a Cron expression in the `<cfschedule>` tag, use the `cronTime` attribute. Listing 14.14 shows how to create a scheduled task using `cronTime` to run the task at 8 a.m. on the fifteenth and thirtieth of every month.

Listing 14.14 /cf10wack/14/cron.cfm

```
<cfschedule
   action="update"
   task="Cut_Paychecks_15th_30th"
   url="http://localhost/cf10wack/14/myTask.cfm"
   crontime="0 0 8 15,30 * ?"
   / >
```

If you don't specify startDate and startTime values for the task (the date and time that ColdFusion considers the task as scheduled, not necessarily the date and time that it executes the task), ColdFusion uses the current date and time. If you use cronTime, other attributes such as interval will be saved by ColdFusion, but they'll be ignored by the scheduler.

Handling Exceptions

Exception handling for scheduled tasks is greatly improved in ColdFusion 10. Sure to disappoint some, it's also an Enterprise-only feature. The exception handler catches HTTP 404 (page not found) and HTTP 500 (internal server error) exceptions, which should cover the majority of the exceptions you're likely to encounter when running scheduled tasks. One small cautionary note: If you use ColdFusion's Site Wide Error Handler (configurable in the ColdFusion Administrator), and your scheduled task calls a page on your server that results in a runtime exception, the scheduled task exception handler will not catch the error because the Site Wide Error Handler returns HTTP 200 (OK).

To implement exception handling, use the new onException attribute of the <cfschedule> tag. The onException attribute accepts three possible values: pause, refire, and invokeHandler. The Pause value temporarily pauses future execution of the task until the task is resumed programmatically or manually via the ColdFusion Administrator. The Refire attribute immediately reexecutes the task. The invokeHandler attribute tells ColdFusion to pass the handling of the exception to a special CFC that you create to handle scheduler-related events. We discuss that feature a bit later, in the section "Event Handling." For now, let's look at an example task that calls a nonexistent page, resulting in an HTTP 404 error (Listing 14.15).

Listing 14.15   /cf10wack/14/onExceptionPause.cfm

```
<cfschedule
  action="update"
  task="OnException_Pause"
  url="http://localhost/cf10wack/14/404.cfm"
  startdate="#now()#"
  starttime="#dateAdd('n', 1, now())#"
  interval="daily"
  onexception="pause"
  / >
```

The code in Listing 14.15 creates a task that's set to run a minute after you create it. It then tries to call a page that doesn't exist, resulting in an HTTP 404 error, which the exception handler catches, causing it to pause the task. If you wait for that minute to pass and then log into the ColdFusion Administrator, you can verify that the task is paused. You can also check the Scheduler.log file from the ColdFusion Administrator, which will show the pause event.

Retry Count

If ColdFusion encounters an error during execution of a scheduled task and you've specified onException="REFIRE_NOW", you can optionally specify the number of times the scheduler should attempt to reexecute the task before giving up by setting retryCount="n ", where n is an integer between 0 and 3 that represents the number of times that you want to try reexecuting the task. If retryCount isn't passed, ColdFusion defaults to three attempts. Listing 14.16 shows an example of how to set up a task that attempts reexecution two times if an exception is encountered.

Listing 14.16   /cf10wack/14/onExceptionRetry.cfm

```
<cfschedule
  action="update"
  task="OnException_Retry"
  url="http://localhost/cf10wack/14/404.cfm"
  startdate="#now()#"
  starttime="#dateAdd('n', 1, now())#"
  interval="daily"
  onexception="refire"
  retrycount="2"
  / >
```

This code sets up a task to execute a minute from the time you run the code. When the code runs, you can verify that the task attempts reexecution twice by checking the Scheduler.log file in the ColdFusion Administrator.

Handling Misfires

A misfire occurs when the scheduler fails to fire a task within 60 seconds of its scheduled start time. There are numerous reasons why this might happen: for instance, the server may be rebooting, the ColdFusion Application Server service may be restarting, or all of the Quartz scheduler worker threads are already being allocated to other tasks. Regardless of the cause, the scheduler is smart enough to know that a particular task failed to fire. Even better for you as a developer, this feature means that you now have some control over how ColdFusion handles the misfire—something that took a lot of custom programming in prior versions of ColdFusion. ColdFusion 10 gives you two options for handling a task misfire: FIRE_NOW and invokeHandler. The FIRE_NOW option causes the scheduler to immediately refire the task, and invokeHandler calls an external event handler, which we discuss later in the chapter. Listing 14.17 shows how to set up a scheduled task that will automatically refire if the scheduler detects a misfire.

Listing 14.17   /cf10wack/14/onMisfire.cfm

```
<cfschedule
  action="update"
  task="OnMisfire_Fire_Now"
  url="http://localhost/cf10wack/14/myTask.cfm"
  startdate="#now()#"
  starttime="#dateAdd('n', 1, now())#"
  interval="daily"
  onmisfire="FIRE_NOW"
  / >
```

You can test the misfire handling yourself by executing the code, waiting a minute for the task to fire, stopping your ColdFusion server, waiting another two minutes, and then restarting the server. After the restart, if you look in the Scheduler.log file in the ColdFusion Administrator, you should see two entries that relate to the task:

```
Task DEFAULT.ONMISFIRE_FIRE_NOW misfired.
Task DEFAULT.ONMISFIRE_FIRE_NOW triggered.
```

These indicate that the scheduled task, which was supposed to execute one minute after it was created, misfired (because the ColdFusion server was stopped). When the server started again, the scheduler realized that the task had misfired and immediately refired (triggered) it.

NOTE

There's currently a bug in ColdFusion 10 (as of Updater 4) that makes the `onMisfire` attribute of the `<cfschedule>` tag case sensitive so that you must use `FIRE_NOW` instead of `fire_now` if you want a task to refire when the scheduler misfires. Normally, ColdFusion does not care about case in tag attributes and values.

Event Handling

While it's certainly easy to handle certain events such as `onMisfire` and `onError` at the individual `<cfschedule>` level by passing them as tag attributes, wouldn't it be even better if ColdFusion provided you with a means of handling those events (and more) that is more flexible and reusable? Well, you're in luck. As part of the scheduler overhaul, you can now create CFC-based event listeners to handle various events associated with the firing of scheduled tasks. Not only does this new function give you more flexibility in the way that your tasks respond to certain events, it also lets you design your application code so that it is much more modular and reusable.

To create an event listener, you first need to create a new CFC and place it in a directory relative to your webroot, in a virtual directory, or in a directory that has a corresponding ColdFusion mapping. Listing 14.18 shows a bare-bones skeleton for a scheduled task event listener.

Listing 14.18 /cf10wack/14/eventListenerSkeleton.cfc

```
<cfcomponent implements="CFIDE.scheduler.ITaskEventHandler">
  <cffunction name="onTaskStart" returntype="boolean">
    <cfargument name="context" type="struct"/>

    <cfreturn true>
  </cffunction>

  <cffunction name="onTaskEnd" access="public" returntype="void">
    <cfargument name="context" type="struct" required="false"/>

  </cffunction>

  <cffunction name="onMisfire" returntype="void">
    <cfargument name="context" type="struct" required="false"/>

  </cffunction>
```

Listing 14.18 (CONTINUED)

```
<cffunction name="onError" returntype="void">
  <cfargument name="context" type="struct" required="false"/>

</cffunction>

<cffunction name="execute" returntype="void">

</cffunction>
</cfcomponent>
```

The first thing you may notice is implements=" CFIDE.scheduler.ITaskEventHandler" in the <cfcomponent> tag. This means that the CFC implements an interface defined in the ITaskEventHandler CFC. Don't worry if you've never worked with interfaces in ColdFusion. All you need to know to create the event handler is that you have to include the line that implements the interface in your CFC.

The next thing you'll notice in our skeleton is that there are five method stubs: onTaskStart, onTaskEnd, onError, onMisfire, and Execute.

- onTaskStart: This method is called before the task executes and can be used to set up variables and determine whether or not the task should fire. If you want the task to fire, return True. If you don't want the task to fire, return False. You can think of onTaskStart as akin to an init() method.

- onTaskEnd: The onTaskEnd method executes after the task has successfully completed. *Successfully* is the operative word here. If the task throws an error while executing, the onTaskEnd method will not fire.

- onMisfire: If you set <cfschedule onMisfire="invokeHandler" ...>, this method will fire in the event that the scheduler misfires. Note that by calling the onMisfire event handler, you're not refiring the task—you're passing control to the onMisfire method, where you can code any behavior you desire. You can still reexecute the task, but you'll need to do so by calling the Execute method (if used) directly, or by rerunning the scheduled task by calling <cfschedule action="run" ...>.

- onError: Don't get stuck on the fact that this method is named onError and not onException to match the onException attribute of the <cfschedule> tag. The onError method executes when you've set <cfschedule onException="invokeHandler" ...> and the task encounters an error such as an HTTP 400 or 500 exception while executing. Like onMisfire, onError won't automatically refire the task. It's up to you to code any error handling behavior you desire.

- Execute: The Execute method lets you encapsulate your task code in a CFC method rather than an external template you have to call with <cfschedule URL="...">. If both the URL parameter <cfschedule> and an Execute event handler are specified, the URL parameter takes precedence, and the code in the Execute event handler will not fire.

Event Handler Arguments

Each event handler method except for Execute accepts a single argument, Context, which is a structure made up of the following keys: group, mode, and task. For the onError event handler, Context contains an additional key: exceptionMessage. You do not have to create these structures yourself; ColdFusion automatically passes them from the values, including default values, specified in the <cfschedule> tag.

Using Event Handlers

Calling event handlers for a scheduled task is a two-step process. First you need to specify the path to your event handler using dot notation in the eventHandler attribute of the <cfschedule> tag. This code associates your event handler with your scheduled task and calls the onTaskStart method each time that your task fires. If you haven't specified a URL in <cfschedule>, the Execute method is called as the code to execute when the task fires. If the task completes successfully, onTaskEnd is called. Listing 14.19 shows how you would call an event handler named taskListener. cfc located in the directory /cf10wack/14.

Listing 14.19   /cf10wack/14/eventHandler.cfm

```
<cfschedule
  action="update"
  task="Event_Handler_Test"
  startdate="#now()#"
  starttime="#dateAdd('n', 1, now())#"
  interval="daily"
  eventhandler="cf10wack.14.taskListener"
  / >
```

Two other methods are also available to the event handler: onError for handling exceptions, and onMisfire for handing scheduler misfires. These two methods must be explicitly called from the <cfschedule> tag with the onException and onMisfire attributes, respectively. Explicit calling is necessary because you have options to specify when you want ColdFusion to handle exceptions and misfired tasks. For example, if you simply want a misfired task to refire, you don't necessarily want to invoke the onMisfire event handler. You might prefer to just use <cfschedule onMisfire="FIRE_NOW" ...>. If, however, you want to call an event handler for onException or onMisfire, simply use <cfschedule onException="invokeHandler"... > to call the onError event handler if an exception is encountered, or <cfschedule onMisfire="invokeHandler" ...> to call the onMisfire event handler if a misfire occurs. Listing 14.20 takes the skeleton event handler from Listing 14.18 and adds some more realistic functionality to it so that each method logs its execution to the Scheduler.log file available in the ColdFusion Administrator. Listing 14.20 shows the code for the improved CFC.

Listing 14.20   /cf10wack/14/taskListener.cfc

```
<cfcomponent implements="CFIDE.scheduler.ITaskEventHandler">
  <cffunction name="onTaskStart" returntype="boolean">
    <cfargument name="context" type="struct"/>

    <!--- use some condition to determine whether to fire the task --->
    <cfset var conditionMet = true>
```

Listing 14.20 (CONTINUED)

```
    <cflog log="scheduler" text="#dateFormat(now(), 'mm/dd/yyyy')#,
      #timeFormat(now(), 'HH:MM:SS')#, #arguments.context.task#,
      #arguments.context.mode#, #arguments.context.group#, Started
      Successfully" />

    <cfreturn (conditionMet ? true : false)>
  </cffunction>

  <cffunction name="onTaskEnd" access="public" returntype="void">
    <cfargument name="context" type="struct" required="false"/>

    <cflog log="scheduler" text="#dateFormat(now(), 'mm/dd/yyyy')#,
      #timeFormat(now(), 'HH:MM:SS')#, #arguments.context.task#,
      #arguments.context.mode#, #arguments.context.group#, Completed
      Successfully" />
  </cffunction>

  <cffunction name="onMisfire" returntype="void">
    <cfargument name="context" type="struct" required="false"/>

    <cflog log="scheduler" text="#dateFormat(now(), 'mm/dd/yyyy')#,
      #timeFormat(now(), 'HH:MM:SS')#, #arguments.context.task#,
      #arguments.context.mode#, #arguments.context.group#, Task Misfired"
      />

    <!--- This is one way to refire the task --->
    <cfschedule
      action="run"
      task="arguments.context.task"
      mode="arguments.context.mode"
      group="arguments.context.group"
      />

    <cflog log="scheduler" text="#dateFormat(now(), 'mm/dd/yyyy')#,
      #timeFormat(now(), 'HH:MM:SS')#, #arguments.context.task#,
      #arguments.context.mode#, #arguments.context.group#, Task Refired"
      />
  </cffunction>

  <cffunction name="onError" returntype="void">
    <cfargument name="context" type="struct" required="false"/>

    <cflog log="scheduler" text="#dateFormat(now(), 'mm/dd/yyyy')#,
      #timeFormat(now(), 'HH:MM:SS')#, #arguments.context.task#,
      #arguments.context.mode#, #arguments.context.group#,
      #arguments.context.exceptionMessage#, Task Exception Caught" />
  </cffunction>

  <cffunction name="execute" returntype="void">
    <cflog log="scheduler" text="#dateFormat(now(), 'mm/dd/yyyy')#,
      #timeFormat(now(), 'HH:MM:SS')#, Task Executed Successfully" />
  </cffunction>
</cfcomponent>
```

There are two other interesting points to note about the code. First, if you look at the onMisfire method, you'll see that we log the misfire and then use the `<cfschedule>` tag to immediately run the task that misfired. Since we're handling the misfire in the onMisfire event handler, there's no built-in way to refire the event as there is when you use `<cfschedule onmisfire="FIRE_NOW">`. The use of `<cfschedule action="run">` gives you equivalent functionality.

The second point to note is that the Execute method doesn't have access to the Context argument. This limitation is unfortunate because it would be handy to have access to the task's name, group, and mode information in the task execution code, especially for our logging purposes.

To see the event handlers in action, run the code in Listing 14.21.

Listing 14.21 /cf10wack/14/invokeHandler.cfm

```
<cfschedule
  action="update"
  task="Call_Event_Handler"
  startdate="#now()#"
  starttime="#dateAdd('n', 1, now())#"
  interval="daily"
  onmisfire="INVOKEHANDLER"
  onexception="INVOKEHANDLER"
  eventhandler="cf10wack.14.taskListener"
  / >
```

This code will set up a task to run one minute in the future. After the task executes, check the Scheduler.log file in the ColdFusion Administrator. You should see entries like these:

```
"Information","DefaultQuartzScheduler_Worker-1","11/13/12","19:07:11",,
➡ "Task DEFAULT.Call_Event_Handler triggered."
"Information","DefaultQuartzScheduler_Worker-1","11/13/12","19:07:11","CF10WACK",
➡ "11/13/2012, 19:07:11, Call_Event_Handler, server, DEFAULT, Started Successfully"
"Information","DefaultQuartzScheduler_Worker-1","11/13/12","19:07:11","CF10WACK",
➡ "11/13/2012, 19:07:11, Task Executed Successfully"
"Information","DefaultQuartzScheduler_Worker-1","11/13/12","19:07:11","CF10WACK",
➡ "11/13/2012, 19:07:11, Call_Event_Handler, server, DEFAULT, Completed
Successfully"
```

The first log entry is created by ColdFusion when the task is triggered. The next three entries are all a result of the logging we created in our event handlers. Notice that neither the onMisfire nor the onError handlers fired. If you want them to fire, you'll need to force a scheduler misfire or an error somewhere in the code.

Listing Scheduled Tasks

One feature that's been sorely missing from `<cfschedule>` is the capability to get a list of tasks that are currently scheduled. This sounds like a basic capability, and it is, but until ColdFusion 10, developers had to resort to Java to interact with the undocumented coldfusion.server.ServiceFactory feature or parse the WDDX-encoded data in ColdFusion's neo-cron.xml file, neither a supported approach. ColdFusion 10 addresses this capability for both ColdFusion Standard and Enterprise with the introduction of a new "List" value for the Action attribute of the `<cfschedule>` tag. Listing 14.22 shows the code for listing both server- and application-level tasks.

Listing 14.22 /cf10wack/14/listAllTasks.cfm

```
<cfschedule
  action="list"
  mode="server"
  result="myServerTasks"
  / >

<cfschedule
  action="list"
  mode="application"
  result="myApplicationTasks"
  / >

<h3>Server Level Tasks</h3>
<cfdump var="#myServerTasks#" />

<h3>Application Level Tasks</h3>
<cfdump var="#myApplicationTasks#" />
```

Execution of this code results in two dumps: one for the server-level tasks and one for any application-level tasks. Each dump is returned as a query object. Notice that there's a lot of metadata returned for each task—pretty much every attribute you can set with the <cfschedule> tag has a corresponding return value. Many of these return values are not well documented; they are defined for you here in Table 14.4.

Table 14.4   Return Values for <cfschedule action="list">

RETURN VALUE	DESCRIPTION
CHAINED_TASK	Indicates whether the task is a chained task. Returns Yes or No.
CLUSTERED	Indicates whether the task is clustered. Returns Yes or No.
CRONTIME	Returns the Cron expression for firing the task. Note that chained tasks do not generally have a Cron expression associated with them because they execute upon completion of their parent task, not on a scheduled basis.
ENDDATE	Returns the end date for the task, if specified.
ENDTIME	Returns the end time for the task, if specified.
EVENTHANDLER	Returns the path to the CFC defined as the event listener for the task. Paths use dot notation.
EXCLUDE	Indicates the date, date range, or comma-delimited list of dates to exclude from the task execution schedule. Note that even if you pass an array of dates for the EXCLUDE attribute of <cfschedule>, the scheduler still stores the dates as a list.
FILE	Indicates the filename to use for task output when PUBLISH is set to Yes.
GROUP	Name of the group to which the task belongs. Returns DEFAULT if the task isn't assigned a user-specified group.
INTERVAL	Interval for which the scheduled task is set to execute. Returns a number of seconds or Once, Daily, Weekly, or Monthly.

Table 14.4 CONTINUED

RETURN VALUE	DESCRIPTION
LAST_FIRE	Returns a time stamp representing the last date and time that the task executed.
MODE	Indicates whether the task is an application-specific or server-specific task.
ONCOMPLETE	Returns the task name, group, and mode in the form task:group:mode for the parent task in a chained task relationship.
ONEXCEPTION	Indicates the action that the scheduler should take if an exception occurs while firing the task. Possible values are Refire, Pause, and InvokeHandler. Returns empty if no exception handling is specified.
ONMISFIRE	Indicates the action that the scheduler should take if a misfire occurs. Possible values are fire_now and InvokeHandler. Returns empty if no misfire handling is specified.
OVERWRITE	Indicates whether to overwrite the file (Yes) created when PUBLISH is also Yes. The value False indicates that a new file should be written each time that the task is run.
PATH	If PUBLISH is Yes, PATH indicates the file system path to which the resulting file should be written.
PRIORITY	Returns the task execution priority. The default priority is 5.
PROXY_PORT	Indicates the port on the proxy server through which the request will be routed. The default is 80.
PROXY_SERVER	Indicates the host name or IP address of the proxy server (if any) through which the task will be routed.
PROXY_USER	Indicates the user name associated with the proxy server listed in PROXY_SERVER.
PUBLISH	Indicates whether task output should be written to a file.
REMAINING_COUNT	Indicates the number of times remaining that a task with ENDDATE and INTERVAL values will execute.
REPEAT	Returns the number of times that a task is set to repeat. For recurring tasks, REPEAT returns -1, indicating forever.
RESOLVE_URL	Indicates whether the scheduler should resolve relative links to absolute URLs in the URL called by the scheduler.
RETRY_COUNT	If ONEXCEPTION is set to Refire, RETRY_COUNT indicates the number of times that the scheduler should attempt to refire the task before giving up.
STARTDATE	Indicates the start date for the scheduled task.
STARTTIME	Indicates the start time for the scheduled task.
STATUS	Indicates whether a task is running or paused.
TASK	Returns the name of the scheduled task.
TIMEOUT	Indicates the time in milliseconds that ColdFusion should wait for an executing task before timing out.
URL	Returns the absolute URL that the scheduler should call when it fires. The URL value may be blank if the task is set to use EVENTHANDLER. If both URL and EVENTHANDLER have values, the scheduler uses URL.
USERNAME	Returns the user name that is used with this task to access secured resources. Note that ColdFusion doesn't return the associated password.

Pausing and Resuming Tasks

In ColdFusion 10, the capability to pause and resume scheduled tasks is no longer limited to individual tasks. You can now pause or resume all tasks, or groups of tasks, at once (both at the server and application levels). Listing 14.23 shows how to pause all server tasks using action="pauseAll".

Listing 14.23 /cf10wack/14/pauseAll.cfm

```
<cfschedule action="pauseAll" />

<cfschedule
  action="list"
  result="myTasks"
  />

<cfdump var="#myTasks#" />
```

Executing the code sets all server tasks as paused. To resume all of the tasks, simply set action="resumeAll". If you want to pause all of the tasks for your application, set mode="application" in your <cfschedule> call.

NOTE

As of Updater 4, in ColdFusion 10, there is a bug in PauseAll; ColdFusion throws an exception if you attempt to pause all tasks and there are chained tasks or tasks that have expired, such as those set to run once.

If you want to pause a group of tasks, as opposed to all tasks, use action="pause" and set the group attribute of the <cfschedule> tag to the name of your task group. Listing 14.24 shows how to do this for a group of server tasks belonging to Group1.

Listing 14.24 /cf10wack/14/pauseGroup.cfm

```
<cfschedule
  action="pause"
  group="Group1"
  mode="server"
  / >

<cfschedule
  action="list"
  result="myTasks"
  />

<cfdump var="#myTasks#" />
```

Running this code pauses all of the tasks in Group1 and then gets a list of all of the tasks on the server, including their status (which should show Paused for any Group1 tasks). To resume the paused tasks, just set action="resume". If you want to pause or resume a group of application-level tasks, set mode="application" in the <cfschedule> tag.

Changes to the ColdFusion Administrator

So far, everything we've covered in this chapter has centered around how to take advantage of the new scheduler features and functions programmatically. Along with the new capabilities added to the `<cfschedule>` tag, the Scheduled Tasks section of the ColdFusion Administrator also got some much needed attention in ColdFusion 10.

The first thing you'll notice is that the navigation link for Scheduled Tasks has moved from the Debugging & Logging section of the ColdFusion Administrator (where it never really belonged) to the Server Settings section. This change should make it much easier to find.

The next thing you'll notice is that the Scheduled Tasks interface has been redesigned and now has different sections for server-level and application-level tasks. Previous versions of ColdFusion had only server-level tasks, so there was only one section.

You'll also notice that the listing for each task contains some new fields that didn't exist in previous versions of ColdFusion. Specifically, ColdFusion 10 adds the following: Group, Next Run, Repeat, Remaining Count, and Cluster.

Group shows the group to which the task belongs. Next Run shows the date and time that the task is set to execute next. Repeat shows the number of times that the task is set to repeat and displays -1 for recurring tasks. Remaining Count is set to Infinite for recurring tasks, or an integer representing the number of times that the task has left to execute if you specify an endDate value for your scheduled task. When you create a task with a repeat value and an endDate value, ColdFusion keeps track of the number of times that the task will execute before you reach the end date and counts down until there are no tasks left to execute. Cluster indicates whether or not the task is a clustered task—something we'll discuss shortly.

Adding and Editing Tasks

The Add/Edit scheduled task has been updated to reflect the additions to the `<cfschedule>` tag that we've discussed throughout this chapter. To see the new interface, click Schedule New Task in the main task listing, or click the edit icon on an existing task.

Right away, you'll notice some differences from previous versions of ColdFusion. New fields including Application, Group, Repeat, Crontime, and Chained Tasks have been added to reflect the new capabilities of the scheduler. You'll also notice a button at the bottom of the page that's labeled Show Additional Settings. Clicking the button reveals additional configuration options for the task, including fields in which you can specify Event Handler, Exclude, On Misfire, On Exception, On Complete, Priority, and Retry Count values, and a checkbox to indicate that the task should be clustered. Figure 14.2 shows these additional settings.

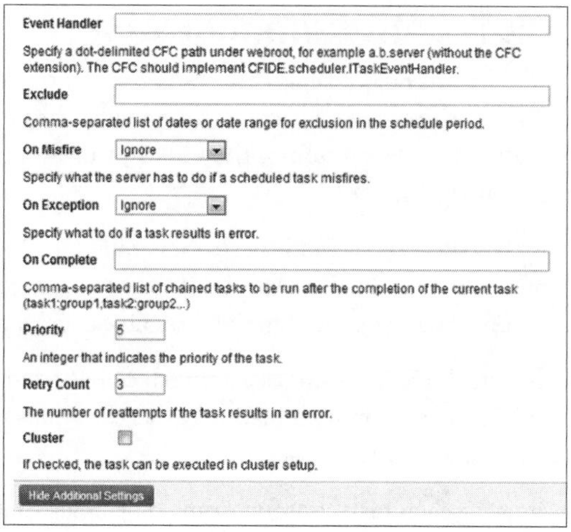

Figure 14.2

Additional settings for
Add/Edit Scheduled
Task.

Clustering Scheduled Tasks

One of the most welcome new scheduling features in ColdFusion 10 is the capability to set up scheduled tasks across a cluster of ColdFusion servers. This is an Enterprise-only feature that lets you make your scheduled tasks cluster aware so that they can be scheduled on any server in the cluster without tying the task's execution to that specific server. This capability is achieved by storing scheduled task information in a central database that is shared by all servers in the cluster.

After clustering is configured, the Quartz scheduler ensures that one and only one node in the cluster fires a given task at a time. Quartz has built-in load balancing algorithms that determine on which node to fire a given task based on scheduler activity. Although node selection for task execution is pseudo-random, the algorithm favors the same node for servers with less scheduler activity than busier servers. Additionally, if you're using chained tasks, the Quartz scheduler executes all of those tasks on the same server.

NOTE

The Quartz scheduler requires the system clocks for all servers participating in a cluster to be synchronized to within a minute of each other. Be sure that your servers use an automated mechanism to keep their clocks in sync to avoid unexpected behavior.

Creating the Shared Database Tables

Before you can start clustering scheduled tasks, you need to create the database tables that Cold-Fusion and the Quartz scheduler use to store task and schedule information. Not to worry: ColdFusion can create the tables for you, provided that you have the data source you want to use already configured in the Data Sources section of the ColdFusion Administrator. As of Cold-Fusion 10, Updater 4, only Microsoft SQL Server, MySQL, and Oracle databases are supported.

To create the tables, log into the ColdFusion Administrator on one of your clustered servers and click Scheduled Tasks in the Server Setting section. You should see the ColdFusion Administrator screen shown in Figure 14.3.

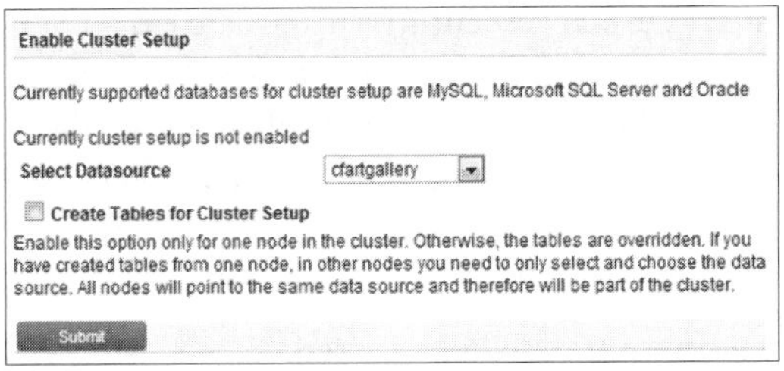

Figure 14.3

Enabling cluster setup in the ColdFusion Administrator.

Choose the data source you want to use for storing information about your clustered tasks. Be sure to check the box labeled Create Tables for Clustered Setup and click Submit when you're ready.

WARNING

Be sure you check the box to create tables only on a single node of your cluster. If you inadvertently check this box on a second node, ColdFusion will overwrite the tables you previously created, wiping out any clustered task information you may have stored.

Adding Servers to the Scheduler Cluster

Now that you have your tables set up for clustered scheduled tasks and you've configured the first server in your cluster to use those tables, it's time to configure the rest of the servers in your cluster to use those tables to store their clustered task information.

Simply log into the ColdFusion Administrator on each of the remaining servers in your cluster and choose the same data source to use for clustered tasks, each time making sure not to check the box to create new tables. That's all there is to it.

Should you want to remove a server from the cluster, simply check the box labeled Disable Cluster in the Scheduled Task section of the ColdFusion Administrator.

Creating Clustered Tasks

After all of the servers in your cluster have been configured for scheduled task clustering, it's time to create a task to ensure that everything is working as expected. To designate a scheduled task as clustered, you set clustered="true" in the <cfschedule> tag, as shown in Listing 14.25.

Listing 14.25 /cf10wack/14/cluster.cfm

```
<cfschedule
  action="update"
  task="Clustered_Task"
  url="http://localhost/cf10wack/14/myTask.cfm"
  startdate="#now()#"
  starttime="#dateAdd('n', 1, now())#"
  interval="10"
  repeat="50"
  cluster="true"
  />
```

This code creates a task that's set to start executing one minute from the time you run the example. It will then repeat every 10 seconds for a total of 50 times. You have to create the task on only a single node of your cluster. ColdFusion will automatically replicate the task to all of the other servers in the cluster that you've added to the scheduler pool. If you open the ColdFusion Administrator on each of the servers in your cluster, you'll see that the same task is shown in the Scheduled Tasks section and that Cluster is set to Yes on each server.

It's worth noting that just because you've set up your servers to cluster scheduled tasks, that doesn't mean that you *have* to cluster all of your tasks. In a clustered environment, you can have a mix of clustered and nonclustered tasks all running in harmony.

Customizing the Quartz Scheduler

While ColdFusion gives you a good degree of control over the Quartz scheduler via the ColdFusion Administrator and the `<cfschedule>` tag, there are additional facets of the scheduler that can be tweaked by more advanced users. One way to do this is with a properties file called quartz. properties, which you can find in /ColdFusion10/cfusion/lib/quartz. Opening the file reveals a number of properties that you can configure, as shown in Listing 14.26.

Listing 14.26 /cf10wack/14/quartz.properties

```
# Default Properties file for use by StdSchedulerFactory
# to create a Quartz Scheduler Instance, if a different
# properties file is not explicitly specified.
#

org.quartz.scheduler.instanceName: DefaultQuartzScheduler
org.quartz.scheduler.rmi.export: false
org.quartz.scheduler.rmi.proxy: false
org.quartz.scheduler.wrapJobExecutionInUserTransaction: false

org.quartz.threadPool.class: org.quartz.simpl.SimpleThreadPool
org.quartz.threadPool.threadCount: 10
org.quartz.threadPool.threadPriority: 5
org.quartz.threadPool.threadsInheritContextClassLoaderOfInitializingThread: true

org.quartz.jobStore.misfireThreshold: 60000

org.quartz.jobStore.class: org.quartz.simpl.RAMJobStore
```

You can modify values such as the worker thread count, the default priority for tasks, and the default 60-second misfire threshold. For a more thorough discussion of what you can configure, see the Quartz documentation.

Security Enhancements

Properly securing your web application is the most crucial aspect of any project. Unfortunately, many people leave this task for the end of development or consider it of lesser importance than other tasks. The truth is, if you aren't thinking about the security of your project from the very first day, then you are going to have problems. ColdFusion has always provided ways to help secure your applications. In this chapter, we'll discuss the new features that ColdFusion 10 adds to help you create more secure websites.

ColdFusion Security Options

Although most of this book is focused on changes in the latest version of ColdFusion, security is an important enough topic that you should refresh your memory about the security-related features available to you already. In general, ColdFusion has three main areas of security support.

The first is resource and sandbox security. This type of security involves restricting access to tags and functions and setting directory-level rules. In ColdFusion Standard, you are limited to one set of rules, referred to as resource security. In ColdFusion Enterprise, you can create multiple sets of rules, referred to as sandboxes. For more information, consult Chapter 55, "Creating Server Sandboxes," in *Adobe ColdFusion 9 Web Application Construction Kit, Volume 3: Advanced Application Development*.

The next area of concern is code-level security. This type of security involves functions such as encryption and hashing (covered in Chapter 52, "Understanding Security") and role-based security (covered in Chapter 54, "ColdFusion Security Options").

ColdFusion also has multiple options to secure the ColdFusion Administrator itself. You can find information about this type of security in Chapter 53, "Securing the ColdFusion Administrator."

The Secure Profile

ColdFusion 10 begins helping you secure your applications and server from the very moment you begin installation. In the installation wizard, you can now enable what is called a secure profile. This secure profile will help ensure that settings related to security default to stronger settings. If you enable the secure profile option, the following changes are made:

- Universal user IDs (UUIDs) are enabled for cftoken.

- Access to internal ColdFusion Java components is disabled. Most developers don't use these components, so this setting should have little impact on the production code.

- Global script protection is enabled. This setting provides automatic cross-site scripting protection for ColdFusion scopes.

- Form POST operations are limited to 20 MB.

- A custom missing-template handler is installed.

- A custom site-wide error template is installed.

- A custom request-queue timeout template is installed.

- The cookies used for memory variables have a lower timeout value set (1440 minutes).

- ColdFusion tags and functions will no longer be able to modify the cookies that ColdFusion uses for session and client scopes.

- The WebSocket server is disabled.

- The Adobe Flash policy server (which is used for clients that can't support WebSocket natively) is disabled.

- The Allowed SQL setting for data sources is modified so that Create, Drop, Alter, Grant, Revoke, and Stored Procedures are disabled.

- The Robust Exception Information setting is disabled.

- The ColdFusion cfstat utility is disabled.

- You must use both a username and password to access the ColdFusion Administrator.

- ColdFusion Remote Development Services (RDS is disabled).

- ColdFusion RDS, if reenabled, will require a username and password.

- Sandbox security is disabled.

- The ColdFusion Administrator has a setting that lets you limit access to a range of IP addresses. This setting is normally available in the Administration interface only, but if you enable the secure profile, you will be able to specify values during installation.

Figure 15.1 shows an example of the secure profile screen during installation.

Figure 15.1

The new Enable Secure Profile option in the installer.

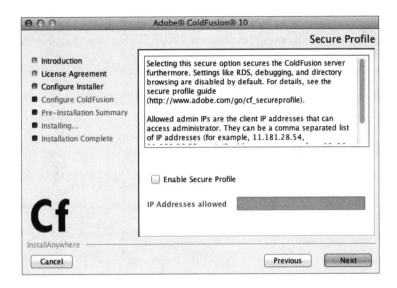

Of course, if you don't select Enable Secure Profile during installation, you can always go back later and make these changes yourself. In fact, you can find an open source project (https://github.com/cfjedimaster/ColdFusion-Security-Profile) to give you an administration extension for checking these settings after installation.

XSS Protection

Cross-site scripting, or XSS, provides one of the easiest ways to attack a site, and therefore you should be sure to protect your code against it. An XSS attack displays user-manipulable code in an insecure manner. Consider the fairly simple dynamic web page shown in Listing 15.1.

Listing 15.1   /cfwack10/15/test1.cfm

```
<cfparam name="url.x" default="">

<h2>Some Random Page</h2>

<cfoutput>#url.x#</cfoutput>
```

All this template does is output the value of url.x. The URL scope is based on the query string, which can be manipulated by the user. Imagine if the URL were changed to something like this:

http://localhost/cfwack10/15/test1.cfm?x=%3Cscript%3Edocument.location.href='google.com'%3C/script%3E

What you see in this URL is an escaped block of JavaScript code that invokes a document location change. Since the ColdFusion code simply outputs it as is, the code is executed as if the page itself were sending the user to Google. This is a trivial example, but there are much more nefarious things that can be done through XSS attacks. (If you can't get the preceding link to work, congratulations. Very recent browsers help by noticing such attacks and blocking them.)

ColdFusion has offered two functions in the past to help deal with XSS: `htmlEditFormat` and `htmlCodeFormat`. ColdFusion 10 expands on these by adding stronger, more targeted encoding functions (Table 15.1).

Table 15.1 New ColdFusion 10 Encoding Functions

FUNCTION	DESCRIPTION
encodeForCSS	Encodes input for use in CSS declarations
encodeForHTML	General-purpose encoder for HTML pages
encodeForHTMLAttribute	Encodes input to be used in an HTML attribute: for example, a dynamic background color
encodeForJavaScript	Encodes input to be used in JavaScript code
encodeForURL	Encodes input to be used in URLs
encodeForXML	Encodes input to be used in XML

Each functions takes in an input argument as well as an optional `strict` argument that restricts any multiple or mixed encoding. These functions all use the Open Web Application Security Project (OWASP) Enterprise Security API for encoding. The functions that you use will depend on your needs. Are you outputting something dynamic in a CSS block? Then you would use `encodeForCSS`. Are you outputting something for XML content? Then use `encodeForXML`. If you aren't sure, you can simply use `encodeForHTML`. In general, though, you should strive to use the appropriate function for the appropriate use case. Listing 15.2 shows a simple example of `encodeForCSS`.

Listing 15.2 /cfwack10/15/test2.cfm

```
<cfparam name="url.bgcolor" default="white">

<!doctype html>
<html lang="en">
<head>
<style>
<cfoutput>
body {
    background-color: #encodeForCSS(url.bgcolor)#;
}
</cfoutput>
</style>
</head>

<body>

<p>
Select the background color:
<ul>
<li><a href="?bgcolor=red">Red</a></li>
<li><a href="?bgcolor=yellow">Yellow</a></li>
<li><a href="?bgcolor=green">Green</a></li>
<li><a href="?bgcolor=blue">Blue</a></li>
```

Listing 15.2 (CONTINUED)

```
    </ul>
    </p>

    </body>
    </html>
```

This example allows users to change the background color by clicking one of four links. The URL variable `bgcolor` is checked and used in the CSS block. If you intentionally modify the value seen in the browser to something unusual, the result, while still invalid CSS, is properly escaped. For instance, if you enter:

```
?bgcolor=blue<b>d
```

the result is properly escaped as follows:

```
body {
    background-color: blue\3c b\3e d;
}
```

Let's look at another example. Listing 15.3 uses a form to prompt the user for various words. The end result will be a dynamic story based on the Mad Libs game.

Listing 15.3 /cfwack10/15/test3.cfm

```
<cfparam name="form.noun1" default="">
<cfparam name="form.verb1" default="">
<cfparam name="form.adjective1" default="">
<cfparam name="form.color1" default="">

<h2>Mad Libs</h2>

<cfoutput>

<form method="post">
Enter a noun: <input type="text" name="noun1"
➥value="#encodeForHTMLAttribute(form.noun1)#"><br/>
Enter a verb: <input type="text" name="verb1"
➥value="#encodeForHTMLAttribute(form.verb1)#"><br/>
Enter an adjective: <input type="text" name="adjective1"
➥value="#encodeForHTMLAttribute(form.adjective1)#"><br/>
Enter a color: <input type="text" name="color1"
➥value="#encodeForHTMLAttribute(form.color1)#">
<input type="submit" name="display" value="Display Mad Lib">
</form>

<cfif structKeyExists(form, "display")>
    <h2>Result</h2>

    <p>
    The #encodeForHTML(form.noun1)# wanted to #encodeForHTML(form.verb1)#
    the car for being #encodeForHTML(form.adjective1)#, but decided to paint
    it #encodeForHTML(form.color1)# instead.
    </p>
</cfif>
```

```
    </cfoutput>
```

As you can see, we used encodeForHTMLAttribute when displaying an existing form value in the various input tags. But in the actual Mad Libs display, encodeForHTML is used instead.

It may be helpful to see how *all* the functions work. Listing 15.4 is a simple utility to let you quickly test various strings and see how they are escaped. To properly see the results, you may want to open Chrome Network Tools and examine the pure HTML result as well (or just choose View Source).

Listing 15.4   /cfwack10/15/generictester.cfm

```
<cfparam name="form.input" default="I like to <b>eat</b> pie and
➥<a href="""" onclick=""javascript:evil()"">drink beer</a>">


<form method="post">
Input string: <br/>
<cfoutput>
<textarea name="input" cols="80" rows="10">#htmlEditFormat(form.input)#</textarea>
</cfoutput>
<input type="submit" value="Test">
</form>

<p>

<cfif len(trim(form.input))>

    <cfoutput>
    naked=#form.input#
    <p/>

    htmlEditFormat=#htmlEditFormat(form.input)#
    <p/>

    encodeForHTML=#encodeForHTML(form.input)#
    <p/>

    encodeForHTMLAttribute=#encodeForHTMLAttribute(form.input)#
    <p/>

    encodeForJavaScript=#encodeForJavaScript(form.input)#
    <p/>

    encodeForCSS=#encodeForCSS(form.input)#
    <p/>

    encodeForURL=#encodeForURL(form.input)#
    <p/>

    encodeForURL=#encodeForXML(form.input)#
    <p/>

    </cfoutput>

</cfif>
```

Before moving on, let's look at another new function related to XSS that may be useful in your development work. The `canonicalize` function is used to *decode* a string. In some ways, it is the opposite of the various encoding functions, but it is more powerful than that. Unicode, for example, presents a problem because there are multiple ways to encode some characters, making properly escaping the output more problematic. The `canonicalize` function can reduce these encodings to only one possible option. Listing 15.5 shows a very simple example form you can use to enter various strings for testing.

Listing 15.5 `/cfwack10/15/test4.cfm`

```
<cfparam name="form.input" default="">

<form method="post">
   <cfoutput>
   <input type="text" name="input" value="#encodeForHTMLAttribute(form.input)#">
   </cfoutput>
   <input type="submit">
</form>

<cfif len(trim(form.input))>

   <cfoutput>
      encoded=#encodeForHTML(form.input)#<br/>
      canonicalize=#canonicalize(encodeForHTML(form.input),false,false)#<br/>
   </cfoutput>

</cfif>
```

CSRF Protection

Cross-site request forgery (CSRF) at its simplest performs an action on some site X that originates on site Y. For example, imagine that site Y contains a form. By default, there is nothing to prevent you from copying that form, putting it on site X, and setting the `action` value of the form tag to point to site Y's location. Site Y receives the form data, and while it certainly could check the headers of the request to see where it came from, almost no sites actually do this.

ColdFusion 10 adds two new features to make it easy to use CSRF protection in your forms: `CSRFGenerateToken` and `CSRFVerifyToken`. Together, these two functions create a virtual bond between one part of your application and another. Listing 15.6 provides a simple example.

Listing 15.6 `/cfwack10/15/csrf_form1.cfm`

```
<form action="csrf_verify1.cfm" method="post">
Your Name: <input type="text" name="name"><br/>
Your Age: <input type="number" name="age"><br/>
<cfoutput>
   <input type="hidden" name="token" value="#CSRFGenerateToken()#">
</cfoutput>
<input type="submit" value="Submit!">
</form>
```

For the most part, this is a fairly typical form, but note the hidden field token. Its value is the result of a call to CSRFGenerateToken.

Now let's look at the file that handles the form post (Listing 15.7).

Listing 15.7   /cfwack10/15/csrf_verify1.cfm

```
<cfif not structKeyExists(form, "token")>
   <cfthrow message="Invalid submit.">
<cfelseif not CSRFVerifyToken(form.token)>
   <cfthrow message="Invalid access.">
<cfelse>
   <!--- Process form as you would normally... --->
   <cfdump var="#form#">
</cfif>
```

This example uses CSRFVerifyToken to verify the token value sent in the form field. Now you may be wondering: Verify what? ColdFusion's CSRF protection uses session management (and therefore sessions must be enabled) to associate the current user with a numeric value. That value is compared to the form field (which can be called anything, not just token). If the values do not match, then the result of CSRFVerifyToken is a false value. At that time, you can do whatever you want, but at minimum you will want to stop the template from working with the form.

You can test this protection by viewing the form in your browser and saving it as HTML. Open the file in an editor and edit the form tag's action value to include a full URL. Then open it in another browser. Submit the form, and you will get the "Invalid access" error (Figure 15.2).

Figure 15.2

An example of a request blocked by CSRF protection.

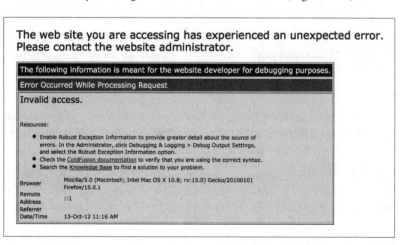

**The web site you are accessing has experienced an unexpected error.
Please contact the website administrator.**

The following information is meant for the website developer for debugging purposes.

Error Occurred While Processing Request

Invalid access.

Resources:

- Enable Robust Exception Information to provide greater detail about the source of errors. In the Administrator, click Debugging & Logging > Debug Output Settings, and select the Robust Exception Information option.
- Check the ColdFusion documentation to verify that you are using the correct syntax.
- Search the Knowledge Base to find a solution to your problem.

Browser	Mozilla/5.0 (Macintosh; Intel Mac OS X 10.8; rv:15.0) Gecko/20100101 Firefox/15.0.1
Remote Address	::1
Referrer	
Date/Time	13-Oct-12 11:16 AM

Although this process works well, you can further lock down access by supplying the key attribute to both CSRF functions. The key value is a free-form string that can be anything you choose. Typically, though, you will want it to match the process you are securing. So, for example, a CSRF token for a registration process should probably use a key called "registration". You aren't required to use sensible names, but your fellow programmers will thank you for doing so (Listing 15.8).

Listing 15.8   /cfwack10/15/csrf_form2.cfm

```
<cfif structKeyExists(form, "submit")>

    <cfif not structKeyExists(form, "token")
    or not CSRFVerifyToken(form.token, "registration")>
        <cfthrow message="Invalid Access!">
    </cfif>

    <!--- more form validation here --->
    <p>Form was sent.</p>

</cfif>


<form action="csrf_form2.cfm" method="post">
Your Name: <input type="text" name="name"><br/>
Your Age: <input type="number" name="age"><br/>
<cfoutput>
    <input type="hidden" name="token" value="#CSRFGenerateToken('registration')#">
</cfoutput>
<input type="submit" name="submit" value="Submit!">
</form>
```

This example shows another form, although we've switched it to a self-posting form. Note the use of the key value in both the CSRFGenerateToken and CSRFVerifyToken functions. If the keys do not match, it doesn't matter whether the user submitting the form is the same user to which the form was presented. The form will not be processed.

You can take this process one step further. The second argument to CSRFGenerateToken specifies whether tokens should be refreshed. By default—and you can verify this yourself by running CSRFGenerateToken many times in a row—the token will not change. It remains unique to each user, and it doesn't change throughout each user's session. You can force this token to change by passing a third argument to CSRFGenerateToken: the forceNew argument. Using this option would simply make your forms that much more secure. Listing 15.9 provides a simple example.

Listing 15.9   /cfwack10/15/csrf_form3.cfm

```
<form action="csrf_verify1.cfm" method="post">
Your Name: <input type="text" name="name"><br/>
Your Age: <input type="number" name="age"><br/>
<cfoutput>
    <input type="hidden" name="token" value="#CSRFGenerateToken("",true)#">
</cfoutput>
<input type="submit" value="Submit!">
</form>
```

This form uses the same code as csrf_form1.cfm, except for the arguments passed to CSRFGenerateToken. Here we've passed an empty string for key and set forceNew to true. Now submit the form and make note of the key value in the dump. Click Back and submit the form again, and you will see a new token value.

File Upload Protection

File uploads provide another vulnerability that wise developers will want to address to secure their applications. Allowing users to upload files to your application isn't too far from letting strangers sleep in your house. Malicious users can upload scripts that, when executed, give them power over your server. One of the best protections you can provide is to simply ensure that file uploads are sent to a folder *outside* the web root. In addition, you can ensure that the files uploaded match your applications' requirements. Are you building an "avatar" upload feature? Then you'll want to ensure that the user uploads a graphic, not a PDF file. ColdFusion's <cffile> tag has always had an accept attribute that specifies a list of file MIME types that are allowed. But this list is only partially effective. You could, for example, take an invalid graphic file and upload it with the right extension, and it would pass the <cffile> "test."

ColdFusion 10 fixes this vulnerability with the addition of a new stricter file check. This new check performs a much deeper file verification process than in previous versions. The best news is that this feature is enabled by default. The <cffile> tag's new attribute, strict, controls this behavior, but you do not have to explicitly use it to get this new level of protection. Listing 15.10 provides an example.

Listing 15.10   /cfwack10/15/file1.cfm

```
<form enctype="multipart/form-data" method="post">
<input type="file" name="file">
<input name="submit" type="submit">
</form>

<cfif structKeyExists(form, "submit")>

    <cffile action="upload" filefield="file" destination="ram:///"
    accept="image/gif" strict="true" nameconflict="overwrite">
    <cfdump var="#cffile#">

</cfif>
```

This simple self-posting form allows you to select a file and upload it. If you select anything but a GIF file, an error occurs. If you want to test this form, try uploading notagif.gif from the code zip file. This is actually just a CFM file that was renamed. If you set strict to false, the file will be allowed as an upload. The default, and better, behavior is the behavior with strict enabled.

This new behavior is also available to you for general file checking. You can use the new fileGetMineType function to check the MIME values of files. Consider Listing 15.11.

Listing 15.11   /cfwack10/15/file2.cfm

```
<cfset files = directoryList(expandPath("./"))>

<cfloop index="f" array="#files#">
    <cfif not directoryExists(f)>
        <cfoutput>
        #listLast(f,"\/")# - mime type is #fileGetMimeType(f)#<br/>
        </cfoutput>
    </cfif>
</cfloop>
```

This script iterates over the files in the current directory and reports the MIME type for each one. Note that it too catches the fake GIF file:

```
Application.cfc - mime type is text/plain
csrf_form1.cfm - mime type is text/html
csrf_form2.cfm - mime type is text/html
csrf_form3.cfm - mime type is text/html
csrf_verify1.cfm - mime type is text/html
file1.cfm - mime type is text/html
file2.cfm - mime type is text/html
generictester.cfm - mime type is text/html
notagif.gif - mime type is text/plain
test1.cfm - mime type is text/html
test2.cfm - mime type is text/html
test3.cfm - mime type is text/html
test4.cfm - mime type is text/html
```

Session Improvements

ColdFusion's Session feature has also been improved in ColdFusion 10. One change is that the cookie values used by session management can be HTTP only (using httponly), so that they cannot be modified on the client side with JavaScript. You can also control the secure, domain, and timeout settings for session cookies. Turning on the secure option sets the cookies to be sent only over HTTPS connections. The domain value specifies a particular domain on which the cookie will be available. All these settings are Application.cfc this scope settings. The following code snippet shows a simple example:

```
this.sessioncookie.httponly="true";
this.sessioncookie.secure="true";
this.sessioncookie.domain="value";
this.sessioncookie.timeout="value";
```

Note that for the timeout value, a setting of -1 creates a session that ends when the browser closes.

Also new to ColdFusion 10 are the SessionInvalidate and SesionRotate functions. Both functions were added to ensure that a previous session could no longer be used and to prevent session fixation attacks. (In fact, the ColdFusion Administrator itself makes use of these methods.) SessionInvalidate simply destroys the existing session. Not only are existing session values removed but even the session markers (CFID and CFTOKEN) are updated. SessionRotate works in a similar way, but it copies existing session values to the new session.

Miscellaneous Improvements

Let's now look at a few more improvements to security in ColdFusion 10. One is a simple update to the Hash() function. A hash is a one-way scrambling of source input. Unlike encrypted passwords, a hash cannot be decrypted. However, since the same string is scrambled the same way, people have created lists of common words and their hash equivalents. One way to protect against such lists is to hash multiple times, so instead of storing the hash of a password in the database, you store the value that results from hashing the password 10 times.

The Hash() function now allows a fourth argument that tells it how many times to iterate. Listing 15.12 shows the difference between hashing a value once and hashing it four times.

Listing 15.12 /cfwack10/15/hash.cfm

```
<cfoutput>
#hash("Hello my name is Raymond Camden","sha")#<br/>
#hash("Hello my name is Raymond Camden","sha","",4)#<br/>
</cfoutput>
```

The result either way is probably equally incomprehensible, but the second version should be harder to guess because of its multiple iterations:

```
E61C2ED6FD73634C8AA35B19E00742D24B5F3009
199BCC77E3488BD6FD37D3C96D083B0B2A290A18
```

Another new security-related function is HMAC(). Hash-based message authentication code, or HMAC, is used to help ensure the authenticity of a message. To use HMAC()in ColdFusion, you simply pass in a message, string, encryption algorithm, and encoding value. Listing 15.13 shows a simple tool that lets you enter strings and see the HMAC output.

Listing 15.13 /cfwack10/15/hmac.cfm

```
<cfparam name="form.input" default="">

<cfoutput>
<form method="post">
<textarea name="input">#form.input#</textarea>
<input type="submit" value="Test">
</form>

<cfif len(form.input)>
    <p>
        #hmac(form.input, "mykeyisbetterthanyourkey")#
    </p>
</cfif>

</cfoutput>
```

Finally, let's look at a how ColdFusion can help address the issue of "clickjacking." Clickjacking refers to an attack based on the addition of fake, or misleading, UI items to a page. When users click them, thinking they are placing an order or performing some other action, the malicious code is executed instead. ColdFusion provides clickjacking protection by using a feature of modern browsers that allows headers to specify whether content can be framed. Unfortunately there is no nice ColdFusion Administrator utility to handle this. You need to edit your web.xml file (located in the WEB-INF folder of your server root) and add a `<filter-mapping>` block. You will see an existing `<filter-mapping>` block related to the ColdFusion Administrator:

```
<filter-mapping>
        <filter-name>CFClickJackFilterSameOrigin</filter-name>
        <url-pattern>/CFIDE/administrator/*</url-pattern>
</filter-mapping>
```

This block defines whether a page under the /CFIDE/administrator URL can frame another page within the same area. You can define a "deny" filter following the same scheme, like this for example:

```
<filter-mapping>
        <filter-name>CFClickJackFilterDeny</filter-name>
        <url-pattern>/cfwack/15/*</url-pattern>
</filter-mapping>
```

Unlike the previous example, which allowed framing from documents in the same host, this filter specifically blocks all framing. If you built a simple page that pointed to a URL in this format using either a frame or an iframe, the content would not load. Note that this process requires cooperation with the browser, but most casual users will not go out of their way to bypass this security feature.

CHAPTER 16

Improving Performance

Performance has been an important focus of ColdFusion in past few releases. ColdFusion 8 worked out of the box several times faster than previous releases, and ColdFusion 9 offered many performance improvements and features and introduced a new caching engine. ColdFusion 10 continues this trend: it adds to enhancements for caching and provides a new underlying engine with Tomcat. This chapter discusses these improvements as well as Java Virtual Machine (JVM) tuning options that you can use in your work.

What Is Caching?

A cache is a temporary storage place that can quickly be accessed for keeping resources and objects that are otherwise expensive to create or access from their original locations. The use of a cache speeds up processing of requests and reduces the wait time for shared resources. Caching helps improve scalability by reducing the load on servers, avoiding database calls, and reducing network bandwidth use. An application can benefit greatly in terms of performance if it uses caching appropriately.

ColdFusion 9 introduced a new caching engine that is based on Ehcache and replaced the underlying implementation of the `<cfcache>` tag. The feature provided better control over template caches, introduced object caches, and provided a new built-in function for using and managing the caches.

Caching Enhancements

ColdFusion 10 added several enhancements related to caching, including the following features detailed in this chapter:

- Application-specific caching

- Cache regions

- Changes to built-in functions

- New cache functions

- Enhanced query caching

- New version of Ehcache: Ehcache 2.5.1

- ColdFusion Server Monitor support for caching

Application-Specific Caching

With application-specific caching, ColdFusion 10 allows finer-grained control over the way that a cache associated with Application.cfc behaves. For example, you may want greater control over eviction policy, time to live, maximum number of elements, and other cache behavior for a specific application.

You achieve this control by creating the application's own copy of ehcache.xml and specifying the location of ehcache.xml in the Application.cfc file. Consider the simple ehcache.xml file shown in Listing 16.1.

Listing 16.1 /cfwack10/16/ehcache.xml

```xml
<?xml version="1.0" encoding="UTF-8"?>
<ehcache xmlns:xsi="http://www.w3.org/2001/XMLSchema-instance"
         xsi:noNamespaceSchemaLocation="ehcache.xsd" >

    <diskStore path="java.io.tmpdir"/>
    <cacheManagerEventListenerFactory class="" properties=""/>

    <!--
    Mandatory Default Cache configuration.
    The defaultCache has an implicit name "default" which is a reserved cache name.
    -->
        <defaultCache
        maxElementsInMemory="10000"
        eternal="false"
        timeToIdleSeconds="86400"
        timeToLiveSeconds="86400"
        overflowToDisk="false"
        diskSpoolBufferSizeMB="30"
        maxElementsOnDisk="10000000"
        diskPersistent="false"
        diskExpiryThreadIntervalSeconds="3600"
```

Listing 16.1 (CONTINUED)

```
            memoryStoreEvictionPolicy="LRU"
            clearOnFlush="true"
            statistics="true"
                />
    </ehcache>
```

After you have created an application's copy of ehcache.xml, you can specify the application-specific cache settings file in Application.cfc, as shown in Listing 16.2.

Listing 16.2   /cfwack10/16/Application.cfc

```
    <cfcomponent>
      <cfset this.name = "appSpecificCache">
      <cfset this.cache.configfile = "ehcache.xml">
    </cfcomponent>
```

You can also specify the absolute path with respect to Application.cfc.

Note that the default OBJECT and QUERY caches are always sandboxed to the application and are created and managed as applicationNameOBJECT and applicationNameQUERY. This sandboxing means that an application cannot access another application's default OBJECT or QUERY cache.

Cache Regions

If you open ehcache.xml from Listing 16.1, you will find another cache, named customcache, defined there. You can then programmatically access this cache and use it in other cache functions. Listing 16.3 provides a simple example that prints the properties of customcache.

Listing 16.3   /cfwack10/16/customcachedump.cfm

```
    <cfdump var="#cacheGetProperties('customcache')#">
```

When you run this file, it dumps the settings that are specified in ehcache.xml (Figure 16.1).

Figure 16.1

The struct showing
the properties of a
custom cache.

MAXELEMENTSINMEMORY	1000
MAXELEMENTSONDISK	100000
MAXENTRIESLOCALDISK	100000
MAXENTRIESLOCALHEAP	1000
MAXMEMORYOFFHEAP	0
MAXMEMORYOFFHEAPINBYTES	0
MEMORYEVICTIONPOLICY	LRU
NAME	customcache
OBJECTTYPE	ANY
OVERFLOWTODISK	YES
OVERFLOWTOOFFHEAP	NO
OVERFLOWTOOFFHEAPSET	NO
STATISTICS	NO
TIMETOIDLESECONDS	720
TIMETOLIVESECONDS	720

A major drawback with this approach is that a custom cache needs to be specified ahead of time in XML—but what if a cache could be specified dynamically using a built-in function? For just this purpose, ColdFusion 10 has added a new function: cacheRegionNew. Listing 16.4 shows an example of the use of cacheRegionNew to create a new cache region.

Listing 16.4   /cfwack10/16/cacheregion.cfm

```
<!--- Defining properties for the struct --->
<cfset defaultCacheProps = StructNew()>
<cfset defaultCacheProps.MAXELEMENTSINMEMORY = "5">
<cfset defaultCacheProps.ETERNAL = "false">
<cfset defaultCacheProps.TIMETOIDLESECONDS = "100">
<cfset defaultCacheProps.TIMETOLIVESECONDS = "50">
<cfset defaultCacheProps.OVERFLOWTODISK = "true">
<cfset defaultCacheProps.DISKEXPIRYTHREADINTERVALSECONDS = "3600">
<cfset defaultCacheProps.DISKPERSISTENT = "false">
<cfset defaultCacheProps.DISKSPOOLBUFFERSIZEMB = "30">
<cfset defaultCacheProps.MAXELEMENTSONDISK = "10">
<cfset defaultCacheProps.MEMORYEVICTIONPOLICY = "LRU">
<cfset defaultCacheProps.CLEARONFLUSH = "true">
<cfset defaultCacheProps.OBJECTTYPE = "OBJECT">

<cfset cacheRegionNew("testregion",#defaultCacheProps#,false)>

<cfdump var="#cacheGetProperties('testregion')#">
```

When you run this file, it dumps the settings, similar to Listing 16.3. The new region is implicitly application specific, and creation of 'testregion' in another application creates a unique region that can be accessed by the application that created it. ColdFusion manages this application sandboxing by adding the application name to the provided region name while creating the cache regions.

ColdFusion 10 also provides a function cacheRegionExists that you can use to check the existence of a region (Listing 16.5).

Listing 16.5   /cfwack10/16/cacheregionexists.cfm

```
cacheregionexists('testregion')
```

To remove a cache region, ColdFusion 10 provides the cacheRegionRemove function, which takes the name of the region to be removed (Listing 16.6).

Listing 16.6   /cfwack10/16/cacheregionremove.cfm

```
<cfset cacheregionremove('testregion')>
```

Note that if no application-specific ehcache.xml is provided in Application.cfc via the this.cache.configfile property, all caches created by cacheRegionNew are serverwide. Such caches can be shared across applications. However, if the this.cache.configfile property is specified, all caches created are sandboxed to their corresponding applications.

Changes to Built-in Functions

Now that you know how to create your own little regions of cache in memory, the next step is to use cache region in the built-in caching functions.

ColdFusion 10 has added a new attribute region to almost all the cache functions to make it easy to use dynamic cache regions. Let us first look at CachePut:

```
CachePut(id, value, [timeSpan], [idleTime], [region], [throwOnError])
```

A custom region created by cacheRegionNew can be used to add objects to the cache. If no region is specified, ColdFusion uses a default cache. A default cache is bound to a named application, and the internal names used by ColdFusion are applicationnameOBJECT and applicationnameTEMPLATE. A default cache is created outside an application and is available to all unnamed applications. In other words, all unnamed applications share the same default cache, and hence unnamed applications should use their own cache regions for better sandboxing.

ColdFusion 10 also introduces the new cache function attribute throwonerror, which also accepts region as a parameter. The throwonerror attribute checks for the existence of a specified region value. If throwonerror is specified as true, an exception is raised if a region does not exist when it should: for example, in the cachePut function. Here the default value of throwonerror is false. Consider the example in Listing 16.7.

Listing 16.7   /cfwack10/16/cacheregionput.cfm

```
<cfset cachePut("123", "foo", "", "", "nonexistentcache", true)>
```

On running this file, it produces an error, as shown in Figure 16.2.

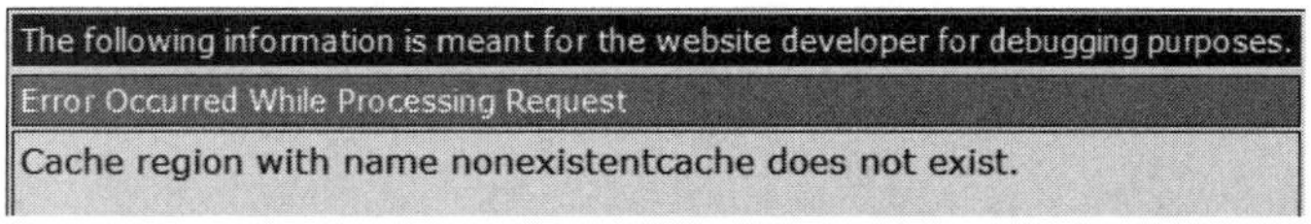

Figure 16.2

The error output when a cache with a given name does not exist.

The following information is meant for the website developer for debugging purposes.

Error Occurred While Processing Request

Cache region with name nonexistentcache does not exist.

What will happen if throwonerror is passed as false in the preceding code? Let's examine the output of the code shown in Listing 16.8.

Listing 16.8   /cfwack10/16/ cacheregionput_f.cfm

```
<cfset cachePut("123", "foo", "", "", "nonexistentcache", false)>
<cfoutput>#cacheGet("123", "nonexistentcache")#</cfoutput>
```

This code will create a new cache region nonexistentcache, and cacheGet will return the foo object.

However, for cacheRegionNew, the behavior of throwonerror is the opposite because the default expectation is that there will not be a region with the same name while a new one is being created. The default value is true, as shown in Listing 16.9.

Listing 16.9   /cfwack10/16/cacheregion_t.cfm

```
<!--- Defining properties for the struct --->
<cfset defaultCacheProps = StructNew()>
<cfset defaultCacheProps.MAXELEMENTSINMEMORY = "5">
<cfset defaultCacheProps.TIMETOIDLESECONDS = "100">
<cfset defaultCacheProps.TIMETOLIVESECONDS = "50">
<cfset defaultCacheProps.DISKEXPIRYTHREADINTERVALSECONDS = "3600">
<cfset defaultCacheProps.MEMORYEVICTIONPOLICY = "LRU">
<cfset defaultCacheProps.OBJECTTYPE = "OBJECT">

<cfset cacheRegionNew("testregion", #defaultCacheProps#, true)>

<cfdump var = #cacheGetProperties('testregion')#>
```

If you run the example in Listing 16.4, or if you run the example in Listing 16.9 twice, you will see the exception shown in Figure 16.3.

Figure 16.3

The error output when a cache with a given name already exists.

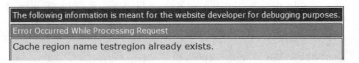

The following information is meant for the website developer for debugging purposes.
Error Occurred While Processing Request
Cache region name testregion already exists.

In ColdFusion 10, all ColdFusion 9 caching functions, including the <cfcache> tag, have been upgraded with the region parameter, and some also have the throwonerror parameter added, as listed here:

- CacheGet(id, [region])

- CacheGetAllIds([region])

- CachePut(id, value, [timeSpan], [idleTime], [region], [throwOnError])

- CacheGetProperties([region])

- CacheSetProperties(propStruct, [region])

- CacheGetMetadata

- CacheRemove(ids, [throwOnError], [region], [exact])

Notice that the CacheRemove method also adds a new parameter: exact. If exact is set to true, ColdFusion will search for an exact match for the ID before removing an item from the cache. Consider the example in Listing 16.10.

Listing 16.10 /cfwack10/16/cacheremove.cfm

```
<!--- Add [123, foo] to somecache --->
<cfset cachePut("123", "foo", "", "", "somecache", false)>

<!--- Retrieve key 123 --->
Before remove:
<cfoutput>#cacheget("123", "somecache")#</cfoutput>

<!--- Remove key 2 performing exact match --->
<cfset cacheremove("2", false, "somecache", true)>

<!--- Retrieve key 123 after remove operation --->
<br>After Remove:
<cfoutput>#cacheget("123", "somecache")#</cfoutput>
```

When exact is specified as true, ColdFusion searches for an exact match. It will not find ID 2 in somecache and hence it will display the output shown in Figure 16.4.

Figure 16.4

The output when a key removal searches for the exact key match.

Before remove: foo
After Remove: foo

However, suppose that exact is specified as false in this example, like this:

```
<cfset cacheremove("2", false, "somecache", false)>
```

ColdFusion will now find all IDs containing 2 and hence will be able to find and remove a key with the ID 123. Figure 16.5 shows the output with the changed code.

Figure 16.5

The output when a key removal searches for a part match.

Before remove: foo
After Remove:

New Cache Functions

ColdFusion 10 adds the following new caching functions:

- cacheIdExists(id [, region])

- cacheRemoveAll([region])

- cacheRegionNew(region,[properties],[throwOnError])

- cacheRegionRemove(region)

- cacheRegionExists(region)

- removeCachedQuery(SQL, datasource, [params], [region])

The `cacheIdExists` function checks whether a cached object with the given ID exists in the specified or default region.

The `cacheRemoveAll` function allows an application to clear the cache from a specified region. If no region is specified, all objects in the default cache are cleared. Use this function with caution when applying it to the default cache because other parts of the application may be dependent on the cached data. Listing 16.11 provides an example.

Listing 16.11   /cfwack10/16/clearcache.cfm

```
<cfset timeToLive = CreateTimeSpan(0, 0, 30, 0)>
<cfset timeToIdle = CreateTimeSpan(0, 0, 30, 0)>

<cfset cachePut("1", "foo1", timeToLive, timeToIdle, "newcache")>
<cfset cachePut("2", "foo2", timeToLive, timeToIdle, "newcache")>
<cfset cachePut("3", "foo3", timeToLive, timeToIdle, "newcache")>

<cfoutput>
  <br>Before cacheRemove() :: Number of objects in the cache:
#ArrayLen(cacheGetAllIds())#
</cfoutput>

<!--- clear all objects from the cache --->
<cfset cacheRemoveAll("newcache")>

<cfoutput>
  <br>After cacheRemove() :: Number of objects in the cache:
#ArrayLen(cacheGetAllIds())#
</cfoutput>
```

Figure 16.6 shows the output.

Figure 16.6

The output after the cache is cleared.

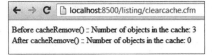

Before cacheRemove() :: Number of objects in the cache: 3
After cacheRemove() :: Number of objects in the cache: 0

The `removeCachedQuery` utility function removes a query from the query cache using the given details. It works on both the internal cache and Ehcache-based caching regions.

The `cacheRegionNew`, `cacheRegionRemove`, and `cacheRegionExists` functions were discussed in the preceding section.

Enhanced Query Caching

ColdFusion 9 added a new caching engine with Ehcache. However, no direct support was provided to use the new caching engine to cache query results from the cfquery tag. A workaround in ColdFusion 9 to use Ehcache-based caching is to run a query and then use cachePut to add the query results to the cache programmatically. Then the program needs to call cacheGet to fetch the results from the cache, as shown in Listing 16.12.

Listing 16.12   /cfwack10/16/querycache_cf9.cfm

```
<!--- check if the query is in the cache--->
<cfset cachedquery = cacheGet("querytocache")/>

<!--- if not in cache fetch from database and add to cache --->
<cfif isNull(cachedquery)>
    <cfquery name=cachedquery datasource="cfartgallery">
    select * from art where artid < 10
    </cfquery>
    <!--- insert the query into the cache --->
    <cfset cachePut("querytocache", cachedquery, CreateTimeSpan(0, 0, 30, 0))/>
</cfif>

<!--- dump the query object --->
<cfdump var="#cachedquery#"/>
```

An interesting artifact of this approach is that the execution time associated with a query object does not show the correct data as the value from the cached object. In this case, this execution time is the time that the query took to run for the first time from the database. Although this approach provides flexibility, a programmer has to manage and maintain the cache.

ColdFusion 10 provides support for the new query cache by introducing two new variables to the cfquery tag: cacheid and cacheregion. Listing 16.13 shows an example.

Listing 16.13   /cfwack10/16/querycache.cfm

```
<cfset cacheRegionNew("testregion", #defaultCacheProps#, false)>

<cfquery name=cachedquery datasource="cfartgallery" cacheid="querytocache"
cacheregion="testregion">
select * from art where artid < 10
</cfquery>

<!--- dump the query object --->
<cfdump var="#cachedquery#"/>
```

The example uses the testregion cache that we created earlier in Listing 16.4, while discussing the CacheRegionNew function. While running this code, ColdFusion will check whether the querytocache ID is present in the testregion cache and, if it is, will return the cached value. If the ID is not present, the query result is added to the cache with the querytocache ID. To use the default cache region, do not provide the cacheregion attribute. Use cacheid to specify whether to retrieve or remove the query from the cache.

Figure 16.7 shows the results of Listing 16.13 after the first execution.

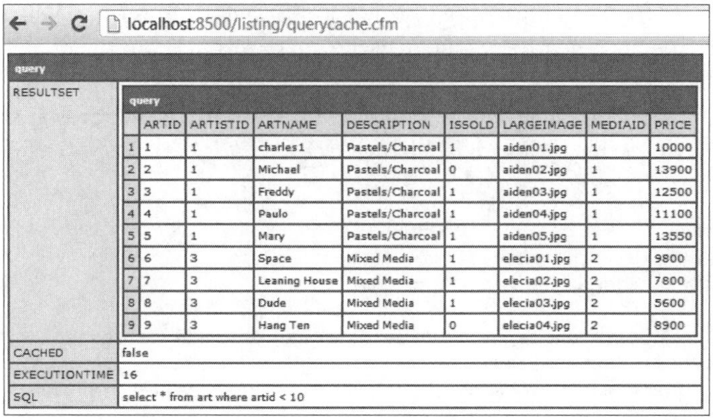

	ARTID	ARTISTID	ARTNAME	DESCRIPTION	ISSOLD	LARGEIMAGE	MEDIAID	PRICE
1	1	1	charles1	Pastels/Charcoal	1	aiden01.jpg	1	10000
2	2	1	Michael	Pastels/Charcoal	0	aiden02.jpg	1	13900
3	3	1	Freddy	Pastels/Charcoal	1	aiden03.jpg	1	12500
4	4	1	Paulo	Pastels/Charcoal	1	aiden04.jpg	1	11100
5	5	1	Mary	Pastels/Charcoal	1	aiden05.jpg	1	13550
6	6	3	Space	Mixed Media	1	elecia01.jpg	2	9800
7	7	3	Leaning House	Mixed Media	1	elecia02.jpg	2	7800
8	8	3	Dude	Mixed Media	1	elecia03.jpg	2	5600
9	9	3	Hang Ten	Mixed Media	0	elecia04.jpg	2	8900

CACHED	false
EXECUTIONTIME	16
SQL	select * from art where artid < 10

Figure 16.7 The output when a query is executed for the first time and the data is retrieved from the database.

The first execution of the query retrieves results from the database and not the cache. Hence, the value of the cached key in the result struct is `false`. As you rerun this page, you will notice that the execution time will be reduced to a fraction of a second—in this example, to 0 seconds—providing a performance boost for your application. The value of the cached key in the result struct changes to `true`, as shown in Figure 16.8.

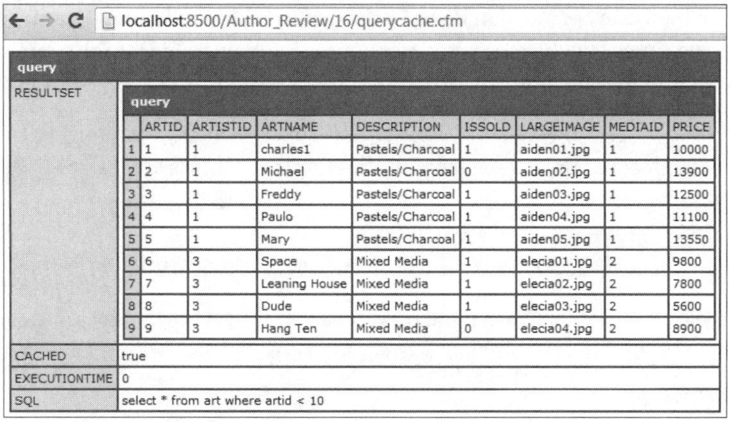

	ARTID	ARTISTID	ARTNAME	DESCRIPTION	ISSOLD	LARGEIMAGE	MEDIAID	PRICE
1	1	1	charles1	Pastels/Charcoal	1	aiden01.jpg	1	10000
2	2	1	Michael	Pastels/Charcoal	0	aiden02.jpg	1	13900
3	3	1	Freddy	Pastels/Charcoal	1	aiden03.jpg	1	12500
4	4	1	Paulo	Pastels/Charcoal	1	aiden04.jpg	1	11100
5	5	1	Mary	Pastels/Charcoal	1	aiden05.jpg	1	13550
6	6	3	Space	Mixed Media	1	elecia01.jpg	2	9800
7	7	3	Leaning House	Mixed Media	1	elecia02.jpg	2	7800
8	8	3	Dude	Mixed Media	1	elecia03.jpg	2	5600
9	9	3	Hang Ten	Mixed Media	0	elecia04.jpg	2	8900

CACHED	true
EXECUTIONTIME	0
SQL	select * from art where artid < 10

Figure 16.8 The output when a query is executed for the second time and the data is retrieved from the cache.

The new query caching offers several advantages. You can use new cache functions such as `timeToIdle` and `timeToLive` and the cache eviction algorithm from Ehcache. By using application-specific or custom cache regions, you have more control over configuration of the cache properties for different types of database access. The new cache also provides fine-grained control over the removal of cached queries, and you can set up your query cache as a distributed cache using Ehcache support.

You can also add the new query cache support to the cfstoredproc tag by adding the `cacheid` and `cacheregion` attributes, as for the `cfquery` tag. If you are using the `cachedWithin` or `cachedAfter` attribute with the new query cache, these attributes are converted to the corresponding `TimeToLive` and `Eternal` properties of the Ehcache element being added to the cache.

If you do not want to use the new query caching, you can go back to the previous default caching architecture by checking a box in the ColdFusion Administrator (Server Settings > Caching), as shown in Figure 16.9.

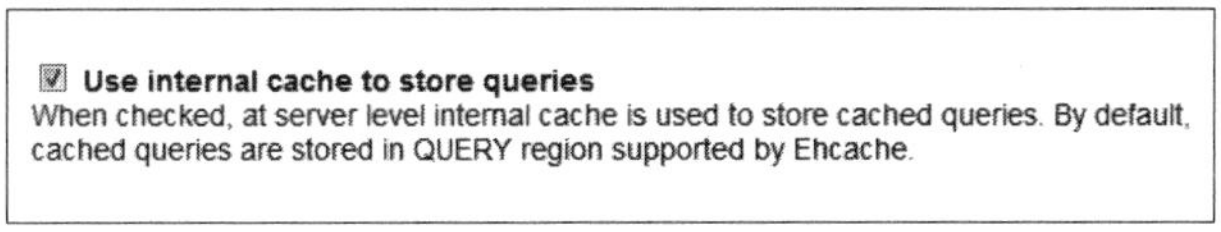

Figure 16.9

Administrator setting to enable internal caching for queries.

> ☑ **Use internal cache to store queries**
> When checked, at server level internal cache is used to store cached queries. By default, cached queries are stored in QUERY region supported by Ehcache.

The setting you specify here is applied serverwide. For application-level settings, use the following specification in Application.cfc:

```
this.cache.useinternalquerycache = true;
```

The application-level setting overrides the value defined in the ColdFusion Administrator for the given application.

Ehcache Version Update

ColdFusion 10 has upgraded the version of Ehcache from 2.0 to 2.5.1. Ehcache is a Java-based caching engine, so you can use Ehcache features that are not available via ColdFusion. A detailed description of the new version of Ehcache is beyond the scope of this book; see http://ehcache.org/ for more information.

Server Monitor Support for Caching

ColdFusion 10 adds two new pages to the Server Monitor. These provide details about the caches in the server. Because you need not start monitoring, profiling, or memory tracking to be able to view this data, you can watch this data in a production system without any impact on your applications.

To launch monitoring, choose ColdFusion Administrator > Server Monitoring > Launch Server Monitor.

After the Server Monitor is launched, you can find caching pages on the Statistics tab.

Figure 16.10 shows information about caches created at the server level.

Figure 16.10

Server Monitor page for the cache regions of the server.

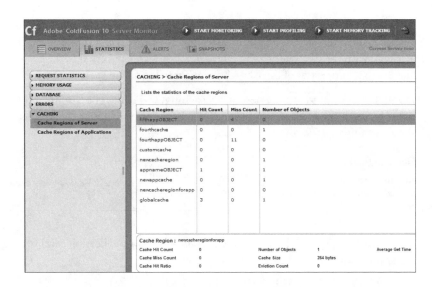

As mentioned earlier, by default all custom caches are created at the server level. The OBJECT and QUERY caches are system caches and by default the application name is prepended to sandbox them the application.

The second page provides details about the cache regions of the various applications (Figure 16.11).

Figure 16.11

Server Monitor details about the cache regions.

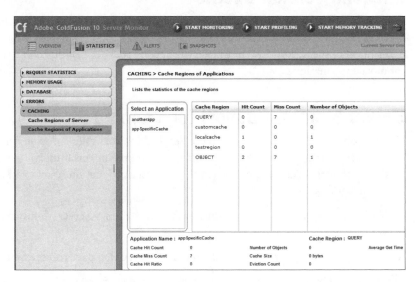

These caches at the application level are created when an application provides its own ehcache.xml file via the `this.cache.configfile` attribute in Application.cfc. These caches are mentioned in the application-level ehcache.xml file or defined for an application using the `cacheRegionNew` function. Because the Server Monitor shows the application-level cache region, the OBJECT and QUERY system caches are not shown prepended with the application name.

The statistics provide valuable information about hit count, miss count, number of objects in the cache, eviction count, and so on that can be used to fine-tune the cache and achieve optimal caching performance.

Other Performance Improvements: JVM Tuning

ColdFusion runs on top of the Java Enterprise Edition (JEE) application server. A JEE application server runs on Java. This means that JEE and Java layers can be tuned and optimized to increase the performance of a ColdFusion application.

First we'll discuss the JEE layer. With ColdFusion 10, the default application server engine is no longer JRun; the default server engine is Tomcat. If you are using the default or standalone configuration for Tomcat, you can refer to several online resources for information about performance tuning; a detailed discussion of Tomcat tuning parameters is beyond the scope of this book.

Now we'll discuss the Java layer. Tuning the Java layer essentially means looking at the performance tuning parameters that JVM provides.

One important parameter that affects application performance is garbage collection (GC): how discarded objects are cleaned up from Java or JVM memory. Consider how the GC process affects performance. During garbage collection, new object creation is halted, and unreferenced objects are marked and memory is reclaimed. Now if all of these activities are happening in parallel with application processing, there is no impact on the performance because the application continues to run as usual while the GC process is underway. In reality, however, almost all GC processes pause the application, even if only for a very short time, mostly to stop new requests for object creation and to reclaim memory.

So if the ColdFusion server receives a ColdFusion template request during GC processing, any pauses on account of GC processing will increase the response time of the request, resulting in lower application performance. Two GC settings in particular affect application performance: the total time needed for GC processing to complete, and the frequency at which GC processing runs.

Fortunately, you can take some steps to tune GC processing to achieve optimal application performance. Unfortunately, there is no flawless recipe or flowchart that can be applied to all GC tuning scenarios, but you can apply some principles and pattern recognition. These are the important questions to answer in GC tuning:

- What triggered GC processing?

- How long is the GC pause time, and how long does GC run?

- How frequently does GC processing occur?

In modern JVM, memory is allocated in three different areas of what is known as the heap:

- Young generation (also called Eden): This is where all new objects are allocated.

- Old generation: Any object that survives a certain number (typically 16 or 32) of GC cycles in the young generation area is promoted to the old generation area.

- Permanent generation: Class files, string interns, and other such data is stored here.

JVM uses different GC algorithms for the young and old generation areas (the permanent generation area typically uses the same algorithm as the old generation area). Note these general guidelines:

- Young generation garbage is collected frequently, and this process is referred to as minor collection. The aim is to maximize the number of objects reclaimed in young generation. Minor collection runs for a shorter duration and hence has less impact on application performance.

- Old generation GC is referred to as major collection and runs for a longer duration than young generation GC. The old generation area should be sized so that it can comfortably hold the application's steady-state live size. You can also consider tuning the sizes and other parameters of the young and old generation areas so that major cycles occur during periods of low load.

- Make sure that the application's memory footprint does not exceed the available physical memory; otherwise, your application may end up performing costly disk operations.

- As a ColdFusion programmer, you have little control over what gets stored in the permanent generation. If the server is running out of memory on account of a permanent generation error, consider increasing the size allocated to permanent generation space.

You also have some tools and techniques that you can use to tune JVM. Listing 16.14 shows jvm.config added to the cfusion/bin folder in a default ColdFusion installation.

Listing 16.14   /cfwack10/16/jvm.config

```
# Arguments to VM
java.args=-server -Xms256m -Xmx512m -XX:MaxPermSize=192m -XX:+UseParallelGC
➡ -Xbatch -Dcoldfusion.home={application.home} -Djava.awt.headless=true
➡ -Dcoldfusion.rootDir={application.home} -Djava.security.policy=
➡ {application.home}/lib/coldfusion.policy -Djava.security.auth.policy=
➡ {application.home}/lib/neo_jaas.policy  -Dcoldfusion.classPath=
➡ {application.home}/lib/updates,{application.home}/lib,{application.home}
➡ /lib/axis2,{application.home}/gateway/lib/,{application.home}/wwwroot/WEB-INF/
➡ cfform/jars,{application.home}/wwwroot/WEB-INF/flex/jars,{application.home}/lib/
➡ oosdk/lib,{application.home}/lib/oosdk/classes -Dcoldfusion.libPath=
➡ {application.home}/lib -Dorg.apache.coyote.USE_CUSTOM_STATUS_MSG_IN_HEADER=true
➡ -Dcoldfusion.jsafe.defaultalgo=FIPS186Random
```

All of these parameters are passed to the JVM when JVM is launched. For garbage collection, the parameters in the first line are relevant. You can add any of the other parameters to the jvm.config file.

- `-server` selects the server virtual machine that is optimized for JVM running in server mode.

- `-Xms` and `-Xmx` define the initial and maximum heap sizes, and you can use them to increase the total heap size. If your system has physical memory (RAM) available and you know that your application will need about 1024 MB, you can specify `1024m` for both parameters. Be careful not to exceed the amount of physical memory available.

- `-XX:MaxPermSize` is used to control the permanent generation space.

- `-XX:+UseParallelGC` allows you to specify an appropriate garbage collection algorithm. With recent advancements in Java, you have many garbage collection algorithms at your disposal. You can refer to the Java documentation for more information about possible values.

- `-Xmn` can be used to control the young generation size. This value generally should be 10 percent of the Java heap size defined using `-Xms` and `-Xmx`. A very small size may lead to too frequent minor collection operations; a size that is too large increases the minor GC collection time.

- `-XX:+PrintGCDetails` can provide useful information about when, what, and how much GC has occurred without any performance impact.

CHAPTER 17

Improved Integration

ColdFusion 8 introduced Microsoft Exchange and SharePoint server integration, and ColdFusion 9 extended the integration support to other Microsoft technologies by providing support for Microsoft Excel operation, PowerPoint creation, and Word conversion to PDF. ColdFusion 10 further enhances this support by providing support for Microsoft Exchange Server 2010, with new features and support for the Microsoft Office 2010 document format. This chapter describes improved integration in ColdFusion 10 with Microsoft Exchange Server and Microsoft Office documents.

Improved Integration with Microsoft Exchange Server

ColdFusion 10 added several enhancements to improve integration with Microsoft Exchange Server.

- Microsoft Exchange Server 2010 support

- Folder operations support

- Conversation operations

- Availability operations

Microsoft Exchange Server 2010 Support

ColdFusion 10 added support to Microsoft Exchange Server 2010. With this support, ColdFusion also changed the underlying implementation of the way that it connects to the Exchange server. When ColdFusion 8 introduced this integration, it used the WebDAV protocol. This is a complicated protocol and does not support many operations, such as attachment operations. It has been deprecated by Microsoft in favor of the Exchange Web Services (EWS) protocol.

EWS was introduced with Microsoft Exchange Server 2007 and includes a set of web services that uses the HTTP and HTTPS standards to connect to Exchange mailboxes.

Although EWS was used in ColdFusion 9 to support attachments with Microsoft Exchange Server 2007, ColdFusion 10 has fully adopted this protocol for all Microsoft Exchange Server 2010 operations. ColdFusion continues to support Microsoft Exchange Server 2003 and 2007 using the WebDAV protocol.

To support multiple Exchange servers, a new attribute, serverVersion, has been introduced for the following cfexchange tags:

- cfexchangeconnection

- cfexchangemail

- cfexchangecalendar

- cfexchangetask

- cfexchangecontact

Listing 17.1 shows a simple use of the serverVersion attribute.

Listing 17.1 /cfwack10/17/version.cfm

```
<cfset user = "sample">
<cfset password = "P@$$w0rd">
<cfset exchangeServerIP = "10.0.0.30">
<cfset version = "2010">

<cfexchangeconnection action="open"
                      username="#user#"
                      password="P@$$w0rd"
                      server="#exchangeServerIP#"
                      serverversion="#version#"
                      connection="wackon">

<cfdump var="#wackon#">

<cfexchangeconnection action="close"
                      connection="wackon">
```

Because Microsoft Exchange Server 2010 is used to run applications provided in Listing 17.1, the value "2010" is used for serverversion. Other valid values are "2003" and "2007", with the default value being "2003".

NOTE

ColdFusion does not automatically close connections that are created using the cfexchangeconnection tag. Demonstrating a good programming practice for managing expensive resources such as Microsoft Exchange Server connections, the example in Listing 17.1 closes the connection when its use is completed. Exchange connections created with cfexchange tags other than cfexchangeconnection are temporary connections that close after the tag's work is complete.

Specifying this information at the tag level is rather cumbersome if all your applications run with Microsoft Exchange Server 2010. ColdFusion 10 allows you to specify exchangeServerVersion at the application level via Application.cfc, as shown in Listing 17.2.

Listing 17.2 /cfwack10/17/Application.cfc

```
<cfcomponent>
  <cfset this.name="exchangeApp">
  <cfset this.exchangeServerVersion = "2010">
</cfcomponent>
```

The `exchangeServerVersion` setting can also be used with Application.cfm.

The `cfexchangefolder` and `cfexchangeconversation` tags are newly added to ColdFusion 10 and support Microsoft Exchange Server 2010 only. Hence, there is no need to specify the `serverVersion` attribute with these two tags.

Folder Operations Support

ColdFusion 10 adds support for folder operations by introducing a new tag, `cfexchangefolder`. This new tag supports operations such as retrieval, creation, deletion, updating, and copying of Microsoft Exchange folders.

Retrieving Folder Information

Listing 17.3 shows how to retrieve important information about folder from a mailbox using `action="getInfo"` with the `cfexchangefolder` tag.

Listing 17.3 /cfwack10/17/folder/getFolderInfo.cfm

```
<cfset user = "sample">
<cfset password = "P@$$w0rd">
<cfset exchangeServerIP = "10.0.0.30">

<cfexchangeconnection action="open"
                      username="#user#"
                      password="P@$$w0rd"
                      server="#exchangeServerIP#"
                      connection="wackon">

<cfexchangefolder action="getInfo"
                  connection="wackon"
                  folderpath="Inbox"
                  name="result">
</cfexchangefolder>

<cfdump var="#result#">

<cfexchangeconnection action="close"
                      connection="wackon">
```

If you run this file, it outputs a ColdFusion struct with the following eight keys:

- `ChildFolderCount` is the number of child folders for the specified folder.

- `DisplayName` is the name of the folder that you see when you open Microsoft Outlook.

- `FolderClass` is the internal class name used by Microsoft Exchange Server.

- `FolderPath` is the path to the folder from one of the top-level folders.

- `UID` is a unique ID that Microsoft Exchange Server associates with each folder.

- `ParentFolderId` is the unique ID of the parent folder.

- `TotalCount` is the total number of items in the specified folder.

- `UnreadCount` is the total number of unread items in the specified folder.

The `UID` value is a long string that is programmatically obtained, and it uniquely identifies a resource in your mailbox on Microsoft Exchange Server. In ColdFusion, it is useful for multistep operations and is a mandatory attribute in many `cfexchange` tags. Other folder operations, such as folder creation and modification, use `UID` to identify a folder. In the example in Listing 17.3, further information about parent folders can be obtained by using the `UID` value of `ParentFolderId`.

If you have never noticed how many default top-level folders are present in Microsoft Exchange Server, the application in Listing 17.4 provides interesting information.

Listing 17.4 /cfwack10/17/folder/topFolderInfo.cfm

```
<cfexchangefolder action="getInfo"
                  connection="request.wackon"
                  folderpath="Inbox"
                  name="result">
</cfexchangefolder>

<cfexchangefolder action="findSubFolders"
                  connection="request.wackon"
                  uid="#result.parentFolderId#"
                  name="parentResult">
</cfexchangefolder>

<cfdump var="#parentResult#"
        show="DisplayName, FolderPath, TotalCount, UnreadCount, ChildFolderCount,
➡FolderClass">
```

Here, `findSubFolders` finds details about child folders and is discussed later in the chapter. When you run this file, it produces output as shown in Figure 17.1.

Figure 17.1

Query result showing top-level folder information for a Microsoft Exchange Server mailbox.

query [Filtered - 6 of 8 columns shown]

	CHILDFOLDERCOUNT	DISPLAYNAME	FOLDERCLASS	FOLDERPATH	TOTALCOUNT	UNREADCOUNT
1	0	Calendar	IPF.Appointment	Calendar	1	0
2	0	Contacts	IPF.Contact	Contacts	0	0
3	0	Conversation Action Settings	IPF.Configuration	Conversation Action Settings	0	0
4	0	Deleted Items	IPF.Note	Deleted Items	0	0
5	0	Drafts	IPF.Note	Drafts	20	0
6	7	Inbox	IPF.Note	Inbox	0	0
7	0	Journal	IPF.Journal	Journal	0	0
8	0	Junk E-Mail	IPF.Note	Junk E-Mail	656	654
9	0	Notes	IPF.StickyNote	Notes	0	0
10	0	Outbox	IPF.Note	Outbox	0	0
11	6	RSS Feeds	IPF.Note.OutlookHomepage	RSS Feeds	0	0
12	0	Sent Items	IPF.Note	Sent Items	34	0
13	3	Sync Issues	IPF.Note	Sync Issues	0	0
14	0	Tasks	IPF.Task	Tasks	2	0

By default, a typical Microsoft Exchange Server installation has 15 top-level folders. The topmost folder can also be reached by using "/" as the value of the folderPath attribute.

The folderPath attribute is important in many cfexchange tags and serves as a user-friendly alternative to UID. A typical folder path starts with one of these top-level folders. For example, the folder path for the foo folder inside Deleted Items in Listing 17.3 can be specified as follows:

```
<cfexchangefolder action="getInfo" connection="wackon"
folderpath="Deleted Items/foo" name="result">
</cfexchangefolder>
```

If folderPath is used, ColdFusion makes additional calls to EWS to first locate the ID and then fetch the results. So it is preferable to use UID if your application is aware of it. By default, ColdFusion uses "/" as the path delimiter to reach the target folder. However, Microsoft Exchange Server allows "/" in the name of a folder. The example, Listing 17.5 shows how you can navigate using a different path delimiter, using the pathDelimiter attribute.

Listing 17.5   /cfwack10/17/folder/delimiter.cfm

```
<cfexchangefolder action="getInfo"
                  connection="request.wackon"
                  folderpath="Inbox,a,b"
                  name="result"
                  pathdelimitter=",">
</cfexchangefolder>

<cfdump var="#result#">
```

When you run this example, ColdFusion will find information about folder named a/b.

NOTE

Code to open and close connection object wackon is moved to onRequestStart and onRequestEnd functions in Application.cfc since the information about connection to Microsoft Exchange Server remains the same throughout this chapter. The use of Application.cfc to manage Exchange connections is not a recommended approach in production code, because all web requests may not use Exchange functionality.

Retrieving Additional Folder Information

The information provided by getInfo is minimal. ColdFusion 10 introduces another value for the action attribute, getExtendedInfo, which provides much more detailed information about a folder. Its use is similar to the use of getInfo in Listing 17.3 and is shown in Listing 17.6.

Listing 17.6   /cfwack10/17/folder/topFolderExtendedInfo.cfm

```
<cfexchangefolder action="getExtendedInfo"
                  connection="request.wackon"
                  folderpath="Inbox"
                  name="result">
</cfexchangefolder>

<cfdump var="#result#">
```

The action `getExtendedInfo` provides a lot more detail about a folder. The structs in the result returned by running Listing 17.6 contain two important structs: `ManagedFolderInfo` and `Permissions`.

The `ManagedFolderInfo` struct provides information such as whether a folder can be deleted and the storage quota of the folder. It also provides information related to the folder size, but often the size information is not populated properly. The code in Listing 17.7 provides folder size information correctly.

Listing 17.7   /cfwack10/17/folder/size.cfm

```
<cfexchangeconnection action="getsubfolders"
                      name="result"
                      connection="request.wackon"
                      folder="Inbox" recurse="true">

<cfdump var="#result#"/>
```

The `Permissions` struct provides information associated with a given folder, such as whether a user can create new items and whether a user is in a delegate role for the specified folder.

You can find more information about `ManagedFolderInfo` and `Permissions` in the ColdFusion 10 documentation here:

http://help.adobe.com/en_US/ColdFusion/10.0/CFMLRef/WSd8001ae4abdbd911-1654a05b1350dc3b20f-8000.html

Retrieving Child Folder Information

The third and last action attribute in the folder retrieval series is `findSubFolders`. It retrieves information about child folders of the specified folder. When this action is used in a `cfexchangefolder` tag, `UID` is a mandatory attribute. See the example in Listing 17.8.

Listing 17.8   /cfwack10/17/folder/findSubFolders.cfm

```
<cfexchangefolder action="findSubFolders"
                  connection="request.wackon"
                  uid="A ..."
                  name="result">
  <cfexchangefilter name="displayname" value="a">
</cfexchangefolder>

<cfdump var="#result#"
        show="DisplayName, FolderPath, TotalCount, UnreadCount, ChildFolderCount">
```

When you run this example, it returns a query object with each row for the child folder containing the same results columns as with the `getInfo` action (Figure 17.2). The returned results are further filtered using the `cfexchangefilter` tag, using the display name as the key and the appropriate value as the display name. Because `parentFolderId` and `UID` are long strings, they are not shown in the result.

Figure 17.2

Query result from a findSubFolder operation.

	CHILDFOLDERCOUNT	DISPLAYNAME	FOLDERPATH	TOTALCOUNT	UNREADCOUNT
1	0	abc	Inbox/abc	0	0

query [Filtered - 5 of 8 columns shown]

Creating Folders

ColdFusion 10 allows you to create folders in a mailbox by using a create action in cfexchangefolder, as shown in Listing 17.9.

Listing 17.9 /cfwack10/17/folder/createFolder.cfm

```
<cfexchangefolder action="getInfo"
                  connection="request.wackon"
                  folderpath="Inbox"
                  name="parentResult">
</cfexchangefolder>

<cfset newfolder = structnew()>
<cfset newfolder.displayname = "CFWACK">
<cfset newfolder.folderclass = "IPF.Note">
<cfexchangefolder action="create"
                  connection="request.wackon"
                  parentfolderid="#parentResult.UID#"
                  folder="#newfolder#"
                  result="uid">
</cfexchangefolder>

<cfdump var="#uid#">
```

The important information required during creation of a new folder is the parent folder's UID, the name of the folder, and a folder class. If you need to perform additional operations on the created folder, you can keep the UID value that is retuned. Figure 17.2, the result of Listing 17.9, shows a list of valid values for folder classes.

NOTE

It is possible to define custom classes for a folder, but this topic is beyond the scope of this book.

Modifying Folders

To modify a folder's name or other properties of a folder, use the modify value for the action attribute. The major difference between create and modify is that a create action requires the parent folder's UID, whereas a modify action requires the UID of the folder being modified. The code snippet in Listing 17.10 provides an example.

Listing 17.10 /cfwack10/17/folder/modifyFolder.cfm

```
<cfexchangefolder action="getInfo"
                  connection="request.wackon"
                  folderpath="Inbox/CFWACK"
                  name="result">
</cfexchangefolder>

<cfset folder = structnew()>
<cfset folder.displayname = "CFWACK-10">
<cfset folder.folderclass = "IPF.Note">
<cfexchangefolder action="modify"
                  connection="request.wackon"
                  uid="#result.UID#"
                  folder="#folder#">
</cfexchangefolder>
```

Copying Folders

You can use a cfexchangefolder tag to copy a folder. You need to specify the UID of the source folder and the UID of the destination folder. The code in Listing 17.11 creates a copy of the source folder in the destination folder.

Listing 17.11 /cfwack10/17/folder/copyFolder.cfm

```
<cfexchangefolder action="getInfo"
                  connection="request.wackon"
                  folderpath="Inbox/CFWACK"
                  name="result">
</cfexchangefolder>

<cfexchangefolder action="getInfo"
                  connection="request.wackon"
                  folderpath="Inbox/dest"
                  name="dest">
</cfexchangefolder>

<cfexchangefolder action="copy"
                  connection="request.wackon"
                  sourcefolderid="#result.UID#"
                  destinationfolderid="#dest.UID#"
                  result="copyId">
</cfexchangefolder>

<cfexchangefolder action="getInfo"
                  connection="request.wackon"
                  uid="#copyId#"
                  name="copyresult">
</cfexchangefolder>
```

NOTE

As of this writing, the result of the **copy** action returns the source UID, which looks incorrect. The product team has been notified about this issue so that the team can evaluate whether to change the result so that the UID of the newly created folder is returned.

Moving Folders

You can use the `cfexchangefolder` tag to move a folder by using `action="move"`. The operation takes a parameter similar to the `copy` action, in which the source and destination UIDs of folders are required. Note that distinguished folders are special, and default folders such as Inbox, Contacts, Calendar, Task, and Deleted Items cannot be moved because Microsoft Exchange relies on the folder's being in the mailbox.

Deleting Folders

You can use the `cfexchangefolder` tag to delete folders from a Microsoft Exchange Server mailbox, as shown in Listing 17.12.

Listing 17.12   /cfwack10/17/folder/deleteFolder.cfm

```
<cfexchangefolder action="getInfo"
                  connection="request.wackon"
                  folderpath="Inbox/dest"
                  name="result">
</cfexchangefolder>

<cfexchangefolder action="delete"
                  connection="request.wackon"
                  uid="#result.UID#">
</cfexchangefolder>
```

Note that the attribute `deleteType="hardDelete"` permanently deletes the folder, `deleteType="moveToDeletedItems"` moves the folder to the Deleted Items folder, and `deleteType="softDelete"` moves the folder to the dumpster if the dumpster is enabled. Items in the dumpster are recoverable in Microsoft Exchange Server.

Emptying Folders

You can use the `cfexchangefolder` tag to empty folders from a Microsoft Exchange Server mailbox, as shown in Listing 17.13.

Listing 17.13   /cfwack10/17/folder/emptyFolder.cfm

```
<cfexchangefolder action="getInfo"
                  connection="request.wackon"
                  folderpath="Inbox/CFWACK"
                  name="result">
</cfexchangefolder>

<cfexchangefolder action="empty"
                  connection="request.wackon"
                  uid="#result.UID#">
</cfexchangefolder>
```

You can also delete the subfolders of the specified folder by using attribute `deleteSubFolders="false"`.

Conversation Operations

Microsoft Outlook clients offer the option to view messages based on conversations. Organizing messages with related topics helps make the conversation easier to follow, with the messages grouped together and sorted, for example, from newest to oldest. Outlook Web App, a browser-based application, also provides this option, as shown in Figure 17.3.

Figure 17.3

View conversation option in Microsoft Outlook Web App.

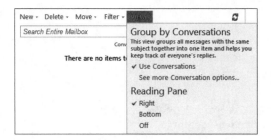

ColdFusion 10 introduces a new tag, cfexchangeconversation, to organize and manage conversations in a Microsoft Exchange Server mailbox. To facilitate conversation management, ColdFusion provides the following actions:

- Retreive conversations using filter criteria

- Change the state of conversations

- Copy conversations

- Move conversations

- Delete conversations

Retrieving Conversations

You can use the cfexchangeconversation tag to retrieve conversations from a Microsoft Exchange Server mailbox, as shown in Listing 17.14.

Listing 17.14   /cfwack10/17/conversation/get.cfm

```
<cfexchangefolder action="getInfo"
                  connection="request.wackon"
                  folderpath="Inbox/CFWACK"
                  name="result">
</cfexchangefolder>

<cfexchangeconversation action="get"
                        connection="request.wackon"
                        folderid="#result.UID#"
                        name="conversations">
    <cfexchangefilter name="topic" value="abc">
</cfexchangeconversation>

<cfdump var="#conversations#">
```

As the example shows, a folder is specified using its UID. The call returns a query object containing all conversations as rows and conversation properties as columns. Table 17.1 lists the conversation properties that are returned, and most of them are self-explanatory. There is a property at the folder level and a property with the same name at the global level that also has "Global" prefixed to it. The folder-level property applies to the conversation messages in the specified folder, and the global properties are applied to all the messages in the conversation across all folders in the mailbox. For example, `HasAttachments` indicates whether any of the messages in the conversation have attachments in the specified folder; `GlobalHasAttachments` indicates whether any of the messages in the conversations have attachments across all folders in the mailbox.

Table 17.1 Conversation Properties

`Categories`	Category that applies to the conversation.
`FlagStatus`	Message status: flagged, not flagged. or comlete.
`HasAttachments`	Boolean value indicating whether at least one message in the conversation has an attachment.
`Importance`	Importance indicated as low, normal, or high.
`ItemClasses`	Classes of the messages in the conversation
`ItemIds`	Unique IDs of the messages in the conversation.
`LastDeliveryTime`	Delivery time of the last message in the conversation.
`MessageCount`	Count of the messages in the conversation.
`Size`	Combined size of the messages in the conversation.
`UniqueRecipients`	Identities of all the receipients in the conversation.
`UniqueSenders`	Identities of all the senders in the conversation.
`UniqueUnreadSenders`	Identities of all the senders whose messages are unread.
`UnreadCount`	Count of the unread messages in the conversation.
`UID`	Unique ID for the conversation; same at the global and folder levels.
`Topic`	Topic of the conversation; same at the global and folder levels.

To filter the query result, you can use one or more `cfexchangefilter` tags on any of the properties in Table 17.1. For the example, here's an example using a code snippet from Listing 17.14:

```
<cfexchangeconversation action="get" connection="request.wackon"
  folderid="#result.UID#" name="conversations">
    <cfexchangefilter name="topic" value="abc">
</cfexchangeconversation>
```

In addition, you can use the `maxRows` property to specify the maximum number of rows to be returned. The default value is 100, and a value of –1 returns all rows.

Performing Actions on Conversation

Just as folders are identified uniquely in a mailbox by their UIDs, conversations are identified by their UIDs in a folder. Any operation on a conversation is performed using its UID, which is obtained using action="get", as shown earlier in Listing 17.14.

You can use the cfexchangeconversation tag to mark a conversation as either read or unread using the isRead attribute, as shown in Listing 17.15.

Listing 17.15 /cfwack10/17/conversation/setRead.cfm

```
<cfexchangefolder action="getInfo"
                  connection="request.wackon"
                  folderpath="Inbox/CFWACK"
                  name="result">
</cfexchangefolder>

<cfexchangeconversation action="get"
                        connection="request.wackon"
                        folderid="#result.UID#"
                        name="conversations">
</cfexchangeconversation>

<cfexchangeconversation action="setReadState"
                        connection="request.wackon"
                        folderid="#result.UID#"
                        uid="#conversations.UID#"
                        isread="true">
</cfexchangeconversation>
```

You can use the cfexchangeconversation tag to copy a conversation to another folder using the action="copy" attribute, as shown in Listing 17.16.

Listing 17.16 /cfwack10/17/conversation/copy.cfm

```
<cfexchangefolder action="getInfo"
                  connection="request.wackon"
                  folderpath="Inbox/CFWACK"
                  name="result">
</cfexchangefolder>

<cfexchangefolder action="getInfo"
                  connection="request.wackon"
                  folderpath="Inbox/dest"
                  name="dest">
</cfexchangefolder>

<cfexchangeconversation action="get"
                        connection="request.wackon"
                        folderid="#result.UID#"
                        name="conversations">
</cfexchangeconversation>
```

Listing 17.16 (CONTINUED)

```
<cfexchangeconversation action="copy"
                        connection="request.wackon"
                        folderid="#result.UID#"
                        destinationfolderid="#dest.UID#"
                        uid="#conversations.UID#">
</cfexchangeconversation>
```

You can use the cfexchangeconversation tag to move a conversation to a different folder using the action="move" attribute, as shown in the code snippet in Listing 17.17. The move operation is similar to the copy operation.

Listing 17.17   /cfwack10/17/conversation/move.cfm

```
<cfexchangeconversation action="move"
                        connection="request.wackon"
                        folderid="#result.UID#"
                        destinationfolderid="#dest.UID#"
                        uid="#conversations.UID#">
</cfexchangeconversation>
```

You can use the cfexchangeconversation tag to delete a conversation using the action="delete" attribute, as shown in the code snippet in Listing 17.18. The deleteType value can be hardDelete, softDelete, or moveToDeletedItems. These options are similar to the options for deleting folders discussed earlier for Listing 17.12.

Listing 17.18   /cfwack10/17/conversation/delete.cfm

```
<cfexchangeconversation action="delete"
                        connection="request.wackon"
                        folderid="#result.UID#"
                        uid="#conversations.UID#"
                        deletetype="moveToDeletedItems">
</cfexchangeconversation>
```

Availability Operations

With the introduction of Microsoft Exchange Server integration in ColdFusion 8, ColdFusion provided operations to create, modify, delete, and respond to Microsoft Exchange calendar events. ColdFusion also provided operations to get calendar event attachments. These operations are provided with the cfexchangecalendar tag. ColdFusion 10 enhances the calendar integration further by providing operations to find user availability, get rooms, and get lists of rooms available on the server.

Find User Availability

You can use the cfexchangecalendar tag in ColdFusion 10 to check availability for one or more users, as shown in Listing 17.19.

Listing 17.19 /cfwack10/17/calendar/availability.cfm

```
<cfset fromDate = #Now()#>
<cfset toDate = DateAdd("d", "1", "#fromDate#")>

<cfexchangecalendar action="getuseravailability"
                    attendees="user1@cfadobe.com, user2@cfadobe.com"
                    startdate="#fromDate#" enddate="#todate#"
                    datarequesttype="FreeBusyAndSuggestions" name="result"
                    connection="request.wackon">
</cfexchangecalendar>

<cfdump var="#result#">
```

This code finds availability for user1 and user2 between now and the same time the next day. You can use a comma-separated list of users or the email address of a distribution list for the attendees attribute. The dataRequestType attribute has three options: to obtain the free and busy status, to obtain suggestions for user availability, or to obtain both the free and busy status and suggestions. ColdFusion 10 returns a large number of properties when user availability is queried, and a good description of the result set is provided in the ColdFusion 10 documentation.

Get Room List

You can use the cfexchangecalendar tag to retrieve lists of rooms that are available on a Microsoft Exchange Server, as shown in Listing 17.20.

Listing 17.20 /cfwack10/17/calendar/roomList.cfm

```
<cfexchangecalendar action="getroomlist"
                    name="result"
                    connection="request.wackon">
</cfexchangecalendar>

<cfdump var="#result#">
```

When you run this code, the result is a ColdFusion query object with each row representing a room list. The properties, represented by column, contain the room list address, the mailbox type, the name of the room list, the routing type (typically SMTP), and the UID.

Get Room

You can retrieve rooms that are associated with a room list by using the `cfexchangecalendar` tag, as shown in Listing 17.21.

Listing 17.21 /cfwack10/17/calendar/rooms.cfm

```
<cfexchangecalendar action="getRooms"
                    emailaddress="GroundFloor@cfadobe.com"
                    name="result"
                    connection="request.wackon">
</cfexchangecalendar>

<cfdump var="#result#">
```

When you run this code, you get a ColdFusion query object similar to the `action="getRoomList"` result shown in Figure 17.4.

Figure 17.4

Query result from a `getRooms` operation.

	ADDRESS	MAILBOX TYPE	NAME	ROUTING TYPE	UID
1	aldan@cfadobe.com	*object of coldfusion.exchange.webservice.MailBoxType*	aldan	SMTP	[empty string]
2	amaravati@cfadobe.com	*object of coldfusion.exchange.webservice.MailBoxType*	amaravati	SMTP	[empty string]
3	alzani@cfadobe.com	*object of coldfusion.exchange.webservice.MailBoxType*	alzani	SMTP	[empty string]

Improved Integration with Microsoft Office Documents

Prior to ColdFusion 10, ColdFusion added comprehensive support for integration with Microsoft Office documents. Table 17.2 provides a quick reference to the added functions in the release prior to ColdFusion 10.

Table 17.2 Microsoft Office Support in ColdFusion

FROM FORMAT	TO FORMAT	COLDFUSION TAG REQUIRED	USES
PowerPoint	Connect presentation	`cfpresentation`	OpenOffice
PowerPoint	HTML	`cfpresentation`	OpenOffice
HTML	PowerPoint	`cfpresentation`	OpenOffice
PowerPoint	PDF	`cfdocument`	OpenOffice
Excel	HTML/Query	`cfspreadsheet`	Apache POI
HTML/Query	Excel	`cfspreadsheet`	Apache POI
Word	PDF	`cfdocument`	OpenOffice

Some PowerPoint operations can also work with the Apache POI library that ships with ColdFusion, but the quality of the converted format is superior with OpenOffice.

ColdFusion 10 has fixed many important bugs related to Microsoft Office integration, but the major improvement is in its support for Microsoft Office 2010 documents. ColdFusion 10 supports interoperability with Office 2010 for Microsoft Word 2010 and Microsoft PowerPoint 2010 with the same tag syntax.

CHAPTER 18

Apache Solr

ColdFusion 10 has added some interesting updates to its embedded full-text search support, provided by Apache Solr. In this chapter, we discuss updates to the indexing and searching functions that can help provide better results for your users. Note that another update, to full-text search of object relational mapping (ORM) entities, is covered in Chapter 9, "Object Relational Mapping Enhancements."

Say Goodbye to Verity

Before we go any further, it's time to say goodbye to an old friend. Users were warned of this in ColdFusion 9, but as of ColdFusion 10, Verity is no longer supported in ColdFusion. If you are currently using Verity with your ColdFusion application, be sure to convert your collection to Solr *before* you upgrade. The ColdFusion Administrator contains a Verity Migration tool that will make this job painless. Also note that the ColdFusion 9 documentation (available online at Adobe.com) contains a section on migration from Verity to Solr that may also be of help to you.

Updates to <cfindex>

The <cfindex> tag is the primary tool for storing data (both file based and dynamic) in Solr collections. This section discusses the primary changes to the tag. Later in the chapter we discuss the new DataImportHandler feature, which deserves a section to itself.

One of the first, and most welcome, updates is the capability to specify custom fields. In the past, ColdFusion supported four custom fields. These fields were used to store whatever you thought necessary. For example, in an index based on product data, you may want to store the prices and sizes of products as well. This information would allow you to display that data in search results without having to access the database. Although this was a useful feature, if you needed more than four fields, you were out of luck.

ColdFusion 10 removes this limitation by allowing any number of custom fields. Even better, the old naming scheme (custom1, custom2, and so on) isn't a requirement anymore. In the product example just mentioned, for instance, you can now store data with much more appropriate names.

Listing 18.1 provides a simple example of this new feature.

Listing 18.1   /cfwack10/18/index1.cfm

```
<!--- Determine if we need to create the collection --->
<cfcollection action="list" name="collections">
<cfif not listFindNoCase(valueList(collections.name), "ows1")>
    <cfcollection action="create" collection="ows1" path="ows1index">
</cfif>

<cfquery name="getFilms">
select filmid, amountbudgeted, dateintheaters,
       movietitle, pitchtext, rating, summary
from films f left join filmsratings fr
on f.ratingid = fr.ratingid
</cfquery>

<cfindex action="update" collection="ows1" body="summary,pitchtext"
         key="filmid" title="movietitle"
         budget_f="amountbudgeted" rating_s="rating"
         released_dt="dateintheaters"
         query="getFilms"
         status="result">

<cfdump var="#result#">
```

Before we really get to the meat of this template, note the code at the top. It uses the <cfcollection> tag to list current collections and create our test index if it doesn't exist. In production code, you would probably just create the collection in the ColdFusion Administrator. Many of the templates in this chapter will use this snippet to quickly set up the collection for you.

After the setup code, a simple query is run against the OWS data source to get film information. Note that a join is used to get film rating values as well. Then we use <cfindex> to store the query. Note the three undocumented attributes: budget_f, rating_s, and released_dt. These attributes represent the custom data we want stored along with the rest of the index. Since we are using a query, the values represent columns in the query. You can name these columns anything you want, but you are probably wondering about the odd naming scheme.

For custom columns to be stored properly within Solr, we have to provide a hint about the type of data being stored. In the example here, _f represents a float value, _s represents a string value, and _dt represents a date value. Table 18.1 lists the available suffixes and their meanings.

Table 18.1   Attribute Suffixes

SUFFIX	MEANING
_i	Integer
_s	String
_l	Long
_t	Text
_b	Boolean
_f	Float
_d	Double
_dt	Date

Listing 18.2 creates a simple search form to test these new custom fields.

Listing 18.2   /cfwack10/18/search1.cfm

```
<cfparam name="form.search" default="">

<cfoutput>
<form method="post">
Enter search:
<input type="search" name="search" value="#encodeForHTMLAttribute(form.search)#">
<input type="submit" value="Search">
</form>
</cfoutput>

<cfif len(trim(form.search))>

    <cfsearch collection="ows1" criteria="#form.search#" name="results">

    <cfif results.recordCount>

        <table border="1">
            <thead>
            <tr>
                <th>Movie</th>
                <th>Budget</th>
                <th>Rating</th>
                <th>Released</th>
            </tr>
            <tbody>
            <cfoutput query="results">
                <tr>
                    <td>#title#</td>
                    <td>#dollarFormat(budget_f)#</td>
                    <td>#rating_s#</td>
                    <td>#dateFormat(released_dt)#</td>
                </tr>
            </cfoutput>
            </tbody>
        </table>
```

Listing 18.2 (CONTINUED)

```
  <cfelse>

    <p>
       Sorry, no results. Try "e*".
    </p>

  </cfif>

</cfif>
```

For the most part, this should be nothing new to you if you have used `<cfsearch>` before. But note that the results now reference the custom columns we created. We can now allow users to search for films using the power of Solr, and you can also include data about the budget, rating, and release date. Technically, since we used only three fields, this same result could have been achieved using the older custom fields. But our code now is a lot more readable.

Even more interesting is that we can implement filters based on this custom data. Again, we could mostly do this before, but with the enhanced data-type help for the index, we can be much more precise. Listing 18.3 creates an enhanced version of the search form.

Listing 18.3 /cfwack10/18/search2.cfm

```
<cfparam name="form.search" default="">
<cfparam name="form.minbudget" default="">
<cfparam name="form.maxbudget" default="">

<cfoutput>
<form method="post">
Enter search:
<input type="search" name="search"
➥value="#encodeForHTMLAttribute(form.search)#"><br/>
Minimum budget: <input type="number" name="minbudget"
                value="#encodeForHTMLAttribute(form.minbudget)#"><br/>
Maximum budget: <input type="number" name="maxbudget"
                value="#encodeForHTMLAttribute(form.maxbudget)#"><br/>
<input type="submit" value="Search">
</form>
</cfoutput>

<cfif len(trim(form.search))>

   <!--- do we have min or max budget? --->
   <cfif len(form.minbudget) or len(form.maxbudget)>
     <cfset form.search &= " AND budget_f:[">

     <cfif not len(form.minbudget) or not isNumeric(form.minbudget)>
       <cfset form.search &= "* ">
     <cfelse>
       <cfset form.search &= "#form.minbudget# ">
     </cfif>

     <cfset form.search &= "TO ">
```

Listing 18.3 (CONTINUED)

```
        <cfif not len(form.maxbudget) or not isNumeric(form.maxbudget)>
          <cfset form.search &= "*">
        <cfelse>
          <cfset form.search &= form.maxbudget>
        </cfif>

        <cfset form.search &="]">

  </cfif>

  <cfsearch collection="ows1" criteria="#form.search#" name="results">

  <cfif results.recordCount>

      <table border="1">
        <thead>
        <tr>
          <th>Movie</th>
          <th>Budget</th>
          <th>Rating</th>
          <th>Released</th>
        </tr>
        <tbody>
        <cfoutput query="results">
          <tr>
            <td>#title#</td>
            <td>#dollarFormat(budget_f)#</td>
            <td>#rating_s#</td>
            <td>#dateFormat(released_dt)#</td>
          </tr>
        </cfoutput>
        </tbody>
      </table>

    <cfelse>

      <p>
        Sorry, no results. Try "e*".
      </p>

    </cfif>

  </cfif>
```

This version of the search form contains two new filtering fields: Minimum budget and Maximum budget. To apply these values to the <cfsearch> tag, we have to work on the search string a bit. An example that searches for only a minimum value looks something like this: x AND budget_f:[Y TO *]. The [and] characters represent a range, with * meaning any value. Therefore, the string to search for only a maximum value looks something like this: [* TO Y]. Finally, if the user provides both values, then the form [Y TO Z] is used. Figure 18.1 shows an example of this advanced search in action.

Figure 18.1

Results from the
search interface.

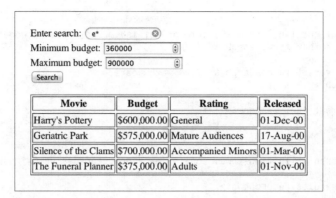

Boosting Fields and Documents

Another interesting new feature is the capability to boost custom fields and whole documents
when indexing. For document indexing, you use the `docboost` attribute. This attribute is useful
only when you are indexing an individual item. You could, for example, use this attribute to boost
the index of a product record that is featured in a monthly promotion, causing the product to rank
higher in search results. You can also boost fields, with `fieldboost`. This attribute allows you to
boost a particular custom field. Listing 18.4 provides an example of `docboost`.

Listing 18.4   `/cfwack10/18/index2.cfm`

```
<!--- Determine if we need to create the collection --->
<cfcollection action="list" name="collections">
<cfif not listFindNoCase(valueList(collections.name), "owsX")>
   <cfcollection action="create" collection="owsX" path="owsXindex">
</cfif>

<cfquery name="getFilms">
select filmid, amountbudgeted, dateintheaters,
      movietitle, pitchtext, rating, summary
from films f left join filmsratings fr
on f.ratingid = fr.ratingid
</cfquery>

<cfquery name="kids" dbtype="query">
select *
from getFilms
where rating = 'Kids'
</cfquery>

<cfquery name="notkids" dbtype="query">
select *
from getFilms
where rating != 'Kids'
</cfquery>
```

Listing 18.4   (CONTINUED)

```
<cfindex action="update" collection="owsX" body="summary,pitchtext"
        key="filmid" title="movietitle"
        budget_f="amountbudgeted" rating_s="rating"
        released_dt="dateintheaters"
        query="kids"
        docboost="5"
        status="result">

<cfdump var="#result#">

<cfindex action="update" collection="owsX" body="summary,pitchtext"
        key="filmid" title="movietitle"
        budget_f="amountbudgeted" rating_s="rating"
        released_dt="dateintheaters"
        query="notkids"
status="result">

<cfdump var="#result#">
```

This example is similar to the original index example, but note that a query of query is used to split the main film data into two separate queries: One contains just the films appropriate for kids, and the other contains everything else. The first <cfindex> tag works with the kids query and contains a docboost value of 5. (The higher the number, the greater the boost.) Listing 18.5 provides an example showing how docboost affects this search.

Listing 18.5   /cfwack10/18/search3.cfm

```
<cfparam name="form.search" default="">

<cfoutput>
<form method="post">
Enter search:
<input type="search" name="search" value="#encodeForHTMLAttribute(form.search)#">
<input type="submit" value="Search">
</form>
</cfoutput>

<cfif len(trim(form.search))>

    <cfsearch collection="ows1" criteria="#form.search#" name="results">
    <cfsearch collection="owsX" criteria="#form.search#" name="results2">

    <cfdump var="#results#" label="NOT Boosted">
    <cfdump var="#results2#" label="Boosted!">

</cfif>
```

Note that we've forgone the "pretty" output of the previous examples and have resorted to the <cfdump> output.

When the user searches, the search is first performed against the unboosted index and then against the boosted collection. If you search for a generic term such as e*, you'll see that kids films are ranked higher in the results.

Ordering Results

Here is one final example of new features in `<cfindex>`: You can now sort the results by your custom fields. This feature allows you still to perform intelligent text-based searching against the data in your collection, but also to sort by anything else you wish. The `orderby` attribute takes the name of a field to search and supports the `asc` or `desc` keyword to specify a direction. You can specify multiple fields by separating each with a comma. Listing 18.6 shows an example of this capability. As before, two searches are performed so you can compare the results.

Listing 18.6   /cfwack10/18/search4.cfm

```
<cfparam name="form.search" default="">

<cfoutput>
<form method="post">
Enter search:
<input type="search" name="search" value="#encodeForHTMLAttribute(form.search)#">
<input type="submit" value="Search">
</form>
</cfoutput>

<cfif len(trim(form.search))>

    <cfsearch collection="ows1" criteria="#form.search#" name="results"
orderby="budget_f desc">
    <cfsearch collection="ows1" criteria="#form.search#" name="results2">

    <cfdump var="#results#" label="Most Expensive">
    <cfdump var="#results2#" label="Regular">

</cfif>
```

Data Import Handlers

If you have ever used ColdFusion's full-text search support (whether with Verity or Solr), then you understand the basic requirement to keep your index up-to-date with your content. When your data changes (whether through additions, updates, or deletions), it is important for you to update your index as well.

ColdFusion 10 adds support for a new way of keeping your index up-to-date. Instead of using ColdFusion to keep your index up-to-date, you can provide data to Solr directly. You can tell Solr where your database is and exactly how to query it for new information. This feature is referred to as DataImportHandler (DIH). DIH is a complex feature, and we will be looking at only a simple example of how to use it. For more information and examples, please see the online documentation at http://wiki.apache.org/solr/DataImportHandler.

Unfortunately, the sample database used for almost all of this book's examples will not work well with this feature. The DIH feature requires you to tell Solr how to connect to your database. The OWS database is meant to be used by one client only. Since ColdFusion is already connected to it, and Solr is, technically, another client, you cannot use the DIH feature with the OWS data. In the zip file you downloaded from this book's website, you will find a MySQL export file zipped as blog.zip. This is a text file that can be unzipped and imported into a new MySQL database. In ColdFusion, create a new data source name, "blog," that points to this database. (The data is an export from the blog at raymondcamden.com.)

Setup

To begin, we are going to create a new ColdFusion collection. You can do this in the ColdFusion Administrator, but Listing 18.7 contains a script that automates the process.

Listing 18.7 /cfwack10/18/collection.cfm

```
<!--- Determine if we need to create the collection --->
<cfcollection action="list" name="collections">
<cfif not listFindNoCase(valueList(collections.name), "blog_dih")>
   <cfcollection action="create" collection="blog_dih"
   ➥path="#expandPath('./blog_dihindex')#">
</cfif>

Collection created.
```

As in many of the previous examples, the script uses the `list` action of `<cfcollection>` to determine whether a particular collection exists. Note, though, the use of the `path` attribute. In this case, we are creating the index below the current script. Why? To properly use DIH, we need to work within the index folder itself. This folder normally is used only by Solr, but you can edit it yourself as well. Run this script and then open this folder yourself. Figure 18.2 shows the folder on a Mac OS X system.

Figure 18.2

Folder structure of the Solr collection.

To configure DIH, we will create a new XML file called data-config.xml. You can find a copy of this in the same folder as collection.cfm, but you must copy this file to the blog_dihindex\blog_dih\conf folder. Listing 18.8 shows you the contents of this file.

Listing 18.8 /cfwack10/18/dih/data-config.xml

```
<dataConfig>

<dataSource driver="com.mysql.jdbc.Driver" url="jdbc:mysql://localhost:8889/blog"
➡user="root" password="" />

<document name="blogentries">
    <entity name="blogentries" query="select * from tblblogentries" pk="id">
    <field column="id" name="uid"/>
    <field column="title" name="title"/>
    <field column="body" name="contents"/>
    </entity>
</document>

</dataConfig>
```

The XML file defines a few important elements. First, notice the URL defined in the dataSource tag. This value defines a JDBC URL for your database. If your MySQL uses a port other than 8889, you will want to edit this. Also note that the password is blank. Most likely, you have a password for your database. Before copying the XML file, you will want to edit the password.

As for the rest of the XML file, what you see is a basic definition indicating how Solr should get content from the database and how it should map the content to index data. Again, there is a *lot* that can be done here, and far more than we can explain here, but for now, you can see that the ID, title, and body columns in the database get mapped to the UID, title, and contents values in the collection. Solr supports both what is called a full import and a delta import. Our XML file defines a full import in that all data is transferred from the database to the index. For the demonstration purposes here, this is fine. In your own applications, you may want to use delta imports to reduce the amount of data that has to be processed.

In the same conf folder, you will see a file called solrconfig.xml. Open this file and remove the comments (<!-- and -->) from this block.

```
<requestHandler name="/dataimport"
➡class="org.apache.solr.handler.dataimport.DataImportHandler">
  <lst name="defaults">
    <str name="config">data-config.xml</str>
  </lst>
</requestHandler>
```

With these two changes, you are almost, but not quite, ready to test. You may have noticed that in the data-config.xml file, you specified the following driver: com.mysql.jdbc.Driver. For Solr to use this MySQL driver, you need to copy the file mysql-connector-java-commercial-5.1.17-bin.jar from the cfusion\lib folder to the cfusion\jetty\lib folder.

Now you need to restart ColdFusion's Solr service. You may find it easier to simply restart Cold-Fusion itself, which should take down the Solr service as well. Otherwise, you can use the cfjetty command-line program in the cfusion\jetty folder.

As you can see, there is a bit of preparation involved in using DIH, but after you get past the initial setup, things get somewhat easier.

Indexing Data

In the previous steps, you modified a Solr collection so that it had, hopefully, enough information to speak to your data directly. To run this handler, though, you still need to run at least one Cold-Fusion command. The <cfindex> tag has been updated with three new features related to DIH support. You can run a fullImport or a deltaImport action to have Solr update the index. You can also ask <cfindex> to return a status report. The fullImport and deltaImport commands both are asynchronous: that is, when they are executed, ColdFusion tells Solr to get busy and then carries on. With the status action, you can see what, if anything, is going on behind the scenes with Solr. Listing 18.9 provides an example.

Listing 18.9 /cfwack10/18/dih/doindex.cfm

```
<p>
<a href="?index=1">Start the index</a>
</p>

<cfif structKeyExists(url, "index")>
    <cfindex collection="blog_dih" action="fullImport" type="dih">
</cfif>

<cfindex collection="blog_dih" action="status" type="dih" status="st">
<cfdump var="#st#" label="Status">
```

The template contains two <cfindex> examples. The first <cfindex> tag performs the actual import operation, but note that it runs only when a link is clicked. The second <cfindex> tag performs a status call on the collection. When you first implement the indexing (and click the link, of course), the status information will show that Solr is busy (Figure 18.3).

Figure 18.3

Status results immediately after indexing.

Status - struct	
TOTAL_DOCUMENTS_PROCESSED	0
TOTAL_DOCUMENTS_SKIPPED	0
TOTAL_ROWS_FETCHED	0
status	busy

If you run the CFM file again but without the URL parameter passed, you can see that Solr is idle but has data indexed (Figure 18.4).

Figure 18.4

Status results after indexing has completed.

Status - struct	
TOTAL_DOCUMENTS_PROCESSED	4526
TOTAL_DOCUMENTS_SKIPPED	0
TOTAL_ROWS_FETCHED	4526
status	idle

To test these results, let's create a simple search form (Listing 18.10).

Listing 18.10   /cfwack10/18/dih/search.cfm

```
<cfparam name="form.search" default="">

<cfoutput>
<form method="post">
Enter search:
<input type="search" name="search" value="#encodeForHTMLAttribute(form.search)#">
<input type="submit" value="Search">
</form>
</cfoutput>

<cfif len(trim(form.search))>

    <cfsearch collection="blog_dih" criteria="#form.search#" name="results">

    <cfif results.recordCount>

        <cfdump var="#results#" top="20">

    <cfelse>

        <p>
            Sorry, no results. Try "e*".
        </p>

    </cfif>

</cfif>
```

All this search form does is present a simple form interface to run a search against our new collection. To keep things simple, <cfdump> is used to render any results.

CHAPTER **19**

Miscellaneous Enhancements

As we reach the final chapter, it may seem that we've covered everything new in ColdFusion 10, but in fact, as is the case with each new release of ColdFusion, there's much more that's new than most people might expect.

In this chapter, we review a couple dozen small but important enhancements, what we might call hidden gems. We'll organize them into the following categories:

- Architectural enhancements
- CFML enhancements
- Administrator enhancements
- Security enhancements

- Logging enhancements
- Updated embedded libraries
- Other enhancements
- Other resources

Each Release Brings Many Enhancements

In each new release of ColdFusion, several major features usually get lots of public discussion, while many other features may go unnoticed. But often some of these "little things" may be just what some people have been awaiting for years.

Some of these changes may be documented, but you might easily miss them. Also, for ColdFusion 10, there was no single release notes document listing all of the changes in the new release. Instead, the various changes are mentioned throughout the ColdFusion documentation (which you can find at http://help.adobe.com/en_US/ColdFusion/10.0/Admin/index.html).

Even with this chapter, this book does not discuss every new enhancement in ColdFusion 10. There are just too many. And, of course, we don't want to just repeat the documentation. So we've highlighted the most significant features in preceding chapters, and will wrap up here with some others that we think you ought not miss.

NOTE

How many total enhancements are there in ColdFusion 10–not every single new tag, function, tag attribute, or function argument, but really, distinct new or changed features? This author counts over 200, as documented in a blog entry "Charlie Arehart's Ultimate List of 200+ New #ColdFusion 10 Features," available at http://tinyurl.com/ultimatecf10list.

Architectural Enhancements

A variety of modest enhancements have to do with some of the architectural changes in ColdFusion 10. Previous chapters focused on the broad topics (the move from JRun to Tomcat and the move from Verity to Solr); this section focuses on some miscellaneous changes related to architectural enhancements, not otherwise yet mentioned.

Verity-Solr Migration

ColdFusion 9 included a migration wizard, to help you convert Verity collections to Solr collections, but what if you did not use that while you were running ColdFusion 9? Or what if you skipped ColdFusion 9 altogether?

Although the migration wizard is not provided with ColdFusion 10, Adobe is offering it separately, as discussed in this blog entry: http://blogs.coldfusion.com/post.cfm/verity-to-solr-migration.

ColdFusion 9.0.2 Replaces 9.0

This change is not technically about ColdFusion 10. The removal of Verity from ColdFusion has a related impact on ColdFusion 9. If you've not noticed, you can no longer obtain ColdFusion 9.0 from the Adobe web site. Instead, you can get 9.0.2, which is a full installer, or 9.0.1, which is an updater to 9.0. What's the difference? And what happened to 9.0?

With the release of ColdFusion 10 and the removal of Verity, the licensing agreement between Adobe and Verity required that Adobe remove any publicly available installers of previous versions that included Verity. This Verity licensing change meant that the ColdFusion 9.0 installer must be removed. (Again, the installer for 9.0.1 is technically an updater for 9.0, so it could, and does, remain. And with support for ColdFusion 8 dropped as of the release of ColdFusion 10, the installer for ColdFusion 8 has been removed.)

So someone wanting to download ColdFusion 9 from the Adobe website is now offered ColdFusion 9.0.2, which is a full installer of ColdFusion (it does not assume a prior ColdFusion 9 installation and in fact cannot coexist with another ColdFusion 9.0 or 9.0.1 installation).

ColdFusion 9.0.2 can be thought of as the accumulation of ColdFusion 9.0, minus Verity, plus the update to 9.0.1, plus all the individual, cumulative, and security hot fixes that existed for 9.0.1 as of May 30, 2012. To learn more about ColdFusion 9.0.2, see the following:

- http://helpx.adobe.com/coldfusion/release-note/coldfusion-9-0-update-2.html

- http://blogs.coldfusion.com/post.cfm/availability-of-coldfusion-9

ColdFusion 9.0.2 even includes at least one new feature introduced in ColdFusion 10. See http://www.raymondcamden.com/index.cfm/2012/6/13/ColdFusion-902-has-one-CF10-tidbit.

Multiserver Enhancements

There are a few enhancements related to multiserver deployments, or what some refer to as multiple instances of ColdFusion (an Enterprise-only feature).

Changes in Installer

While running the ColdFusion 10 installer, you may notice that you are no longer offered a separate option to install ColdFusion in multiserver mode. (You did not see this option if you provided a Standard license key during installation of previous releases of ColdFusion.)

Instead, the ColdFusion 10 installer presents only the options Server and JEE, both of which have been offered for several releases. The Server option previously installed only a single instance, and the JEE option deployed ColdFusion as an EAR or WAR file (and still does).

In ColdFusion 10, if you choose the Server form of deployment during installation, the ColdFusion 10 (Enterprise) Administrator will offer an Instance Manager option to create and manage instances (and clusters). The means of creating new instances has not changed significantly in ColdFusion 10 Enterprise and is beyond the scope of this book. For more information, see the chapter "Using Multiple Server Instances" in the manual, *Configuring and Administering ColdFusion 10*, or the *Adobe ColdFusion 9 Web Application Construction Kit, Volume 3: Advanced Application Development*, Chapter 48, "Scaling with ColdFusion."

NOTE

This multiserver support (or multiple instances, as enabled using the Instance Manager) is still supported only in ColdFusion Enterprise. Technically, it's also available in the trial or developer editions, but if you provide a ColdFusion 10 Standard key (whether during installation or later using the Administrator System Information screen), the Instance Manager option is removed from the Administrator.

Changes in File Locations and Arrangements

As was true in multiserver deployments in previous releases, the main instance name is cfusion, and this is true even for ColdFusion 10 Standard deployments (in which only one instance is supported). The files for this cfusion instance are found (in all ColdFusion 10 deployments) in the [cf10]\cfusion directory.

If you create a new instance, the files for that instance are now no longer buried deep in a servers directory, but instead can be found at [cf10]\[instance]. (More information about changes related to ColdFusion 10 folders for logging is offered later in this chapter, in the "Logging Enhancements" section.)

Each Instance Has Its Own jvm.config File

In ColdFusion 10, if you do create multiple instances, each instance has its own jvm.config file, which is a great enhancement if you want different instances to use different heap size settings, JVM versions, garbage collection algorithms, or other JVM settings.

Note as well that a Java & JVM page is now available within each instance's Administrator.

Obtaining the Instance Name Programmatically

In previous releases, if you wanted to obtain the instance name (at runtime), you had to call a JRun library method. In ColdFusion 10, the Admin API has a new method called getInstanceName(), found in the Admin API's runtime.cfc file. For more information about this new method, see http://www.carehart.org/blog/client/index.cfm/2012/6/30/get_instancename_in_cf10.

Lost: Deploying an Instance Using an EAR or WAR File

One feature related to multiserver deployment was lost in the move to ColdFusion 10: during the creation of a new instance, you can no longer deploy an EAR or WAR file in that instance. See the blog entry at http://blogs.coldfusion.com/post.cfm/what-s-the-deal-with-tomcat-in-coldfusion-10 for more information about this change.

You can, of course, still use the JEE deployment option during installation to create an EAR or WAR version of ColdFusion, which can be used to deploy ColdFusion on any JEE application server, such as JBoss, Tomcat, GlassFish, Jetty, or WebSphere. (You can also still create an EAR or WAR file from an existing ColdFusion instance using the Administrator Packaging & Deployment section's J2EE Archives page, for the Enterprise, Trial, and Developer editions of ColdFusion, but not the Standard edition.)

CFML Enhancements

There are a number of CFML enhancements that you might miss. For more details about these, see the corresponding section for each tag or function in the ColdFusion documentation.

- CFIMAGE action="resize" now includes the INTERPOLATION attribute. This attribute previously was offered only as an argument to the imageresize() function. Both the tag and function have a default value of "highestquality"; for increased performance, consider using "highestperformance" instead.

- The CFMap and CFMapItem tags now offer an optional ShowUser attribute. For HTML5 browsers, this attribute displays the user's current location on a map (the user is prompted to authorize this display). For other browsers, this feature uses the value of the CenterAddress attribute.

- The CFInclude tag offers a new RunOnce attribute, which causes the named file to be included only once in a request, regardless of the number of times an attempt is made to include it in the request.

- The CFFILE tag now supports output content within its tag body, as an alternative to the previously available OUTPUT attribute, as in the following example:

```
<cffile action="write" file="#filename#">
some tag body
</cffile>
```

- You can now define an onAbort method in Application.cfc, to intercept any calls made to a CFABORT or abort script statement.

- The CFParam tag offers a new attribute for MAXLENGTH validation.

- The CFPOP tag offers a new SECURE attribute for SSL processing.

- New tags are available for Microsoft Exchange integration: CFExchangeConversation and CFExchangeFolder. ColdFusion 10 also offers Microsoft Exchange 2010 support, including support for Microsoft Exchange Web Services (EWS). There are also some new attributes for CFExchangeCalendar as well as a new ServerVersion attribute for all Cold-Fusion tags related to Microsoft Exchange.

- The new dateTimeFormat()function returns a formatted value for both the current date and the current time in a single function call. There is a corresponding locale-specific variation: lsDateTimeFormat().

- The new DirectoryCopy() function allows you to make a copy of a directory, as does the corresponding new Action="copy" action for CFDirectory.

- The new getApplicationMetaData() function returns the settings specified in the application framework for the current application, whether specified in that application in Application.cfc or Application.cfm, or inherited as defaults, as might be set in the Cold-Fusion Administrator.

- The new sessionGetMetaData() function returns the start time of the current session.

- The new callStackGet() and callStackDump() functions return the current call stack (a stack dump as of the current line of code), which can be useful during debugging. It identifies the calling template name, line number, and function name (if any) at that point in code. Whereas CallStackGet returns an array of structs, CallStackDump returns a string.

- Several new functions return system-level information, including GetCpuUsage(), which returns CPU use as a percentage over a specified time period (defaulting to 1 second); GetSystemTotalMemory(), which returns available total memory in the operating system; GetSystemFreeMemory(), which returns available free memory in the operating system; GetTotalSpace(), which returns total disk space for a given path (hard drive or Cold-Fusion Virtual File System, or VFS, path); and GetFreeSpace(), which returns free disk space for a given path (hard drive or VFS path).

- The Expandpath() function can now resolve the paths for files located in custom tag paths.

- The `arrayAppend()` function has a new `merge` argument.

- The `replaceList()` function now takes delimiters (for its search and replace operations).

- The `LSParseDateTime()` function has a new format argument.

- The `arraySort()`, `listSort()`, and `structSort()` functions have been modified to support all Java-supported locale-specific characters.

- The `queryAddRow()` and `queryNew()` functions accept new arguments that let you initialize the query data to be simulated with the functions.

- The `CFLOOP` tag supports dynamic references when naming a query to be looped over (as opposed to the more traditional approach of naming a query as a string that is the name of a query result). For instance, you can now use `<cfloop query = "#getEmployees()#">` to refer to a function or method named `getEmployees()` that returns a query.

- A new `fetchClientInfo` attribute is provided for all query-related tags (`cfquery`, `cfinsert`, `cfstoredproc`, etc.) to be used with information that can also be provided in settings defined in the ColdFusion Administrator data source Advanced Settings.

- The `CFStoredProc` tag now supports a `Timeout` attribute specifying the number of seconds that each action (in the stored procedure call) is permitted to execute before an error is returned. Note that the cumulative time of all actions in the procedure can exceed the specified value.

Administrator Enhancements

There are a number of Administrator enhancements that you might miss.

Some Modest Administrator Enhancements

Let's start with a few simple enhancements.

- Have you been annoyed by the Java applet that has been used until now in the Cold-Fusion Administrator for choosing files and folders? It's replaced in ColdFusion 10 with a nicer jQuery control.

- A ColdFusion Administrator can now disable creation of any unnamed application scopes (instancewide), by using the Server Settings section's Settings page and selecting Disable Creation of Unnamed Applications.

- You can now specify web service proxy details in the ColdFusion Administrator (whereas previously you could define them only when invoking the web service, such as with `CFINVOKE`). This service is configured in the Data & Services section on the Web Services page.

Only One Administrator Logon at a Time

One additional change, which may or may not be considered an enhancement by some, is a security change. Only one login at a time is permitted for a given ColdFusion Administrator user account. If you or others find yourselves getting logged out of the administrator unexpectedly, this is the likely explanation. Note that the limit is per Administrator user account. It is possible to define new users in the Administrator. For more information about this enhancement and how to resolve issues relating to it, see this blog entry:

http://www.carehart.org/blog/client/index.cfm/2012/6/13/cf10_admin_allows_one_logon_at_a_time.

This is actually a change in the function of the CFLOGIN tag, which the Administrator uses. If you have applications that also use CFLOGIN, this change affects those as well.

Admin API Enhancements

There are several additions to the Admin API (a set of CFCs in the CFIDE/adminapi/directory that you can use to programmatically perform functions normally performed in the Administrator). Here are the names of the CFCs, followed by any new methods:

- Runtime.cfc: getInstanceName and clearQueryCache

- Administrator.cfc: getUpdates, getUpdateCount, and getBuildNumber

- Extensions.cfc: Various methods related to REST

- Scheduler.cfc: New; various methods related to Scheduler

- ServerMonitoring.cfc: getAllApplicationCacheMetadata and getAllServerCacheMetadata

Security Enhancements

Chapter 15 covers security enhancements. However, ColdFusion 10 includes some miscellaneous related to security that bridge coding and configuration and so are discussed here.

Single-User CFLOGIN

As mentioned in the previous section, the function of the CFLOGIN tag has changed so that now only one user at a time (for a given account used in a CFLOGIN action) can be logged in. If a request comes from another browser for the same CFLOGIN account, the first user will be logged out.

Sandbox Permissions for RDS

ColdFusion 8 introduced the option to configure different accounts in the ColdFusion Administrator, for defining both different users of the Administrator (and Admin API) and different RDS users. (RDS is a feature used to connect ColdFusion Builder and Dreamweaver to ColdFusion, as an aid in development.)

The process for defining RDS permissions for an account on the ColdFusion Administrator (Security > User Manager) page has changed. Prior to ColdFusion 10, a given RDS user could be connected to a given sandbox. In ColdFusion 10, when you define permissions for a given RDS user, you will now see two new sections: Sandboxes: Data Source Permissions and Sandboxes: Add/Edit Secured Files and Directories. You need to grant appropriate access for that RDS user to the required data sources and files and directories. For more information about this change, see http://www.shilpikhariwal.com/2012/03/new-way-to-add-sandbox-permissions-for.html.

Backward-Compatibility Issues

ColdFusion 10 includes some changes that were introduced originally as security hotfixes in Cold-Fusion 8 and 9. ColdFusion users who have not yet applied those hotfixes to those releases should be aware of these changes if they move to ColdFusion 10, because they can affect the compatibility of some code and some functions.

Limitation in the Number of Form Fields Posted

ColdFusion 10 now limits the number of form fields that can be posted to ColdFusion from an HTML form. The default is 100, and this value can be changed in the ColdFusion Administrator, on the Server Settings section's Settings page, using the Maximum Number of POST Request Parameters setting.

This change was introduced as a security hotfix in ColdFusion 8 and 9, as alluded to earlier and as discussed in this tech note: http://helpx.adobe.com/coldfusion/kb/coldfusion-security-hotfix.html.

The higher you raise this value beyond the default of 100, the greater the risk that you will open your server to the vulnerability it was protecting against. Raise this value only as high as needed for your applications to function, or modify your applications so that they do not require so many form fields.

Session-Fixation Protection

ColdFusion 10 now includes protection against a web application security attack called session fixation (for more information, see https://www.owasp.org/index.php/Session_fixation). This protection, however, can make it appear in some applications that users are losing their session and being forced to log in frequently.

If that problem is indeed caused by this built-in protection against session fixation, the protection can be disabled by adding a new argument for the JVM configuration underlying ColdFusion:

```
-Dcoldfusion.session.protectfixation=false
```

This argument can be added on the ColdFusion Administrator's Java & JVM page (available in ColdFusion 10 within each instance, if multiple instances are deployed), or it can be added to the jvm.config file found in each instance at [cf10]\[instance]\jvm.config. You must restart Cold-Fusion for this change to take effect.

This JVM argument was introduced as a security hotfix in ColdFusion 8 and 9, as discussed in this tech note: http://helpx.adobe.com/coldfusion/kb/security-hotfix-coldfusion-8-8.html.

Of course, removing this protection will open your server to the session-fixation vulnerability that the feature addresses, but if your users appear to be losing their sessions and you can't solve that problem otherwise, consider trying this JVM argument.

Logging Enhancements

There are several enhancements related to ColdFusion logging. Before exploring the enhancements, it's important to note where logs are stored now in ColdFusion 10.

Log Locations

As mentioned in a previous section of this chapter, ColdFusion 10's logs are stored in the [cf10]\cfusion\logs directory, or if you are using an instance, [cf10]\[instance]\logs. To simplify things, we'll refer to the logs as [cf10]\[instance]\logs for both single and multi-instance deployments.

Also, previously, if ColdFusion was run as a Microsoft Windows service, the console logs (with lots of potentially useful diagnostic and troubleshooting information) were written to the [cf]\runtime\logs or [jrun]\logs. In ColdFusion 10, this log (ColdFusion-out.log) is now written in the same directory as the other ColdFusion logs just mentioned. (Web server connector logs remain elsewhere, in [cf10]\config\wsconfig\.)

New Metrics Logging

Some readers may have known about JRun Metrics logging, available since ColdFusion 6, which allowed a set of server diagnostic metrics to be written to a log on a periodic basis, such as every minute. Enabling this capability required you to edit a particular XML file.

In ColdFusion 10, such logging can be enabled on the Debugging Output Settings page, by selecting Enable Metrics Logging. This selection causes ColdFusion to write a line of metrics information every minute (configurable with the Metrics Frequency setting) to [cf10]\[instance]\logs\metrics.log. If you start ColdFusion from the command line, the information is logged to the console; otherwise, it is also duplicated in the aforementioned ColdFusion-out.log file.

Here's an example of a line from that file:

```
"Information","scheduler-2","08/06/12","16:08:50",,"Max threads: 150 Current
➡thread count: 4 Current thread busy: 1 Max processing time: 279876 Request count:
➡748 Error count: 3 Bytes received: 281578 Bytes sent: 7375153 Free memory:
➡120128728 Total memory: 442957824 Active Sessions: 9
```

New Request Logging (Access Logs)

Those using an external web server such as IIS or Apache may have request logging enabled there for all files of all extensions in a site, and ColdFusion 10 now automatically logs all requests that ColdFusion processes (typically, .cfm and .cfc file requests).

These access logs are not found in the traditional logs location, but are instead found in [cf10]\ [instance]\runtime\logs, with a filename in the form of localhost_access_log.yyyy-mm-dd.txt. Note that that the file extension is .txt, so you might miss these files if you search the entire [cf10] directory to find any and all logs that ColdFusion 10 creates.

The lines in this access log have the form:

```
Format: [ip]-[date/time] "GET [path/file] HTTP/1.1" [statuscode] [bytessent]
```

Also, you can configure this logging, including the file location and name and the content that is logged. Configuration is beyond the scope of this book, but the logging is actually being performed by Tomcat, using a valve called AccessLogValve. To learn more about the concept of valves and how to configure this particular one, see http://tomcat.apache.org/tomcat-7.0-doc/config/valve.html.

The file in which such valves (and other aspects of Tomcat) are configured in ColdFusion 10 is [cf10]\[instance]\runtime\conf\server.xml.

Solr Access Logs

The Solr search service also has access logs that track all requests made to Solr, which means any Solr-based processing in your ColdFusion code (the CFCOLLECTION, CFINDEX, and CFSEARCH tags, or the corresponding new CFC-based script equivalents for them, discussed in Chapter 8, "CFScript Enhancements").

These logs are enabled by default and are found in [cf10]\[instance]\jetty\logs\, with filenames in the form yyyy_mm_dd.request.log. To change the filename, location, or format of the content in the files, see the file [cf10]\[instance]\jetty\etc\jetty.xml. (This directory also contains a pair of logs that hold any Solr error information and that are created each day that ColdFusion runs. If there are no Solr errors, the log files will be empty.)

NOTE

Are you wondering about the reference to jetty with respect to the directory holding these Solr logs? Just as in ColdFusion 9, Solr is deployed on its own Java application server, deployed within the ColdFusion directory. In ColdFusion 9, that directory location was [cf9]\solr; in ColdFusion 10, the location has been changed to [cf10]\[instance]\jetty. Similarly, the name of the Microsoft Windows service (if used) has been changed from ColdFusion 9 Solr Service to ColdFusion 10 Jetty Service.

Updated Embedded Libraries

ColdFusion embeds many different technologies, and with each new release, those underlying libraries are updated.

Web Services and Axis

The underlying web services library has been updated to Axis 2, which adds the following features:

- Support for SOAP 1.2 and WDSL 2.0

- Capability to create and publish REST-based services (using JSON and XML)

- Capability to consume and publish RPC, document-literal, and document-literal wrapped web services

Support for these features and enhancements can be specified variously at the component, application, or server levels. See the ColdFusion 10 documentation for more information.

Also see the following blog entries:

- "Using Axis2 Web Services with ColdFusion 10" (http://www.adobe.com/devnet/coldfusion/articles/axis2-web-services.html)

- "ColdFusion 10 WebServices—Axis2 vs. Axis1" (http://blogs.coldfusion.com/post.cfm/coldfusion-10-webservices-axis2-vs-axis1)

- "Axis-2 and Axis-1 Compatibility Issues" (http://blogs.coldfusion.com/post.cfm/axis-2-and-axis-1-compatibility-issues)

XML Support

The XML functions `xmlSearch` and `xmlTransform` now support XPath 2.0 syntax.

Underlying Java Architecture

ColdFusion 10.0 is built-in atop Oracle JVM Version 1.6.0_29, with Tomcat Version 7.0.23. Adobe has stated that it plans to support new and updated versions of both Java and Tomcat over time, whether through the new update mechanism or new installers or updaters.

This version information is viewable in the ColdFusion Administrator, via the System Information screen (accessible via the *i* icon on the top right of the Administrator interface).

Other Libraries

Other embedded libraries that have been updated include the following:

- Solr, which has been updated from Version 1.4 to Version 3.4

- Derby, which has been updated from Version 10.5 to Version 10.8

- EhCache, which has been updated from Version 2.0 to Version 2.5.1

- Lucene, which has been updated from Version 2.3.2 to Version 3.4.0

Other Enhancements

A handful of remaining enhancements don't fit neatly into categories.

Query-Caching Enhancements

Cached queries are now stored in ehCache by default. If you want to change this to the behavior of previous releases (storing the query cache in the Java heap), you can add `this.cache.useinternalquerycache=true` in Application.cfc.

And as discussed in Chapter 16, "Improving Performance," the ehCache is now application specific, so this query caching is now unique to each application, whereas previously query caching was shared serverwide.

Similarly, you can set the maximum number of cached queries (per application) in Application.cfc with `this.cache.querysize`.

Virtual File System Enhancements

ColdFusion 9 introduced the Virtual File System (VFS) feature through which various CFML tags and functions that typically processed local files could also refer to files and directories defined in a virtual remote location, by using the `ram:///` prefix. For instance, the tag `<cffile action="write" file="ram:///a.txt" output="Testing the function FileSetLastModified">` would write to this VFS a file named a.txt.

In ColdFusion 9, this VFS storage location was serverwide (shared by all users of the given ColdFusion instance). In ColdFusion 10, it is now application specific. This behavior can be changed or managed using the following statements in Application.cfc: `this.inmemoryfilesystem.enabled` and `this.inmemoryfilesystem.size`.

Another enhancement in ColdFusion 10 is support (wherever VFS can be used) to access files over a network via FTP or HTTP or in a zip file, using corresponding new prefixes: `ftp:`, `http;`, and `zip:`. Other supported file types include SFTP, FTPS, Https, JAR, TAR, and GZ.

For more information about VFS, see the chapter "Working with In-Memory Files" in the ColdFusion manual *Developing ColdFusion 10 Applications*.

Note also that there is a new Admin API method related to VFS, `getGlobalVFSMemoryStats`, in servermonitoring.cfc.

Solr Enhancements

On the ColdFusion Administrator page for managing Solr collections, ColdFusion Collections, a new Reload option is offered. This option is useful when you need to reload just a single collection, when the schema.xml file related to that collection has changed, without restarting the Solr server (which is named the Jetty service in Microsoft Windows) as was required in ColdFusion 9.

You also can now secure communications between ColdFusion and the Solr server (or Jetty service).

ColdFusion 10 now also supports additional languages.

For more information, see the chapter "Solr Enhancements in ColdFusion 10" in the ColdFusion manual *Developing ColdFusion 10 Applications*.

Differences Between Enterprise and Standard Editions

ColdFusion comes in two commercial editions: Standard and Enterprise (and the free Trial and Developer editions, which function like Enterprise but with the Developer edition having a connection limitation as discussed in this section).

Of the new features in ColdFusion 10, the following are available only in the Enterprise (or Trial or Developer) edition:

- Some (though not all) scheduling improvements (listeners, chaining, application-specific tasks, clustering, and exception handling)

- HTML 5 charting

- ORM search

- Data import handler for Solr

And with respect to the new Web Socket feature, the Standard edition limits you to 100 simultaneous requests (not 5, as is stated in the documentation).

Besides noting these differences in the ColdFusion documentation, Adobe identifies them in its Buying Guide; see http://www.adobe.com/products/coldfusion-enterprise/buying-guide.html.

Developer Edition Restrictions Eased

Speaking of the free Developer edition, previously it limited the number of individual IP addresses that could access it before it blocked additional visitors (until a ColdFusion restart).

In ColdFusion 10, visitors from any number of different IP addresses can access a Developer edition of ColdFusion, but no more than two at once. This more flexible restriction allows you to show your work to clients, colleagues, and testers, while also protecting Adobe's interests.

Licensing

There have been some modest changes in ColdFusion 10 licensing; in particular, in the definitions of CPUs and cores, staging servers, and backup and disaster recovery, and in virtual machine and cloud licensing. (Note that testing, staging, development, and disaster recovery capabilities all continue to be free.)

For more information, see this blog post: http://blogs.coldfusion.com/post.cfm/coldfusion-10-eula.

Other Resources

Many references have been made throughout this book to the ColdFusion documentation, but there also are some additional resources that will help as you explore ColdFusion 10.

Adobe ColdFusion 10 Documentation

As with previous releases, the ColdFusion 10 documentation set contains four manuals (don't be misled to believe that there is only a single manual, the CFML Reference):

- *Configuring and Administering Adobe ColdFusion 10*

- *Adobe ColdFusion 10 CFML Reference*

- *Developing Adobe ColdFusion 10 Applications*

- *Installing Adobe ColdFusion 10*

Each manual is available online, in both HTML and PDF formats (click the View Help PDF link at the top right of each manual). There is no single link to a page listing all the manuals, but the front page of each manual offers a link at the left to the other manuals, such as that at http://help. adobe.com/en_US/ColdFusion/10.0/Admin/index.html.

Adobe ColdFusion Blog

Most important in terms of staying up-to-date on the latest information about ColdFusion 10 is the Adobe ColdFusion team's blog, at blogs.coldfusion.com. A few representative entries show the value and importance of the information shared here:

- "ColdFusion 10 Hotfix Installation Guide" (http://blogs.coldfusion.com/post.cfm/ coldfusion-hotfix-installation-guide)

- "ColdFusion 10 Server Lockdown Guide" (http://blogs.coldfusion.com/post.cfm/ coldfusion-10-server-lockdown-guide)

- "Tuning ColdFusion 10 IIS Connector Configuration" (http://blogs.coldfusion.com/ post.cfm/tuning-coldfusion-10-iis-connector-configuration)

- "Minor Java Upgrades in ColdFusion" (http://blogs.coldfusion.com/post.cfm/ minor-java-upgrades-in-coldfusion)

- "Product Roadmap for ColdFusion" (http://blogs.coldfusion.com/post.cfm/ product-roadmap-for-coldfusion)

Adobe ColdFusion Developer Center

See the Adobe ColdFusion Developer Center, at http://www.adobe.com/devnet/coldfusion.html. This page offers not only new information about ColdFusion 10 but also getting-started resources (for those new to ColdFusion), videos on beginner and advanced topics, feature overviews, tutorials, case studies, and more.

The page also highlights recent updates in the Adobe ColdFusion blog, the Adobe ColdFusion forums, and other resources and provides links to ColdFusion documentation and updates, so it can serve as a landing page for all things ColdFusion.

"Adobe ColdFusion 10 Tutorials and Resources"

Separate from Adobe's resources are, of course, hundreds of valuable blog entries, presentations, and more created by people throughout the ColdFusion community. It's impractical to list them all here, but fortunately we can turn to the work of one community member, Akbar Sait, who has created his own compilation of ColdFusion 10 resources, which he labels "Adobe ColdFusion 10 Tutorials and Resources," available at http://www.akbarsait.com/cf10tutorials.cfm.

INDEX